ELECTRIC PIONEER
AN ARMCHAIR GUIDE TO GARY NUMAN

Printed in the UK.
Published by Helter Skelter Books,
Southbank House, Black Prince Road, London SE1 7SJ.
www.helterskelterbooks.com
Copyright 2004 © Paul Goodwin. All rights reserved.

Cover design by Chris Wilson. Typesetting by Caroline Walker.

Printed in Great Britain by CPI, Bath.

The right of Paul Goodwin to be identified as author of this work has been
asserted in accordance with the Copyright, Design and Patents Act, 1988.

A CIP record for this book is available from the British Library.

This author thanks the following record companies for the use of their artwork
throughout this book: **BEGGARS BANQUET, NUMA, IRS, POLYDOR, EAGLE,
ARTFUL/ UNIVERSAL, G.F.M./THE RECORD COMPANY, BBC, STRANGE FRUIT,
CLEOPATRA, RSO, JAMBO, A&M, FOX, TVT, CASTLE, FLAG, ISLAND,
SURVIVAL, NORTHWEST ELEKTRO, FOOD, INTERSCOPE, CAPITAL,
ROADRUNNER, REMILLE PLATEAU, ORCHARD, XL, WEA, SCRATCH, ROCKET,
CARRERE, JVO, MINORITY ONE, MERGE and FLR.**

The author would also like to thank the following video and movie companies for
the use of their artwork seen throughout this book: **WARNERS/ BEGGARS
BANQUET VIDEO, PALACE, PEPPERMINT, VIDEO COLLECTION, 4FRONT
VIDEO, CASTLE HENDRING, PMI, TRIMARK, RCA, SANCTUARY, NEW
HORIZON, BBC, VIDEO and CLASSIC ROCK PRODUCTIONS.**

In addition, this author would like to thank the following companies for the use of
their logos seen in this book: **RIMMEL, AMERICAN EXPRESS, 7UP** and
CARLING BEERS.

Front cover photo taken by Joseph Cultice.

Special note: whilst every attempt to properly trace, acknowledge and credit all
the photographers, record and video companies whose work has been used in
this book I'd like to apologise should there have been any errors or omissions. In
this event, please contact the publishers.

ISBN 1-900924-95-1

ELECTRIC PIONEER
AN ARMCHAIR GUIDE TO GARY NUMAN

by

PAUL GOODWIN

Helter Skelter Publishing

This book is dedicated to:
My long-suffering family (Sarah, James and Kathy) who had to live a year of their lives surrounded by piles of records, photographs and videos.

I'd especially like to dedicate this book to my partner Kathy who not only had to put up with my endless Numan biased conversation for months on end but also had nothing but the back of my head to speak to during the creation of this manuscript, a manuscript that for me steadily became an obsession (a fact she was acutely aware of, though I was not). I owe her many thanks for gently and quite rightfully pointing out to me that after a solid year of writing, followed by endless month's of re-writes, corrections, additions and bouts of rising in the middle of the night to, as I would often put it, 'jot something down', that enough was enough and it was not only time to stop, it was also time to let it go.

...INTRO

'Now I'm behind glass,
I'll talk to you.'
(lyric taken from the *Telekon* track, 'Please Push No More' from 1980.)

Ask any hardcore Numan devotee about the complexities of Gary's vast and growing recording catalogue and the response would likely be one of exasperation and mock despair. Trying to keep track of Numan's prolific 26-year voyage through the music business, one that has seen the star signed either directly or indirectly to a staggering seven different record companies (including his own Numa imprint) requires a degree of patience and determination that, if truth be told, few people apart from dedicated fans possess.

Frustrated with my own efforts to keep track, I finally decided to sit down and compile a thorough and in-depth career overview that would truly be the most accurate and definitive Gary Numan discography of them all. The one thing I didn't plan to do, however, was set myself on a path that would ultimately result in the publication of my first book.

Electric Pioneer took over a year to write and is the sum total of my exhaustive and concise trawl through every facet of Numan's extensive and at times bewildering musical archive. However, I believe the book is more than just a 'warts and all discography': *Electric Pioneer* is designed to operate on a number of different levels and compiled in a way that I hope will appeal to fans both old and new. For those new to the Numan cause, the book is a unique, year-by-year, history lesson, one that tells the real story of Numan's unique and often bizarre career. For older fans, those that were there at the very beginning, the book is a virtual treasure trove of memories.

Electric Pioneer successfully brings out into the open Gary's rich and varied musical catalogue, a catalogue that has, for far too long, skulked in the shadows of the music industry away from the glare of the media spotlight. With the addition of videos, concert guides and a wealth of artefacts and memorabilia, Electric Pioneer is, I believe, the definitive and ultimate collectors guide to Gary Numan.

'Remember we toured the skies.'
(lyric taken from the 1981 single 'Love Needs No Disguise.')

FOREWORD BY GARY NUMAN

I clearly remember sitting at home in 1977 and looking for the first time at a copy of my debut single, 'That's Too Bad.' It was something I'd dreamed about for as long as I could remember. I didn't expect to be sitting down, many years later, looking at a meticulously researched book detailing the enormous catalogue of Numan releases that have followed that first rough and ready single.

At the time many people gave me two albums at the most before I'd be swept to one side like so many other would-be pop stars before and since. It was a very reasonable point of view to be honest so I'm as surprised as anyone to find myself still here, still making chart music and reading a book like this.

In fact, looking through these pages, I'm amazed at just how much music I've released over the years since 'That's Too Bad.' A few of the songs detailed here I can barely remember, some I genuinely don't remember at all. But then it seems that I've written quite a few so, perhaps, forgetting some of them isn't quite as surprising as it might seem. Others of course are like old friends, friends that continue to give me a most exciting and rewarding life.

Songwriting is an art you never stop trying to master, knowing always that mastering is impossible. Making mistakes is almost essential, because sometimes the mistakes made on one forgettable song can help turn the next one into something far more special. How else can you learn and improve? So, good or bad, they all have a part to play in any songwriting career. This book details them all, good, bad and middling. It chronicles the ebb and flow of my so-called creativity and isn't afraid to say where I succeeded and where, perhaps, I did not.

The amount of work that Paul has put into Electric Pioneer is enormous. It is, without doubt, the most complete and thorough discography of my music that I've ever seen and I'm very grateful to him for making the huge effort required to put it together. I only hope that I can carry on for another 25 years and have the pleasure of, one day, reading Volume 2. I certainly intend to try.

I can't imagine doing anything else.

Gary Numan.

July 2004.

CONTENTS

HOW TO USE THIS BOOK

The following explains how to accurately interpret some of the terminology used within this book.

ALBUM AND SINGLE RE-ISSUES

Re-issues are listed as two separate formats, CD and vinyl. As CD only properly took off in the mid to late 80s, all Numan's vinyl releases pressed onto that format are listed separately (this occurs primarily in both the Beggars Banquet and Numa sections of this book). Known and significant vinyl re-issues have been added to the information text with each originally released recording.

FOREIGN FORMATS

Singles, albums and videos released or re-issued in other territories have been added to each of the original recordings when significant differences have been detected.

PROMO'S

Although promo's are commonplace, they are only included here if they are significantly different to the eventually issued recording.

INTERVIEW RECORDINGS

This book does not include the many interview recordings that have surfaced on vinyl and CD over the years. The only exception to this rule has been the inclusion of the 'Images' interview albums Gary issued throughout the 80s and early 90s via his fan club.

GREATEST HITS COMPILATION ALBUMS

A number of Numan's songs and singles have been included on industry compilation albums over the years, however, Numan tracks included on any given album are only highlighted when significant alterations, edits or remixes have occurred.

FANZINES AND FAN PRODUCED BOOKS

Since Gary's 1979 breakthrough many excellent (and some not so excellent) fanzines have come and gone. In addition, independent works like *The Red Book* and *The Numan A To Z Directory* have also provided fans with early attempts at compiling Numan's recorded output. Sadly, with so many fan-produced magazines appearing over the course of the last 26 years, a genuine lack of space prevented this edition of *Electric Pioneer* from covering this off-shoot of the Gary Numan phenomenon. Hopefully future editions of this book will rectify this intended omission.

Some of the many Numan fanzines from the 80s.

SECTION ONE

MUSIC

SECTION ONE

PART ONE

THE BEGGARS BANQUET YEARS

When Tubeway Army signed to Beggars Banquet Records in the early part of 1978, there wasn't a lot to distinguish the group from the hundreds of other punk rock hopefuls that had emerged in the wake of that scene's explosion the previous year. However, as a punk band, Tubeway Army were not particularly convincing with Gary only adopting this style of music in the belief that a recording contract would follow soon after. Nevertheless, in the space of a few months, Tubeway Army issued two punk-flavoured singles earning modest sales for a relatively unknown group. More demos were recorded but Gary Valeriun (Gary had yet to christen himself Numan at this point) was less than thrilled with the results and when the group's line-up splintered, he quickly reverted the band back to its original Paul Gardiner, Jess Lidyard, Gary Numan power trio axis, shelving the previously recorded material in favour of beginning again from scratch. It is during these sessions that the discovery of a rented synthesizer (left behind in the studio), and its subsequent integration into the demos recorded, would prove to be a career defining moment for the band, one ultimately responsible for permanently reshaping the group's sound. The resulting album, released at the tail end of 1978, complete with Gary's quickly added synthesised embellishments, got the band some recognition and into the UK's independent album charts. However, it was the group's next record that would be responsible for elevating them out of their garagey confines and into the big league when that album's keyboard-heavy second single 'Are "Friends" Electric?' shot, unexpectedly, to No1 in the UK singles chart. Suddenly, virtually overnight, Tubeway Army found themselves catapulted from relative obscurity to the very forefront of a new musical movement: the all synthesiser pop act. It was this point that Gary chose to dispense with the Tubeway Army moniker in favour of launching himself as a solo artist and any doubts from either Gary or his label over this decision proved unfounded as Numan's success continued unabated.

Although regarded as pioneering, innovative and futuristic by the media in foreign territories, in the UK, Numan's heavily synthesised music made him an instant bitter enemy of the press who lashed out at every opportunity to both ridicule and rubbish him to the British record-buying public. However, unjustified as this was, press hatred in the UK (a feeling largely borne out of the media's whimsical notion that Numan had become successful not only against their wishes but against the very tide of fashion) could do little to halt Numan's global commercial rise. Indeed, by the end of 1981, Gary had sold 10 million records worldwide and was a huge international star. Sadly though, Numan's good fortune and high profile couldn't be sustained, although in a break from the norm, drugs, alcohol and poor songwriting were not factors in Gary's fall from grace: it would be his own questionable decisions over his career that would set the wheels in motion for his subsequent downfall. Perhaps Numan's most glaring mistake was to announce his retirement from touring. As a result, following three spectacular farewell shows at Wembley Arena in April 1981, Numan's record sales plummeted as seemingly significant sections of his audience were swiftly spirited away by the inevitable lure and attraction of a new breed of pop stars in waiting. By early 1982, it had become apparent that with no tours in place to promote his new music, his records were beginning to occupy progressively lower and lower chart positions: worse still, Numan's record company, much like the radio, had turned their attentions to newer acts to promote, practically writing him off as yesterday's news. Attempts to address these matters in 1983 proved to be in vain as Numan discovered to his horror that his big comeback was viewed as being far from a priority at his label, despite a sold out UK tour and a strong-selling album in the shops, Numan's relationship with his record company began to crumble, so much so that by the end of the year, both parted ways.

Although Numan went on to pastures new, Beggars Banquet, on the other hand, chose to dip into the vaults, eventually unearthing nearly two album's worth of unreleased material. In 1987, the label decided to transfer, for the first time, Numan's eight studio albums to CD: however, this venture wasn't entirely successful. What was successful though was a heavily remixed 'Cars' finding itself high in the top 20 in the autumn of 1987. Come 1993 (and in direct response to the successful, Japanese CD re-issue campaign of 1990) Beggars Banquet decided to give Numan's catalogue another makeover, this time transferring full albums as well as B-sides onto twin CD sets.

Again, another remix of 'Cars' was commissioned along with another 'best of' collection. Unfortunately, these fared less favourably as, by the 90s, Gary was swiftly heading into a cult bracket and facing something of an unknown future. Thankfully, Numan's lean times were brought to an end in 1996 when 'Cars' rocketed back into the top 20 again on the back of a beer commercial. A year later and with a high profile tribute album in the shops, Numan suddenly found himself being name-checked by artists as diverse as David Bowie and Marilyn Manson. With Gary seemingly relevant again, Beggars Banquet used these more favourable times to finally give their Numan back catalogue the justice it deserved. From 1998 until 2002, virtually all the Tubeway Army and Gary Numan albums recorded under the Beggars Banquet/ WEA umbrella were re-issued on single CDs featuring beautifully reproduced artwork, new detailed sleeve notes, vintage photographs and vastly improved sound levels via a re-mastering process undertaken on the original studio cutting tapes. These CDs are now much prized by fans. The future looks even more promising as rumours suggest that Beggars Banquet have, as yet, more un-issued recordings on the way comprising more previously unreleased studio material as well as more, rare, live recordings from Gary's time on the label.

ORIGINAL ALBUMS
Part One: TUBEWAY ARMY 1978-1979

TUBEWAY ARMY
(**Cat No:** UK Bega 4, US Atco SD 32-106)
Formats: vinyl (gatefold sleeve) and cassette.
Released: November 1978.
Foreign formats: issued in a number of European territories featuring a cover sticker stating the release was a Ltd edition, blue vinyl print run. Germany issued the record in a single sleeve (all gatefold sleeves featured lyrics printed within).

Re-issued August 1979 in a new cover and credited to 'Tubeway Army featuring Gary Numan' (see 'Re-issued albums' section). Second re-issue via the Fame label in May 1983 (FA 3060-LP and CA 3060), this re-issue was also joined by a rare vinyl, two-LP (each one-sided) promo. Each vinyl LP featured a green label. A third re-issue via Beggars Banquet in July 1988 came complete with a newly commissioned back cover featuring four relevant studio photos: cassette featured the debut of a lyric inlay card. This release credited to 'Gary Numan and Tubeway Army' (BBL4, BBLC4).

Special note: First 5000 copies appeared on blue vinyl, subsequently dubbed by fans as 'the blue album.'

Group Line-up: Gary Numan* – Vocals, guitars and keyboards/ Paul Gardiner – Bass and backing vocals/ Jess Lidyard – Drums.

Engineered and mixed by Mike Kemp.

Produced by Gary Numan.

Recorded at Spaceward studios, Cambridge.

* Changed surname for the release of this record.

Side One, Tracks: 'Listen To The Sirens' 3.06/ 'My Shadow In Vain' 2.59/ 'The Life Machine' 2.46/ 'Friends' 2.31/ 'Something's In The House' 4.15/ 'Every Day I Die' 2.25.

Side Two, Tracks: 'Steel And You' 4.45/ 'My Love Is A Liquid' 3.33/ 'Are You Real?' 3.26/ 'The Dream Police' 3.39/ 'Jo The Waiter' 2.41/ 'Zero Bars (Mr Smith)' 3.11. All songs by Gary Numan.

Singles: none, although 'Every Day I Die' was rumoured to be being considered.

Videos: none.

The release of Tubeway Army's self-titled, debut album showcased a group in the midst of a musical transition, as punk rock itself was, by the end of 1978, evolving into a style much more geared towards mass acceptance (*New Wave*). Tubeway Army too were also morphing into an altogether more experimental, more forward thinking type of outfit. The one thing the band had never been accepted as was as the archetypal British punk rock group (indeed, Gary had earlier shelved a whole album's worth of punky flavoured material in favour of continuing to develop the group signature sound). Gary's 'sci-fi' tinged lyrics as well as his unusual look and vocal style had never fit seamlessly into the punk rock framework and Tubeway Army, set adrift from the hordes of bratty, punk rock hopefuls were resigned to going it alone. When released, *Tubeway Army* attested to a group badly in need of a set direction, the record's twelve tracks lurched wildly from nihilistic punk rock to more world-weary acoustic numbers. The bulk of the material for Tubeway Army's debut album was recorded in July and August of 1978 and bar one or two tracks, little of the recorded material had much in common with the group's two earlier singles ('That's Too Bad' and 'Bombers' – neither included here). Tubeway Army's former punk rock bluster had here been joined by both a neo-acoustic slant as well as an embryonic interest in synthesisers (the latter brought on by Numan's chance encounter with the instrument when the hire company failed to collect it following an earlier recording session in the same studio). Despite the record's lack of any clear direction, *Tubeway Army* was still a good, solid record, littered with strong material. Fans of the group's aforementioned earlier, grittier sound would've found comfort in the record's heavier, more guitar-oriented moments with the likes of the art school raunch of 'My Shadow In Vain', the gonzoid, balls out fury of 'Friends' and the riffy pop of 'Are You Real?' all being propelled by big rock riffs and brash arrangements. However, the group's identity crisis was no better typified than with lone acoustic numbers like 'Jo The Waiter' and 'The Life Machine' being pitched against the experimental futurisms of tracks like 'Zero Bars (Mr Smith)' and 'My Love Is A Liquid.' Numan also revealed flickers of a morbid, yet humorous side to his writing with the slow burning 'Every Day I Die' being a dark paean to the joys of the 'little death.'

With the group's manifesto anchored in three distinct musical areas, choosing a single to accurately represent the album proved impossible. However, both the catchy 'Something's In The House' and the startlingly effective 'Listen To The Sirens' would've been ideal had a single from the record been required. In the end, Gary effectively abandoned the project in favour of recording a wealth of new material curtailing any plans to perform live.

Tubeway Army failed to chart nationally but did feature highly on a number of independent album listings.

Original gatefold, blue vinyl issue.

REPLICAS
(**Cat No:** UK Bega 7, US Atco 38-117)
Formats: vinyl, cassette and US 8 track tape.
Released: April 1979.
Foreign formats: America, Canada and Italy credited the record to 'Gary Numan – Tubeway Army', New Zealand and Australia issued the record in a gatefold, alternative sleeve*, Saudi Arabia issued the record with a revised track order (cassette also featured new artwork). Greece issued the record with an enclosed press release written in Greek. Spanish issue printed 'Includes 'Are 'Friends' Electric?'' on the front cover.
* Two versions exist, one featuring Gary sporting black lapels and one with red.
Re-issued September 1988 as 'Gary Numan and Tubeway Army' (BBL 7, BBLC 7).
Group Line-up: Gary Numan – Vocals, keyboards and guitars/ Paul Gardiner – Bass/

Jess Lidyard – Drums.
Engineered by John Caffery – assisted by Harvey Ishiki.
Mixed by Rikki Sylvan/ John Caffery/ Gary Numan at Marcus music, A.B.
Produced by Gary Numan.
Recorded at Gooseberry studios, London in late December 1978/ early January 1979.
Side One, Tracks: 'Me! I Disconnect From You' 3.22/ 'Are "Friends' Electric?" 5.24/ 'The Machmen' 3.07/ 'Praying To The Aliens' 3.59/ 'Down In The Park' 4.24.
Side Two, Tracks: 'You Are In My Vision' 3.14/ 'Replicas' 5.00/ 'It Must Have Been Years' 4.00/ 'When The Machines Rock' 3.14/ 'I Nearly Married A Human' 6.31.
All songs by Gary Numan.
Singles: 'Down In The Park' and 'Are "Friends" Electric?'
Videos: none, however, both singles were performed live in the studio on UK music show *The Old Grey Whistle Test* prior to the group's breakthrough. The show also screened an animated video for the track 'Praying To The Aliens' later in the year. The group also made several appearances on UK pop show *Top Of The Pops* to perform a mimed version of 'Are "Friends" Electric?' (one of the performances was remixed by the programme's producers to add some spacey embellishments).
Special note: Initial copies in the UK came with a free poster.

Recorded in a matter of days, *Replicas* was an assured, planet sized leap forward for the group, with synthesisers now taking on a more prominent role. Gary's musical and lyrical aspirations soared. Numan's 'sci-fi' themed lyrics blended perfectly with the deep, analogue boom of the synths creating a unique, otherworldly sound. However, the album was not completely dominated by electronics with tracks like 'You Are In My Vision' and 'It Must Have Been Years' being the album's two, hard driving, riffy rockers. Both tracks showed that had one particular song on *Replicas* not gone on to change everything for the group, Tubeway Army could well have developed into a slick, guitar-heavy pop act. Elsewhere though, Gary boldly embraced the new technology being woven into the group's sound with 'The Machmen' and album opener 'Me! I Disconnect From You' being dizzying welds of space age electronics and riffy rock power. However, neither of these could hope to match the sheer power of the album's two standout moments, 'Down In The Park' and 'Are "Friends" Electric?' Each song, though texturally polar opposites, were classic examples of Gary's knack of penning cold, off kilter pop music. 'Down In The Park', despite its sinister charm, was almost cinematic in its approach with much of the track possessing an almost orchestral beauty. 'Are "Friends" Electric?' on the other hand hit like a runaway freight train, the track's raw, pulsing, uncompromising synths virtually steam-rolled the listener into submission with its bowel-loosening Moogs and cold, detached vocals. 'Are "Friends" Electric? was a call to arms, a song that, when issued as a single, quickly elevated Tubeway Army to the forefront of the burgeoning electronic rock movement, then populated by a number of other synthetic obsessed luminaries like Simple Minds, Fad Gadget and Ultravox as well as the seminal German outfit Kraftwerk.

To compliment the bleak mood of the record, for the cover, Gary depicted himself as a stark, ghostly figure stood motionless in a grimly lit bare room: this picture alone echoed many of the songs that featured within the record.

Replicas became one of the first records that successfully combined guitars with

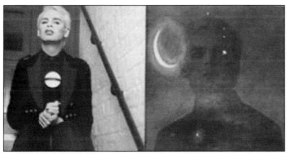

New Zealand/ Australian (black lapel) gatefold sleeve.   *Japanese issue.*

synthesisers to break through into the mainstream public domain, the record's focus and conviction were both instrumental in thrusting Tubeway Army onto international success and Gary Numan (who was just 21 at the time) as the world's first synthesiser rock star.

Again, as with *Tubeway Army*, no tour took place with Gary resisting pressure to appear live in the wake of the group's phenomenal success, preferring instead to dispense with the Tubeway Army moniker and prepare to re-launch himself as a strictly solo artist from this point on.

Replicas entered the UK album charts in April 1979 just inside the top 200 ultimately following 'Are "Friends" Electric?' to the No1 slot in June spending a total of 31 weeks on the listings.

ORIGINAL ALBUMS
Part Two: GARY NUMAN 1979-1983

THE PLEASURE PRINCIPLE
(**Cat No:** UK Bega 10, US Atco SD 38-120)
Formats: vinyl*, cassette and US 8 track tape.
Released: September 1979.
Foreign formats: Canadian and Korean sleeve feature both 'Cars' and 'Complex' printed on the cover. In addition, a further variation of the Korean issue saw this album released with a sleeve shaded red and a fold out lyric sheet. Saudi Arabian version features an alternative track order. German version featured a sticker that read, 'Gary Numan is Tubeway Army.' Hong Kong version printed the lyrics to the album on the back cover and advertised 'Cars' on the front cover. Argentinean sleeve featured the album title printed in Spanish ('*El Principio De Placer*'). Australian cover included a removable sticker that stated 'Includes the hits "Cars" and "Complex."' Japanese vinyl issue included an insert. Cassette issue also featured new artwork. Early US issues came with press kit (two page biography and photo).
* Full colour, fold out poster included with debut pressing.
Re-issued September 1988 (BBL 10, BBLC 10).
Group Line-up: Gary Numan – Vocals, keyboards and synthetic percussion/ Paul Gardiner – Bass/ Christopher Payne – Keyboards and viola/ Cedric Sharpley – Drums/ Billy Currie – Violin ('Tracks' and 'Conversation')/ Gary Robson – Backing

vocals on 'Conversation.'
Engineered and mixed by Rikki Sylvan and Harvey Webb.
Produced by Gary Numan.
Recorded at Marcus Music AB, London.
Side One, Tracks: 'Airlane' 3.18/ 'Metal' 3.33/ 'Complex' 3.14/ 'Films' 4.09/ 'M.E' 5.37.
Side Two, Tracks: 'Tracks' 2.52/ 'Observer' 2.53/ 'Conversation' 7.38/ 'Cars' 3.53/ 'Engineers' 4.00.
All songs by Gary Numan.
Singles: 'Cars' and 'Complex' ('Metal'/ 'Airlane' – issued in the Philippines only).
Videos: 'Cars', 'Complex' and 'Metal.'* In addition, 'Cars' was performed on *TOTP* when released and again alongside 'Are "Friends" Electric?' on a special Christmas show at the end of the year. 'Are "Friends" Electric?' was performed on German TV during 'The Touring Principle.' The band also performed 'Cars' and *Replicas* album track 'Praying To The Aliens' on the American TV show *Saturday Night Live* during the US leg of 'The Touring Principle' shows in early 1980.
* 'Metal', it should be pointed out, was not a proper Beggars Banquet funded promo video: this clip (featuring Gary moodily wandering around an electricity installation) was filmed by a local UK TV company especially for inclusion on one of their shows. In addition, the song was also slightly edited.

The Pleasure Principle was Gary's most easily identifiable, all electronic rock record: here the synths dominated throughout. Numan's three-album transition from abstract, experimental *New Wave* to full-on electronic pop was now complete. The record itself did not disappoint, kicking off in dramatic style with the soaring, adrenalin packed instrumental 'Airlane'. This track though quickly gave way to the icy, analogue stomp of 'Metal', a throbbing slice of exquisite cyber rock. Elsewhere, both 'Films' and 'M.E.' buckled under the weight of skyscraper, epic synths. Both tracks had US critics proclaiming Numan's 'march of the machines' sound-bites could well hold the key to the very future of rock and roll in the coming decade (a feeling shared by Gary's US label Atco who promoted *The Pleasure Principle* and 'Cars' through the early spring of 1980 as just that). With 'Cars', an instantly acknowledged synth-pop classic, invading the pop charts and dance floors the world over, it was perhaps, understandably, this album's most recognisable and

Left: Original US magazine advert.

Above: Original UK issue with free poster.

most memorable track, yet 'Cars' wasn't the record's only out and out pop song. 'Tracks' was also equally radio friendly and along with the aforementioned 'Metal', provided *The Pleasure Principle* with a further two potential smash hit singles in waiting. However, Gary ignored them both (although 'Metal' did feature as an A-side in the Philippines – Cat No: Atlantic ATR 0158-plain sleeve) and chose this album's standout track, the gorgeous synth ballad 'Complex' as the second and penultimate single from the record.

Any lingering tensions between either Gary or his label (now under the wing of the mighty WEA music group) over the change from Tubeway Army to Gary Numan were quickly put aside when both The Pleasure Principle and the album's first single 'Cars' hit the No1 spot when released in September of 1979. This event gave Numan the unique distinction of scoring four straight No1's in a row.

To support the record, Gary finally set out on his first major headlining tour, a trek that took him all over the globe as the Gary Numan phenomenon began to spread.

The Pleasure Principle debuted at No1 on the UK album chart spending 21 weeks on the top 75 listings. This album was also a major hit internationally, especially the all important US market where both the album and its attendant single 'Cars' soared into the American top 20.

TELEKON
(**Cat No:** UK Bega 19, US Atco SD 32-103)
Formats: vinyl, cassette and 8-track tape.
Released: September 1980.
Foreign formats: Australian, Japanese and American releases replaced the track 'Sleep By Windows' with former single 'I Die: You Die.' Canadian release featured a slightly different coloured sleeve. Saudi Arabian and Italian versions featured the same tracks as the US / Far East versions except in an alternative order. Japanese issue* included a black and white insert along with the standard Obi.

★★★★★

* Cassette version issued featuring new artwork (see 'Memorabilia').
Special note 1: UK cassette version added, 'We Are Glass' and 'I Die: You Die' to the album's running order. European territories issued coloured vinyl editions of the album, variations being: red, green, yellow, blue, orange, dark blue, white, marble and opaque. Initial copies also included a free, plain sleeved live single that featured: 'Remember I Was Vapour' as its A-side and 'On Broadway' on the flip (Cat No: SAM 126). Both these tracks were taken from the Gary Numan video cassette *The Touring Principle '79*, some copies of the 7-inch were also pressed onto deep red vinyl. Cover featured a peel-off sticker that stated 'Includes free live single', later copies of *Telekon* replaced the live single with a free poster.
Re-issued October 1988 (BBL19, BBLC 19).
Group Line-up: Gary Numan – Vocals, Minimoog, Polymoog, A.R.P., Pro-soloist, Jp4 Piano, Prophet 5, Cp30, Compurhythm, Synare and guitar/ Paul Gardiner – Bass and backing vocals/ Cedric Sharpley – Drums, backing vocals and percussion/ John Webb – Hand claps/ James Freud – Handclaps/ Chris Payne – Viola, solo piano, Minimoog and backing vocals/ RRussell Bell – Claves, Rhythm guitar, Lead guitar ('The Joy Circuit') and backing vocals/ Denis Haines – Prophet 5, piano, Cp30, Minimoog, Polymoog, whistle and backing vocals/ Simple Minds – Handclaps.

Engineered by Nick Smith, Steve Smith, Graham Myhre and Jess Sutcliffe.
Mixed at Rock City and Matrix.
Recorded at Rock City.
Produced by Gary Numan.

In-store poster.

Original album poster.

Original album advert.

Side One, Tracks: 'This Wreckage' 5.27/ 'The Aircrash Bureau' 5.41/ 'Telekon' 4.27/ 'Remind Me To Smile' 4.05/ 'Sleep By Windows' 5.00.
Side Two, Tracks: 'I'm An Agent' 4.26/ 'I Dream Of Wires' 5.11/ 'Remember I Was Vapour' 5.12/ 'Please Push No More' 5.40/ 'The Joy Circuit' 5.14.
All songs by Gary Numan.
Singles: 'This Wreckage' (previous singles 'We Are Glass' and 'I Die: You Die' had a limited availability, see above). In addition, an edited 3.18 mix of 'Remind Me To Smile' (Beg 1001) was issued in the US as a promo single. 'Remember I Was

Vapour' was also issued as a single in Germany. This was, however, only released on the 12-inch format backed up with a live rendition of the A-side residing on the flip.
Videos: 'This Wreckage', 'We Are Glass' and 'I Die: You Die.' In addition, 'This Wreckage' was performed on *TOTP* (an appearance that saw the brief return of Numan's long time friend Garry Robeson guesting on guitar) and 'I Die: You Die' was also performed on *The Kenny Everett TV Show*. This version of 'I Die: You Die,' however, was another alternative mix that, like the video version, has so far not surfaced officially.
Special note 2: the promo video for 'This Wreckage' actually formed part of a trio of live 'Teletour' clips, the others being 'Down In The Park' and 'Remind Me To Smile.'
Special note 3: promo copies of this album appeared minus the interlocking red stripes, print run limited to as little as two. Track list included 'I Die: You Die.'
Special note 4: a rather badly edited version of 'The Aircrash Bureau' was included on the Virgin Records

compilation *Machines* (Cat No: Virgin V2177). This 2 minutes, 22 seconds edit was also joined by the full, uncut version of 'Down In The Park.'

Recorded in the spring of 1980, *Telekon* was the fourth studio effort from the pen of the clearly prolific Gary Numan in as little as two years. This latest recording though found Numan in a different frame of mind to his previous releases, angry and frustrated by the relentless attacks from the press, weary from the constant media attention and disillusioned with the cold, hard realities of fame and its pitfalls. The sessions for *Telekon* found Numan alternating from licking his wounds to vowing his revenge. Although lyrically the record was dark and fairly downbeat, musically, *Telekon* featured some of Gary's most inspired work to date. *Telekon* was an album that bristled with jaw-dropping, lush atmospherics, beautiful melodies and ethereal synthesiser passages. Quality songs were also in abundance, ranging from the anthemic Numan pop of 'Remind Me To Smile' to the edge of the seat drama of 'The Aircrash Bureau.' Other highlights included the tear-jerking ballad 'Please Push No More', the catchy 'Remember I Was Vapour' (issued as a '12-inch only' single in Germany – see 'Memorabilia' section), the stunning 'I Dream Of Wires' and the riffy, in-your-face crunch of 'I'm An Agent.'

Numan's new image for this period saw him clad in leather boiler suits topped of with interlocking red belts and for a brief period Gary also sported a red flash in his hair. This dark man image was immediately embraced by fans and has become one of Gary's best-loved and most enduring images.

Oddly, despite the record rewarding Gary with yet another chart-topper in the UK and the subsequent 'Teletour' raising Numan's worldwide profile to even greater heights, no single was lifted from the record until a full month after the tour had concluded. When one did emerge, Numan confounded everyone by selecting the relatively lengthy and rather dour 'This Wreckage' over the album's most obvious choice 'Remind Me To Smile' (this track though was eventually issued as a limited edition 'promo only' single in the US). Not surprisingly 'This Wreckage' struggled to attain the dizzying heights achieved by previous Numan releases and stalled at the No 20 slot in early January 1981.

Telekon showed Numan had grown into an artist who was quickly becoming a master craftsman when it came to texturising his songs. On *Telekon*, the opulent synth work sang in unison with Gary who, by this record, had also taken to adding electronic effects to his already machine-like voice. The overall effect though was a far less abrasive, almost soothing musical experience than any of Gary's previous studio outings.

Telekon entered the UK album charts at No1 giving Gary his fifth and final chart topper with the album spending 11 weeks on the listings.

LIVING ORNAMENTS '79 AND '80
(**Cat No:** UK Bega BOX-1, European Cat No: K 68035)
Formats: flip top, LP sized cardboard box containing two live records and double cassettes (Cat No: BOXC1). This release was also backed up with a limited edition, 3D shop display that featured: four 12-inch by 12-inch cubes with photos on each side as well as two pyramids placed on top.
Released: April 1981.
Foreign formats: New Zealand and Australia issued both records as a gatefold double album set, the artwork

though was a brighter shade than other territories with the cover photo used for LO '79 printed in reverse (see below). The gatefold sleeve idea was repeated in Canada: however, the cover was shaded identical to the UK. In addition, the cover featured a gold stamp. Australia also issued double cassettes of both albums much like the UK. Japan issued the box-set featuring a career biography, printed in Japanese, along with the lyrics printed in English to all the songs on the two albums. In addition, a free live single was also included with the set in the Far East. Finally a special promo edition of the box-set was also issued containing a pair of white label promos of the two live records. Saudi Arabian double cassette (featuring both live albums) issued with alternative artwork.

Special note: vinyl copies had messages etched into the run off grooves with *LO* '79 marked with 'Nothing more than memories GN' and *LO '80* marked with 'Thanks, Gary Numan.'

Deleted after one month and never re-issued.

Singles: none, although fans were surprised that Beggars Banquet didn't issue a four track live EP from the set featuring perhaps the stunning 1980 re-workings of 'Down In The Park' and 'Every Day I Die' as well as two further tracks from *LO '79*.

Videos: Aside from *The Touring Principle '79* videocassette, a number of additional live clips from both 'The Touring Principle '79/ '80 World Tour and the 1980 'Teletour' emerged. Following Gary's appearance at *The Year Of The Child* concert at Wembley Arena in November 1979, the two songs performed ('Metal' and 'Down In The Park') were shown on UK TV (none of these clips feature the computer generated images that featured so heavily on the *Touring Principle '79* videocassette). A further three live clips taken from Gary's 29th of March 1980 concert in Paris were also shown on television. The clips aired from this show were 'Replicas', 'I Die: You Die' and 'Down In The Park.' Professionally filmed concert footage from Gary's show at The Toronto Music Hall in February 1980 was also aired: footage from this show was screened alongside an interview with Gary from the same venue prior to the show. Finally another trio of live clips, this time originating from the 'Teletour' were screened. The songs aired were 'Down In the Park', 'Remind Me To Smile' and 'This Wreckage' (the latter was used as a promo video). All three clips from this show were taken from the Hammersmith Odeon on the 16th of September 1980.

Japanese booklets included with the box set.

To coincide with Gary's farewell concerts at the end of April, Beggars Banquet issued two commemorative live albums available to buy either separately or contained within a unique vinyl box set. Fans opting for the more expensive boxed version found inside: order forms for official fan club merchandise as well as a four page glossy booklet that detailed every Numan concert to date as well as text from

Gary himself explaining his decision to cease touring.

The majority of fans opted to buy the boxed version of the albums with the whole set entering the UK album charts at No 4 peaking at No 2 the following week before quickly sliding down, spending a mere four weeks on the listings.

  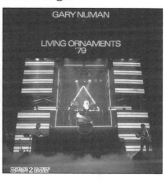

Some of the merchandise advertisements that appeared at the time of the release of the Living Ornaments box set along with the Canadian gatefold issue of the box set.

LIVING ORNAMENTS '79
(**Cat No:** UK Bega 24, European **Cat No:** K58295)
Formats: vinyl and cassette (Begac 24).
Released: April 1981.
Deleted after one month.
Group Line-up: Gary Numan – Vocals/ Paul Gardiner-Bass/ Cedric Sharpley – Drums/ Billy Currie – Keyboards/ Chris Payne – Keyboards/ RRussell Bell – Guitar.
Engineered by Tim Summerhayes, assisted by Phil Thornalley.

Mixed by Gary Numan and Tim Summerhayes, assisted by Will Gosling at the RAK studios.

Produced by Gary Numan.
Recorded on the 28th of September 1979 at the Hammersmith Odeon, London. Recorded on the RAK mobile.
Side One, Tracks: 'Airlane' 3.17/ 'Cars' 3.27/ 'We Are So Fragile' 2.39/ 'Films' 3.56/ 'Something's In The House' 4.05.
Side Two, Tracks: 'My Shadow In Vain' 2.35/ 'Conversation' 7.43/ 'The Dream Police' 4.17/ 'Metal' 3.30.
All songs by Gary Numan.
Singles: none (see box set).
Videos: none (see box set).

Tasters from this tour had previously been released (in edited form) on the B-side of the single 'Complex' ('Bombers' and 'Me! I Disconnect From You') and the free live single given away with *Telekon*, ('Remember I Was Vapour' and 'On Broadway') however, none of those tracks appeared on this album. Although this album featured just nine tracks from Gary's first headlining tour, fans were pleased to finally have an audio alternative to the 1980 released live video cassette *The Touring Principle '79*. Of the nine tracks on this record, only three ('My Shadow In

Vain', 'Conversation' and 'We Are So Fragile') had been repeated on both. In concert, Numan was obviously in his element, any critics hoping that Gary would not be able to reproduce the synthesiser wizardry from his recordings would've been instantly silenced following the melodramatic overtones of 'Airlane' (included here). In fact, quite to the contrary, live, Numan was able to add both depth and body to his already amped up, synth rock sound as the nine tracks selected for this record so admirably demonstrated. For this record, five of its tracks came from *The Pleasure Principle,* a further three originated from *Tubeway Army* with only one track emerging from the *Replicas* sessions (B-side 'We Are So Fragile'). Pitching Numan's powerhouse, synth rock work outs against the rockier *Tubeway Army* era material made for an intriguing juxtaposition emphasising that there was more to the Gary Numan phenomenon than just electronics. In all, *Living Ornaments '79* was a welcome release and a fine souvenir of Numan's first big tour.

   Living Ornaments '79 entered the UK album chart at No 47 climbing no higher with three weeks on the listings.

LIVING ORNAMENTS '80
(Cat No: UK Bega 25, European **Cat No:** K58296)
Formats: vinyl and cassette (Begac 25).
Released: April 1981.
Deleted after one month.
Group Line-up: Gary Numan – Vocals/ Paul Gardiner – Bass/ Cedric Sharpley – Drums/ RRussell Bell – Guitars/ Roger Mason – Keyboards/ Chris Payne – keyboards.
Engineered by Tim Summerhayes, assisted by Phil Thornalle.

★★★★★ Mixed at the RAK studios by Gary Numan and Tim Summerhayes, assisted by Will Gosling.
Produced by Gary Numan.
Recorded on the 16th of September 1980 at the Hammersmith Odeon, London. Recorded on the RAK mobile.
Side One, Tracks: 'This Wreckage' 5.26/ 'I Die: You Die'* 3.53/ 'M.E'. 4.36/ 'Every Day I Die' 4.35/ 'Down In The Park' 5.57.
Side Two, Tracks: 'Remind Me To Smile' 3.34/ 'The Joy Circuit' 5.56/ 'Tracks' 3.05/ 'Are "Friends" Electric?' 5.45/ 'We Are Glass' 4.42.
All songs by Gary Numan.
Singles: none (see box set).
Videos: none (see box set).
* Fans noted that Beggars Banquet had not been entirely successful in re-editing this track in to the position of track two on this record as the opening strains of the original set's next track 'I Dream Of Wires' could clearly be heard at the end of track two.

   Living Ornaments '80 featured ten incredible live tracks culled exclusively from the tenth date of Numan's 1980 'Teletour.' This show, performed as part of the UK leg saw Numan leaving behind his previous awkward and somewhat wooden live persona to emerge here as a much more confident and consummate performer. Numan was, by the end of 1980, a huge international star with a string of hit singles and albums to his name both here in the UK and across the globe and with four studio records to draw from, the set-list for the 'Teletour' was, for any devoted

Numan fan, a mouth-watering proposition. True to form, Numan did not disappoint, delivering both his emotionally charged music and his futuristic stage set and light show with considerable verve and aplomb. As this record so aptly illustrated, Numan was hitting a career peak in 1980 with suitably turbo-charged versions of 'This Wreckage', 'Remind Me To Smile', a gloriously, OTT rendition of 'The Joy Circuit' and the now virtually unrecognisable 'Every Day I Die' whizzing past in a blur of heart-stopping, keyboard based power chords and adrenalin driven nervous energy. Indeed, from the overdriven synth pop of 'I Die: You Die' to the masterful re-workings of both 'Are "Friends" Electric?' and 'Down In The Park' (both arguably sounding better here than their studio counterparts), *Living Ornaments '80* succeeded in delivering up an extraordinary, somewhat jaw-dropping snapshot of an artist at his commercial zenith.

Living Ornaments '80 entered the UK album charts at No 39 climbing no higher, spending three weeks on the listings.

DANCE
(**Cat No:** UK Bega 28, US Atco SD 38-143)
Formats: vinyl (gatefold sleeve) and cassette.
Released: September 1981.
Foreign formats: US, Brazil, Argentina and Israel released the album in a single sleeve with the latter released with a different back cover to the UK Japanese cassette issued featuring new artwork and a revised track list.
Re-issued January 1989. (BBL 28, BBLC 28).

★★★☆☆

Special note: Initial copies came with a front cover peel-off sticker advertising the enclosed free poster: later copies dropped both the gatefold sleeve and poster.

Musicians: Gary Numan – Vocals, Polymoog, Prophet 5, Roland JP4, Cp30, Claptrap, percussion, Cr78, Odyssey bass, LM 1 drum computer, piano, guitar, claves and handclaps/ Paul Gardiner – Guitar and Odyssey/ Mick Karn – Saxophone and bass/ Mick Prague – Bass/ Sean Lynch – LM1 programming/ John Webb – Handclaps, computer and JP4 operation/ Roger Mason – Prophet 5 and Cp30/ Chris Payne – Viola/ Nash the Slash – Violins/ Tim Steggles – Percussion/ Cedric Sharpley – Drums/ Jess Lidyard – Drums/ Roger Taylor – Drums and Tom toms/ Rob Dean – Guitars/ Connie Filapello – Vocals.
Engineered by Nick Smith, assisted by Sean Lynch and Juliet Brown.
Produced by Gary Numan.
Recorded at Rock City Sound Studios, Shepperton.
Side One, Tracks: 'Slowcar To China' 9.07/ 'Night Talk' 4.30/ 'A Subway Called You' 4 41/ 'Cry The Clock Said' 9.59.
Side Two, Tracks: 'She's Got Claws' 5.00/ 'Crash' 3.41/ 'Boys Like Me' 4.17/ 'Stories' 3.13/ 'My Brother's Time' 4.38/ 'You Are, You Are' 4.04/ 'Moral' 4.34.
All songs by Gary Numan, except 'Night Talk' – music by Paul Gardiner/ Gary Numan, lyrics by Gary Numan.
Singles: 'She's Got Claws.'
Videos: 'She's Got Claws.'

After all the pomp and ceremony of the farewell concerts earlier in the year and with ten million sales behind him, Numan set about crafting a record that would be a departure from all that had gone before, and with the charts full of synthesiser based acts by 1981, Gary made a conscious decision to distance himself from the now mainstream, electronic pop scene. In truth, 1981 found the singer in a sombre, more reflective mood and the resulting sessions for *Dance* revelled in a looser, jazzier, more self-indulgent theme. However, the album's moody atmospherics and lengthy songs left the finished record sounding rather awkward and uncommercial. Gary's two-year rollercoaster ride had seemingly left the singer drained and emotional and he poured these feelings into the record. *Dance* may have been the wrong record at the wrong time but that's not to say it wasn't without its merits: aside from the stellar 'She's Got Claws' other notable highlights came in the shape of the subdued pop of 'A Subway Called You', the epic 'Slowcar To China', the dreamy 'Boys Like Me' and the bizarre, carnival-like pop of 'Stories.' However, perhaps the album's two strongest tracks were a perfect example of the diversity included on the record, 'Cry The Clock Said', at ten minutes in length, beautifully summed up Numan's desire to create longer, more atmospheric, oriental mood pieces. The exact polar opposite could be found in the record's closing track, 'Moral.' This loose re-write of Gary's 1979 classic 'Metal' now came complete with new lyrics as well as a beefier, more hard rock approach. For the lyrics, Numan took a cynical swipe at the prevalent *New Romantic* scene as well as expressing his feeling of relief over turning his back on aspects of his career he had seemingly long found distasteful. Elsewhere, both the pseudo, loud and bratty hard rock of 'Crash' and the sad, reflective, torch-like ballad 'My Brothers Time' further emphasised the conflicting emotions and material served up on the record. Not surprisingly, with the general awkward and

Japanese tape issue

Above: Japanese issue.
Left: UK issue with poster

self-indulgent nature of the resulting opus and no tour to promote the project, *Dance* performed poorly when released and signalled a steep slide in Numan's fortunes from this point on. No further singles were lifted from the record (a rumoured single release for either 'Crash' or 'Moral' did not in the end materialise) and Gary effectively abandoned the project preferring to concentrate and plough his energies into a long dreamed ambition away from the music business, a solo flight around the world.

   Dance entered the UK album chart at No 4 peaking one place higher the following week before dropping away with just eight weeks on the listings.

★★★☆☆

I, ASSASSIN

(**Cat No:** U.K. Bega 40, US Atco 90014-1)
Formats: vinyl and cassette.
Released: September 1982.
Foreign formats: Japanese cassette issued featuring new art work; album also mistakenly re-titled as simply 'I.'
Special note: initial copies included a poster.
Re-issued January 1989 (BBL40, BBLC 40).
Group Line-up: Gary Numan – Vocals, keyboards and guitar/ Roger Mason – Keyboards/ Pino Palladino – Fretless bass and guitar/ Chris Slade – Drums and percussion/ John Webb – Percussion/ Mike* – Saxophone and harmonica.

* Surname unknown.
Engineered by Nick Smith, assisted by Sean Lynch.
Produced by Gary Numan.
Recorded at Rock City Studios, Shepperton, London.
Side One, Tracks: 'White Boys And Heroes' 6.27/ 'War Songs' 5.10/ 'A Dream Of Siam' 6.17/ 'Music For Chameleons' 6.07.
Side Two, Tracks: 'This Is My House' 4.57/ 'I, Assassin' 5.28/ 'The 1930's Rust' 3.58*/ 'We Take Mystery (To Bed)' 6.13.
* Slightly longer intro for the cassette issued recording.
All songs by Gary Numan.
Singles: 'Music For Chameleons,' 'We Take Mystery (To Bed)' and 'White Boys And Heroes.'
Videos: 'Music For Chameleons' and 'We Take Mystery (To Bed).' In addition, 'Music For Chameleons' was performed twice on UK pop show *TOTP* and once on *Late Night On 2, Jim'll Fix It* and *Razzamatazz*. 'We Take Mystery (To Bed)' and 'White Boys And Heroes' were performed especially for *TOTP* on location in Los Angeles and New York. Numan also appeared on the American *Merv Griffin Show* performing both 'White Boys And Heroes' and 'Cars.'

Recorded in January, the sessions for *I, Assassin* steered Numan back into more commercial waters with the tracks recorded basking in an up-tempo, danceable groove. With fretless bass now deputising as the dominant instrument, Gary's former synth heavy backdrop gave way to a bass led/electro dance approach.

Early single, 'Music For Chameleons' was an accessible slice of Numan pop and fans were confident Gary was back on course to deliver a good, solid record. Prior to the release of the record (despite Gary residing in the United States), 1982 saw Numan score three top twenty hit singles from his long awaited new studio opus (one of which, the dance floor smash 'We Take Mystery (To Bed)' even managing to breach the top ten). Sadly, when the album emerged, *I, Assassin* merely continued Numan's sliding commercial fortunes, barely making the top ten in his homeland and performing even worse just about everywhere else. This was something of a shame as *I, Assassin* was clearly a much more accessible record than *Dance*. Aside from the three excellent singles, other notable highlights were the anthemic 'This Is My House', the groove laden and riffy 'War Songs', and the atmospheric, dream-like slowie 'A Dream Of Siam.' Better still, the record wasn't without its surprises. In 'The 1930's Rust' Gary had conjured up a finger-clicking slice of jazzy blues complete with harmonica and saxophone solos, certainly Numan's most drastic musical deviation thus far (a fact not lost on Beggars

Banquet who pointed to the track as a brave and potential single, though Gary ultimately rejected this idea releasing no further singles once the album emerged in the Autumn).

Japanese tape issue.   *Japanese vinyl issue.*

1982 yearbook.

1982 also saw Numan reversing his decision to quit the road and go out on a short club tour in his temporarily adopted US homeland. These dates were Gary's first concerts on US soil since the conclusion of the 1980 'Teletour' and his first concert dates since his farewell shows of 1981. With the trek an enjoyable, though far from financially rewarding experience, Gary quietly set about planning his return to the live circuit the following year with a comeback tour scheduled for the UK in the autumn.

I, Assassin entered and peaked at No 8 on the UK album chart spending just six weeks on the listings.

WARRIORS

(**Cat No:** UK Bega 47)

Formats: vinyl and cassette.

Released: September 1983.

Foreign formats: Australian vinyl and cassette issue had a slightly different cover. Japanese issue included a black and white insert.

Re-issued January 1989 (BBL 47, BBLC47).

Group Line-up: Gary Numan – Vocals, guitar, keyboards and percussion /John Webb – Keyboards and percussion /Cedric Sharpley – Drums and percussion /Chris Payne – Viola and keyboards /RRussell Bell – Guitar /Joe Hubbard – Bass /Dick Morrissey – Saxophone /Tracy Ackerman – Vocals /Bill Nelson – Guitar and keyboards /Terry Martin – Keyboards ('Tick Tock Man').

Produced by Gary Numan.

Engineered by Pete Buhlmann, assisted by John Webb and Nick Smith.

Mixed by Pete Buhlmann and Gary Numan.

Recorded at Rock City Studios, Shepperton, England.

Special note 1: Bill Nelson, who co-produced this project with Gary requested that his production credit be removed from the finished recording (See Numan's autobiography *Praying To The Aliens* for details), this occurred on re-pressings of the *Warriors* album.

Special note 2: prior to the release of the album, fans were given the opportunity to vote for one of three potential album titles. Out of the three provided ('This Prison Moon', 'Glasshouse' and 'Poetry And Power') 'This Prison Moon' fared the best, however, Gary overrules this preferred choice and ultimately chose *Warriors* as the title for his long-awaited comeback album.

Side One, Tracks: 'Warriors' 5.49/ 'I Am Render 4.58'/ 'The Iceman Comes' 4.22/ 'This Prison Moon' 3.13/ 'My Centurion' 5.20.

Side Two, Tracks: 'Sister Surprise' 8.26/ 'Tick Tock Man' 4.20/ 'Love Is Like Clock Law' 4.00/ 'The Rhythm Of The Evening' 5.53.

All songs by Gary Numan except 'I Am Render', music by John Webb, lyrics by Gary Numan.

Singles: 'Warriors' and 'Sister Surprise.'

Videos: 'Warriors.' In addition, 'Warriors' was performed on *TOTP*, *Saturday Superstore* and *Crackerjack*. 'Sister Surprise' was also performed on *TOTP.*

The arrival of *Warriors* in September of 1983 ended an agonising, year-long wait for fans, desperate for new material. Upon hearing the staccato, apocalyptical title track, most were in no doubt that Numan was back to his menacing best. *Warriors* was an altogether tougher sounding record relying on a more traditional sound of bass, drums and guitars and with a clutch of great songs on board, the record was certainly Gary's best and most consistent album for some time. Aside from the title track itself, other notable highlights came in the shape of the effortless pop suss of 'This Prison Moon', the rockier 'My Centurion' (a track inspired by Gary's near fatal 1982 plane crash) and 'The Iceman Comes', the latter, a beautiful, windswept ballad that, in a similar fashion to the 1982 *I, Assassin* album track 'The 1930's Rust', continued Numan's drive to record material that was outside the framework of his publicly perceived sound. Elsewhere, the stripped back, haunted ballad 'Love Is Like Clock Law' showcased Gary at his most bare and honest. 'Sister Surprise' however, seemed more like a work in progress, unfinished demo, lacking much of the spark that ran through the album's eight other tracks. In addition, and throughout the disc, Gary's usual melodic sensibilities were frequently punctuated with bursts of rock guitars and thunderous drums making the record vibey and at times aggressive.

Image-wise, Numan had changed yet again: gone was the trilby hat and three-piece suits replaced by a *Road Warrior/ Mad Max* creation (a look also favoured by the likes of Duran Duran, The Police and American rockers Kiss at the time). *Warriors* was also supported by an extensive, forty-date UK tour: Gary's first live dates on UK soil in two years. With the album selling well and the tour a huge success, on the surface, Gary's comeback appeared to be going according to plan. However, behind the scenes and unknown to fans at the time, Numan's relationship with his label was quickly unravelling. With Gary's cold realisation that he was now far from a priority with the company, coupled with his frustrations over the apparent lack of promotion for his new record, when the second single from *Warriors*, the drastically re-recorded 'Sister Surprise' failed to emulate the success of the first by stalling just outside the top 30, Numan and Beggars Banquet/ WEA parted company for good.

Warriors entered the UK album chart at No 12 climbing no higher with a six week run on the listings.

FROM THE VAULTS

With Numan no longer signed to Beggars Banquet/ WEA, a cursory look into the vaults unearthed a wealth of material that, for a variety of reasons, had been shelved. These recordings were swiftly dusted down with a view to releasing them later in the year and the end result delivered one full album and a flurry of 12-inch mini-albums.

THE PLAN – 1978

(**Cat No:** UK Bega 55)
Formats: vinyl and cassette.
Released: October 1984.
Foreign formats: same as UK.
Group Line-up: Gary Numan – Vocals, keyboards, lead guitar and bass guitar/ Paul Gardiner – Bass/ Jess Lidyard – Drums.
Re-issued July 1988 (BBL55, BBLC55).

★★★☆☆ Produced by Gary Numan.

Recorded at Spaceward Studios 7th to the 9th of March 1978.
Special note: still operating under the name Valeriun at this point.
Picture disc issued limited to 4800 copies.
Side One, Tracks: 'This Is My Life'* 2.14/ 'My Shadow In Vain'** 4.03/ 'Critics'* 1.30/ 'Mean St'* 3.12/ 'Thoughts No 2'* 3.22/ 'Bombers'** 3.51.
Side Two, Tracks: 'Basic J'* 2.49/ 'Ice'* 2.12/ 'Something's In The House'** 4.05/ 'Do Your Best' (original version of 'Friends')* 2.30/ 'Check It'* 3.33/ 'This Machine' (original version of 'Steel And You')** 3.54.
* Previously unreleased track.
** Original demo recording, previously unreleased.
All songs by Gary Numan/ Valeriun.
Singles: 'This Is My Life' released as a double sided, promo 7-inch limited to 300 copies only (Cat No: TUB1).
Videos: none.

First fruits of this campaign delivered a whole album of previously unreleased material dating from the early days of Tubeway Army. The twelve tracks on the disc all predated the band's official debut album and were much more in tune with the

Left: Early '78 Tubeway Army gig poster.
Above: Both sides of The Plan – 1978 *picture disc.*

group's two early singles, 'That's Too Bad' and 'Bombers' (the latter track included here in its original demo form). The recordings themselves appeared to have been an early attempt at assembling an album and unusually for record company exercises like this, the discovered material was, on the whole, rather good, highlighting Gary's flair for penning great material even at this early stage of his career.

Annoyingly (for fans as well as Gary), this project surfaced mere weeks before Numan's long anticipated comeback with his first release on his own imprint Numa Records, effectively leaving fans with little choice but to buy two new album's in the space of a month.

The Plan-1978 entered the U.K. album chart at No 29 climbing no higher spending four weeks on the listings.

1978-1979 VOLUME TWO
(**Cat No:** UK Bega 123E)
Formats: red and black vinyl only.
Released: March 1985.
Foreign formats: none.
Special note: bizarrely, *Volume two* didn't appear until after *Volume's One and Three*. *Volume One* was a re-issue of the same 12-inch mini-album released in March 1983 (albeit with one minor difference – see 'Re-issued albums' for this release).

★★☆☆☆

Group Line-up: for 'Fade Out 1930's': Gary Numan/ Valeriun – Vocals and guitar/ Paul Gardiner – Bass/ Bob Simmonds – Drums. Line-up for remaining tracks: Gary Numan – Vocals, keyboards and guitars/ Paul Gardiner – Bass/ Jess Lidyard-Drums.
All tracks produced by Gary Numan ('Valeriun' in the case of track one).
Studio information for track one, (see *The Plan-1978*).
Studio information for Tracks two to four, (see *Replicas*).
Side One, Tracks: 'Fade Out 1930's' 3.10 (demo 1978)/ 'The Crazies' 2.56 (out-take from the *Replicas* sessions).
Side Two, Tracks: 'Only A Downstat' 3.38 (out-take from the *Replicas* sessions)/ 'We Have A Technical' 8.03 (out-take from the *Replicas* sessions).
All tracks previously unreleased.
Credited to 'Numan – Tubeway Army.'

At the same time Numan was back in the UK top 20 singles chart with the Sharpe and Numan track 'Change Your Mind', Beggars Banquet continued their look into the vaults by issuing three 12-inch mini-albums. Aside from *Volume One*, which had previously been released, the other two contained hitherto unheard recordings. Although essentially off-cut material, fans were nevertheless highly impressed with *Replicas* out-take 'We Have A Technical' and rightfully questioned its exclusion from the finished album.

★★☆☆☆

1978-1979 VOLUME THREE

(**Cat No:** UK Bega 124E)
Formats: blue and black vinyl.
Released: February 1985.
Foreign formats: none.
Group Line-up: for Side one (see 'Fade Out 1930's').
Group Line-up: for Side two 'A Game Called Echo': this track was recorded at Rock City Studios and was an early recording from the *Telekon* sessions, musicians other than Gary Numan and Paul Gardiner are unknown.

Both 'Random' and 'Oceans' date from the early sessions for *The Pleasure Principle* and are likely to feature most, if not all of the musicians connected with that album.
All tracks produced by Gary Numan (Valeriun in the case of 'The Monday Troop' and 'Crime Of Passion').
Studio information for side one (see *The Plan – 1978*).
Studio information for 'A Game Called Echo' (see *Telekon*).
Both 'Random' and 'Oceans' were recorded in the early part of April 1979 at Freerange studios, London.
Side One, Tracks: 'The Monday Troop' 3.00/ 'Crime Of Passion' 3.38/ 'The Life Machine'*1.55.
Side Two, Tracks: 'A Game Called Echo' 5.10/ 'Random' 3.50/ 'Ocean' 3.02 (both instrumentals).
All tracks previously unreleased.
* Original demo recording, previously unreleased.
Credited to 'Numan – Tubeway Army.'

Third and final mini-album of rare and lost recordings with the main talking point of this release falling to both 'The Monday Troop' and 'Crime Of Passion', two early Tubeway Army recordings that saw the group adopting a world-weary, street-busker sound. Also worthy of note was the instrumental 'Random.' Although previously unreleased this track had originally been aired in 1979 on the UK leg of 'The Touring Principle.'

All three mini-albums were also gathered together at this point and released as a cassette only compilation album (see 'Compilation albums – Beggars Banquet').

Numan-themed mirror.

European ad for Replicas.

ORIGINAL SINGLES
Part One: TUBEWAY ARMY 1978-1979

THAT'S TOO BAD
1. 'That's Too Bad' 3.17 (non-album track) 2. 'Oh! Didn't I Say' 2.20 (non-album track).
(**Cat No:** UK Beg 7)
Formats: 7-inch vinyl only.
Released: February 1978.
Foreign formats: none.
Special note: re-issued as a special edition double-pack in June 1979 (see 'Re-issued singles').

★★★★☆ No promo video.

Tubeway Army's debut single was a typical, post-Sex Pistols slab of 70s punk rock, a snotty, lairy, adrenalin packed anthem that was one of three tracks on the group's original demo and acknowledged by Beggars Banquet at the time as one of the group's strongest early recordings. 'That's Too Bad' was an unashamed attempt by Gary to create a recognisable punk rock anthem, the track's raucous, buzz-saw riffs and phlegm-spattered chorus saw the song immediately embraced by the UK punk scene, selling well enough to guarantee the group further recording opportunities.

Gary had also yet to choose Numan as his professional name at this point and chose, along with the rest of the group (now including Bob Simmons who replaced the departed Jess Lidyard), spacey synonyms. 'Valeriun' for Gary, 'Scarlett' for Paul Gardiner and 'Rael' for Bob (who lasted for this record only). Over on the flip side was 'Oh! Didn't I Say', a track fans have long pointed out was actually far better than the chosen A-side.

'That's Too Bad' failed to chart.

BOMBERS
1. 'Bombers' 3.48 (non-album track) 2. 'O.D. Receiver' 2.39 (non-album track) 3. 'Blue Eyes' 1.47 (non-album track).
(Cat No UK Beg 8)
Formats: 7-inch vinyl only.
Released: July 1978.
Foreign formats: none.
Special note: re-issued in June 1979 with 'That's Too Bad' (see 'Re-issued singles').

★★★☆☆ No promo video.

With a revised line-up now including additional guitarist Sean Burke and new drummer Barry Benn (replacing the departed Bob Simmons) Tubeway Army issued their second single. For this release, the band were joined by the debut of producer Kenny Denton (a record label request, however, this liaison didn't last and Gary himself produced all subsequent recordings issued by the band). 'Bombers' was a much more restrained offering from the group lacking much of the pent-up fury of the band's debut 'That's Too Bad.' In addition, the track's smooth and commercial production job did not sit well with the group's early punk rock fan base. Although 'Bombers' would equal the sales of 'That's Too Bad', Gary was now more convinced than ever that the punk rock bubble had burst and what the public really wanted was a return to good old-fashioned show business. Following the release of this single, the Tubeway Army line-up splintered with both Gary and Paul re-uniting with Jess Lidyard and Barry and Sean forming a new group going by the name of Tubeway Patrol (one single issued in 1981 on the Carrere label entitled 'Do Eyes Ever Meet?').

'Bombers' failed to chart.

DOWN IN THE PARK
1 'Down In The Park' 4.20. 2. 'Do You Need The Service?' 3.36 (non-album track).
(**Cat No:** UK Beg 17)
1. 'Down In The Park' 4.20. 2. 'Do You Need The Service?' 3.36 (non-album track) 3. 'I Nearly Married A Human 2' 6.40 (non-album track).
(**Cat No:** UK Beg 17T – Limited edition, 5000 copies only).
12-inch cover different to the 7-inch (see 'Memorabilia').
Formats: 7-inch and 12-inch vinyl.
Released: March 1979.
Foreign formats: none.
No promo video though the song was performed on *The Old Grey Whistle Test*.

Original magazine advert.

'Down In The Park' was the perfect introduction to the group's new record: its atmospheric, neo gothic chill beautifully conjured up the cold, bleak nightmare world of *Replicas*, 'Down In The Park's' grandiose instrumental flourishes and moody synths were in stark contrast to Numan's otherworldly narrative of androids, shadowy figures and rape machines.

The track's icy desolation struck an instant chord with the group's previously small but dedicated following swelling the fan base as a result.

Although the single failed to chart nationally, 'Down In The Park' sold three times as many copies as the band's two previous singles and neatly paved the way for the group's groundbreaking next release.

ARE 'FRIENDS' ELECTRIC?
1. 'Are "Friends" Electric?' 5.19. 2. 'We Are So Fragile' 2.39 (non-album track).
(**Cat No:** UK Beg 18)
Formats: 7-inch vinyl.
Released: May 1979.
Foreign formats: 12-inch version issued in Germany (Intercord INT 126-501). Japanese 7-inch sleeve different. Spanish 7-inch sleeve different. French 7-inch sleeve different, also features an alternative B-side:

'Down In The Park.' Italian 7-inch sleeve different, in addition, Italy issued a special 7-inch promo featuring an edited 4.00 version of it's A-side. Canadian 7-inch featured an alternative B-side: 'I Nearly Married A Human.' American 7-inch featured an alternative B-side: 'You Are In My Vision' (some copies of this single actually played the track 'Me! I Disconnect From You' despite stating otherwise), in addition, US 7-inch and 12-inch promo issued with a different sleeve (12-inch issued in both a black and white sleeve and a rarer die cut sleeve. This single was credited to Gary Numan only – see Memorabilia) and edited down to 3.46 minutes (Atco DMD235). Also extremely rare US picture disc released. South African 7-inch featured an alternative B-side: 'Replicas' (WBS323).

Special note: UK 7-inch picture disc issued (Beg 18P), print run limited to 20,000. No promo video though the song was performed on German TV and *TOTP*
Music sheet for this song issued following the release of the single.

The second single selected from *Replicas* continued the band's synthesised manifesto, however, unlike the classical, delicate strains of 'Down In The Park', 'Are "Friends" Electric? was powered full tilt by a driving, throbbing wall of synth riffs, the song's steamrolling pace and energy was both hypnotic in its execution and relentless in its pursuit. The track itself was a masterful mix of astute pop aesthetics and space age dynamics intercut with a brace of spoken word passage all topped off with Gary's disaffected, icey vocals. Within weeks the song had breached the top fifty putting it under the watchful gaze of the UK's premier pop show *Top Of The Pops*, who duly invited the band on to the show to perform. Their debut appearance was both mesmerising and entrancing. The band's striking, unified look and futuristic, synthesised sound immediately captured the public's imagination and with the help of a limited edition 7-inch picture disc single (itself a relatively new and desirable vinyl format), 'Are "Friends" Electric?' was quickly inside the top 30 and picking up sales fast. More startling performances on *Top Of The Pops* followed and with the single selling at a phenomenal rate, it finally soared into the top ten before finally dislodging Anita Ward's disco hit 'Ring My Bell' from the top spot.

'Are "Friends" Electric?' turned Tubeway Army and Gary Numan into household names virtually overnight: the track's stirring electronics and pulsing drone immediately opened the floodgates for the electronic rock movement finally bringing synthesisers into the public's consciousness and into the pop charts.

'Are "Friends" Electric?' entered the charts at No 72 reaching No1 on the 30th of June spending 4 weeks at the top of the charts and 16 weeks on the top 75 listings.

 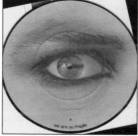 

Above: 12-inch and picture disc version of 'Are "Friends" Electric?'
Right: Original music sheet.

Special note: 'Are "Friends" Electric?' would prove to be the group's final single and swan song with Gary opting to present himself as a solo artist from this point on

ORIGINAL SINGLES
Part Two: GARY NUMAN 1979-1983

CARS
1. 'Cars' 3.53. 2. 'Asylum' (non-album track) 2.30.
(**Cat No:** UK Beg 23)
Formats: 7-inch and 12-inch* vinyl.
Released: September 1979.
Foreign formats: Spanish and Holland back sleeve different. Italian sleeve different. South African (Zimbabwe): 7-inch B-side – 'Airlane.' US: 7-inch B-side – 'Metal.' Canadian: 7-inch B-side – 'Are "Friends" Electric?' Brazilian: 7-inch-poster sleeve (Cat No: PRO 11025). Japanese: 7-inch sleeve different. French: 12-inch B-side – Airlane – also featured a third track by another artist (Cat No: PRO 508). Issued in Peru as 'Carros.'

Promo video shot.
* German: 12-inch issued (Cat No: INT 126-502), tracks same as UK: 7-inch, cover featured two peel-off slickers that stated 'Gary Numan is Tubeway Army' and 'Maxi-single.'
Music sheet for this song issued following the release of this single (see below).

Having abandoned the Tubeway Army pseudonym to begin a solo career, Gary's first solo single (this time aided by the debut of a glossy, slick promotional video) wasted no time in duplicating the success of 'Are "Friends" Electric?' by instantly rocketing to the No 1 spot in the UK singles chart when released.

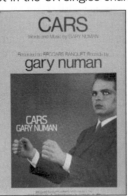

Alternative 'back sleeve' for the Spanish issue of 'Cars.'

Original magazine advert and music sheet.

Numan's phenomenal success story was now no longer confined to just the U.K., with 'Cars', Gary was able to tap into the international market (thanks in part to the rise of *New Wave*) with the single going top ten all over the world including the lucrative US market who, like the UK, quickly succumbed to Numan's monolithic, robo-rocking synth-rock sound. 'Cars' was a compelling, infectious piece of music complimented by an irresistible hook and beat providing Numan with a global smash.

However, although a hero to some, these feelings were not shared by the written media (especially the punk rock obsessed UK press) who balked at the idea of a synthesised pop star and roundly dismissed and demonised him from this point on.

'Cars' entered the UK singles chart at No 20 reaching No 1 with an 11 week run on the top 75.

COMPLEX

1 'Complex' 3.09. 2. 'Bombers' (live 1979) 5.48 (non-album track).
(**Cat No:** UK Beg 29)
1. 'Complex' 3.09. 2. 'Bombers' (live 1979). 5.48 (non-album track) 3. 'Me! I Disconnect From You' (live 1979) 3.05 (non-album track).
(**Cat No:** UK Beg 29T)
Formats: 7-inch and 12-inch* vinyl.
Released: November 1979.
Foreign formats: Dutch sleeve, different colour.

★★★★★

Japanese sleeve different.
* Artwork slightly different.
Promo video shot.**
** Video revealed the Gary Numan band had been trimmed to a five-piece following the departure of keyboard player Billie Currie.

Numan concluded a very successful year by issuing the semi-autobiographical 'Complex' as the second single from *The Pleasure Principle*. The track was, itself, a beautiful ballad shot through with Gary's innate sense of melody and was perhaps the ideal track to show another side to the Numan cannon. Fans, however, would have perhaps preferred to see 'Metal' released as the next single (indeed a low key promo video was shot for this track). As it was, Numan's surprise choice paid off as 'Complex' joined Both 'Cars' and 'Are "Friends" Electric?' in the upper most reaches of the charts.

'Complex' entered the UK charts at No 15 peaking at No 6 with a 9-week chart run.

End of the year magazine advert.

WE ARE GLASS

1. 'We Are Glass' 4.40 (non-album track). 2. 'Trois Gymnopedies (First Movement)' 2.44 (non-album track).
(**Cat No:** UK Beg 35)
Formats: 7-inch vinyl only.
Released: May 1980.
Foreign formats: Spanish, Italian and Japanese sleeves all different to the UK. Holland sleeve shaded blue: in addition, this single was issued as a series of coloured vinyl (blue, red, green, white and yellow).

★★★★★

Promo video shot.

Special note 1: the video was banned by UK music show *Top Of The Pops* due to what the show's producers saw as unnecessary acts of violence during scenes depicting Gary smashing televisions and large mirrors with a sledgehammer.

Special note 2: originally a four-track, live EP was scheduled to be issued in May. Tracks scheduled for inclusion were: 'Down In The Park (alternative live mix)', 'On Broadway', 'Every Day I Die' and 'Remember I Was Vapour.'

Upon completion of the 'Touring Principle' world tour in Australia, a new single emerged. 'We Are Glass' was a noticeably tougher sounding song from Numan: laced with powerful, choppy bursts of electric guitar as well as his now trademark anthemic synths. This new single also ushered in a new image for fans to digest with Gary clad in all-in-one leather boiler suits complimented with interlocking red belts. This design also formed part of the framework for the artwork on the next couple of singles as well as the upcoming new album and tour.

'We Are Glass' entered the UK charts at No 10 peaking at No 5, with a 7-week run on the top 75.

I DIE: YOU DIE
1. 'I Die: You Die' 3.40 (non-album track). 2. 'Down In The Park (piano version)' 4.16 (non-album track).
(**Cat No:** UK Beg 46)
Formats: 7-inch vinyl only.
Released: August 1980.
Foreign formats: American and Canadian B-side-'Sleep By Windows.' Japanese sleeve different.
A rather badly edited version of 'I Die: You Die' appeared on the compilation album *Chart Explosion* (Cat No: 'KTEL' NE 1103).

Special note: This single also emerged on a variety of coloured vinyl formats, 'I Die: You Die' was issued as green, yellow, red, orange, white and blue as well as the standard black vinyl release. Holland issued yet more variations.

Promo video shot.

Special note: video for 'I Die: You Die' featured an unreleased, alternative take of the song. A second, alternative take of this song was issued as an extremely rare, limited edition (six copies only) promo 7-inch – (Cat No: UK Beg 46 A1).

'I Die: You Die' proved to be an immediate hit with fans who quickly acknowledged the song as another fine addition to Numan's growing and impressive back catalogue, clearly Gary had hit a rich seam of creativity and 'I Die: You Die' was yet another stunning piece of music. From its handclapped, electric piano intro to its glorious, melodramatic, feedback laden conclusion, 'I Die: You Die' saw Numan reaching the very pinnacle of his powers.

For the lyrics, Numan took a long overdue swipe at the ever vitriolic UK press whose unwanted and vicious, written attacks had clearly shocked the star. In the song, Numan retaliated with a mixture of anger and resentment before rightfully pointing out that, in any case, they were all too late anyway. Quickly hailed as a classic, Numan's expanding fanbase sent this single crashing into the UK top 10 a mere week after its release.

Gary also continued to defy convention by including neither this single nor the previous top 5 smash 'We Are Glass' on the vinyl version of *Telekon*.

'I Die: You Die' entered the UK charts at No 8 peaking at No 6 with a 7 week run on the top 75.

THIS WRECKAGE

1. 'This Wreckage' 5.10. 2. 'Photograph' (instrumental) 2.29 (non-album track).
(**Cat No:** UK Beg 50)
Formats: 7-inch vinyl only.
Released: December 1980.
Foreign formats: Japanese sleeve different.
Promo video shot.
Special note: A rather poorly edited version of 'This Wreckage' was included on the 'KTEL' compilation album *Hit Machine*.

★★★☆☆

Music sheet for this song issued following the single's release (see below).

Telekon's opening track was issued as a single following the conclusion of the 'Teletour' in late 1980, however, 'This Wreckage' with its mildly nihilistic lyrics ('And what if God's dead, we must have done something wrong') and plodding pace was perhaps not the best track to issue as the first single from *Telekon,* especially with the December singles chart traditionally overrun with festive novelty singles and charity releases. 'This Wreckage' was also a bizarre choice in itself as most fans were fully expecting the UK to follow the American lead by issuing 'Remind Me To Smile' – itself another classic slice of Numan pop – as the first real single from the album. 'This Wreckage,' although catchy and edgy, didn't really cut it as a single and ended Numan's unbroken raids on the British top 10.

'This Wreckage' entered the UK charts at No 35 peaking at No 20 with a 7 week run on the top 75.

Original music sheet.

STORMTROOPER IN DRAG

1. 'Stormtrooper In Drag' 4.53 (non-album track).
2. 'Night Talk' 4.30.
(**Cat No:** UK Beg 61)
Formats: 7-inch vinyl only.
Released: July 1981.
Foreign formats: none.
This single was credited to Paul Gardiner alone.
Special note: 12-inch white label promo also released (Cat No: UK Beg 61T), rumours that this edition of the single featured an alternative mix of the A-side sadly proved to be incorrect.

★★★★★

First new material from Numan following his much publicised farewell concerts arrived in the shape of this low-key single release. 'Stormtrooper In Drag' was an ominous and moody track powered by hypnotic, shimmering, melodic guitars and swooping synths that ghosted in and out of the mix. The song was further enhanced by an unusually loose, less stylised vocal performance from Gary.

Fans have since speculated that aside from helping long time Numan ally Paul Gardiner kick-start a solo career, 'Stormtrooper In Drag' was an attempt to revisit the era of the pre-success Tubeway Army axis of Gary, Paul, and Jess Lidyard (although for this project Gary's younger brother John substituted for Jess behind the drum kit). 'Stormtrooper In Drag' was certainly much closer in spirit to Tubeway Army than the heavily synthesised sound that Numan had become famous for. In addition, by crediting the single to Paul Gardiner, it guaranteed its anonymity and passed by largely unnoticed by Gary's fan base slipping quietly and quickly in and out of the lower reaches of the UK singles chart.

'Stormtrooper In Drag' entered the UK singles chart at No 68 climbing to a peak position of No 49 with a 4-week run on the top 75.

SHE'S GOT CLAWS
1. 'She's Got Claws' 4.43. 2. 'I Sing Rain' 2.34 (non-album track).
(**Cat No:** UK Beg 62)
1. 'She's Got Claws' 4.43. 2. 'I Sing Rain' 2.34 (non-album track). 3. 'Exhibition' 4.30 (non-album track).
(**Cat No:** UK Beg 62T).
Formats: 7-inch and 12-inch vinyl.
Released: August 1981.

★★★★★ **Foreign formats:** Italian, Spanish and Japanese* sleeves all different. In addition, a bootleg three track tape emerged from Saudi Arabia.

* Lyrics also printed on the back sleeve of the Japanese issue.
Special note: Some mis-pressed British copies of the 7-inch version of this single actually played a former single by the UK pop duo Dollar ('Hand Held In Black and White'). In addition, single sleeves were printed in lighter and darker shades.

An edited version of 'She's Got Claws' can also be found on the 'KTEL' compilation album *Modern Romance* (**Cat No:** KTEL NE 1156).
Promo video shot.

'She's Got Claws' heralded in a new musical era for Gary, gone was the strict, bombastic, electronic backdrop, replaced here with a looser, jazzier, more spontaneous sound. Fans had earlier heard a tantalising and very much work in progress preview of this song at Numan's three farewell concerts: however, the finished article, complete with re-worked lyrics and some fairly bizarre yet inspired saxophone playing courtesy of Japan's Mick Karn provided them with another fine single and Numan yet another career highlight.

Image-wise, Numan ditched the previous 'Dark man' look for a more relaxed, almost 'Bogart' era style complete with a three-piece suit and trilby hat.

'She's Got Claws' entered the UK singles chart at No 15 climbing to a peak position of No 6 with a 6 week run on the top 75.

LOVE NEEDS NO DISGUISE
1. 'Love Needs No Disguise' 4.58. 2. 'Take Me Home' 5.33 (non-album track).*
(**Cat No:** UK Beg 68)
1. 'Love Needs No Disguise' 4.58. 2. 'Take Me Home' 5.33 (non-album track)* 3. 'Face To Face' (non-album track).

★★★★☆

(**Cat No:** UK Beg 68T)
Formats: 7-inch and 12-inch vinyl.
Released: December 1981.
Foreign formats: Japanese sleeve different. In addition, some sleeves were textured.
Promo video shot.
Group Line-up: Chris Payne – Viola and keyboards /RRussell Bell – Guitar /Dennis Haines – Keyboards (lead vocals on 'Take Me Home') /Cedric Sharpley – Drums/ Gary Numan – Guest vocalist.
This single credited to 'Gary Numan – Dramatis.'

* Credited to Dramatis only.
Special note: The Dramatis band performed this single without Gary Numan on the UK chart show Top Of The Tops but sadly this performance was never screened.

Following the much publicised farewell concerts in April 1981, most of the former members of Numan's backing group (with the exception of bassist Paul Gardiner) re-grouped and re-emerged as Dramatis. The group swiftly signed to Elton John's label Rocket Records and issued a trio of excellent though poor selling singles throughout the summer of 1981. The group's bid for stardom though was given a significant boost when a chance studio visit from Gary himself in the late Autumn resulted in the star laying down guest lead vocals on one of the tracks the band were working on at the time. The completed song was deemed so good that it was quickly issued as the group's fourth single (though this one-off release emerged through Gary's label Beggars Banquet and not Rocket Records) and resulted in a modest, debut hit for the group. The song itself was a pretty, mid-tempo, melodic anthem featuring lyrics that were part love song, part celebration of the glory days of the early 80s Gary Numan band. For the accompanying promo video Gary and the Dramatis band performed the track in front of a specially invited audience, mostly made up of members of the Gary Numan fan club.

Sadly, subsequent releases from Dramatis failed to match this single's success and the band eventually faded from view.

'Love Needs No Disguise' entered the UK charts at a peak position of No 33 spending a total of 7 weeks on the top 75.

★★★★☆

MUSIC FOR CHAMELEONS
1. 'Music For Chameleons' (single edit) 3.35. 2. 'Noise Noise'* 3.39 (non-album track).
(**Cat No:** UK Beg 70)
1. 'Music For Chameleons' (extended version). 2. 'Noise Noise'* 3.39 (non-album track) 3. 'Bridge? What Bridge?'** 4.27. (non-album track).
(**Cat No:** UK Beg 70T)
Formats: 7-inch and 12-inch vinyl.
Released: March 1982.
Foreign formats: German sleeve different. Italian back sleeve of the single different.
Promo video shot.

This single marked the beginning of extended and edited versions of Numan's singles being released.

Music sheet for this single was available to buy shortly after the single's release.
*Features Teresa Bizarre as guest vocalist.
**Features both Teresa Bizarre and David Van Day as guest vocalists.
Special note 1: Teresa and David make up the UK pop duo Dollar.
Special note 2: Numan's first single of 1982 was originally scheduled to be 'The 1930's Rust', however, Gary overruled his record label and issued 'Music For Chameleons' instead.

With his round-the-world flight concluded, Gary got back to the business of making music, the first fruits of which arrived with the release of this new single in the spring of 1982. 'Music For Chameleons' stuck close to the blueprint laid down by 'She's Got Claws', propelled by an accessible, danceable groove yet all the while moody enough in sound to be recognisably Gary Numan.

'Music For Chameleons' found Gary still using a variation of his *Dance* image and fans catching a glimpse of the video for this track saw Numan playing out a somewhat fantasy gangster role.

On the flipside to the single was another new track, entitled 'Noise Noise', a fantastic, spiky Numan anthem that fans argued was far too good to have been relegated as a mere B-side as it was clear that the song was easily strong enough to have been released as a single in its own right.

'Music For Chameleons' entered the UK singles chart at No 35 climbing to No 19 with a 7-week run on the top 75.

Original music sheet.

Promo video shot.

WE TAKE MYSTERY (TO BED)
1. 'We Take Mystery (To Bed)' 3.31 (single edit). 2. 'The Image Is' 5.59 (non-album track).
(**Cat No:** UK Beg 77)
1. 'We Take Mystery (To Bed)' 7.42 (extended version). 2. 'The Image Is' 5.59 (non-album track) 3. 'We Take Mystery (To Bed) (early version)' 5.58 (non-album track).
(**Cat No:** UK Beg 77T – cover slightly altered)
Formats: 7-inch and 12-inch vinyl.
Released: June 1982.
Foreign formats: matched the UK

Never one to take the easy root, 'We Take Mystery (To Bed)' was a classic example of Numan's unique approach to pop music and as Numan singles went, this was the oddest yet. For not only did it sport a somewhat eyebrow raising, cryptic title but its frantic rhythm track and soaring anthemic synth riffs were bizarrely offset with an affected, almost mumbled vocal delivery making the song both commercial and obscure at the same time. As strange as it was it didn't stop Numan's die-hard fan base from buying it in droves and within a week of release 'We Take Mystery (To Bed)' had debuted inside the British top 10.

'We Take Mystery (To Bed)' entered the UK singles chart at No 9 climbing no higher with a 4-week run on the top 75. This single was also Gary's 7th and final top 10 hit in the UK.

WHITE BOYS AND HEROES
1. 'White Boys And Heroes' (single edit) 3.30. 2. 'Wargames' 3.58 (non-album track).
(**Cat No:** UK Beg 81)
1. 'White Boys And Heroes' (extended version) 6.27. 2. 'Wargames' 3.58 (non-album track). 3. 'Glitter And Ash' (instrumental) 4.49 (non-album track).
(**Cat No:** UK Beg 81T)
Formats: 7-inch and 12-inch vinyl.
Released: August 1982.

★★★☆☆

Foreign formats: Special 12-inch issued in the US featuring extended mixes of both 'White Boys And Heroes' and 'We Take Mystery (To Bed)' – (Cat No: Promo 468).
No promo video.

Prior to the release of the album *I, Assassin*, a new single emerged. This new track continued Numan's drive to inject a danceable, groove-oriented edge into his music without compromising his trademark menacing attack. Although this was achieved, 'White Boys And Heroes' made for a somewhat unusual single release with its intentional droning chorus and lop-sided rhythm track being bolstered by some superb soaring synth riffs and a particularly inspired saxophone outro. However, of the three singles that emerged from *I, Assassin,* fans viewed this one to be the weakest.

'White Boys And Heroes' entered the UK singles chart at No 20 climbing no higher with a 4-week run on the top 75.

WARRIORS
1. 'Warriors' (single edit) 4.03. 2. 'My Car Slides 1' 3.02 (non-album track).
(**Cat No:** UK Beg 95)
1. 'Warriors' (album version) 5.47. 2. 'My Car Slides 1' 3.02 (non-album track). 3. 'My Car Slides 2' 4.45 (non-album track).
(**Cat No:** UK Beg 95T-alternative sleeve)

★★★★★

Formats: 7-inch and 12-inch vinyl.
Released: September 1983.
Foreign formats: matched the UK.
Promo video shot.
Special note: Aeroplane shaped 7-inch picture disc released. (Beg 95P).

From its ghostly, windswept and eerie intro, 'Warriors' introduced a far tougher, earthier sound for the Numan army to digest. The song's clipped, rhythmic grooves and deeply melodic atmospherics proved Numan's year long sabbatical had not seen the star laid idle, far from it, 'Warriors' was an inspired re-invention, the song's doomsday overtures, hard rock guitars and driving rhythms, all topped off with Gary's cool and dusky vocals proved Numan was not only keen to move forward musically but was still very much a force to be reckoned with five years after his initial chart breakthrough. Over on the flip side to this single was yet another superb new track. 'My Car Slides 1' was a somewhat ethereal and seductive ballad that was clearly far too good to be languishing as an overlooked B-side and fans were baffled as to why it hadn't been selected for the forthcoming *Warriors* album.

Sadly, despite 'Warriors' being a world away from the likes of 'Cars' and 'Are "Friends" Electric?', the time away had done nothing to soften the hostility of the British media who merely picked up where they left off and launched a fresh attack on the star. Worse still, bad luck was now beginning to figure into the equation with 'Warriors' being denied its No 17 chart position due to the sales of picture discs being discounted in the one week the single was due to climb into the top 20. With the single repositioned further down the chart, to all intents and purposes, Numan's big comeback suddenly looked like a flop.

'Warriors' entered the UK singles chart at No 30 climbing to No 20 the following week. The week after that the single climbed into the top 20 but was re-positioned back one place to the No 21 slot following the one week picture disc ban. 'Warriors' spent a total of 5 weeks on the top 75.

SISTER SURPRISE
1. 'Sister Surprise' (new version) 4.58. 2. 'Poetry And Power' 4.28 (non-album track).
(**Cat No:** UK Beg 101)
1. 'Sister Surprise' (new version) 4.58. 2. 'Poetry And Power' 4.28 (non-album track). 3. 'Letters'* (non-album track).
(**Cat No:** UK Beg 101)
Formats: 7-inch and 12-inch vinyl.
Released: October 1983.
Foreign formats: matched the UK.

★★★☆☆

No promo video.
* This track actually turned out to be a mis-pressing and was in reality the 1981 B-side 'Face To Face' that had previously occupied the flip side of the 12-inch version of 'Love Needs No Disguise', the collaboration between Dramatis and Gary Numan.
Special note: The 12-inch version of 'Sister Surprise' claimed to include an extended mix of the single's A-side, however, this turned out to be incorrect as only the newly recorded 7-inch mix appeared.

This muscular, aggressive re-recording of 'Sister Surprise', although better than it's somewhat unfinished album counterpart, was still something of a mess, sounding at times like two separate songs desperately jockeying for centre stage at once. 'Sister Surprise' found Numan straying into the unlikely world of hard rock with Gary's trademark synths being relegated to the background behind a heavy onslaught of slamming beats, pounding drums and bursts of wild and manic saxophones flourishes. 'Sister Surprise' was also quite a bizarre and unexpected choice for a single in the first place with fans initially pointing to 'The Iceman Comes' as the preferred and likely follow up to 'Warriors.' Sadly this did not materialise. With no video, radio play and little in the way of promotion from Beggars Banquet/ WEA, 'Sister Surprise' made only a brief appearance in the lower reaches of the top 40 before vanishing for good.

'Sister Surprise' entered the UK single chart at No 36, climbing to a peak position of No 32, spending 3 weeks on the top 75.

This would turn out to be the final single from Gary under contract to Beggars Banquet/ WEA as by the year's end artist and label parted ways bringing to an end Numan's six year tenure with the company.

COMPILATION ALBUMS
Part One: BEGGARS BANQUET

1978-1979
(**Cat No:** UK Begc 78/79)
Formats: Cassette only.
Released: April 1985.
Foreign formats: none.
Deleted soon after release.
Credited to 'Gary Numan – Tubeway Army.'
Tracks – Side One: 'That's Too Bad' (single mix) 3.22/ 'Oh! Didn't I Say' 2.20/ 'The Monday Troop' 3.00/ 'Bombers' (single mix) 3.55/ 'O.D. Receiver' 2.39/ 'Blue Eyes' 1.47/ 'Crime Of Passion' 3.38/ 'Fadeout 1930's' 3.10/ 'The Life Machine' (early version) 1.55/ 'That's Too Bad' (original demo) 3.14.
Tracks – Side Two: 'Random' (instrumental) 3.50/ 'The Crazies' 2.56/ 'Only A Downstat' 3.38/ 'We Have A Technical' 8.03/ 'Do You Need The Service?' 3.43 (slightly longer version than original B-side)/ 'A Game Called Echo' 5.10/ 'Oceans' (instrumental) 3.02.
Singles: none.
Videos: none.

This briefly available cassette compiled *Volume's One* to *Three* of the 1985 12-inch mini-albums. The tracklist though failed to list the demo version of 'That's Too Bad.' This compilation has since been dubbed by fans as 'The plan 2.'

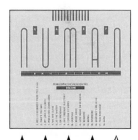

EXHIBITION
(**Cat No:** UK Bega 88)
Formats: Cassette, vinyl, and compact disc.
Released: September 1987.
Re-issued in the UK in a slimline 2CD case.
Special note: 'Cars (original version),' 'We Are Glass,' 'I Die: You Die', 'She's Got Claws' and 'Are "Friends" Electric?' all featured on a double vinyl album entitled *History Of Rock Volume 40*. The album surfaced at roughly the same time as *Exhibition* (HRL040).
Foreign formats: Canadian version released in a single sleeve featuring an alternative track list, dropping: 'Remind Me To Smile', 'We Are So Fragile', 'Engineers', 'Remember I Was Vapour', and 'White Boys And Heroes' in favour of 'Change Your Mind', 'No More Lies', and 'Voices', all three tracks originally recorded by Sharpe and Numan. (**Cat No:** 'PolyGram'/ 'Vertigo' 832 993-2). In addition, this release also included the extended E Reg remix of 'Cars.' Issued in Greece featuring yet another tracklist.
CD1/ Cassette, Side 1: 'Me! I Disconnect From You (live '79)' 3.03/ 'That's Too Bad' 3.17/ 'My Love Is A Liquid' 3.28/ 'Music For Chameleons' 3.35/ 'We Are Glass' 4.40/ 'Jo The Waiter' 2.39*/ 'On Broadway (live '79)' 4.42*/ 'Are "Friends" Electric?' 5.19/ 'I Dream Of Wires' 5.05/ 'Complex' 3.09/ 'Noise Noise' 3.39/ 'Love Needs No Disguise' 4.35*/ 'Remind Me To Smile' 3.59*/ 'We Are So Fragile' 2.49*/ 'Bombers' 3.48/ 'Moral' 4.29*/ 'Warriors' 4.03/ 'Every Day I Die (live '80)' 4.32.
CD2/ Cassette, Side Two: 'Cars (E Reg Model)' 3.35/ 'We Take Mystery (To Bed)'

3.36/ 'I'm An Agent' 4.17/ 'My Centurion' 5.20/ 'Metal' 3.25/ 'You Are In My Vision' 3.10/ 'This Wreckage' 5.10/ 'Sister Surprise' 4.52/ 'Engineers' 3.57*/ 'I Die: You Die' 3.39/ 'She's Got Claws' 4.43/ 'Stormtrooper In Drag' 4.52*/ 'My Shadow In Vain' 2.57/ 'Down In The Park' 4.20/ 'Remember I Was Vapour (live '79)' 4.41*/ 'Do You Need The Service?' 3.36*/ 'White Boys And Heroes' 3.31*/ 'The Iceman Comes' 4.23.

* These 11 tracks were omitted from the 2-disc vinyl version of this release.

Special note: Text and photos contained within the CD's booklet claimed to have been lifted from a 'book' by Francis Drake and Paul Gilbert entitled *Decade*: to date this has never materialised.

Singles: 'Cars (E Reg Model).'

Videos: aside from the original promo video, Gary performed this new version of 'Cars' on both *Top Of The Pops* and *The Roxy* (ITV's rival music show).

Exhibition was Beggars Banquet's first serious compilation of material from the years Gary recorded with the label. This expansive release was a fair representation all round and ran from Numan's earliest recordings as Tubeway Army in 1978 right up to his final solo outing with *Warriors* in 1983. Aside from being a powerful documentation of Gary's recorded (both studio and in concert) works, *Exhibition* had been assembled with another motive in mind. With all Gary's eight studio albums being transferred and re-issued on CD for the first time, Beggars Banquet found themselves facing a rather awkward dilemma. Due to two albums being included on one disc, the CD's time constraints meant that, unfortunately, some tracks had to be omitted. *Exhibition* was assembled to address that problem by providing a home for all the tracks that had to be regrettably removed from the original albums as well as serving as a genuine 'greatest hits' collection.

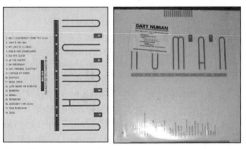

The only sweetener on *Exhibition* was the newly commissioned remix of 'Cars': everything else had previously been released going some way to explaining the record's modest chart placing.

Exhibition entered the charts at a peak position of No 43, with 3 weeks on the charts.

Canadian cassette and vinyl issue.

SELECTION
(Cat No: BBP5CD)
Formats: CD only.
Released: November 1989.
Foreign formats: none.
Special note: limited edition picture disc mini-album.
Tracks: 'Cars (E Reg Extended Model)' 6.14/ 'Down In The Park' 4.22/ 'Are "Friends" Electric?' 5.19/ 'I Die: You Die' 3.40/ 'We Are Glass' 4.42/ 'Music For Chameleons' 3.36. Released as a taster from the *Exhibition* set. A bit of a pointless release with its only redeeming feature being the extended 1987 remix of 'Cars' making its way to CD in the UK for the first time.

Selection failed to chart.

THE BEST OF GARY NUMAN 1978 – 1983

(**Cat No:** Bega 150)

Formats: CD and cassette.

Released: September 1993.

Foreign formats: matched the UK.

Re-issued September 1998.

Special note: CD booklet identical to *Exhibition*.

CD1/ Cassette, Side One: 'Cars' (original version)* 3.47/ 'We Are Glass'*4.43/ 'Are "Friends" Electric?'* 5.19/ 'My Love Is A Liquid' 3.32/ 'Music For Chameleons'* 3.35/ 'Complex'* 3.09/ 'Me! I Disconnect From You' 3.20/ 'Love Needs No Disguise'* 4.33/ 'Bombers'* 3.50/ 'The Joy Circuit' 5.10/ 'We Are So Fragile' 2.51/ 'Films' 4.07/ 'Warriors'* 4.03/ 'That's Too Bad'* 3.18/ 'Every Day I Die'* 2.23/ 'On Broadway (live '79)' 4.29/ 'Please Push No More'5.40.

At the end of side one was the piano version of 'Down In The Park.' This track was not listed on the disc or the accompanying album artwork.

CD2/ Cassette, Side Two: 'Cars (93 Sprint Mix)'* 3.49/ 'We Take Mystery (To Bed)'* 3.37/ 'I Die: You Die'* 3.41/ 'Down In The Park'* 4.21/ 'She's Got Claws' 4.54/ 'Stormtrooper In Drag'* 4.56/ 'My Shadow In Vain' 2.58/ 'This Wreckage'* 5.22/ 'Sister Surprise' 4.57/ 'M.E.' 5.34/ 'You Are In My Vision' 3.11/ 'Metal'/ 'I'm An Agent' 4.18/ 'White Boys And Heroes'* 3.30/ 'The Life Machine' 2.42/ 'My Centurion' 5.18/ 'Remember I Was Vapour' 5.12.

Singles: 'Cars' (93 Sprint Mix).

Videos: none, although Numan did perform a mimed version of the Sprint remix of 'Cars' on the TV show *It's Bizarre*.

* These 19 highlighted tracks were the only ones to feature on the cassette version of this compilation.

With a second attempt by Beggars Banquet to re-issue their Numan back catalogue onto CD underway, and a new dance mix of 'Cars' in the lower end of the UK singles chart, a new compilation emerged to tempt fans. *The Best Of Gary Numan 1978-1983* was, like *Exhibition*, another 2CD affair: however, there were differences evident between the two. The track list was revised to include: 'Every Day I Die' (original studio version)/ 'The Life Machine'/ 'Me! I Disconnect From You' (original studio version)/ 'Cars' (original version)/ 'M.E.'/ 'The Joy Circuit'/ 'Please Push No More'/ 'Remember I Was Vapour' (original studio version) as well as the newly remixed version of 'Cars.' These were included at the sacrifice of: 'Jo The Waiter'/ 'Do You Need The Service?'/ 'Me! I Disconnect From You' (live '79)/ 'Engineers'/ 'Remember I Was Vapour' (live '79)/ 'Remind Me To Smile'/ 'I Dream Of Wires'/ 'Moral'/ 'Noise Noise'/ 'The Iceman Comes'/ 'Cars' (E Reg Model) and 'Every Day I Die' (live '80) – the loss of this latter track meant that *Living Ornaments '80* was now completely unrepresented.

With the dance mix of 'Cars' failing to set the chart alight, this compilation slipped quietly in and out of the lower reaches of the UK album charts.

The Best Of Gary Numan 1978-1983 entered the charts at No 70, spending one week on the chart.

COMPILATION ALBUMS
Part Two: LICENCED

Over the years Beggars Banquet have given permission to a small number of other record companies to use their Numan back catalogue for compilations and so forth. This venture has resulted in some interesting releases and in one particular case, quite a controversial one.

PHOTOGRAPH
(**Cat No:** Intercord 146 606)
Formats: cassette and vinyl (gatefold sleeve-see below).
Released: January 1981. *
Special note: this was a German only release imported into the UK.
* Actual release date was unclear but this was the point that copies began appearing in the UK.
Side One: Tracks: 'Films' 4.11/ 'Are "Friends" Electric?' 5.19/ 'Replicas' 4.57/ 'Every Day I Die' 2.23/ 'Down In The Park' 4.21.

★★★★★

Side Two: Tracks: 'This Wreckage' 5.01/ 'Cars' 3.5/ 'Metal' 3.33/ 'Remember I Was Vapour' 5.08/ 'Complex' 3.10.

Vinyl gatefold sleeve and back cover as well as the extremely rare cassette issue.

Fans were surprised to see this compilation on sale in the UK in the early part of 1981, as were Gary's label Beggars Banquet who quickly had it withdrawn due to the illegal nature of the record. Mint copies are now rare and can command a hefty price tag.

NEW MAN NUMAN – THE BEST OF GARY NUMAN
(**Cat No:** UK TV Records/Virgin TVA7)
Formats: vinyl and cassette (TVC7).
Released: November 1982.
Foreign formats: none.
Special note: released simultaneously along with the video compilation of the same name.
Side One: Tracks: 'Are "Friends" Electric?' 5.19/ 'Cars' 3.53/ 'We Are Glass' 4.46/ 'Complex' 3.11/ 'Me! I Disconnect From You' 3.22/ 'Down In The Park' 4.20/ 'I Die: You Die' 3.40.

★★★★★

Side Two: Tracks: 'She's Got Claws' 4.56/ 'Love Needs No Disguise' 4.38/ 'This Wreckage' 5.23/ 'Stormtrooper In Drag' 4.53/ 'We Take Mystery (To Bed)' 3.42/ 'Music For Chameleons' 3.40/ 'White Boys And Heroes' 3.36.

Fairly straightforward singles collection that excluded Tubeway Army's two early, punk flavoured singles – 'That's Too Bad' and 'Bombers' – in favour of adding 'Replicas' album track 'Me! I Disconnect From You' in their place. With no UK tour, new single or exclusive material to promote, *New Man Numan,* despite the addition of a short TV advert, made little impression on the charts.

New Man Numan entered the UK album charts at No 63 climbing to a peak position of No 45 before departing after 7 weeks.

THE COLLECTION
(Cat No: UK Castle Communications CCSCD 229)
Formats: vinyl, cassette and CD.
Released: October 1989.
Foreign formats: none.
Tracks: 'Cars' 3.53/ 'Tracks' 2.50/ 'Down In The Park' 4.22/ 'This Wreckage' 5.25/ 'Random' 3.57*/ 'My Shadow In Vain' 3.01/ 'She's Got Claws' 4.56/ 'Music For Chameleons' 3.39/ 'Remind Me To Smile' 4.03/ 'Stories'

3.10/ 'A Game Called Echo' 5.06*/ 'Complex' 3.13/ 'On Broadway (live-'79)' 4.41/ 'The Aircrash Bureau' 5.37/ 'M.E.' 5.25/ 'Are "Friends" Electric?' 5.20/ 'Photograph' 2.25*/ 'We Are Glass' 4.39.

* First time on CD at this point.
Singles: none.
Videos: none.

Surprise was expressed by fans when Castle Communications licensed a selection of Gary's early work for this one-off compilation, as the label was mainly the preserve of long washed up heavy metal bands and similar artists. It came across as rather bizarre that they would even be interested in compiling material from an artist more associated with electronic and synthesiser music than straight-ahead rock. However, aside from the strength of the music selected, and the fact that one or two tracks were appearing on CD for the first time, there wasn't much to recommend about it.

Gary Numan The Collection failed to chart.

DOCUMENT SERIES PRESENTS GARY NUMAN
(Cat No: UK Connoisseur Collections CCSAP CD 113)
Formats: CD and cassette.
Released: October 1992.
Foreign formats: none.
Sleeve notes by Dominic Jones.
Special note: this compilation included the out of print, ultra rare 12-inch version of 'We Take Mystery (To Bed)', previously unavailable on CD.

Tracks: 'Mean St' 3.19/ 'Jo The Waiter' 2.41/ 'You Are In My Vision' 3.14/ 'Cars' 3.53/ 'Complex' 3.13/ 'She's Got Claws' 5.00/ 'Exhibition'* 4.30/ 'A Subway Called You' 4.41*/ 'Face To Face'* 3.39/ 'Noise Noise' 3.49/ 'We Take Mystery (To Bed)' 7.45 (extended version)/ 'The Image Is'* 5.59/ 'White Boys And Heroes' 6.27 (extended/ album version)/ 'A Dream Of Siam' 6.17/ 'The Tick Tock Man' 4.21.

* First time on CD, in addition, 'A Subway Called You' incorrectly spelt on all album artwork as 'Subway I Call You.'
Singles: none.
Videos: none.

Fairly unusual compilation that not only took an alternative look at the Beggars Banquet years but also managed to transfer a couple of old B-sides and one rare UK 12-inch remix to CD for the first time in the UK.

Document Series Presents Gary Numan failed to chart.

THE PREMIER HITS

(**Cat No:** UK PolyGram TV 531 149-2)
Formats: CD and cassette.
Released: March 1996.
Foreign formats: US version issued in March 1997 in a different sleeve, copies of which were imported into the UK in April 1999.
Credited to 'Gary Numan – Tubeway Army.'
Sleeve notes by Steve Malins.

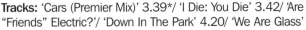

Tracks: 'Cars (Premier Mix)' 3.39*/ 'I Die: You Die' 3.42/ 'Are "Friends" Electric?'/ 'Down In The Park' 4.20/ 'We Are Glass' 4.46/ 'Bombers'** 3.48/ 'We Take Mystery (To Bed)' 3.42/ 'She's Got Claws' 4.56/ 'Complex' 3.11/ 'Music For Chameleons' 3.40/ 'That's Too Bad'** 3.20/ 'This Wreckage' 5.23/ 'Warriors' 4.08/ 'Love Needs No Disguise' 4.38/ 'White Boys And Heroes' 3.36/ 'Sister Surprise' 5.01/ 'Stormtrooper In Drag' 4.53/ 'Cars ' (original version) 3.55.

* This is the 1987 'E Reg model' simply re-titled 'The Premier mix.'
** Both tracks also included as part of a Beggars Banquet themed 'Punk' retrospective entitled *The Punk Singles Collection* (see below).
Special note: Rumours of a similarly titled video cassette compilation of all Gary's early 80s promos proved to be unfounded. In addition, the back cover included printed copies of all but three of the eighteen Gary Numan/ Tubeway Army single sleeves issued in the UK by Beggars Banquet. Sleeves omitted were: 'Love Needs No Disguise '81', 'Stormtrooper In Drag '81' and 'Cars (E Reg Model) '87.' These same single sleeves were also reprinted within the artwork for the March 1997 US issue of this compilation, however, an unsuccessful attempt to re-instate at least one of the omitted sleeves had obviously been tried with a blank space having been allocated between the sleeves for 'Are "Friends" Electric?' and 'Cars.'
Singles: 'Cars.'
Videos: aside from the original promo for 'Cars', none, however, the return of 'Cars' to the top 20 sparked a flurry of TV appearances for Gary performing both 'Are "Friends" Electric?' and 'Cars' as well as interview segments. Album itself also had a short TV ad shot.

With 'Cars' making an unexpected return to the British top 20 on the back of all things, a beer commercial (ironic in itself as Numan does not drink), PolyGram licensed all Gary's Beggars Banquet singles for an accompanying compilation CD.

Premier Hits entered the charts at a peak position of No 21 with a three week run on the charts.

Issued in March 1996.

RE-ISSUE CAMPAIGN
Part One: ALBUMS

Re-issuing albums as well as singles is usually standard record company policy and Beggars Banquet have engaged in a number of notable Numan re-issue campaigns to date. This section will take a look at these re-promotions.

TUBEWAY ARMY
(**Cat No:** UK Bega 4)
Formats: vinyl and cassette.
Re-issued August 1979.
Foreign formats: Canadian version credited the record to 'Gary Numan and Tubeway Army.' US issue via Atco marked as 'The first album.' Issued in New Zealand featuring a peel-off sticker that stated 'Re-issue – the first album.' Issued in Japan as Tubeway Army, however, the cassette version featured 'Cars' as a bonus track (747 new wave label). Japanese vinyl issue also included a black and white insert alongside the regular issued Obi. Issued in Australia featuring a green, peel-off sticker crediting the record to 'Tubeway Army featuring Gary Numan.'
Tracks – same as the original album.

Following Numan's chart-topping success, Beggars Banquet re-issued Tubeway Army's two early singles (see 'Re-issued singles') as well as the group's debut album. Gone was the original blue sleeve, replaced here with a black and white drawing of Gary's face (done by Numan's long time friend Garry Robson). The record was also, like the re-issue of *Replicas* re-credited to include Gary Numan into the artwork.

Tubeway Army entered the charts for the first time peaking at No 14 with a 10-week run on the charts.

Japanese issue complete with Obi and insert.

NUMAN/ TUBEWAY ARMY – 1978
(**Cat No:** UK Beg 92E)
Formats: 12-inch vinyl mini-album complete with insert.
Re-issued March 1983.
Foreign formats: none.

Second re-issue: March 1985 on yellow vinyl as part of a trio of 12-inch mini-albums (see right). In addition, the cover was marked 'Volume One.'

This release substituted the original single version of 'That's Too Bad' with the previously unreleased demo version.

Tracks: 12-inch version of Tubeway Army's first two singles. In addition to the five tracks included, Beggars Banquet added a slightly longer mix of the *Replicas* era B-side 'Do You Need The Service?'

1985 re-issued version.

CD TRANSFER
UK CAMPAIGN: ONE

Beggars Banquet's first attempt to move Numan's back catalogue to CD in the UK was not as successful as fans would have hoped. By placing two albums on one CD, some of them lost the odd track here and there from their original running orders. Worse still, the original artwork all but disappeared leaving the finished product looking more like bankrupt stock than official re-issues. Although Gary's eight studio albums were transferred, neither *Living Ornaments '79* nor *'80* surfaced in this venture. All these CDs are now deleted.

TUBEWAY ARMY/ DANCE
(**Cat No:** UK Bega CD4)
Released: December 1987.
Special note: 1979 re-issued artwork for Tubeway Army's debut album used as opposed to the original blue cover.

For this CD, Gary's 1981 album *Dance* lost one track ('Moral') in the transfer process and *Tubeway Army*, the 1978 debut album lost two tracks ('My Shadow In Vain' and 'Jo The Waiter').

All three missing tracks were included on the Beggars Banquet commissioned compilation *Exhibition*.

REPLICAS/THE PLAN-1978
(**Cat No:** UK Bega CD7)
Released: December 1987.
Special note: *Replicas* cover on this CD was not the original: rather one of the re-issued prints that re-credited the record to 'Gary Numan – Tubeway Army.'

This CD, not surprisingly, featured *Replicas* in full. *The Plan-1978*, however, made its first appearance on CD in a radically different form to its original vinyl outing. Removed from the original track listing were the early versions of: 'My Shadow In Vain', 'Bombers', 'Something's In The House', 'Friends' (original title 'Do Your Best') and 'Steel And You' (original title 'This Machine') replaced here with: 'The Monday Troop' and 'Crime Of Passion' (both originally from *Volume Three* of the 12-inch mini-album released in 1985). Another addition to *The Plan-1978* and this CD was a previously unreleased track entitled 'Out Of Sight.' This discovery turned out to be the original version of 'Fade Out 1930's', itself a track unearthed and included on *Volume Two* of the 12-inch mini-album released in 1985.

THE PLEASURE PRINCIPLE/WARRIORS
(**Cat No:** UK Bega CD10)
Released: December 1987.
This CD featured *The Pleasure Principle* minus one track ('Observer') and *Warriors* minus two tracks ('My Centurion' and 'The Iceman Comes').

All three missing tracks were included on the compilation *Exhibition*.

TELEKON/ I, ASSASSIN
(**Cat No:** UK Bega CD19)
Released: April 1988.

For this CD, (arriving much later than the others) *Telekon* lost both 'Remind Me To Smile' and 'I Dream Of Wires' whilst *I, Assassin* lost the album version of 'White Boys And Heroes.'

Both tracks from *Telekon* were included on *Exhibition*: however, the album version of 'White Boys And Heroes' from *I, Assassin* remained un-transferred.

CD TRANSFER
THE FAR EAST CAMPAIGN
In 1990, Japanese record company Alfa Records licensed Numan's Beggars Banquet back catalogue with a view to re-issuing it on to CD. The resulting *Asylum* series – conceived by Steve Webbon and Nobi Tagoh – far outstripped the 1987 UK attempt by transferring full albums as well as including all relevant B-sides (many of which were being issued on CD for the first time). Also transferred for the first time was both Numan's early 80s live albums *Living Ornaments '79* and *'80* which were by-passed in the UK. This project also yielded a single that preceded the re-issues. Each of the sets came with a glossy booklet featuring rare and unreleased photos.

ASYLUM 1
(**Cat No:** Alfa 6 to 9)
Formats: 4 CD set.
Released: January 1990.
Disc 1 – THE PLAN – 1978 (**Cat No:** JA BB ALCB-6)
Tracks: 'That's Too Bad' 3.17/ 'Oh! Didn't I Say' 2.20/ 'Out Of Sight' 3.30/ 'That's Too Bad' (original demo) 3.14/ 'Bombers' (original demo) 3.55/ 'My Shadow In Vain' (original version) 4.09/ 'This Machine' ('Steel And You') 3.55 (original version)/ 'Thoughts No 2' 3.26/ 'Something's In The House' 4.08 (original version)/ 'Check It' 3.38/ 'The Monday Troop' 3.00/ 'This Is My Life' 2.19/ 'Mean St' 3.19/ 'Ice' 2.17/ 'Crime Of Passion' 3.38/ 'The Life Machine' 1.55 (original version)/ 'Critics' 1.54/ 'Friends' ('Do Your Best') 2.33 (original version)/ 'Basic J' 2.54/ 'Bombers' 3.54 (single version)/ 'Blue Eyes' 1.47/ 'O.D. Receiver' 2.39.

This CD was a fairly comprehensive snapshot of the early stages of the Tubeway Army group. Included on the disc was the originally released version of *The Plan – 1978* as well as relevant tracks that surfaced on the 1985 12-inch mini-albums. Also included were early singles 'That's Too Bad' and 'Bombers' as well as each of those singles' B-sides.

Disc 2 – TUBEWAY ARMY (Cat No: JA BB ALCB-7)
This CD featured the debut *Tubeway Army* album in full with the addition of six bonus tracks: 'Fade Out 1930's' 3.10/ 'Me! I Disconnect From You (live '79)' 3.05/ 'Something's In The House (live '79 4.05/ 'Every Day I Die (live '79)' 3.29/ 'Down In The Park (live '79)' 4.33 / 'Bombers (live '79)' 5.48.

Of the five live tracks from 1979 included on this CD, two were previously unreleased namely: 'Every Day I Die' and 'Down In The Park', both of these were taken from the early 80s video *The Touring Principle '79*. Of the remaining three tracks: 'Something's In The House' was taken from the album *Living Ornaments '79* with 'Bombers' and 'Me! I Disconnect From You' being originally the B-sides to the 12-inch version of 'Complex.'

Disc 3 – REPLICAS (Cat No: JA BB ALCB-8)

This CD featured the original album in full with the addition of six bonus tracks: 'Do You Need The Service?' (B-side to 'Down In The Park'), 'The Crazies', 'Only A Downstat', 'We Have A Technical' (all three tracks out-takes from the sessions for this record and originally found on *Volume Two* of the mini-album released in 1985), 'We Are So Fragile' (B-side to 'Are "Friends" Electric?' and 'I Nearly Married A Human 2' (bonus track originally included on the 12-inch version of 'Down In The Park' and originally credited to Gary Numan and not Tubeway Army).

Disc 4 – THE PLEASURE PRINCIPLE (Cat No: JA BB ALCB-9)

This CD featured the original album in full with the addition of six bonus tracks: 'Random', 'Oceans' (both out-takes from the sessions for this record and originally included on *Volume Three* of the mini-album released in 1985), 'Asylum' (B-side to 'Cars'), 'Remember I Was Vapour' (live '79)*, 'On Broadway' (live '79)* and 'Conversation' (live '79).**

* Two live tracks originally included on a 7-inch single given away free with *Telekon* in 1980.

** This live track taken from *Living Ornaments '79* album.

Special note: B-sides to 'Complex', the final single drawn from this album can be found on Disc 2 in this 4 CD set.

ASYLUM 2
(**Cat No:** Alfa 10 to 13)
Formats: 4 CD set.
Released: January 1990.

Disc 1 – TELEKON (Cat No: JA BB ALCB 10)

This CD featured the original *Telekon* album in full with 'We Are Glass' included into the running order between the tracks 'Sleep By Windows' and 'I'm An Agent.' In addition, the disc featured a further five bonus tracks, namely former single: 'I Die: You Die', B-sides: 'Photograph', 'Trois Gymnopedies (First Movement)' and 'Down In The Park (Piano Version)' as well as 'A Game Called Echo', a track that originally surfaced on *Volume Three* of the 12-inch mini-album released in 1985.

Disc 2 – DANCE (Cat No: JA BB ALCB 11)

This CD featured the *Dance* album in full with the addition of four bonus tracks namely two B-sides: 'I Sing Rain' and 'Exhibition' as well as both the Paul Gardiner single 'Stormtrooper In Drag' and the Dramatis single 'Love Needs No Disguise.' One other B-side from this era ('Face To Face' – flip side to the 12-inch version of 'Love Needs No Disguise') was not included on this CD, this track was added to Disc 4 – the *Warriors* CD.

Disc 3 – I, ASSASSIN (Cat No: JA BB ALCB 12)

Although this CD featured the full *I, Assassin* album, one variation occurred. The album version of 'We Take Mystery (To Bed)' was replaced with the longer 12-inch mix. In addition, six bonus tracks were added including B-sides 'Noise Noise', 'Bridge? What Bridge?', 'Wargames,' 'Glitter And Ash,' 'The Image Is' and 'We Take Mystery (To Bed)' – early version. Omitted due to time limitations of the CD itself were the aforementioned album mix of 'We Take Mystery (To Bed)' as well as the 12-inch mix for 'Music For Chameleons.' Also not included were the regular 7-inch versions of all three singles lifted off the album. Another omission from this CD was the rare US mix of 'White Boys And Heroes' that was floating around as a promotional 12-inch in the United States at the time of Numan's short US club tour.

Disc 4 – WARRIORS (Cat No: JA BB ALCB 13)

This CD featured the *Warriors* Album in full with six bonus tracks namely B-sides: 'My Car Slides1', 'My Car Slides 2' (both songs now joined together), 'Poetry And Power' and the track entitled 'Letters' (which actually turned out to be 1981 B-side 'Face To Face'). Also included were the 'Motorway Mix' and the 'E Reg Extended Model Mix' of 'Cars' from 1987. The single mixes of 'Warriors' and 'Sister Surprise' were both omitted for this disc.

ASYLUM 3

(LIVING ORNAMENTS '79 AND '80)
(Cat No: JA BB ALCB 31)
Released: January 1990
Special note: *Asylum 3* included documentation of Gary's tours.

To round the *Asylum* project off, a 9th and final disc appeared housing both Numan's two long deleted live albums. However, whereas *Living Ornaments '80* was included in its full ten track mode, the '79 concert had two tracks removed from its original running order namely: 'Something's In The House' and 'Conversation' (both of these were re-allocated to two earlier discs – See discs 2 and 4 on *Asylum 1*). A proposed *Asylum 4* housing all Gary's Numa recordings running up to 1986 has so far failed to materialise.

Asylum 3 CD.

CD TRANSFER
UK CAMPAIGN: TWO

Following the well-received and far superior Japanese *Asylum* CD transfer, the UK end of Beggars Banquet opted to take another crack at the project and re-issued, for the second time, Numan's eight studio albums on to CD. This time, two discs were housed inside each release along with a booklet of lyrics and photos. Bizarrely (and for the second time), neither *Living Ornaments '79* nor *'80* were included in this re-issue campaign despite their appearance in the Far East three years back.

TUBEWAY ARMY/ DANCE
(**Cat No:** UK Bega 151CD)
Released: December 1993.

CD 1 – TUBEWAY ARMY
This CD features the original album in full, along with five bonus tracks: 'Fade Out 1930's', 'Down In The Park' (live '79), 'Every Day I Die' (live '79), 'On Broadway' (live '79) and 'Remember I Was Vapour' (live '79). Of the live tracks, both 'Down In The Park' and 'Every Day I Die' were previously unreleased in the UK. Also worthy of note was the inclusion of the 'Lee Cooper Jeans' TV ad that Gary had sung back in the early part of 1979: here it was included at the end of the disc as a hidden/unlisted extra.

CD 2 – DANCE
This CD was identical to the Japanese *Asylum* disc (**Cat No:** JA BB ALCB 11).

REPLICAS/THE PLAN-1978
(**Cat No:** UK Bega 152CD)
Released: December 1993.

CD 1 – REPLICAS
This CD was identical to the Japanese *Asylum* disc (**Cat No:** JA BB ALCB 8).

CD 2 – THE PLAN-1978
Aside from losing the track 'Out Of Sight', this CD was identical to the Japanese *Asylum* disc (**Cat No:** JA BB ALCB 6).

THE PLEASURE PRINCIPLE/ WARRIORS
(**Cat No:** UK Bega 153CD)
Released: December 1993.

CD 1 – THE PLEASURE PRINCIPLE
This CD features the original album in full as well as five bonus tracks: 'Asylum', 'Random', 'Oceans', 'Bombers' and 'Me! I Disconnect From You' (the latter, both live).

CD 2 – WARRIORS
This CD was identical to the Japanese *Asylum* disc (**Cat No:** JA BB ALCB 13).

TELEKON/ I, ASSASSIN
(**Cat No:** UK Bega 154CD)
Released: December 1993.
Special note: catalogue number: BEGA 155CD was set aside for the *Living Ornaments* albums, their non-appearance made this double-pack the concluding re-issue of 1993.

CD 1 – TELEKON
This CD was identical to the Japanese *Asylum* disc (**Cat No:** JA BB ALCB 10).

CD 2 – I, ASSASSIN

This CD was virtually identical to the Japanese *Asylum* disc except for one minor change, that being, the extended version of 'We Take Mystery (To Bed)' that found its way on to the Far East version of *I, Assassin* was here replaced by the correct album version. In addition, Beggars Banquet had managed to unearth a previously unreleased new track entitled 'This House Is Cold' that originated from the session for the album and was included here as the last track on the disc.

CD TRANSFER
UK CAMPAIGN: THREE

20th ANNIVERSARY EDITIONS

Following the top 20 success of the re-issued remix of 'Cars' in 1996 and the high profile tribute album *Random* a year later, Beggars Banquet, sensing Numan's years of critical exile were at an end, opted to return to the companies vaults and fully restore their Numan back catalogue for a third UK re-issue campaign commencing in early 1998. This time the label went to great lengths to truly do justice to the Numan back catalogue by not only re-instating the original artwork on each album, but adding to and expanding them by including, extensive sleeve notes (courtesy of Steve Malins), original record labels*, relevant archive photographs, brand new covers and in some cases even the odd comment from Gary himself. Beggars Banquet also went back to the original studio cutting tapes, the re-mastering process undertaken on those resulted in a far superior sound quality than had been achieved before.

* Japanese issues featured picture disc CD labels.

   The first wave of re-mastered CDs appeared in the early part of 1998, although the original intention of re-issuing both *Living Ornaments '79* and *Living Ornaments '80* alongside a previously unreleased audio version of the long deleted *Micromusic* video cassette did not go according to plan. Attempts to locate the full master tapes for *Living Ornaments '80* proved fruitless. In the end only *Living Ornaments '79* made it into the high street with the new take of *Micromusic*, re-titled *Living Ornaments '81* being only available via mail order.

LIVING ORNAMENTS '79
(Cat No UK Bega 155CD)
Released: January 1998.
Deleted December 1999.
Remixed by Tim Summerhayes at Fleetwood studios 1997.
Digital mastering by John Dent at Loud mastering.
Special note: on stage photo printed within the CD jewel case featured Jess Lidyard on drums and originated from 'The Year Of The Child' concert performed at the end of 1979.

This CD was deleted at the end of the year for good.

CD 1 – Tracks: 'Intro' 2.32/ 'Airlane' 3.07/ 'Me! I Disconnect From You' 3.02/ 'Cars' 3.25 / 'M.E.' 4.42/ 'You Are In My Vision' 3.11/ 'Something's In The House' 3.55/ 'Random' 3.38 / 'Every Day I Die' 3.36/ 'Conversation' 7.51/ 'We Are So Fragile' 2.46.

CD 2 – Tracks: 'Bombers' 5.30/ 'Remember I Was Vapour' 4.51/ 'On Broadway' 4.38/ 'The Dream Police' 4.19/ 'Films' 3.49/ 'Metal' 3.25/ 'Down In The Park' 5.38/ 'My Shadow In Vain' 2.34/ 'Are "Friends" Electric?' 5.33/ 'Tracks' 3.10.

Originally only boasting nine tracks, this re-mastered, re-issued version of *Living Ornaments '79* was a dream come true for fans as the full concert (spread out over two CDs) was finally available to buy. This release also gave fans access to six tracks that were completely new to CD ('M.E'*, 'Are "Friends" Electric?'* and 'Tracks'*, 'Intro', 'You Are In My Vision' and 'Random.' The latter three had never been issued on any format until now). Also included were additional photographs and a run down of the full UK autumn tour of 1979.

* These three tracks had previously been issued as part of the long form video *The Touring Principle '79.*

LIVING ORNAMENTS '81
(**Cat No:** UK Bega 157CD)
Released: January 1998.
Special note: this two CD live recording was basically an audio release of the now, long deleted early 80s videocassette *Micromusic*, essentially a re-issue and included here.
Recorded at Wembley Arena, London on the 28th of April 1981.

Group Line-up: see 'Official video cassettes.'
Recorded on the RAK mobile.
Engineered by Tim Summerhayes, assisted by Phil Thornalle.
Mixed at the RAK studios by Gary Numan and Tim Summerhayes, assisted by Will Gosling.
Digital mastering by John Dent at Loud Mastering.
Produced by Gary Numan.
CD 1 – Tracks: 'Intro'-'This Wreckage' 7.40/ 'Remind Me To Smile' 3.22/ 'Metal' 3.14/ 'Me! I Disconnect From You' 3.03/ 'Complex' 3.10/ 'The Aircrash Bureau' 5.24/ 'Airlane' 3.24/ 'M.E.' 4.3/ 'Every Day I Die' 4.38/ 'Films' 5.47/ 'Remember I Was Vapour' 4.34/ 'Trois Gymnopedies (First Movement)' 3.04/ 'Conversation.'*
CD 2 – Tracks: 'She's Got Claws' 4.51/ 'Cars' 3.39/ 'I Dream Of Wires' 4.37/ 'I'm An Agent' 3.57/ 'The Joy Circuit' 5.56/ 'I Die: You Die' 3.43/ 'Cry The Clock Said' 5.26/ 'Tracks' 2.19/ 'Down In The Park' 5.59/ 'My Shadow In Vain' 2.38/ 'Please Push No More' 5.20/ 'Are "Friends" Electric?' 5.40/ 'We Are Glass' – 'Outro' 7.43.
* Monitor mix from a previous show.

Living Ornaments '81 was less available to buy than its predecessor, only obtainable via mail order (from Beggars Banquet and later Numan's own web site NuWorld) as well as a few specialist stores. It came housed in a 2CD jewel case with a glossy booklet that featured a selection of photographs from the shows along with comments from Gary that originally appeared as part of a 4 page, LP sized booklet inside the boxed version of *Living Ornaments '79 and '80.*

Although fans were delighted with this release, some reservations were voiced over the inclusion of the track 'Conversation.' Of the three farewell shows, 'Conversation' was performed on the first two nights then dropped and replaced with 'Complex' on the penultimate night. In a bid to make this release a comprehensive one, Beggars Banquet un-earthed a 'Monitor mix' from a previous show and added it to the end of CD 1 explaining that they couldn't re-sequence it into the show itself due to the 'different sonic balance.' This was basically a fancy way of describing what was, in essence, a rather unflattering 'lo-fi' recording that was more karaoke than rock concert.

Living Ornaments '81 is of course of considerable historical value due to the three farewell shows being the very pinnacle of Numan mania during the early 80s, and for those reasons alone this release is a worthy addition to the Numan cannon.

The second stage of the 20th anniversary re-masters arrived in the middle of 1998, this wave delivered Numan's first official four studio albums.

TUBEWAY ARMY
(**Cat No:** UK Bega BBL 4 CD)
Released: June 1998.

Featured the original *Tubeway Army* album in full along with an unexpected bonus section. Tagged onto the end of the CD is the early 80s bootleg, *Live At The Roxy 1977* (see 'Bootlegs' section), this show is the only known recording of the Tubeway Army band live and was added here under the heading 'Living Ornaments '78.'

Bizarrely, Beggars Banquet opted to use the re-issued cover from 1979 for this re-mastered CD instead of resurrecting the original 1978 blue sleeve preferring instead to print a small photograph of it inside the accompanying booklet.

REPLICAS
(**Cat No:** UK Bega BBL 7 CD)
Released: 1998.
Album cover unchanged from original issue. This CD was correctly credited to Tubeway Army alone and featured within the CD booklet the original poster.
Special note: this album had briefly been available to buy on CD and tape through the record label Music Collection (INT MUSCD 509 and MUSMC 509) in April 1995, however, this was only the original 10 track album. CD artwork also included sleeve notes from Steve Malins as well as a slightly altered cover that saw the removal of the light bulb. This re-issue was identical to the CD found on the December 1993 UK double-pack CD re-issues. However, one minor difference should be pointed out. Fans noted that one of the bonus tracks ('We Have A Technical') sounded

US 8 track tape.

somewhat different to the originally released version discovered in 1985, suggesting that it was a previously unreleased, alternative take. This wasn't the case, by going back to the original studio masters, Beggars Banquet were able to re-master and release the recordings as they originally were. Its from this point that slight tweaking had previously taken place on a few select recordings hence the incorrect belief that alternative takes were being unearthed.

Above: Japanese CDs featured photos instead of the reprinted record label idea. Each CD also came with the standard Japanese Obi.

THE PLEASURE PRINCIPLE

(**Cat No:** UK Bega BBL 10 CD)
Released: June 1998.
Album cover unchanged from the original.

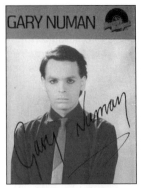

This re-mastered CD features the album's original 10 tracks in full with the addition of 7 bonus tracks: 'Random', 'Oceans', 'Me!, I Disconnect From You'*, 'Bombers'*, 'Remember I Was Vapour'* and 'On Broadway.'* The last four tracks were all live recordings edited from the 28th of September at the Hammersmith Odeon in London 1979. They were included here in their originally released mixes.

   * Full, un-edited versions available on the re-mastered version of *Living Ornaments '79.*

Original '79 signed poster.

TELEKON

(**Cat No:** UK Bega BBL 19 CD)
Released: June 1998.
Album cover unchanged, original poster printed within the CD booklet.

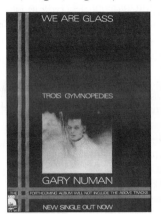

Telekon era magazine advert as well as the April 1981 issue of Italian magazine 'Ciao 2001.'

This release marked the end of phase one of the re-masters campaign, the disc itself was virtually identical to the CD found on the UK double-pack re-issue of December 1993 except for one major alteration. For this release, the single mix of 'I Die: You Die' was removed to make way for the ultra rare, white label promo mix that was briefly floating around at the time of this album's original appearance (this take though was not the promo video version, that mix/ recording, along with the version performed on *The Kenny Everett Video Show* are still currently unreleased). In addition, due to the re-mastering process on the studio tapes, three tracks: 'Remind Me To Smile', 'The Joy Circuit' and 'Remember I Was Vapour' altered slightly with fans expressing dismay as well as delight. Although both 'Remind Me To Smile' and 'The Joy Circuit' benefited from this process, 'Remember I Was Vapour' unfortunately lost a short keyboard solo in its mid-section.

   CD booklet included a lyrical error for the song 'I Die: You Die', reprinted lyric stated that the final line of the song was 'I'm still running from the telephone' when in fact Gary originally sang 'I'm still frightened by the telephone.'

The third phase of the re-mastered project appeared just over a year later, this time delivering a further two albums.

DANCE
(**Cat No:** UK Bega BBL 28 CD)
Released: August 1999.
Album cover unchanged, original poster printed within the CD booklet.

This CD was virtually identical to the disc that emerged as part of a double-pack in December 1993, the difference this time being the loss of the track 'Love Needs No Disguise', dropped from this re-issue to make way not only for the welcome return of 'Face To Face' but the discovery of a previously unreleased track, a gentle, melodic, torch-like ballad entitled 'Dance.'

THE PLAN
(**Cat No:** UK Bega BBL 55 CD)
Released: August 1999.
Special note: this album was re-titled simply *The Plan* and re-credited to 'Tubeway Army.' The record was also re-issued in a newly commissioned sleeve.

This CD was virtually identical to the disc released in Japan in 1990 (*Asylum 1*, disc 1) with this version including two bonus tracks namely: 'Fade Out 1930's' and the 'Lee Cooper Jeans' TV ad that surfaced on disc originally in the UK in December 1993 (see *Tubeway Army/ Dance* CD double-pack-Bega 151 CD).

In addition, the original version of 'That's Too Bad' was moved from the position of track 4 to track 19. The 4th wave of re-masters appeared three years later in 2002, this time delivering the final two studio albums recorded for Beggars Banquet/ WEA.

I, ASSASSIN
(**Cat No:** UK Bega BBL 40 CD)
Released: December 2002.
Album cover unchanged, original poster printed within the CD booklet (see right).

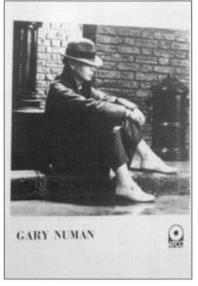

This CD was virtually identical to the disc issued as part of a double-pack in the UK in December 1993, the only alterations occurring with the seven bonus tracks being changed to new positions in the running order. In addition, it was revealed within the extensive sleeve notes that not only did the track 'Noise Noise' originate from 1981 but was also being considered at the time for release as a single. However, this idea was nixed by Numan once the sessions for *I, Assassin* got underway. Also included within the sleeve notes was text from Numan himself with Gary finally quashing the long running rumour that the *I, Assassin* album track 'The 1930's Rust' had originally been penned for UK singer (the late) Marti Caine.

Original Atco poster.

WARRIORS
(**Cat No:** UK Bega BBL 47 CD)
Released: December 2002.
Special note: this re-issue of *Warriors* dropped the original album's sleeve for a newly commissioned one. (original sleeve printed within the CD booklet).

This re mastered version of *Warriors* included the original nine-track album in full along with six bonus tracks. Of the additional material, three were former B-sides: 'My Car Slides 1', 'My Car Slides 2' and 'Poetry And Power' (the latter track was slightly longer than previous versions and no longer faded out, this was due to the re-mastering process under taken on the original studio tapes). The final three tracks included were the single mix of 'Sister Surprise' and two previously unreleased songs. Of those, the first was a newly discovered, vaguely *New Romantic* sounding item, originally titled 'Gangster Strut', but re-titled here as 'Nameless And Forgotten.' The second was a slightly different mix of the album's title track. Fans have speculated that it was a surviving Bill Nelson co-production: unfortunately, the track in question had been rather badly edited in a bid to make it appear longer. The exact date for this edit was unknown with no real clues given within the sleeve notes. Both *I, Assassin* and *Warriors* came with a detailed discography for the years 1982 and 1983, something that was missing from the previous re-masters.

RE-ISSUE CAMPAIGN
Part Two: SINGLES

THAT'S TOO BAD/ BOMBERS
1. 'That's Too Bad' 3.17. 2. 'Oh! Didn't I Say' 2.20
1. 'Bombers' 3.55. 2. 'O.D. Receiver' 2.39. 3. 'Blue Eyes'
1.47.
(**Cat No:** UK Back 2 – Beg 5 and Beg 8)
Released: June 1979.
Special note: some copies were mis-pressed and did not
feature the track 'O.D. Receiver.' In addition, cover included
a sticker that stated 'Beggars backfire, double-pack.'

With 'Are "Friends" Electric?' and *Replicas* at No1 in the UK, Beggars Banquet
went back to Gary's first two singles with Tubeway Army with a view to re-issuing
them. They re-emerged here as a special edition double-pack single.

'That's Too Bad'/ 'Bombers' double-pack failed to chart.

CARS (E REG MODEL)
1. 'Cars (E Reg Model)' 3.35. 2. 'Are "Friends" Electric?'
(**Cat No:** UK. Beg 199)
1. 'Cars (E Reg Extended Model)' 6.16. 2. 'Are "Friends"
Electric?' 5.24. 3. 'We Are Glass' 4.46. 4. 'I Die: You Die'
(US version)* 3.40.
(**Cat No:** UK Beg 199T)

1. 'Cars (E Reg Extended Model)' 6.16. 2. 'Are "Friends"
Electric?' 5.24. 3. 'Cars (E Reg Model)' 3.35. 4. 'Cars
(Motorway Mix)' 4.31.
(**Cat No:** UK Beg 199TR)
Formats: 7-inch, 12-inch (two versions) and 4 track
cassette (track list same as Beg 199T except with the
extended version replaced with the regular single edit –
Beg 199C).
* This was expected to be either the rare video version or
the limited edition 7-inch promo that was issued in 1980, in actual fact this turned
out to be nothing more than the standard single version.
Released: September 1987.
Foreign formats: none.
Special note: 7-inch picture disc issued (Beg 199P) as well as a 7-inch promo
featuring a stickered sleeve.
Promo video same as the original 1979 clip, however, the remixed version was
substituted over the original recording when transmitted on television.
Remixed by Zeus B Held.

When news emerged that 'Cars' was to be remixed as a sweetener for an
impending 'best of' collection, fans feared the worst, however, the results far
exceeded their expectations by actually improving over the original. In its turbo
charged new skin, 'Cars' the 'E Reg Model' effectively made a great song even
better, fans were delighted and when released 'Cars' became a huge hit going top
20 eight years after its initial chart appearance.

'Cars (E Reg Model)' entered the charts at No 35 peaking at No 16 with a 7-week run on the top 75.

EXHIBITION
1. 'Cars (E Reg Model)' 3.35. 2. 'We Take Mystery (To Bed)' 3.42. 3 'I'm An Agent' 4.26. 4. 'Complex' 3.11. 5. 'Trois Gymnopedies (First Movement)' 2.44.
(**Cat No:** JA BB ALDB 10)
Formats: picture disc CD single issued with a foldout sleeve and lyric sheet (see below).
Released: 1990.
    This was the single that was issued in the Far East to precede the *Asylum* series.

Left: full foldout sleeve.

Japanese re-issue of 'Cars' in 1990 complete with lyric sheet as well as the rare 1993 12-inch promo of the 'Multivalve' mix of 'Cars.'

CARS (93, SPRINT)
1. 'Cars (93, Sprint)' 4.01. 2. 'Cars (Multivalve Mix)' 5.47. 3. 'Cars (Classic)' 3.48. 4. 'Cars (Endurance Mix)' 6.45. 5. 'Cars (Top Gear Mix)' 4.13. 6. 'Cars (Motorway Mix)' 6.12.* 7. 'Cars (E Reg Model)' 3.35.
(Cat No. UK Beg 264 CD, also special auto sports awards edition CD released with a different sleeve)
Formats: CD single (two versions), Cassette single (Beg 264C), 7-inch picture disc (Beg 264L – Features 'Sprint' and 'Endurance' mixes). This was available as a poster sleeve that unfolded to reveal on one side, a 1976 picture of Formula 1 world champion racing driver James Hunt. On the other side was a picture of a McClaren sports car surrounded by pictures of Numan throughout his career.
Special note: 12-inch promo released featuring the 'Multivalve', 'Endurance' and 'Top gear' mixes of 'Cars' (Beg 264T), this was issued in a plain black sleeve with the addition of a press release.
All new mixes undertaken by Charles Pierre and Francis Usmar of Native Soul.
* The time for this track was incorrect, it should have read 4.31, the time 6.12 belongs, in fact, to the 'E Reg Extended Model,' which was not included on this single.

With a second wave of Beggars Banquet backed CDs on the way, another remix of 'Cars' was quickly commissioned. However, when released, this third take on the song was met with indifference with fans noticeably less enthusiastic about a poppy/ dance version of the song. Of the four new mixes commissioned, most fans felt the 'Multivalve' version worked the best and some questioned why it hadn't been promoted as the single's lead track. Within the CD single's sleeve there was a three-questioned competition that allowed winners access to three top prizes, the first prize being an exclusive flight with Gary. For the second prize the winner was taken on a trip with Gary around Silverstone race-track and finally the third prize offered the opportunity for the winner to be the guest courtesy of Gary at the 'Fuji film race day', again at Silverstone.

'Cars (93, Sprint)' entered the charts at a peak position of No 53 with a 1-week chart run.

CARS (PREMIER MIX)
1 'Cars (Premier Mix)'* 3.35. 2. 'Cars (Extended Premier Mix)'* 6.12. 3. 'Down In The Park (live '80)'**5.59. 4. 'Are "Friends" Electric? (live '80)'**5.39.
(Cat No. UK PolyGram T.V. PRMCD 1)
Formats: CD single, cassette single (PRMCS 1), picture disc 7-inch single featuring the 'Premier Mix' and the live version of 'Are "Friends" Electric?' (PolyGram T.V. PRM 1).
* Both 'Premier' mixes were actually the 1987 'E Reg Model' versions of 'Cars' simply re-titled to promote the TV advert.
** Taken from the album *Living Ornaments '80*, both tracks released on CD for the first time in the UK.
Released: March 1996.
Special note: promo CD issued featuring: 'Cars', 'Are "Friends" Electric?' and 'We Are Glass' (GNRAD 1).
All music licensed to PolyGram Records.

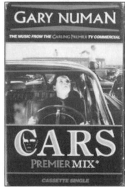

After featuring in a heavily aired UK television advert promoting Carling Beers new 'Premier Lager', 'Cars' was re-issued once again and immediately leapt into the top 20: this event gave Numan the unique accolade of having the same song a hit three times in three different decades. Ironically 'Cars' has not only been the song that made Numan a worldwide household name but can now be attributed to being the very song that successfully resurrected Gary from a decade of cult obscurity. Following this, PolyGram licensed all Numan's Beggars Banquet singles for a complimentary 'greatest hits' collection (see 'licensed compilation albums').

'Cars (Premier Mix)' climbed to a peak position of No 17 with a 4-week run on the top 75.
Special note: in addition, three 7-inch double A-side singles were issued in the UK during 1990, the first two were released through Old Gold and featured 'Are "Friends" Electric?' paired with 'I Die: You Die' and 'Cars' also paired with 'I Die: You Die.' The remaining 7-inch was issued through Old Silver and featured 'Cars' paired with 'We Are Glass.'

MEMORABILIA

The final pages of 'The Beggars Banquet Years' will take a look at some of the memorabilia that appeared during Gary's time spent on the label and it is split into three separate sections.

Part One: MAGAZINE COVERS

Although vilified by the press in the late 70s/ early 80s, it didn't stop the leading magazines of the day from adding Numan to their front covers on a regular basis and the following pages take a look back at some of those front covers.

UK –June 28th 1979, Numan's first cover following the success of Replicas.

UK Sounds *magazine 1979.*

Record Mirror, *September 1979.*

Words, *October 1979.*

Melody Maker, *October 1979.*

Smash Hits, *November the 15th 1979.*

Pop Rock, *1979.*

In The City, *1979.*

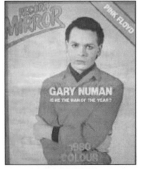
Record Mirror, *December 1979.*

Look-In, *December 1979.*

Superpop, *December 1979.*

New Music News, *24th of May 1980.*

Record Mirror, *July 19th 1980.*

Look-In, *September 20th 1979.*

Smash Hits, *October 20th 1980.*

Pop Rock, *October 1980.*

Melody Maker, *October 18th 1980.*

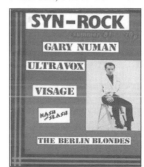

Syn-Rock, *1981*

Trouser Press, *Jan 1981.*

Melody Maker, *May 1980.*

Record Mirror, *June 1981.*

Smash Hits, *17th of Sept 1981.*

Pop Tops, *Sept 1981.*

My Guy, *Nov 1981.*

My Guy, *Jan 1982.*

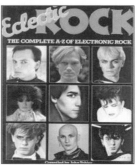

Electric Rock, *1982.*

Electronics And Music Maker, *Dec 1983.*

Electronic Soundmaker, *Dec 1983.*

Mail Spin, *Aug 1983..*

The History Of Rock, *1984*

Part Two: MERCHANDISE

Gary Numan was no different to any other artist in respect of the amount of merchandise that entered the market place immediately after his 1979 breakthrough; this section gathers together some of the more notable items that would be of historical interest to collectors and fans alike.

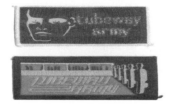

Early Tubeway Army/
Gary Numan sew-on patches.

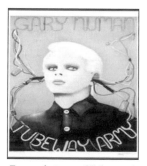
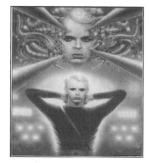

Two early items of Tubeway Army artwork.

Gold disc awarded to The Pleasure Principle.

Two of the very first fan club newsletters.

Two rare greeting cards.

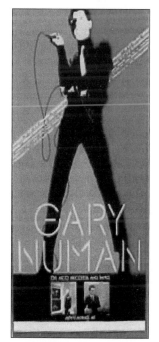

Two "Numan" themed cushions.

In-store poster.

Pair of "Numan" themed mirrors.

Telekon *embossed purse.*

"Hit Pops" bubblegum album sleeve, featured the lyrics to "This Wreckage" printed within.

Brazilian poster sleeve for "Cars."

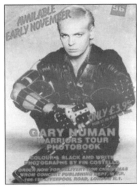

Magazine advert for the Warriors *photo book.*

Poster advert for the '83 air display.

Argentinean issue.

Mirror prints of Replicas *and* The Pleasure Principle.

Debut yearbook.

Alternative Korean issue. Cat No WEA LIFE86.

Argentinean issue.

Left: Selection of badges, pins and sew-on patches. Above: variations of the Telekon *album.*

Part One: ALTERNATIVE ARTWORK AND RELEASES FROM AROUND THE WORLD

Shown below are a number of the different picture sleeves and alternative releases that emerged during Gary's days signed to the Beggars Banquet/ WEA label.

SINGLES

UK 12-inch version of "Down In The Park."

Spanish version of "Are "Friends" Electric?"

Italian version of "Are "Friends" Electric?"

US 12-inch double sided promo (mono and stereo) of "Are "Friends" Electric?", both tracks edited down to 3.45 minutes.

Japanese issue of "Are "Friends" Electric?"

French issue of "Are "Friends" Electric?"

US issue of "AFE", credited to Gary Numan. Back cover printed above.

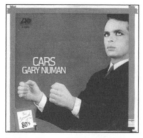

Italian issue of "Cars."

Japanese issue of "Cars", lyrics printed on the back.

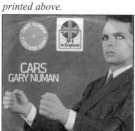

German issue of "Cars."

Brazilian issue of "Cars", picture sleeve opened up to reveal a B&W poster.

UK 12-inch issue of "Complex", note the altered artwork.

Japanese issue of "Complex", B-sides both live (plays at 33 rpm).

Spanish issue of "We Are Glass."

Italian issue of "We Are Glass."

Japanese issue of "We Are Glass", as always the lyrics on Japanese singles are included with each single.

Ultra rare US only 12-inch Atlantic issue of "Are "Friends" Electric?", this issue was, although minus a picture sleeve, also edited down to 3.45 minutes.

Japanese issue of "I Die; You Die."

North American issue of "Remind Me To Smile" B-side: "I Dream Of Wires."

7-inch free live single given away with initial copies of Telekon.

Japanese issue of "This Wreckage."

German 12-inch featuring both the live and studio version of 'Remember I Was Vapour' (INT 126-600).

Japanese issue of "She's Got Claws."

Spanish issue of "She's Got Claws."

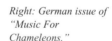

Special edition cassette only releases, each tape included two of Gary's early 80s singles. Tape one included both 'AFE' and 'Cars' (Cat No: SPC4), tape two included both 'Down In The Park' and 'We Are Glass' (Cat No: SPC7) released in the UK and Europe in April 1981. Both issued as 'cigarette style' flip-top boxes.

Italian issue of "She's Got Claws."

Japanese issue of "Love Needs No Disguise."

Right: German issue of "Music For Chameleons."

Left: specially commissioned US only 12-inch promo featuring the original 12-inch mix (7.42) of 'We Take Mystery (To Bed)' and a US only extended (8.20) remix* of 'White Boys And Heroes' (Atco PR468).
* Remixed by Chris Nelson.

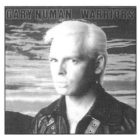

UK 12-inch version of "Warriors."

Picture disc issue of the "Warriors" single.

7-inch promo featuring "This Is My Life", only 300 copies made (Cat No: TUB1).

Cassette issue of the 1987 "E Reg Model" issue of "Cars."

Picture disc issue of the 1993 remix of "Cars."

Picture disc issue of the 1996 re-issue of "Cars."

ALBUMS

Original US cassette and vinyl issue.

New Zealand issue.

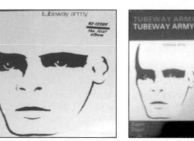

UK '79 issue.

UK '83 re-issue.

Japanese issue featuring "Cars."

UK '79 issue.

Australian issue.

US/ Canadian/ Italian issue.

Japanese '79 issue.

UK '79 issue.

Japanese '79 issue.

US '79 issue.

Canadian/ Korean issue, Korean Cat No: OLW 10.

Taiwanese issue.

US 8 track tape.

Saudi '79 issue.

Canadian '79 issue.

Japanese issue.

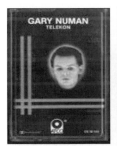

US '80 issue.

Canadian '80 issue.

UK original cassette and vinyl issue.

Saudi '80 issue.

Japanese '80 issue.

Australian/ New Zealand '81 issue.

Japanese '81 issue.

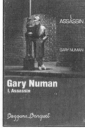

Original UK cassette releases.

Japanese issue.

Australian/ Canadian issue, note the altered artwork.

One of only two promo versions of Telekon issued minus the interlocking red strips.

Above and below: 1988 vinyl and cassette issue of the debut Tubeway Army album, note new artwork.

Left: German '82 issued cassette compilation

US issue of Premier Hits.

Left: Rare Australian issue featuring a peel-off sticker
Right: Second Australian/ NZ gatefold sleeve.

SECTION ONE

PART TWO

THE NUMA YEARS

When news filtered out in early 1984 that Gary had left Beggars Banquet, fans assumed Numan would quickly sign a new deal and be back in action soon after. It came then as something of a surprise to learn that Gary had in fact decided to launch his own record label designed to be independent and free from any major label interference. Christened Numa and taking its company logo from the cover of the 1979 re-issue of the *Tubeway Army* album, the label aimed to operate as a vehicle, not only for Numan's work, but others too. To that end, Gary spent the summer months assembling a wide and varied roster of artists.

Part way through the year, long time Numan cohort Paul Gardiner sadly passed away and as a tribute to him Numa's first release was a single featuring two songs he recorded shortly before his death. Come November though, Gary finally released his first new material in a year. However, neither the single nor album (both entitled *Berserker*) made much of an impression on the nation's charts, barely grazing the top 50 upon release. Subsequent releases from Gary running up to the end of 1986 also struggled to emulate his early 80s successes and after 21 singles and 4 albums (none of which reached the top 20) Numa closed its doors and was quietly wound up in the early part of 1987. Gary found a new home for his work at IRS Records but this tenure lasted barely three years and following a label re-shuffle, Gary found himself label-less once more.

Gary re-activated Numa Records midway through 1991 but unfortunately this second phase of the label saw his fortunes dwindle even further as Gary began to slip from the mainstream and into a cult bracket. The year 1994 saw Gary finally turn things around with his new studio record *Sacrifice* being hailed by fans as a genuine return to form, seeing thousands of previously disillusioned fans flooding back to the fold. Encouraged by this and with a re-issued 'Cars' back in the top 20 singles chart two years later, Gary opted to dispense with Numa for the second and final time and go once more in search of a new recording contract, following a number of leads (including a proposed return to Beggars Banquet). Gary eventually inked a new deal with Eagle Records midway through 1997.

ORIGINAL ALBUMS
Part One: 1984-1986

★★★☆☆

BERSERKER
(**Cat No:** UK Numa 1001)
Formats: vinyl and cassette (Numac 1001).*
Released: November 1984.
Foreign formats: matched the UK.
Re-issued: 1991** and December 1995 on CD (see 'Numa albums re-issued'). Also re-issued February 1999 on CD in the UK through Eagle Records and April 1999 on CD in the US through Cleopatra Records (see 'The Eagle Records Years').
* The cassette version of this album featured six of its tracks extended namely: 'Berserker' 6.40, 'This Is New Love' 8.45, 'The Secret' 6.40, 'My Dying Machine' 9.04, 'Cold Warning' 6.57 and 'The Hunter' 6.47. The remaining three tracks were identical in length to the vinyl issue.
** Extended version issued on CD for the first time. Fan club only release.

Musicians: Gary Numan – Vocals and keyboards/ Chris Payne – Viola and keyboards/ Cedric Sharpley – Drums/ RRussell Bell – Guitars/ John Webb – Keyboards and programming/ Martin Elliott – Bass/ Andy Coughlan – Bass ('Cold Warning')/ Pat Kyle – Saxophone/ Tessa Niles – Vocals/ Tracy Ackerman – Vocals/ Zaine Griff – Vocals ('The Secret')/ Mike Smith, Ian Herron – PPG programming.
Engineered by Pete Buhlmann.
Mixed by Pete Buhlmann and Gary Numan.
Recorded at Rock City Sound Studios.
Produced by Gary Numan.
Side One, Tracks: 'Berserker' 5.50/ 'This Is New Love' 6.15/ 'The Secret' 5.45/ 'My Dying Machine' 5.33.
Side Two, Tracks: 'Cold Warning' 4.03/ 'Pump It Up' 4.45/ 'The God Film' 4.41/ 'A Child With A Ghost' 4.04/ 'The Hunter' 4.31.
All songs by Gary Numan.
Singles: 'Berserker' and 'My Dying Machine.'
Videos: initially none, however, following the release of the long form video *The Berserker Tour*, both singles were commissioned promo's featuring footage from the concert video. In addition, 'Berserker' was performed on UK music shows *TOTP* and *Razzamatazz*: 'My Dying Machine' was also performed on *Razzamatazz*. Both singles were performed on German TV.
Special note 1: an alternative and edited version of 'Berserker' was performed on Swiss and German TV. In addition, the German performance of 'My Dying Machine' saw Gary dispensing with the 'white face/ blue hair' image in favour of an early *Fury* look. This performance saw Gary sporting black hair.
Special note 2: part way through the year Gary appeared on *The Leo Sayer Show*. Following an interview, two songs were performed: one was a duet with Leo on the old standard 'On Broadway' and the other was a brand new Numan penned track entitled 'This Is New Love', a catchy up tempo slice of Numan pop that fans assumed was to be Gary's comeback single. Later in the year a second and vastly different version of this track was aired on *The Main Attraction*, this mix was an edited version of the messy and mangled take that ended up on the *Berserker* album.
Special note 3: prior to its release, Gary's first Numa studio album went through a number of alternative titles with both 'The Hunter' and 'The Promise' being put forward.

For fans, another agonising, year long wait for new material finally came to an end in late 1984 when Numan finally released his first new album on his own imprint, Numa Records. In the time away Gary had altered his sound quite dramatically, *Berserker* was a bold, purposeful move into a harder, more metallic sound incorporating a new technology called sampling. *Berserker* was also a fairly rhythmically aggressive record and by far the least commercial music from Numan thus far. With no obvious hits on board, when released, the record received a cautious and lukewarm reaction from fans, selling nowhere near as much as previous releases. However, admittedly, Gary's former record label Beggars Banquet could be blamed in part for *Berserker's* poor chart showing when they issued their Tubeway Army out-takes album *The Plan-1978* in the month running up to its release. As hard hitting as it may have been, *Berserker* did offer up some choice moments with 'Cold Warning,' 'The Hunter' and the album's title track working the best. Also special note should be given to the track 'A Child With A Ghost', a haunting ballad that was Gary's own personal tribute to the sadly deceased Paul Gardiner. Overall though, *Berserker* was a fairly patchy and disappointing offering and only succeeded in getting Numa off to a relatively poor start.

Berserker entered the charts at No 51 climbing to a peak position of No 45 with a 3-week run on the top 75.

WHITE NOISE
(**Cat No:** UK Numad 1002)

Formats: double vinyl and single cassette (Numac 1002*).

Released: April 1985.

Foreign formats: Finland issued the record in a single sleeve. Australian issue featured a slightly different sleeve. European label Teldec issued the record with a free sticker.

Re-issued May 1993 on CD for the first time (see 'Numa albums re-issued'). Also re-issued January 1998 for the first time on CD in the US through Cleopatra Records. Finally re-issued in the UK, March 2003. This release was also on CD and included a brand new cover (see 'The Eagle Records Years').

* Cassette sleeve featured a mis-pressing that omitted the track 'The Iceman Comes', however, this mistake was not repeated within the sleeve's inlay card itself.

Special note: 12-inch, four-track, white label sampler also released.

Musicians: Gary Numan – Vocals/ Chris Payne – Keyboards and viola/ John Webb – Keyboards and saxophone/ RRussell Bell – Guitars and violin/ Andy Coughlan – Bass guitar/ Karen Taylor – Backing vocals/ Cedric Sharpley – Drums.

Engineered by Tim Summerhayes.

Mixed at Rock City Studios.

Mixed by Tim Summerhayes and John Webb.

Produced by Gary Numan.

Recorded at the Hammersmith Odeon, London in December 1984.

Record One, Side One, Tracks: 'Intro' 1.58/ 'Berserker' 5.42/ 'Metal' 3.32/ 'Me! I Disconnect From You' 3.21/ 'Remind Me To Smile' 3.21/ 'Sister Surprise' 6.11 Side Two, Tracks: 'Music For Chameleons' 6.10/ 'The Iceman Comes' 4.37/ 'Cold Warning' 6.09/ 'Down In The Park' 5.28.

Record Two, Side One, Tracks: 'This Prison Moon' 3.28/ 'I Die: You Die' 3.55/ 'My Dying Machine' 5.42/ 'Cars' 3.38/ 'We Take Mystery (To Bed)' 6.31

Side Two, Tracks: 'We Are Glass' 4.57/ 'This Is New Love' 6.21/ 'My Shadow In Vain' 5.45/ 'Are "Friends" Electric?'

Australian issue of White Noise, released via Powderworks Records.

All songs by Gary Numan.

Singles: 'The live EP' (featured four cuts from the album).

Videos: footage shown at the time of the EP's release had been taken from one of the two December dates at the Hammersmith Odeon and was itself released as part of a long form video in early 1986 (see 'Official video cassettes').

Released in the spring of '85 as a souvenir from the 'Berserker Tour', *White Noise* –Numan's first live record since the classic coupling of *Living Ornaments '79 and '80* – quickly leapt into the British top 30 surprisingly out-performing Gary's first record for Numa (the *Berserker* album) in the process. However, unlike the two previous classic live outings, *White Noise* struggled to reach the dizzying heights attained by those albums. The 18 songs included on the record were a balanced assembly of past classics with all of Gary's previous studio albums (except *Dance*) being plundered for the odd track here and there. However, *Berserker,* the recent studio album, was represented by just four cuts and although 'Cold Warning' had all the makings of a Numan classic, 'Berserker', My Dying Machine' and the truly dire 'This Is New Love' struggled to impress even in this live setting hinting that perhaps even Numan himself was less than thrilled with the finished album. One month after *White Noise*, Gary issued a souvenir live EP featuring four tracks cut from the album. Tellingly, only one of the new songs performed (*Berserker)* was included with this release.

'White Noise' entered the charts at No 60 climbing to a peak position of No 29 with a 5-week run on the top 75.

THE FURY

(**Cat No:** UK Numa 1003)

Formats: vinyl, cassette* and CD.**

Released: September 1985.

Foreign formats: German sleeve featured 'Includes "Your Fascination" and "Call Out The Dogs"' printed on the cover, in addition, the record's inner sleeve was shaded pink.

Special note 1: limited edition 2000 print run released in the US.

★★★☆☆

Special note 2: two vinyl picture discs issued (Numax 1003 and Nump 1003).

Re-issued in December 1996 (see 'Numa albums re-issued'), November 1998 and February 1999 (see 'The Eagle Records Years').

* Available as an extended recording (Numac 1003) as well as a later standard issue.

** CD issue released with a new catalogue number (CDNuma 1004), this was issued in early 1986 and was not extended.

Musicians: Gary Numan – Vocals and keyboards/ Mike Smith – Keyboards/ Dick Morrissey – Saxophone/ Andy Coughlan – Bass/ Tracy Ackerman – Backing vocals/ Tessa Niles – Backing vocals/ Mike Smith – PPG and keyboards/ Ian Herron – PPG/ Ian Ritchie – Saxophone on 'Miracles.'

Engineered by Peter Buhlmann, assisted by Andy Reilly.

Recorded and mixed at Rock City Studios by Pete Buhlmann and Gary Numan.

Produced by Gary Numan and The Wave Team, except 'Your Fascination', produced by Colin Thurston and Gary Numan.

Side One, Tracks: 'Call Out The Dogs' 4.39/ 'This Disease' 4.03/ 'Your Fascination' 4.44/ 'Miracles' 3.38/ 'The Pleasure Skin' 4.08.
Side Two, Tracks: 'Creatures' 5.08/ 'Tricks' 5.42/ 'God Only knows' 5.25/ 'I Still Remember' 4.03.
All songs by Gary Numan except 'This Disease' and 'Tricks' (Gary Numan, Andy Coughlan).
Singles: 'Your Fascination', 'Call Out The Dogs' and 'Miracles.'
Videos: videos shot for all three singles. In addition, both 'Your Fascination' and 'Call Out The Dogs' were performed on Italian TV.
Special note: Running times for extended mixes: 'Call Out The Dogs' 6.41/ 'This Disease' 5.14/ 'Your Fascination' 5.10/ 'Miracles' 4.18/ 'The Pleasure Skin' 4.52/ 'Creatures' 6.35/ 'Tricks' 6.14/ 'God Only Knows' 6.36/ 'I Still Remember' 5.20.

When released, *The Fury* revealed itself to be an album of contradictions, whilst the music contained within contorted and twisted under Numan's new found move into a proto-industrial backdrop. Outwardly Gary looked for all the world like a cast off from the 80s US crime show *Miami Vice*. The image may have suited the times but what it didn't do was accurately represent or compliment the hard attack of the music within. Overall, musically, *The Fury* was a better record than *Berserker*, however. Song-wise, Gary was moving ever further from the mainstream into lengthier and more atmospheric music. None of the singles from this album breached the top 40 and in truth, none of them possessed the stellar pop suss of the Sharpe and Numan mega hit 'Change Your Mind.' Notable tracks from the record though were the anthemic 'Tricks', the slow burning 'God Only Knows' and the sadly ignored first single 'Your Fascination.' However, not all Gary's new material sat comfortably within his new musical framework with 'This Disease' finding Gary clearly out of his depths and as for 'Miracles', no amount of seductive saxophone playing could hide the fact that this song was never destined to be spoke of in the same breath as past classics like 'I Die: You Die' and 'Cars.' The final track on *The Fury*, a smokey, mournful ballad called 'I Still Remember' raised fans eyebrows when Gary ended the track by singing that this could be his final song. For fans, this was the last thing they needed to hear, with Numan's career in freefall and a string of flop singles to his name, some began to speculate that Gary was once again pre-warning fans (like he had on the 1980 single 'This Wreckage') that he was about to say farewell once more.

The Fury entered the charts at No 29 peaking at No 24 with 5 weeks on the listings.

STRANGE CHARM
(**Cat No:** UK Numa 1005)
Formats: vinyl, cassette (Numac 1005*) and CD (CDNuma 1005).
Released: November 1986.
Foreign formats: Finland cover altered slightly (see below).
* Included the 12-inch mix of the *Blade Runner* influenced track 'Time To Die' at the end of side one.

Special note: the version of 'New Thing From London Town' found on *Strange Charm* was a new recording featuring revised lyrics from Numan.

Re-issued: December 1996 (see 'Numa re-issued albums') and February 1999 and April 1999 (see 'The Eagle Records Years').

Musicians: Gary Numan – Vocals, guitar and keyboards/ Mike Smith – PPG and keyboards/ Ian Herron – PPG/ Dick Morrissey – Saxophone/ Ade Orange – Guitar and keyboards/ Chris Payne – Violin/ Bill Sharpe – Keyboards/ Roger Odelle – Drum programming/ Mark Railton – Guitar/ RRussell Bell – Guitar/ Jess Lidyard – Percussion/ Martin Elliott – Bass/ Tessa Niles – Backing vocals/ Linda Taylor – Backing vocals.

Engineered by Tim Summerhayes.

Mixed by Tim Summerhayes and Gary Numan.

Recorded at Rock City Sound Studios.

Produced by Gary Numan and The Wave Team except 'My Breathing' (Ade Orange and Gary Numan), 'Strange Charm' (Gary Numan, The Wave Team and Ade Orange) and 'New Thing From London Town' (Bill Sharpe and Nick Smith).

Side One, Tracks: 'My Breathing' 6.36*/ 'Unknown And Hostile' 4.27/ 'The Sleeproom' 5.16/ 'New Thing From London Town' 5.53.

Side Two, Tracks: 'I Can't Stop' 5.45**/ 'Strange Charm' 5.45/ 'The Need' 7.04/ 'This Is Love' 4.30.

* This track sadly suffered from a short mid-song sound problem.

** Picture disc mix.

All songs by Gary Numan except 'New Thing From London Town' – music by Bill Sharpe, lyrics by Gary Numan.

Singles: 'This Is Love', 'I Can't Stop' and 'New Thing From London Town.'

Videos: promos shot for all three singles with two versions shot for 'I Can't Stop.' A special video was also shot for the RSPCA charity single 'I Still Remember' that emerged following the album's release. In addition, 'I Can't Stop' was performed on *Wogan* and 'This Is Love' was performed on *Nightline*.

With Gary's career problems taking centre stage, his enthusiasm for his 1986 studio album *Strange Charm* (a record Gary recorded twice) all but melted away with the record eventually slipping quietly onto the market place at the tail end of the year to little fanfare. Even in its abandoned form *Strange Charm* was one of Gary's best mid period albums, awash with great material like the eastern flavoured anthem 'My Breathing' and the criminally overlooked 'Unknown And Hostile.' Other notable tracks, aside from the three classic singles on board, were the chunky, energetic title track and the ballad like, sublime pop of 'The Sleeproom.'

Superbly produced and certainly one of Gary's most commercial records, it's a pity that the record emerged at such a critical point in his career.

Finnish issue of Strange Charm released via Polarvox Records.

Following this, Gary abandoned Numa and went in search of a new deal eventually signing with IRS Records in 1988: *Strange Charm* would prove to be the final commercially available Numa endorsed album for many years.

Strange Charm entered and peaked at the No 59 position spending just 2 weeks on the top 75.

ORIGINAL ALBUMS
Part Two: 1992-1995

Following his sudden and shock departure from IRS Records in the middle of 1991,

Gary immediately re-activated his mid-80s label Numa Records, this time, however, Numan was the label's only signing.

MACHINE + SOUL*
(**Cat No:** UK NumaCD 1009)
Formats: CD, vinyl and cassette.
Released: September 1992.
Foreign formats: none.
Re-issued: September 1993**, February 1999 and April 1999 (See 'The Eagle Records Years').
* Front cover artwork printed the title of the record as *Machine + Soul*: however, inner sleeve, back sleeve and CD disc printed the album title (and title track) as *Machine And Soul*.

★★☆☆☆

** Released as an extended version featuring extra tracks (NumaCDX 1009), some copies of this release were mis-pressed and didn't feature the bonus material despite the tracks being listed on the back cover.

Musicians: Gary Numan – Vocals, guitar and keyboards/ Kipper – Guitars, keyboards and backing vocals/ Mike Smith – Keyboards/ Ade Orange – Keyboards/ Keith Beauvais-Guitars/ Jackie Rawe – Backing vocals/ Cathi Ogden – Backing vocals/ Susie Webb – Backing vocals/ Zoe Nicholas – Backing vocals.

Engineered by Gary Numan.

Mixed by Gary Numan.

Recorded at Outland studios.

Tracks: 'Machine And Soul' 5.57/ 'Generator' 6.08/ 'The Skin Game' 6.23/ 'Poison' 5.02/ 'I Wonder' 4.28/ 'Emotion' 5.31/ 'Cry' 4.45/ 'U Got The Look' 3.57/ 'Love Isolation' 4.38.

All songs by Gary Numan except 'Generator': Music by Gary Numan and Kipper, Lyrics by Gary Numan. 'U Got The Look' written by Prince.

Produced by Gary Numan except tracks 1, 2, 4, 5, 7 and 9 (Kipper and Gary Numan)

Singles: 'Emotion', 'The Skin Game' and 'Machine + Soul/ Machine And Soul.'

Videos: 'Emotion' and 'Machine + Soul/ Machine And Soul.'

Special note: Running times for the extended mix album were: 'Machine And Soul' 7.33/ 'Generator' 9.51/ 'The Skin Game' 7.41/ 'Poison' 6.39/ 'I Wonder' 6.33/ 'Emotion' 8.00/ 'Cry' 7.31/ 'Love Isolation' 6.30 ('U Got The Look' remained unchanged). Extra tracks included on the extended mix CD were all B-sides unique to this project and included: 'Dark Mountain', 'The Haunting', 'In A Glasshouse' and 'Hanoi.'

In *Machine + Soul*, Gary had made a record that managed somehow to straddle the middle ground between Prince and En Vogue: two of America's biggest dance/ funk acts of the early 90s and as a result delivered a thoroughly modern pop record. Although musically *Machine + Soul* could not be faulted, fans were horrified with Gary's latest direction declaring it the worst record so far to bare the Numan name. Over the course of the album's nine tracks, Numan virtually disappeared behind a barrage of bouncy synths and overpowering backing vocals. Bizarrely, the record began with a blinder, title track 'Machine And Soul', that got the elements Numan was after: big fat grooves and hard rock guitar riffs, all glued to a killer chorus. In addition to that, the album's second track 'Generator' was also worthy of note being a somewhat inspired, anthemic dance track. Sadly the rest of the album nose-dived with Prince cover 'U Got The Look' being one of the worst Numan recordings thus far. Two ballads, 'I Wonder' and 'Love Isolation' did manage to bring the record momentarily back from the brink but in reality it was all too little too late.

Machine + Soul entered the charts at No 42 spending just one week on the top 75.

DREAM CORROSION
(**Cat No:** UK NumaCD 1010)
Formats, 2 CD set, twin cassette (Numac 1010)* and triple vinyl gatefold sleeve (NUMA 1010**).
Released: August 1994.
Foreign formats: none.
Re-issued: April 2003 (see 'The Eagle Records Years').
Musicians: Gary Numan – Vocals and guitar/ John Webb – Keyboards and saxophone/ Ade Orange – Keyboards and bass/ Kipper – Guitar/ Richard Beasley – Drums/ T.J. Davis – Backing vocals.
Mixed and produced by Gary Numan at Outland studios.
Recorded at the Hammersmith Apollo, London November 6th 1993.
Recorded on the Zipper mobile.
Special note: Initial copies included a signed poster.
* Cassette featured different artwork.
** Omits the track 'It Must Have Been Years.'
CD 1, Tracks: 'Mission' 2.17/ 'Machine And Soul' 6.15/ 'Outland' 4.10/ 'Me! I Disconnect From You' 3.14/ 'We Are So Fragile' 3.02/ 'Respect' 4.12/ 'Shame' 4.32/ 'Films' 5.16/ 'Dream Killer' 4.41/ 'Down In The Park' 6.13/ 'My World Storm' 5.11/ 'The Machmen' 3.43/ 'Generator' 5.25/ 'Noise Noise' 4.21.
CD 2, Tracks: 'Cars' 5.16/ 'Voix' 5.33/ 'You Are In My Vision' 3.41/ 'It Must Have Been Years' 4.32/ 'That's Too Bad' 3.42/ 'Remind Me To Smile' 3.50/ 'I'm An Agent' 4.44/ 'Are "Friends" Electric?' 7.05/ 'My Breathing' 7.10/ 'I Don't Believe' 4.36/ 'Bombers' 4.46/ 'Jo The Waiter' 6.33/ 'We Are Glass' 5.59.
All songs by Gary Numan except 'Generator' (Numan/ Kipper).
Singles: 'The Dream Corrosion EP.'
Videos: full concert released via Numan's fan club (see 'Official video cassettes').

Having reached his lowest point with the release of the ill advised *Machine + Soul* album, this two week tour undertaken a year later provided fans with the first chinks of light on an ever darkening career. Perhaps realising at last the folly of the last few years, Gary performed a lengthy two hour set that re-introduced a large chunk of the material that he was best known for, some of which had never been performed live before.

The shows themselves were psyched and vibey, with

Original gatefold sleeve.

Numan clearly enjoying the tour every bit as much as the fans were. The set list was vintage Gary Numan as classics from his heyday rubbed shoulders with the best of his more recent material. Gary was also not afraid of taking a calculated risk when he performed a lone acoustic rendition of the *Tubeway Army* rarity 'Jo The Waiter.' This tour found Gary relaxed and in a positive and playful frame of mind even causing a gasp or two from the assembled crowd as he joked he was considering retiring before quickly rubbishing the idea in dismissive defiance. *Dream Corrosion* was a fine souvenir of one of Gary's best latter day tours but most important of all, it was clearly a major step back in the right direction.

   Dream Corrosion failed to chart.

SACRIFICE
(**Cat No:** UK NumaCD 1011)
Formats: CD, vinyl (Numa 1011) and cassette (Numac 1011).
Released: October 1994.
Foreign formats: issued in the US in February 1997 re-titled *Dawn* (see 'Eagle Memorabilia'). In addition, re-issued January 1995*, August 1998 and February 1999 (see 'The Eagle Records Years').

★★★★☆ * Released as an extended version, cover artwork altered to include the words 'Extended mixes' underneath the title of the album (NumaCDX 1011).
Musicians: Gary Numan – Vocals, keyboards and guitars/ Kipper – Synth bass on 'Love And Napalm' and extra guitar and solo on 'Scar'/ T.J. Davis – Backing vocals on 'Scar.'
Engineered by Gary Numan, assisted by Gemma O'Neill.
Mixed and produced by Gary Numan.
Recorded at Outland studios.
Tracks: 'Pray' 3.55/ 'Deadliner' 4.29/ 'A Question Of Faith' 4.52/ 'Desire' 3.47/ 'Scar' 3.25/ 'Love And Napalm' 5.08/ 'You Walk In My Soul' 4.39/ 'Magic' 4.42/ 'Bleed' 6.10/ 'The Seed Of A Lie' 5.26.
Special note: also included within the vinyl version of this album was a double-sided 7-inch single featuring the regular mix of 'The Seed Of A Lie' and an extended one on the flipside (this version could also be found on the extended version of *Sacrifice*).
All songs by Gary Numan.
Singles: 'A Question Of Faith' and 'Magic' (US only).
Videos: none, although Gary did manage to squeeze 'Scar' on to the *VH1* show *In Bed With Me Dinner* ('Are "Friends" Electric?' and 'Cars' were also performed).
Special note: Running times for the extended tracks were: 'Pray' 5.57/ 'Deadliner' 8.45/ 'A Question Of Faith' 8.43/ 'Desire' 5.33/ 'Scar' 5.25/ 'Love And Napalm' 8.26/ 'You Walk In My Soul' 6.54/ 'Magic' 6.29/ 'Bleed' 7.41/ 'The Seed Of A Lie' 7.07.

   In addition, a further UK version of *Sacrifice* was released featuring the original 10-track album as well as two extra tracks ('A Question Of Faith' 8.43 and 'Love And Napalm' 8.26 – both of these were the extended mixes).

   Sacrifice was Gary's best album in 10 years and a powerful reminder as to just what it was that captured the public's imagination all those years ago. Much of the material on this album recalled the halcyon days of the late 70s to early 80s, with Gary at last back to recording music to please himself rather than later albums that included the odd track or two that slotted into a 'radio friendly' format just to appease the ever hits-obsessed major label record companies that Numan signed with.

Sacrifice was an inspired return, heavy with chiming, gothic melodies and all wrapped in a contemporary, industrial canvas. From the chilly intro, 'Pray' with it's distorted, ghostly narrative, to equally stellar tracks like the towering 'Bleed', the cathedral like noir of 'Magic' (released as a single in the US in early 1997, see 'The Eagle Records Years') and the moody melodic closer 'The Seed Of A Lie.'

The album was a real turning point for Gary, word spread quickly throughout his fan base convincing those that had been disillusioned with his late 80s and early 90s recordings to consider returning to the fold in this new chapter in Gary's career.

Warmly received by fans, *Sacrifice* marked the beginnings of the long claw back from the edge for the one time dark lord of pop.

Sacrifice failed to chart.

DARK LIGHT
(**Cat No:** UK NumaCD 1012)
Formats: 2 CD set and twin cassettes (Numac 1012).
Released: June 1995.
Foreign formats: none.
Re-issued: August 1998, February 2001 and April 2003 (see 'The Eagle Records Years').
Special note: this tour was plagued with technical demons, from mysterious power cuts to faulty equipment, some of the songs on this album had obviously been either musically or vocally 'fixed', none more so than 'Stormtrooper In Drag' which suffered from a number of microphone problems during the tour.

Musicians: Gary Numan – Vocals and guitar/ John Webb – Keyboards/ Ade Orange – Keyboards, bass and vocals/ Kipper – Guitars and vocals/ Richard Beasley – Drums

Mixed and produced by Gary Numan at Outland Studios.

CD 1, Tracks: 'Pray (Intro)' 2.18/ 'A Question Of Faith' 4.58/ 'I Dream Of Wires' 5.04/ 'Noise Noise' 4.11/ 'Listen To The Sirens' 3.11/ 'Every Day I Die' 4.27/ 'Desire' 4.12/ 'Friends' 3.29/ 'Scar' 3.31/ 'Magic' 4.57/ 'Praying To The Aliens' 3.39/ 'Replicas' 5.22/ 'Mean St' 3.43.

CD 2, Tracks: 'Stormtrooper In Drag' 4.53/ 'Deadliner' 4.48/ 'Bleed' 6.03/ 'The Dream Police' 4.45/ 'I Die: You Die' 3.37/ 'The Hunter' 5.33/ 'Remind Me To Smile' 3.59/ 'Are "Friends" Electric?' 6.11/ 'Do You Need The Service?' 3.00/ 'Love And Napalm' 5.28/ 'Jo The Waiter' 3.21/ 'I'm An Agent' 5.02.

Recorded at Labatts Hammersmith Apollo on the 5th of November 1994, although the date is incorrectly listed on the sleeve as November the 12th.

Recorded on the Fleetwood mobile.

All songs by Gary Numan.

Singles: 'The Dark Light EP.'

Videos: none.

If *Sacrifice* had been the album that saw Numan's star begin to rise again, the accompanying tour was yet another positive step back up the ladder. Performed before a fired up, electrified crowd, listening to the opening strains of 'Pray', one got the impression that 'The Sacrifice Tour' was, in reality, the sound of an artist hell bent on resurrecting his career. Sure enough, second track in 'A Question Of Faith' literally exploded into life and from there on in it was wall to wall classics at every turn. Admittedly some of the resurrected material sounded somewhat forced with Gary sounding a little uncomfortable at times, but these minor niggles did little to dampen Numan's new found enthusiasm, a feeling not lost on long time fans either. Of the eight tracks culled from the *Sacrifice* album, all fitted seamlessly into the set highlighting an important fact that Numan's future lay not in his past but in his future. However, Gary also used this tour to delve deeper still into his 16-year career and air material that either hadn't been played in years or hadn't been played at all. Two tracks making a welcome return to the set were Tubeway Army oldies 'The Dream Police' and 'Replicas.' Both had been updated since their last airing on the 'Touring Principle' and sounded all the better for it. Making their concert debut alongside tracks from the *Sacrifice* record were: an energetic romp through the early Tubeway Army classic 'Friends,' a breathless rendition of 'Listen To The Sirens', as well as further, long lost rarities like 'Mean St,' 'Stormtrooper In Drag' and 'Do You Need The Service?' All the songs chosen for this tour received a rapturous welcome from fans and with a return to form album already in the shops, Numan not only seemed reborn, but for the first time in years, relevant again.

Dark Light failed to chart.

HUMAN
(**Cat No:** UK NumaCD 1013)
Formats: CD and cassette (Numac 1013).
Released: October 1995.
Foreign formats: none.
Never re-issued.
Credited to Gary Numan and Michael R Smith.
Tracks: 'Navigators' 2.12/ 'Bombay' 2.30/ 'We Fold Space' 1.10/ 'A Cry In The Dark' 2,45/ 'Manic' 1.37/ 'Empire' 2.19/ 'A Little Lost Soul'* 2.42/ 'The Visitor' 1.09/ 'Magician' 2.13/ 'Undercover' 1.28/ 'Halloween' 1.13/ 'Embryo'** 1.59/ 'Elm St' 1.27/ 'Harmonos' 2.20/ 'Big Alien'*** 1.48/ 'Blind Faith' 1.09/ 'New Life' 4.02/ 'Fairy Tales' 2.52/ 'Disease' 2.22/ 'Tidal Wave'**** 1.22/ 'Alone And Afraid' 1.19/ 'Sahara' 1.35/ 'Cold' 1.41/ 'Do You Wonder' 1.32/ 'Betrayal' 1.01/ 'Suspicion' 1.04/ 'The Unborn' 1.59/ 'Lethal Injection' 1.44/ 'Frantic' 1.04/ 'Mother'*** 0.57/ 'Black Heart' 1.43/ 'Thunder Road' 0.34/ 'Law And Order' 2.02/ 'Needles'***** 2.27/ 'Climax' 0.35/ 'Inferno' 0.48.

* Semi-instrumental version of *Outland* album track 'Soul Protection.' ** This track provided the backbone for the *Sacrifice* track 'The Seed Of A Lie.' *** Both these tracks are virtually instrumental versions of the 1991 single 'Heart.' **** This track formed the basis for the *Outland* album track 'From Russia Infected.' ***** This track formed the backbone for the *Sacrifice* album track 'Pray.'

Special note 1: 'Big Alien' incorrectly listed on the CD label as 'Big Alten.'

Special note 2: IRS Records decision to pass on this release was in itself odd as they had originally approached Gary in early 1988 to record a series of instrumental albums entitled 'No Speak' for them (none of which were ever made).

All the music contained within this album (of which 75 different pieces of music were originally recorded) was taken from the low budget horror movie of the early 90s, *The Unborn* (see 'Official video cassettes') and had never been released before. All the tracks are instrumentals and originated from Gary's days signed to IRS Records. This album emerged at a time when Gary was re-issuing all his Numa recordings onto CD.

Human failed to chart. This album was the final commercially available release from Numa Records with Gary signing to Eagle Records in 1997.

ORIGINAL SINGLES
Part One: 1984-1986

BERSERKER

1. 'Berserker' (edit) 4.05. 2. 'Empty Bed, Empty Heart' 3.10 (non-album track).
(**Cat No:** UK NU4)
1. 'Berserker' (extended) 6.40. 2. 'Empty Bed, Empty Heart' 3.10 (non-album track). 3. 'Berserker' (edit) 4.05.
(**Cat No:** UK NUM4)
Formats: 7-inch and 12-inch vinyl.
Released: October 1984.

★★★★☆

Foreign formats: German back sleeve different to UK issue.

Special note: 7-inch double-sided picture disc released (NUP4).
Promo video shot.

For a comeback single, 'Berserker' was certainly an odd choice. Its dense wall of shuddering, stomping synths and bizarre reversed guitar riffs resulted in a single that was about as fiercely uncommercial as you could get and with the hopes of a new record company behind it, in hindsight, perhaps 'Berserker''s rampaging, industrial assault was not the best way to allay Numan's financial worries at this critical point. Gary also found himself at odds with the pop charts of 1984. Heavily made-up in white make-up, blue lips, eyeliner and hair, it was certainly an arresting sight but not one guaranteed to win the hearts of a nation more used to the clean-cut likes of Duran Duran and Wham! In truth, 'Berserker' was a brave yet ultimately disappointing comeback possessing none of the accessible charm of earlier singles. However, for Gary and Numa, it was nothing short of a disaster.

'Berserker' entered the charts at No 38 peaking the following week at No 32 before dropping away with just 5 weeks on the top 75.

Picture disc issue (both sides).

MY DYING MACHINE

1. 'My Dying Machine' (edit) 3.22. 2. 'Here Am I' 5.36 (non-album track).
(**Cat No:** UK NU6)
1. 'My Dying Machine' (extended) 9.16. 2. 'Here Am I' 5.36 (non-album track). 3. 'She Cries' 5.52 (non-album track).
(**Cat No:** UK NUM6)
Formats: 7-inch and 12-inch vinyl.

★★★★☆ **Released:** December 1984.

Foreign formats: 7-inch German sleeve slightly different (see below). Italian 12-inch featured a previously unreleased extended remix. Promo video shot.

Special note: German version of 'Here Am I' edited down to 3.45.

With its late-night dance grooves, sweetened synths and stuttered sampling throughout, 'My Dying Machine' was a much more accessible single from the Numan camp, unfortunately, the song fell on deaf ears and even with two superb new tracks added as B-sides (one of which 'She Cries' was a remixed, previously unreleased *I, Assassin* demo) as well as a short TV advert, this single achieved the sad accolade of being the first Numan single to fail to grace the British top 50 since Gary's 1979 breakthrough.

German sleeve.

'My Dying Machine' entered and peaked at No 66 spending just 1 week on the top 75 singles chart.

★★★★★

THE LIVE EP

1. 'Are "Friends" Electric?' 5.40. 2. 'Berserker' 5.36. 3. 'Cars' 3.25. 4. 'We Are Glass' 4.50.
(**Cat No:** UK NU7 and NUM7)
Formats: 7-inch and 12-inch.
Released: May 1985.
Foreign formats: German 12-inch sleeve slightly different. Australian label Powerworks issued similar UK style coloured vinyl editions of the live EP.
Special note: both 7-inch and 12-inch format available on coloured vinyl (blue, white and standard black).

Promo video shot.

With the live album *White Noise* achieving a respectable top 30 placing a month earlier (itself following hot on the heels of Gary's return to the top 20 singles chart with the Bill Sharpe collaboration 'Change Your Mind'), Numan decided to release a special souvenir live EP from the album featuring four of his past hits. Not surprisingly, former No1 'Are "Friends" Electric?' took the lead spot, the track having long become a staple of Gary's live shows. This recording was, however, a little different as halfway through Numan dissolved into a fit of laughter brought on by end of tour, on stage hi-jinks. Despite the usual zero airplay and limited publicity 'The

Australian sleeve

Live EP' did rather well by quickly rocketing into the British top 30. Unfortunately, without vital exposure the single soon fell away and ultimately out of the charts denying Gary of a much needed, and in this case, much deserved top 20 hit.

'The Live EP' entered the charts at No 40 climbing to its peak position of No 27 the following week before dropping back with just four weeks on the top 75.

YOUR FASCINATION

1. 'Your Fascination' (edit) 3.40. 2. 'We Need It' (edit) 3.34 (non-album track).
(**Cat No:** UK NU9)
1 'Your Fascination' (extended) 5.10. 2. 'We Need It' (extended) 6.50 (non-album track) 3. 'Anthem' 3.23 (non-album track).
(**Cat No:** UK NUM9)
Formats: 7-inch and 12-inch vinyl, also 7-inch and 12-inch-picture discs released (Cat-No: NUP7 and NUMP7).
Released: July 1985.

★★★★☆

Foreign formats: German sleeves features the words 'Top UK hit', also the 12-inch version released via Teldec came as an orange vinyl edition (**Cat No:** 620481). Promo video shot.

'Your Fascination' was one of Numan's best mid-period singles. For this track, Gary enlisted the help of The Human League producer Colin Thurston who offered the song a stark, abrasive sound complete with Gary's rasping vocals upfront in the mix. The result was a classic slice of sublime Numan pop. It was then something of a mystery as to why this single stalled just outside the British top 40 when released. Aside from that, it was also the last thing Gary needed at this point, with his record company already struggling after a year in operation as well as a new album waiting in the wings. The failure of 'Your Fascination' was a major blow. It entered the charts at No 47 peaking one place higher the following week, spending a total of 5 weeks on the top 75.

Original poster ad.

CALL OUT THE DOGS

1. 'Call Out The Dogs' (edit) 3.13. 2. 'This Ship Comes Apart' 3.55 (non-album track).
(**Cat No:** UK NU11)
1. 'Call Out The Dogs' (extended) 6.42. 2.'This Ship Comes Apart' 3.55 (non-album track). 3. 'No Shelter' 1.49 (non-album track).
(**Cat No:** UK NUM11)
Formats: 7-inch and 12-inch vinyl.
Released: September 1985.

★★★☆☆

Foreign formats: none.
Promo video shot.

From its eerie *Blade Runner* sampled intro to Numan's cool and husky vocal performance, 'Call Out The Dogs' had all the makings of a classic Numan single.

Unfortunately, the song soon spiralled into a rather freakish and somewhat chaotic and disjointed attempt at a Numan anthem. When released, 'Call Out The Dogs' shared a similar fate to previous single 'Your Fascination' by hovering briefly just outside the top 40 before departing for good giving Numan and fans two straight flops in the space of a few weeks.

'Call Out The Dogs' entered the charts at No 51 before climbing to a peak position of No 49 the following week, spending only two weeks on the top 75.

MIRACLES
1. 'Miracles' 3.38. 2. 'The Fear' 4.24 (non-album track).
(**Cat No:** UK NU13)
1. 'Miracles' (extended) 4.18. 2. 'The Fear' (extended) 6.14 (non-album track).
(**Cat No:** UK NUM13)
Formats: 7-inch and 12-inch vinyl.*
Released: November 1985.
Coloured vinyl releases were printed on the single sleeves.
Foreign formats: none.

Special note: both formats were available in white, red and standard black vinyl.
* Some of the 12-inch covers where mis-pressed in black and white with the back sleeve left completely blank.
Promo video shot.

Surprise was expressed when 'Miracles' was issued as the third single from *The Fury* album, its arrival also did little to calm fans' nerves that Gary was about to throw the towel in. Lyrically the song caught the star in a downbeat mood whilst accompanied by a beautiful, dreamlike backdrop enhanced towards the end by a superb saxophone solo. Unfortunately, the track was delivered a fatal blow right from the start with Gary delivering one of his harshest vocals to date: this removed any possible chance of the song entering the charts any higher than the two previous singles thus ending the year with a trio of flop singles.

'Miracles' entered the charts at No 51 climbing to a peak position of No 49 with a three week run on the top 75.

THIS IS LOVE
1. 'This Is Love' (edit) 3.12. 2. 'Survival' 5.02 (non-album track).
(**Cat No:** UK NU16)
1. 'This Is Love' (album version) 4.30. 2. 'Survival' 5.02 (non-album track).
(**Cat No:** UK NUM16)
Formats: 7-inch and 12-inch Vinyl.
Released: April 1986.
Foreign formats: none.
Special note: both formats were available as picture

discs (NUP16 and NUMP16): in addition, the 7-inch version came with a free flexi-disc that featured excerpts from the 12-inch versions of 'Call Out The Dogs' and 'This Is Love.' Also included were clips from one of the recently released fan club only interview albums.

Another simultaneous release of the 12-inch version of this single appeared shrink-wrapped to the 12-inch version of 'Call Out The Dogs' (Cat No, NUMX16).

Promo video shot.

Numan's first new material since the release of *The Fury* album appeared as a single in the spring of 1986, entitled 'This Is Love'. The song heralded in a change of pace for Gary that saw him strip away his former trademark synth-drenched sound to revisit the torch-like, piano-led balladry of the 1980 classic 'Please Push No More.' Dreamlike and gothic, 'This Is Love' seduced the listener with an inspired saxophone solo courtesy of Dick Morrissey and an emotive vocal performance from Gary. On sheer strength alone 'This Is Love' leapt into the top 40 climbing the following week to the No 28 position. Unfortunately, with UK radio ignoring the track completely and media exposure virtually non-existent, 'This Is Love' slipped back and quietly out of the charts just as quickly as it had arrived. The failure of this single enraged fans who felt Numan had yet again been denied a sizable and well deserved hit. The bulk of this bad feeling though was directed firmly at Radio One with fans frustrated with the station's blanket refusal to play any of Gary's chart singles as well as their increasingly pop biased play list. Without the backing of a major record label, Numan was now slipping further and further from the spotlight looking ever increasingly like a fading star of yesteryear.

'This Is Love' entered the charts at No 34 peaking the following week at No 28, spending three weeks on the top 75.

Trio of picture discs.

I CAN'T STOP
1. 'I Can't Stop' (edit) 3.25. 2. 'Faces' 4.42 (non-album track).
(**Cat No:** UK NU17)
1. 'I Can't Stop' (extended) 6.58. 2. 'Faces' 4.42 (non-album track).
(**Cat No:** UK NUM17)
Formats: 7-inch and 12-inch vinyl.
Released: June 1986.
Foreign formats: German release featured the words 'Top UK hit.'

★★★★★

Special note: 7-inch copies came with a free flexi-disc featuring excerpts from other artists signed to Numa, also both formats were released as picture discs with the 7-inch version being available shaped as an aircraft (NUP17) and the 12-inch version featuring a picture disc mix of 'I Can't Stop' with a running time of 5.45 (NUMP17). In addition, a rare 10-inch version of this single was released featuring a 6.32 club mix (NUM17DJ). All formats retained the same B-side.

Promo video shot (two versions).

If 'Cars' was the single universally acknowledged as Numan's finest pop song then 'I Can't Stop' was surely his second. Like 'Cars', 'I Can't Stop' was naggingly catchy but whereas the former was a glorious exercise in synthesizer wizardry, the latter was a spectacular weld between the worlds of hard rock and disco. Armed with choppy guitar riffs, strident female backing vocals and a thumping great chorus, 'I Can't Stop' was quickly proclaimed by the Numan faithful as one of his finest singles to date. Yet despite prime time appearances on *Top Of The Pops, The Chart Show* and *Wogan* as well as PRT (Numan's distribution company) and radio pluggers all in agreement that this single was going to be a smash 'I Can't Stop' failed to break out of a depressingly familiar sales pattern that had befallen much of Numan's releases of late, angering fans who, again, felt Gary had been robbed of a genuine hit single.

'I Can't Stop' entered the charts at No 32 peaking the following week at No 27 with a 4 week run on the top 75.

Following this single on the 9th of August, fans voiced their mounting anger and frustration by organising a day of protest outside the building used by Radio One.

Sadly however, the media at large simply interpreted it as a Numan-instigated scam and used it as the perfect excuse to further ridicule the star.

NEW THING FROM LONDON TOWN

1. 'New Thing from London Town'* (edit) 3.30. 2. 'Time To Die' (edit) 3.00.

(**Cat No:** UK NU19)

1. 'New Thing From London Town' (extended) 8.00. 2. 'Time To Die' (extended) 4.10.

(**Cat No:** UK NUM19)

Formats: 7-inch and 12-inch vinyl.

Released: September 1986.

Foreign formats: none.

This single was credited to 'Sharpe and Numan.'

Special note: both formats were released as picture discs (NUP19 and NUMP19). * A re-recorded version of this song was included on the album *Strange Charm*.

Promo video shot.

Taking time away from his own struggling career and mounting worries, Numan re-united with Bill Sharpe to record a follow up to the pair's mega hit 'Change Your Mind.' The result, 'New Thing From London Town' (a song that had originally been rejected by Polydor) was a world away from the superbly executed polished pop of their earlier single being this time much more in tune with Numan's hard hitting and menacing cyber rock style. The response from the media at large was rather uncharacteristically positive with the song not only picking daytime airplay but also being voted 'Single of the week' by one of the UK's leading music magazines. With all this it came as a shock when the single stalled outside the UK top 50 indicating that perhaps Numan's fiercely loyal fan base were, after so many years, finally beginning to crack. The failure of 'New Thing From London Town' initially delayed the release of Gary's new album with it finally slipping out virtually un-noticed at the tail end of the year.

'New Thing From London Town' entered the charts at No 53 peaking one place higher before departing with just three weeks on the top 75.

I STILL REMEMBER

1. 'I Still Remember' 4.00 (newly recorded version). 2. 'Puppets' 4.00 (non-album track).
(**Cat No:** UK NU21)
1. 'I Still Remember' (extended) 5.20 (newly recorded version). 2. 'Puppets' (extended) 5.20 (non-album track).
(**Cat No:** UK NUM21)
Formats: 7-inch and 12-inch vinyl.
Released: December 1986.
Foreign formats: none.
Special note: both formats were issued as picture discs (NUP21 and NUMP21). Promo video shot.

'I Still Remember' had originally appeared as the penultimate track on Numan's 1985 album *The Fury*: here the song had been re-recorded featuring new lyrics that delved into the appalling world of animal cruelty. The single was in aid of the *RSPCA* with all proceeds from it going direct to help the organisation fund their operations. As noble a cause as it was, the single was utterly depressing and not surprisingly barely grazed the charts upon release effectively driving the final nail into Numa's coffin. Weeks later Gary folded the label preferring to cut his losses while he could and search instead for a new recording contract.

'I Still Remember' entered and peaked at No 74 spending just 1 week on the top 75.

ORIGINAL SINGLES
Part Two: 1991-1995

After a label reshuffle at IRS Records left Numan without a deal in the summer of 1991, Gary quickly re-activated his mid-80s independent label Numa, this time however, the only artist on board was Gary himself.

EMOTION

1. 'Emotion' (edit) 4.00. 2. 'In A Glasshouse' 4.12 (non-album track).
(**Cat No:** UK NU22)
1. 'Emotion' (extended) 7.40. 2. 'In A Glasshouse' 4.12 (non-album track). 3. 'Hanoi' 2.06 (non-album track).
(**Cat No:** UK NUM22)
1. 'Emotion' (edit) 4.00. 2. 'In A Glasshouse' 4.12 (non-album track). 3. 'Hanoi' 2.06 (non-album track) 4. 'Emotion' (CD mix) 8.00.
(**Cat No:** UK NUCD22)
Formats: 7-inch and 12-inch vinyl, CD single and cassette single (same tracks as

the 7-inch – NUC22).
Released: September 1991.
Foreign formats: none.
Promo video shot.

If much of the music offered up on Numan's last album *Outland* had been a bridge too far for many fans, then the release of this single saw Numan's fan base fracture yet further still. Fans were aghast at this latest recording (released to co-inside with a similarly titled short UK tour) with most declaring it the worst recording from Gary thus far. With Numan's trademark sound and style now completely vanished, his worsening choice of direction led him to the kind of no-brainer dance pop peddled by any number of manufactured rubbish drifting in and out of the UK top 40 at any given time. 'Emotion' sounded like an artist down the darkest of dead ends and with fans shaking heads in disbelief, when released, perhaps not surprisingly, 'Emotion', despite its multi formats, failed to chart.

THE SKIN GAME
1. 'The Skin Game' (Nu mix) 4.09. 2. 'Dark Mountain' 3.13 (non-album track).
(**Cat No:** UK NU23)
1. 'The Skin Game' (Lycra mix) 7.41. 2. 'Dark Mountain' 3.13 (non-album track). 3. 'The Skin Game' (Nu mix) 4.09.
(**Cat No:** UK NUM23)
1. 'The Skin Game' (Nu-mix) 4.09. 2. 'Dark Mountain' 3.13 (non-album track) 3. 'U Got The Look' 4.00. 4. 'The Skin Game' (Digi-mix*) 6.23.
(**Cat No:** UK NUCD23)
Formats: 7-inch and 12-inch vinyl, CD single and cassette (Same tracks as the 7-inch – NUC23).
Released: March 1992.
Foreign formats: none.
* Digi-mix same as the album version.
No promo video.

'The Skin Game' was released at the same time Gary set out on another short UK tour entitled 'Isolate' (named after the recently released Numa compilation album of the same name). This new single found Gary still actively pursuing his Prince-influenced, shiny, dance pop sound, although for this recording Numan managed to at least inject an element of power as well as a fair degree of menace back into his music. 'The Skin Game' was, in itself, a significant improvement over Numan's previous single 'Emotion' displaying something approaching a recognisable Numan sound again. On the musical front, 'The Skin Game' couldn't be faulted. Fans, however, felt that this direction change was about as close to career suicide as you could get and what was left of Numan's once solid fan base were now abandoning the star in clearly worrying

Official T-shirt from "The Isolate Tour"

numbers. Interestingly, time has been fairly kind to this single with the track's mean and moody stance, slamming beats and overall synth dominated feel earning the song a somewhat underground appeal amongst Numan's hardcore fan base.

Sadly, 'The Skin Game' barely grazed the charts when released and its failure lit the fires that signalled the end of Numan's reign as a mainstream artist for many years.

'The Skin Game' entered and peaked at the No 68 position spending just one week on the top 75.

MACHINE + SOUL (Parts One and Two)
1. 'Machine And Soul' (Mix 1) 4.54. 2. 'Soul Protection' 3.17 (live 1991 – non-album track). 3. 'Confession' 4.15 (live 1991 – non-album track). 4. 'From Russia Infected' 5.19 (live 1991 – non-album track). All three live tracks recorded at The King Georges Hall, Blackburn in October 1991 – 'Interval 3' was also included at the end of 'From Russia Infected.'
(**Cat No:** UK NUM124)

★★★★★ 1. 'Machine And Soul' (Mix 3) 7.33. 2. 'Cry Baby' 4.17 (non-album track). 3. 'Wonder Eye' 4.02 (non-album track) 4. 'Machine And Soul' (Promo mix1) 4.09.
(**Cat No:** UK NUCD124)
Above two formats prefixed as 'Part One.'

1. 'Machine And Soul' (Mix 2*) 5.54. 2. 'Your Fascination' 4.26 (live 1991 – non-album track) 3. 'Outland' 3.55 (live 1991 – non-album track) 4. 'Respect' 4.03 (live 1991 – non-album track). All three live tracks recorded at The Club Ancienne Belqique, Brussels in September 1991.
(**Cat No:** U.K. NUM224)

1. 'Machine And Soul' (Mix 4) 8.57. 2. '1999' 4.53 (non-album track) 3. 'The Hauntings' 4.10 (non-album track) 4. 'Machine And Soul' (Promo mix 2) 4.29.
(**Cat No:** U.K. NUCD224)
* 'Mix 2' same as the album version.
Above two formats prefixed as 'Part Two.'
Formats: 2 x 12-inch vinyl and 2 x CD singles. In addition, two vinyl promo's were issued (one 12-inch + press release and a two track 7-inch).
Special note 1: Both 'Cry Baby' and 'Wonder Eye' were early demo recordings of Machine + Soul album tracks 'Cry' and 'I Wonder.'
Special note 2: As with the Machine + Soul album, this single was also known as 'Machine And Soul' (CD disc also printed this track as 'Machine & Soul' just to further confuse fans!).
Released: August 1992.
Foreign formats: None
Promo video shot.

'Machine + Soul' went some way to appeasing fans who had watched with some dismay Numan issue a steady stream of dubious singles in recent years to ever worsening chart positions and sales, this single though managed to pull Numan's career, temporarily, back from the brink by being the closest thing to a return to form for some time. 'Machine + Soul' was an inspired slice of muscular dance/rock, laced with slashing metallic guitars topped off with an assured vocal performance. In essence 'Machine + Soul' was the most commercial single from Gary since his 1988 single 'America.' Sadly it could do little to halt the downward spiral and even with a number of different formats to choose from, 'Machine + Soul' limped weakly into the charts for one week at No 72 finally bringing to an end Numan's 13-year run as a mainstream chart act. Aside from the 1996 re-issue of 'Cars', it would be another 10 years before Gary would be sufficiently recovered to enjoy a return to the British top 40 singles chart.

DREAM CORROSION (THE LIVE EP)
1. 'Noise Noise' 4.00. 2. 'It Must Have Been Years' 3.54. 3. 'I'm An Agent' 4.30. 4. 'Jo The Waiter' 2.48.
(**Cat No:** UK NUCD25 and NUM25)
Formats: CD single and 12-inch vinyl.
Released: August 1994.
Foreign formats: none.
Promo video shot: The full concert was filmed and released through Numan's fan club (see 'Official video cassettes').
Released: as a taster to the double live album of the same name, the tour performed the year previous marked the start of a Gary Numan re-birth with hitherto rare and obscure material being performed live for the first time in years (in some cases, the first time ever). This EP featured four tracks culled from the album and tour with only one ever performed live previously (1980's 'I'm An Agent'). Taking the place of the lead track was the overlooked 1982 classic B-side 'Noise Noise'; this track had long been championed by fans and most were pleased that at long last it was released as a single in its own right. Another debut live performance came in the shape of 'It Must Have Been Years', a semi-forgotten track from the *Replicas* album. The final track on the EP was the song that got everybody talking on the 'Dream Corrosion Tour.' 'Jo The Waiter', an old *Tubeway Army* track, had never been aired live before and was, without doubt, the high point of the tour as Gary initially took centre stage to sing over the acoustic portion of the track before the rest of the band joined in halfway through. A truly magical moment.

Through revisiting his legendary back catalogue, Numan had not only re-discovered himself but also realised the strengths (and weaknesses) of his unique style and sound. With that knowledge on board, Gary had all the tools he needed to fight his way back into the mainstream and attempt to become a success all over again.

'Dream Corrosion – The Live EP' failed to chart.

A QUESTION OF FAITH
1. 'A Question Of Faith' (Agnostic edit) 3.45. 2. 'Play Like God' 6.55 (non-album track). 3. 'Whisper Of Truth' 4.21 (non-album track) 4. 'A Question Of Faith' (Devout edit) 8.43.
(**Cat No:** UK NUCD26 and NUM26)
Formats: CD single and 12-inch vinyl.
Released: October 1994.
Foreign formats: none.

No promo video.

Brittle and rampaging, 'A Question Of Faith' snarled and dripped with a menacing edge that had long been absent from Numan's material. Fans were in no doubt that sonically and lyrically Gary was finally back in a place he should have never left and the 1993 'Dream Corrosion Tour' had been no mere fluke. 'A Question Of Faith' was a stunning return to form for Numan, the song's nasty and aggressive stance complete with Gary's rasping, metallic voice quickly paved the way for his long awaited new studio record. Although the single failed to chart, it did succeed in bringing long time fans back to the fold helping to turn Numan's ailing career around in the process. Indeed, on the strength of this single and the accompanying return to form studio album *Sacrifice*, Numan's days at a cult level looked like they were going to be, if anything, short lived.

ABSOLUTION

1. 'Absolution' 4.08 (non-album track). 2. 'Magic' (Trick mix) 4.08 (non-album track). 3. 'Magic' (extended edit) 6.29.
(**Cat No:** UK NUCD27 and NUM27*)
Formats: CD single and 12-inch vinyl.
Released: March 1995.
Foreign formats: none.
Special note: 'Magic' (extended edit) same as extended album version.
* 12-inch picture disc also released.

No promo video.

Bleak, gloomy and ominous, 'Absolution''s broody, funereal pace picked up where *Sacrifice* had left off by continuing Gary's move into a gothic-edged industrial rock sound. Lyrically, the song was a harrowing journey into the dark and disturbing world of obsession and paranoia. It's sluggish pace, locked around a chiming melodic hook was haunting, overpowering and suffocating.

Released shortly after the *Sacrifice* album, 'Absolution' further re-enforced Numan's commitment to his swelling fan base that the days of pandering to the radio were well and truly over.

'Absolution' failed to chart.

Sacrifice era fridge magnet.

DARK LIGHT (THE LIVE EP)

1. 'Bleed' 6.03. 2. 'Every Day I Die' 4.27. 3. 'The Dream Police' 4.45. 4. 'Listen To The Sirens' 3.11.
(**Cat No:** UK NUCD28 and NUM28)
Formats: CD single and 12-inch vinyl.
Released: June 1995.
Foreign formats: none.
No promo video.

Released as a souvenir from the *Dark Light* double album, this four track, live EP featured one track lifted from Numan's comeback album *Sacrifice* and three tracks taken from the 1978 *Tubeway Army* debut. Lead track 'Bleed' was a faithful and suitably loud rendition of one of the standout tracks on Gary's latest album. Of the *Tubeway Army* tracks, both 'Every Day I Die' and 'The Dream Police' hadn't been performed since the early 80s, whilst 'Listen To The Sirens' was completely new to the live arena. 'Dark Light (The Live EP)' was the final single to emerge via Numa Records with Gary opting to seek out a new recording contract following the massive, unexpected success of both 'Cars' and the resulting compilation album *Premier Hits* in 1996.

'Dark Light (The live EP)' failed to chart.

COMPILATION ALBUMS
Part One: NUMA

NUMA RECORDS YEAR 1
(**Cat No:** UK Numa 1004)
Formats: vinyl and cassette (Numac1004). In addition, a promo album was released entitled *Numa Various* featuring a selection of Numa artists as well as the previously unreleased demo for 'My Dying Machine' (Cat No; NUMPRO).
Released: February 1986.
Foreign formats: none.
Special note: vinyl copies of this album came complete with a free 12-inch remix of 'My Dying Machine' (Cat No: ZIG 20007), the A-side had been extended to 7.17 and re-mixed by Massimo Carpani with the B-side being an instrumental version extended to 6.12. In addition, the vinyl version included an insert and omitted the track 'Cold Warning' whilst the cassette version included an edited version (5.20) of the 'My Dying Machine' remix as well as the 'vinyl' omitted 'Cold Warning.'
Tracks, Side One: 'I Still Remember' 4.00 (Gary Numan)/ 'Venus In Furs' 3.25 (Paul Gardiner)/ 'King' 3.45 ('Hohokam')/ 'When I See Your Eyes' 3.45 (Steve Braun)/ 'Asleep' 3.35 ('Grey Parade')/ 'A Child With A Ghost' 4.04 (Gary Numan)
Tracks, Side Two: 'Harlequin Tears' 3.26 ('Hohokam')/ 'Cold Warning' 4.01*/ 'Pump Me Up'**3.51 (Caroline Munroe)/ 'Creatures' 5.09 (Gary Numan)/ 'The Experiment (Of Love)' 4.10 (John Webb)/ 'My Dying Machine' 5.20 (Gary Numan).
*Time incorrect on cassette version of this album, actual time 6.01.
** Original *Berserker* album version entitled 'Pump Me Up.'

Fairly low-key assemblage of various Numa artists, of interest to fans due to the previously unreleased remix of 'My Dying Machine.'

Numa Records Year 1 failed to chart.

ISOLATE – THE NUMA YEARS
(**Cat No:** UK Numa 1008)
Formats: vinyl, cassette (Numac 1008) and CD – (NumaCD1008).
Released: March 1992.
Foreign formats: none.
Cover photo taken from the sessions for *Metal Rhythm*.
Tracks for cassette, Side One: 'My Breathing' 6.35/ 'Call Out The Dogs' (album version)/ 'Emotion' (7-inch mix)*/ 'My Dying Machine' (7-inch mix-previously unreleased on

cassette)/ 'Time To Die' (extended mix).

Side Two: 'Berserker' (7-inch mix-previously unreleased on cassette)/ 'Your Fascination' (7-inch mix)*/ 'The Secret' (album version)/ 'Creatures' (album version)/ 'This Is Love' (album version).

* Incorrect time given for 'Emotion' (4.38, should read 4.00). Also incorrect time for 'Your Fascination' (3.31, should read 3.40).

Special note: some of the tracks included on the CD version of this compilation were different mixes to the cassette issue. Tracks altered were 'Call Out The Dogs' 6.41 (extended/ 12-inch mix-previously unreleased on CD), 'Emotion' 8.00 (CD mix), 'My Dying Machine' 9.04 (extended/ 12-inch mix), 'Berserker' 6.40* (extended/ 12-inch mix), 'Your Fascination' 5.10 (extended/ 12-inch mix-previously unreleased on CD), 'The Secret' 6.40 (extended mix) and finally 'Creatures' 6.36 (extended mix-previously unreleased on CD). Vinyl version of this album featured the regular mixes of all the songs.

* Incorrect time (6.04) printed on the CD label.

   With only a handful of tracks selected from Gary's previous three Numa studio albums and nothing taken from either *White Noise* or *Ghost*, *Isolate* was hardly looked upon by fans as a comprehensive Numa compilation. However, this release (originally planned as a two volume set) was initially of interest to fans, as much of the material on it had long been out of print; in addition, the extended mixes were also being made available commercially for the very first time.

COMPILATION ALBUMS
Part Two: LICENCED

Following the release of the poorly received *Machine + Soul* album, Numan began to allow his Numa recordings to be licensed out to other record companies. What started out as an opportunity for fans and public alike to view the Numa catalogue in a different light ended up spiralling out of control as week in week out, album after album flooded on to the market with virtually every one released as wretched as the last (this was much to Gary's dismay who stated in an online interview in 1996 that he viewed many of these compilations as not a part of his licensing agreement and thus highly illegal). Collectively, they have succeeded in totally devaluing Gary's Numa endorsed recordings and none have displayed any real care or interest in either the music or the artist represented. Fans are warned to approach with caution before parting with money for any of these relatively worthless enterprises.

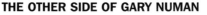

THE OTHER SIDE OF GARY NUMAN
(**Cat No:** Receiver Records RRCD 170)
Formats: CD and vinyl.
Released: November 1992.
Foreign formats: matched the UK.
Special note: half the photos adorning the cover did not originate from the time period that the music on this CD was compiled from. In addition, CD version included four extra tracks.
Sleeve notes also included.

★★★☆☆

Tracks: 'I Can't Stop'***/ 'Tricks'**/ 'Miracles'**/ 'The Sleeproom'***/ 'Machine + Soul' ****/ 'Rumour' (1987 B-side)/ 'The Skin

Game'****/ 'A Child With A Ghost'*/ 'This Disease'** (some copies of this CD misspelt this track as 'The Disease')/ 'The Need'***/ 'I Still Remember'**/ 'Strange Charm'***/ 'The Hunter' */ 'Empty Bed, Empty Heart' (1984 B-side).
* Taken from the album *Berserker*, ** Taken from the album *The Fury*, *** Taken from the album *Strange Charm* and **** Taken from the album *Machine + Soul*.

This was the first licensed Numa compilation to enter the market place appearing six months after the relatively disappointing *Isolate* set. Like that album, the only redeeming feature here was the fact that much of the material included was out of print and fairly new to CD. *The Other Side Of Gary Numan*, like *Isolate*, fell well short of being anything like a comprehensive Numa compilation but was nowhere near as desperate as some of the albums that were to come.

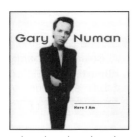

HERE I AM
(**Cat No:** UK Receiver Records FRRRCD 186)
Formats: CD.
Released: July 1994.
Foreign formats: French import.
Re-issued May 1996 following the top 20 success of 'Cars.'
Photo unrelated to the music within and album bizarrely titled 'Here I Am' when track included was titled 'Here Am I.'

★★★☆☆

Tracks: 'Emotion'***/ 'The Skin Game'***/ 'In A Glasshouse' (1991 B-side)/ 'Confession' (live 1991/ 92-no date or venue given, likely to be from either the 1991 'Emotion Tour' or the 1992 'Isolate Tour')/ 'America' (live – 1991 or 1992)/ 'Your Fascination'*/ 'Time To Die'**/ 'Are "Friends" Electric?' (live – 1991 or 1992)/ 'My Dying Machine' (7-inch mix)/ 'Here Am I' (1984 B-side)/ 'She Cries' (1984 B-side)/ 'We Need It' (1985 B-side)/ 'London Times' (extended mix-1987 Radio Heart single)/ 'Rumour' (1987 B-side)/ 'Berserker' (7-inch mix).
* Taken from album *The Fury*, ** Taken from album *Strange Charm* and *** Taken from album *Machine + Soul*.

Much like the previous compilation, this album managed to get a selection of Gary's post Beggars Banquet music onto CD for the first time. This album also included three live tracks that appeared to originate from the official live tapes that were made available through Numan's fan club. However, no dates or venues were given.

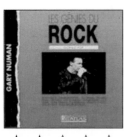

LES GENIES DU ROCK
(**Cat No:** Atlas RKCD511))
Formats: CD.
Released: 1995.
Foreign formats: none.
Tracks: 'I Can't Stop'/ 'Machine + Soul'/ 'This Disease'/ 'The Skin Game'/ 'The Need'/ 'I Still Remember'/ 'Strange Charm'/ 'The Hunter'/ 'Tricks'/ 'Miracles'/ 'The Sleeproom'/ 'Rumour'/ 'A Child With A Ghost'/ 'Empty Bed Empty Heart.'
Information about this French issue compilation is

scarce, nevertheless the track list was hardly awe-inspiring and like many of the other Numa based compilations *Les Genies Du Rock* also failed to accurately represent Gary's Numa years.

THE STORY SO FAR

(**Cat No:** UK Receiver Records RRXCD 505)
Formats: 3 CD box set.
Released: June 1996.
Foreign formats: none.
Box set cover photo unrelated to the music within.

The release of this 3 CD box set came hot on the heels of 'Cars' and the *Premier Hits* compilation denting the UK top 20 in early 1996. Any hopes that this release would mirror the *Premier Hits* set and provide fans with a comprehensive Numa based compilation were quickly dashed when fans viewed the three CDs within.

CD 1 MY DYING MACHINE

(**Cat No:** UK Receiver Records RRCD 221)
Tracks; 'Berserker' (12-inch mix)/ 'My Dying Machine' (12-inch mix)/ 'Call Out The Dogs'**/ 'Your Fascination'**/ 'Miracles'**/ 'I Still Remember'**/ 'I Can't Stop'***/ 'This Is Love'***/'Machine + Soul'****/ 'My Breathing'***/ 'Emotion'****/ 'The Skin Game'****/ 'A Child With A Ghost'*/ 'Generator.'****

★★☆☆☆ * Taken from album *Berserker*, ** Taken from album *The Fury*, *** Taken from album *Strange Charm* and **** Taken from album *Machine + Soul*.

For this CD, an attempt to compile a Numa singles compilation went badly off course by not only failing to locate the single mixes but even including tracks that weren't released as singles in the first place, frustratingly poor.

CD 2 THE SLEEPROOM

(**Cat No:** UK Receiver Records RRCD 222)
Tracks: 'Poison'****/ 'In A Glasshouse' (1991 B-side)/ 'She Cries' (1984 B-side)/ 'Time To Die'***/ 'We Need It' (1985 B-side)/ 'Strange Charm'***/ 'The Need'***/ 'Creatures'**/ 'Pump It Up'*/ 'The God Film'*/ 'Cold Warning'*/ 'The Sleeproom'***/ 'God Only Knows'**/ 'Love Isolation.'****

★★☆☆☆ * Taken from album *Berserker*, ** Taken from album *The Fury*, *** Taken from album *Strange Charm* and **** Taken from album *Machine + Soul*.

Another pointless compilation of Numa album tracks and B-sides, some copies appeared wrongly labelled as *The Sleeproom Live*.

CD 3 TIME TO DIE

(**Cat No:** UK Receiver Records RRCD 223)
Tracks: 'Me! I Disconnect From You'/ 'Call Out The Dogs'/ 'Emotion'/ 'Are "Friends" Electric?' / 'We Are Glass'/ 'U Got The Look'/ 'Your Fascination'/ 'Time To Die'/ 'Cars'/

'The Skin Game'/ 'I Die; You Die'/ 'My Breathing'/ 'Down In The Park'/ 'My Shadow In Vain'/ 'We Take Mystery (To Bed)'/ 'I Can't Stop.'

This CD took a number of tracks from the fan club only live album *Ghost* with the remainder taken from either 'The Emotion tour' or 'The Isolate Tour.'

From the inaccurate sleeve notes to the poor track selections and shoddy packaging, the 3 CDs contained within 'The Story So Far' had little to recommend in the end and only really succeeded in being an exercise in futility.

THE BEST OF GARY NUMAN 1984-1992
(**Cat No:** UK Emporio Records EMPRCD 666)
Formats: CD and cassette.
Released: September 1996.
Foreign formats: none.
Cover photo was from 1981 and didn't represent the music contained within.
Tracks: 'I Can't Stop'***/ 'Berserker'*/ 'The Skin Game'****/ 'I Still Remember' **/ 'Machine + Soul'****/ 'Empty Bed, Empty Heart' (1984 B-side)/ Are "Friends" Electric?' (live 1991 or 1992, date and venue unknown)/ 'Your Fascination'**/ 'This Disease'**/ 'Miracles'**/ 'A Child With A Ghost'*/ 'Strange Charm'***/ 'London Times' (1987 Radio Heart single)/ 'Time To Die'***/ 'America' (live 1991 or 1992, date and venue unknown)/ 'My Dying Machine.'*
* Taken from album *Berserker*, ** Taken from album *The Fury*, *** Taken from album *Strange Charm* and **** Taken from album *Machine + Soul*.

Bearing a title that that bore no relevance to the material included on the disc, *The Best Of Gary Numan 1984-1992* was, in reality, just another poorly assembled compilation. The two live tracks included were previously unreleased and were likely sourced from either 'The Emotion Tour' or 'The Isolate Tour.'

ARCHIVE
(**Cat No:** UK Rialto Records RMCD 205)
Formats: CD.
Released: October 1996.
Foreign formats: none.
Re-issued 1997 complete with a new cover (see below). Cover artwork was of Gary from 1979 and therefore didn't accurately represent the music assembled on the CD. Cover for the re-issued version featured a photo of Gary from 1982 again completely unrelated to the music included.
Tracks: Are "Friends" Electric?' (live)*/ 'Me! I Disconnect From You' (live)*/ 'U Got The Look' (live)*/ 'Berserker' (1984 12-inch mix)/ 'The God Film' (from the album *Berserker*)/ 'We Are Glass' (live)*/ 'Poison' (from the album *Machine + Soul*)/ 'Creatures' (from the album *The Fury*)/ 'Cars' (live)*/ 'Call Out The Dogs'/ 'God Only

Knows' (both tracks from the album *The Fury*)/ 'Down In The Park' (live)**/ 'We Take Mystery (To Bed)' (live)**/ 'My Shadow In Vain' (live)**/ 'Love Isolation'/ 'Generator' (both from the album *Machine + Soul*).

* Five tracks taken from 'The Isolate Tour.'

** Three tracks taken from the live album *Ghost*.

None of the live tracks have dates or venues included within the sleeve notes; the rest was made up of the usual jumble of Numa album tracks, a waste of plastic really.

Re-issued cover

BLACK HEART

(**Cat No:** UK Culture Press Records CP 1004)

Formats: CD.

Released: April 1997.

Foreign formats: none.

Cover photo was from 1979 and therefore didn't represent the music assembled within.

Tracks: 'Are "Friends" Electric?' (live)/ 'We Are Glass' (live)/ 'I Die; You Die' (live)/ 'Cars' (live)/ 'Call Out The Dogs' (live) – All five tracks taken from the fan club only album *Ghost* / 'Berserker' (7-inch mix)/ 'Emotion' (7-inch mix)/ 'Machine + Soul' (taken from the album of the same name)/ 'Pray' (extended version)/ 'The Seed Of A Lie' (extended version-both tracks taken from the extended version of the album *Sacrifice*)/ 'A Little Lost Soul'/ 'Black Heart' (both tracks taken from the instrumental album *Human*).

Numan's 1994 return to form album *Sacrifice* was plundered for the first time on this compilation, as was the soundtrack to the early 90s movie *The Unborn*. The rest, however, was the usual motley collection of live tracks in amongst the odd album track. A slight improvement over previous albums displaying something approaching care and attention although by no means is that a recommendation.

ARCHIVE VOLUME 2

(**Cat No:** UK Rialto Records RMCD 225)

Formats: CD.

Released: February 1998.

Foreign formats: none.

Cover photo was from 1979 and didn't represent the music on the CD.

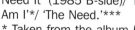

Tracks: 'In A Glasshouse' (1991 B-side)/ 'Confession' (live 1991-'Emotion Tour' or 1992 'Isolate Tour')/ 'Down In The Park' (live-taken from the album *Ghost*)/ 'Tricks'**/ 'Rumour' (1987 B-side)/ 'I Die; You Die' (live-taken from the album *Ghost*)/ 'The Sleeproom'***/ 'My Breathing'***/ 'This Is Love'***/ 'We Need It' (1985 B-side)/ 'Emotion'****/ 'Time To Die' ***/ 'I Can't Stop'**/ 'Here Am I'*/ 'The Need.'***

* Taken from the album *Berserker*, ** Taken from the album *The Fury*, *** Taken from the album *Strange Charm* and **** Taken from the album *Machine + Soul*.

Yet another pointless compilation of Numa album tracks and live material.

STRANGE CHARM – LIVE CUTS, HITS AND RARITIES
(**Cat No:** UK Castle Communication PIESDO 55)
Formats: CD.
Released: September 1999.
Foreign formats: none.
For once the cover photo of Numan in his *Berserker* era was representative of some of the music contained within. **Tracks:** 'We Take Mystery (To Bed)' (live)/ 'We Are Glass' (live – both tracks taken from the live album *Ghost*)/ 'Call Out The Dogs'**/ 'Your Fascination'**/ 'This Is Love'***/ 'Emotion'****/ 'Empty Bed, Empty Heart' (1984 B-side)/ 'This Disease'**/ 'Strange Charm'***/ 'London Times' (1987 Radio Heart single)/ 'She Cries' (1984 B-side)/ 'Generator'****/ 'Confession' (live – sourced from either 'The Emotion Tour' or 'The Isolate Tour')/'My Dying Machine'*/ 'Here Am I' (1984 B-side).
* Taken from album *Berserker*, ** Taken from album *The Fury*, *** Taken from album *Strange Charm* and **** Taken from album *Machine + Soul*.

The CD with perhaps the most brazen cheek of them all by naming itself after Numan's 1986 studio album! Aside from that, it was identical to all the rest before it.

DOWN IN THE PARK – THE ALTERNATIVE ANTHOLOGY
(**Cat No:** UK Castle Music Ltd ESACD 785)
Formats: 2 CD.
Released: October 1999.
Foreign formats: none.
Re-issued months later featuring a front cover sticker stating that the music had been re-mastered. Also included new sleeve notes from Paul Lester of *Uncut* magazine. Music compiled by Steve Malins.
CD 1: Studio disc.
Tracks: 'My Breathing'***/ 'A Child With A Ghost'*/ 'The Skin Game'****/ 'Call Out The Dogs'**/ 'Berserker'*/ 'She Cries' (1984 B-side)/ 'Time To Die'***/ 'In A Glasshouse' (1991 B-side)/ 'Rumour' (1987 B-side)/ 'Here Am I' (1984 B-side)/ 'God Only Knows'**/ 'Cold Warning'*/ 'Creatures'**/ 'Tricks'**/ 'Empty Bed, Empty Heart' (1984 B-side).
* Taken from the album *Berserker*, ** Taken From album *The Fury*, *** Taken from album *Strange Charm* and **** Taken from album *Machine + Soul*.
Special note: Both 'Berserker' and 'Cold Warning' taken from the extended version of the *Berserker* album.
CD 2: Live.
Tracks: 'Confession'*/ 'America'*/ 'Me! I Disconnect From You'/ 'Call Out The Dogs'/ 'Emotion'*/ 'Are "Friends" Electric?' / 'We Are Glass'/ 'U Got The Look'**/ 'Your Fascination'*/ 'Time To Die'**/ 'Cars'/ 'The Skin Game'**
* All these tracks were sourced from an unknown date and venue on either the 1991 'Emotion Tour' or the 1992 'Isolate Tour.'
** These tracks taken from the 1992 'Isolate Tour.'
Remaining live tracks taken from the album *Ghost*.

The studio disc was a familiar recycled collection of album tracks and B-sides. As for the live disc, at least some attempt had been made to include more of the generally unavailable 1992 'Isolate Tour' recordings. Unfortunately, even with two

CDs to choose from it was still a very poor package.

DESIRE
(**Cat No:** UK Armoury ARMCD 051)
Formats: CD.
Released: August 2001.
Foreign formats: none.
Cover photo was completely unrelated to the music assembled within.
Tracks: 'Deadliner'*****/ 'Love Isolation'****/ 'Whisper Of Truth' (1994 B-side)/ 'Puppets' (1986 B-side)/ 'My Breathing'***/ 'Love And Napalm'*****/ 'I Wonder'****/ 'Berserker'*/ 'This Is New Love'*/ 'You Walk In My Soul'*****/ 'The Seed Of A Lie'*****/ 'The Pleasure Skin'**/ 'Desire'*****/ 'Absolution' (1995 single).
* Taken from album *Berserker*, ** Taken from album *The Fury*, *** Taken from album *Strange Charm*, **** Taken from album *Machine + Soul* and ***** Taken from album *Sacrifice*.

Basically half the *Sacrifice* album from 1994 mixed in with the usual past plundered album tracks, completely pointless.

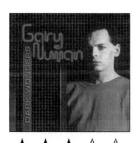

DARK WONDER
(**Cat No:** UK Navarre 372)
Formats: 2CD.
Released: January 2002.
Foreign formats: none.
Cover photo was completely unrelated to the music contained within.
CD 1, Tracks: 'Call Out The Dogs' (1985 single mix)/ 'The Pleasure Skin'**/ 'My Breathing'***/ 'Strange Charm'***/ 'I Wonder'****/ 'Cold Warning'*/ 'The Skin Game'****/ 'Your Fascination'**/ 'Berserker'*/ 'A Child With A Ghost'*/ 'Survival' (1986 B-side)/ 'Puppets' (1986 B-side)/ 'Cars' (live – date, venue and year unknown).
* Taken from album *Berserker*, ** Taken from album *The Fury*, *** Taken from album *Strange Charm* and **** Taken from album *Machine + Soul*.
CD 2, Tracks: 'Rip'****/ 'Dark'***/ 'A Question Of Faith'**/ 'An Alien Cure'***/ 'Pure'****/ 'Bleed'**/ 'This Is Love'*/ 'The Angel Wars'***/ 'The Seed Of A Lie'**/ 'Dominion Day'***/ 'Pray'**/ 'I Can't Breathe'****/ 'I Die; You Die' (live – date, venue and year unknown).
* Taken from album *Strange Charm*, ** Taken from album *Sacrifice*, *** Taken from album *Exile* and **** Taken from album *Pure*.

CD 1 was the usual collection of past album tracks and B-sides whilst CD 2 selected tracks from more recent albums like *Exile* and *Pure*.

DISCONNECTION
(**Cat No:** UK Sanctuary/ Castle SACA812142)
Formats: 3CD Box set.
Released: April 2002.

Foreign formats: none.

CD 1, Tracks: Features the *Berserker* album minus two tracks ('This Is New Love' and 'The Secret') as well as three of that projects B-sides ('Empty Bed, Empty Heart', 'Here Am I' and 'She Cries'). Also featured Gary's 1985 album *The Fury* minus one track ('The Pleasure Skin') as well as including one B-side from that project ('We Need It').

CD 2, Tracks: Features two tracks from 1987 (The Radio Heart single 'London Times' and B-side 'Rumour') as well as the 1986 album *Strange Charm* minus two tracks ('Unknown And Hostile' and 'New Thing From London Town'). Also featured five tracks from the album *Machine + Soul* (The title track, 'Generator', 'The Skin Game', 'Poison' and 'Love Isolation') as well as one B-side from the project ('In A Glasshouse').

CD 3 (Live disc) Tracks: 'Call Out The Dogs'/ 'I Die; You Die'/ 'I Can't Stop'/ 'Me! I Disconnect From You'/ 'My Breathing'/ 'Cars'/ 'We Take Mystery (To Bed)'/ 'We Are Glass'/ 'Are "Friends" Electric?' / 'Down In The Park'/ 'My Shadow In Vain' – all tracks taken from the live album *Ghost*. 'Emotion'/ 'Your Fascination'/ 'Time To Die'/ 'The Skin Game' – final four tracks taken from 'The Isolate Tour', date and venue unknown.

Another pointless exercise and nothing that hasn't been done before, avoid.

U GOT THE LOOK
(Cat No: UK Delta CD 47104)
Formats: CD.
Released: October 2002.
Foreign formats: none.
Photo used for the cover was from 1979 and did not represent the music assembled within.

Tracks: 'Cars' (live)/ 'Rumour' (1987 B-side)/ 'Anthem' (1985 B-side)/ 'I Die; You Die' (live) / 'U Got The Look'****/ 'New Anger' (1988 single)/ 'Machine + Soul'****/ 'Down In The Park' (live)/ 'Absolution' (1995 single)/ 'Desire' (taken from the album *Sacrifice*)/ 'Your Fascination'**/ 'A Child With A Ghost'*/ 'Strange Charm'***/ 'I Can't Breathe' (taken from the album *Pure*)/ 'Are "Friends" Electric?' (live).
* Taken from album *Berserker*, ** Taken from album *The Fury* *** Taken from album *Strange Charm* and **** Taken from album *Machine + Soul*. All live tracks taken from the album *Ghost*.

More of the same except for the inclusion of one IRS Records track from 1988 ('New Anger').

ANTHOLOGY
(Cat No: UK Silverline Entertainment)
Formats: DVDA.
Released: November 2002.
Foreign formats: none.
Cover photo was from 1980 and didn't represent the music contained within. CD bizarrely credited to 'Gary Nvman.'

Tracks: Features three tracks from *Berserker* (title track, 'My Dying Machine' and 'The Hunter'), one track from *The*

Fury ('This Disease'), the title track from *Machine + Soul*, one B-side from that project ('In A Glasshouse') and finally four tracks from the live album *Ghost* ('I Die; You Die', 'Me! I Disconnect From You', 'Cars' and 'Are "Friends" Electric?'

The first of a new breed of compilation, the only difference here being the inclusion of a DVD section where fans could access photographs and an enhanced digital 5.1 surround sound. However, the track selection was still very poor.

RUMOUR

(**Cat No:** Artikel NR 6615705)
Formats: CD.
Released: December 2002.
Foreign formats: this was initially issued in Germany before receiving a full British release in August 2003.
Cover photo taken from the sessions for *Pure*.
Tracks: 'Are "Friends" Electric?' (live)/ 'Anthem' (1985 B-side)/ 'Machine + Soul'****/ 'Your Fascination'**/ 'Absolution' (1995 single)/ 'I Die; You Die' (live)/ 'Desire' (taken from the album *Sacrifice*)/ 'Pure' (taken from the album of the same name)/ 'A Child With A Ghost'*/ 'U Got The Look'****/ 'I Can't Breathe' (taken from the album *Pure*)/ 'Berserker'*/ 'Rumour' (1987 B-side)/ 'Strange Charm'***/ 'Cars' (live).

* Taken from album *Berserker*, ** Taken from album *The Fury*, *** Taken from album *Strange Charm* and **** Taken from album *Machine + Soul*. All live tracks taken from the album *Ghost*.

Yet another pointless compilation, 'Your Fascination' misspelt on this CD as 'You Fascination.'

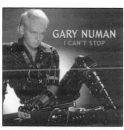

I CAN'T STOP

(**Cat No:** UK Delta Deluxe 4719900)
Formats: 2CD.
Released: August 2003.
Foreign formats: none.
Cover photo taken from the sessions for *Warriors* and therefore didn't represent the music contained within.
CD1, Tracks: 'Berserker'*/ 'My Dying Machine'*/ 'A Child With A Ghost'*/ 'The Skin Game'****/ 'Call Out The Dogs'**/ 'Your Fascination'**/ 'This Is Love'***/ 'I Still Remember.'**
CD2, Tracks: 'Miracles'**/ 'I Can't Stop'***/ 'Machine + Soul'****/ 'Me! I Disconnect From You'/ 'Are "Friends" Electric?'/ 'We Are Glass'/ 'Down In The Park'/ 'My Shadow In Vain.'

* Taken from the album *Berserker*. ** Taken from the album *The Fury*. *** Taken from the album *Strange Charm*. **** Taken from the album *Machine + Soul*.
Special note: final five tracks on CD2 are live recordings taken from the fan club album *Ghost*. In addition, both *Berserker* tracks taken from the extended release.

Yet another poor quality compilation to add to the dozens that preceded it, *I Can't Stop* was littered with spelling mistakes and inaccuracies. 'Me! I Disconnect From You' was incorrectly listed as 'Me I Disconnect' and 'I Can't Stop' was listed as 'I Can t Stop.' In addition, the sleeve notes state that Gary's 1980 classic 'I Dream Of Wires' was co-written with the late Robert Palmer, in fact, Palmer only covered the track for his own 1980 album *Clues*.

RECONNECTED LIVE, N' MORE
(**Cat No:** Music Club MCCD529)
Formats: 2CD.
Released: September 2003.
Foreign formats: matched the UK.
Cover photo was taken from the sessions for *Sacrifice.*
CD 1, Tracks: 'Are "Friends" Electric?'/ 'Cars'/ 'We Are Glass'/ 'I Die; You Die'/ 'Down In The Park'/ 'Me! I Disconnect From You'/ 'We Take Mystery (To Bed)'/ 'Music For Chameleons'/ 'Sister Surprise' – All these tracks were live and originated from the Numa live album *White Noise.* / 'I Can't Stop'**/ 'Berserker'*/ 'My Dying Machine'*/ 'Cold Warning'*/ 'Call Out The Dogs.'**

CD 2, Tracks: 'Your Fascination'**/ 'Miracles'**/ 'The Pleasure Skin'**/ 'My Breathing'***/ 'The Sleeproom'***/ 'New Thing From London Town'***/ 'This Is Love'***/ 'Machine + Soul'****/ 'A Child With A Ghost'*/ 'I Still Remember'**/ 'The Seed Of A Lie' (taken from the album *Sacrifice*)/ 'Rip'/ 'I Can't Breathe' – latter two tracks taken from the album *Pure.*
* Taken from the album *Berserker*. ** Taken from the album *The Fury*. ***Taken from the album *Strange Charm*. ****Taken from the album *Machine + Soul*.

Another desperately poor assemblage of the Numa years and beyond, avoid.

NUMAN FACTOR
(**Cat No:** Direct Source 2880)
Formats: CD.
Released: December 2003.
Foreign formats: none.
Cover photo taken from the sessions for *Pure.*
Tracks: 'Cars' (live 2000)/ 'Pure'/ Walking With Shadows'*/ 'Rip'/ 'One Perfect Lie'/ 'Torn'/ 'Puppets' (1986 B-side)/ 'Creatures' (1985 album track)/ 'Replicas' (live 2000)/ 'Down In The Park' (live 2000).
* Incorrectly titled as 'Walking In The Shadows.'

Although thankfully brief, this Canadian compilation at least managed to compile the bulk of its material from more recent recordings.

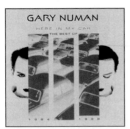

HERE IN MY CAR THE BEST OF GARY NUMAN 84-98
(**Cat No:** Cleopatra)
Formats: CD
Released: July 2004
Tracks: 'Metal ('98)'/ 'Down In The Park ('98)'/ 'A Question Of Faith' 4.52/ 'The Hunter' 4.32/ 'Deadliner' 4.29/ 'Magic' 4.43/ 'You Walk In My Soul' 4.42/ 'Stormtrooper In Drag' (live '94)/ 'Replicas' (Live '94)/ 'I Die; You Die' (live '94)/ 'Me! I Disconnect From You' (live '84)/ 'Cars' (live '84)/ 'We Are Glass' (live '84)/ 'Are "Friends" Electric?' (live '84)/ 'Dominion Day' 4.50/ 'Dark'

4.29/ 'Dead Heaven.' 5.52.

Artwork for this CD neglects to mention that most of the songs are actually live.

RE-ISSUE CAMPAIGN
Albums: UK

Unlike Beggars Banquet, Numa's re-issue campaigns were nowhere near as extensive. All Numa albums released by the label in its initial 80s period of activity were re-promoted on CD in the early 90s with the original extended cassette version of *Berserker* appearing on CD (2000 copies pressed) in 1991. Many of the re-issues on CD that followed were also the extended versions (most of these releases were limited to a print run of 2000 copies only). The Numa catalogue was finally re-issued on CD in the UK and the US via Eagle and Cleopatra Records, although these re-issues were mainly limited to the standard recordings (see 'The Eagle Records Years'). In addition, both Numa live albums were re-issued in the early part of the '90's. *Ghost* had initially emerged via Gary's fan club on vinyl and in October of 1992, the album was re-promoted onto CD (baring the slightly altered catalogue number of; NumaCD 1007) with some copies even appearing in a few selected specialist shops. The other live recording to be re-issued was *White Noise*; like *Ghost*, this record had never previously appeared on CD. Catalogue number for this release was NumaCD 1002. In both cases the packaging remained unchanged.

The next recordings to be re-promoted were a flurry of Gary's studio albums, almost all of them were new to CD.

MACHINE + SOUL – EXTENDED
(**Cat No:** UK NumaCDX 1009)
Formats: extended CD.
Released: October 1993.
Foreign formats: none.
Special note: 'Emotion' features a slightly different ending to the previously released 8.00 CD mix version.
Track list: see original album for tracks and extended new times.

Many fans were more than a little surprised to see an extended version of this album materialise, especially in light of it being shunned when it originally appeared the previous year. This album also carried an error with the packaging that stated that four extra tracks (former B-sides to this project) were included. Initial copies did not include them although later copies rectified this mistake.

SACRIFICE – EXTENDED
(**Cat No:** UK NumaCDX 1011)
Formats: Extended CD.
Released: January 1995.
Foreign formats: none.
Track list: see original album for tracks and extended new times.

This version of *Sacrifice* appeared two months after the initial original release and like the extended version of *Machine + Soul* featured the word 'Extended' under the album title. Aside from the songs being longer, no further differences could be detected.

More re-issues emerged throughout 1995, a series of seven mini-albums entitled *Babylon* were issued featuring long lost and deleted B-sides as well as 12-inch mixes of past Numan singles released through Numa (see 'Fan Club Releases').

BERSERKER – EXTENDED
(Cat No: UK NumaCDX1001)
Formats: extended CD.
Released: December 1995.
Foreign formats: none.
Track list: see original album for tracks and extended new times.
Special note: Gary confirmed in an online interview that the original artwork for this album had been lost; this re-issue featured reprinted versions of the original photographs.

This was the second appearance of the extended version of *Berserker* on CD and although the cover photo and packaging remained true to the original, the music on the disc was identical to the original tape released in 1984 that featured six of the album's nine tracks in an extended form (the first Numan album to utilize this practice). The original vinyl mix of *Berserker* would eventually see the light of day once again in June of 1998 when it was featured as part of a five CD box set (see 'The Eagle Records Years').

THE FURY – EXTENDED
(Cat No: UK NumaCDX1003)
Formats: extended CD.
Released: December 1996.
Foreign formats: none.
Special note: album title abbreviated from the World War Two fighter 'The Sea Fury.'
Track list: see original album for tracks and extended times.

Released with a new cover featuring an alternative photo from the sessions for this album's artwork.

The Fury, in extended form, had previously been issued in this guise as an extended cassette; this was its first appearance on CD. Some later copies of this CD included the song 'Tribal', a track that first appeared on the *Babylon 3* mini-CD that was released through Gary Numan's fan club the year previous.

GARY NUMAN

Original 1985 Fury era poster.

STRANGE CHARM
(Cat No: UK NumaCDX1005)
Formats: CD.
Released: December 1996.
Foreign formats: none.
Track list: see original album.

This CD was a straight forward re-issue of the previous one originally issued in 1986 alongside the cassette and vinyl versions, the only minor differences here were firstly, the cover now featured the album's title under Gary's name as apposed to the other way round. This was probably done so fans could at least differentiate between the old version and the new. Secondly, two of the album's tracks were different for this re-issue with the original mix of 'I Can't Stop' here replaced by the extended 12-inch version and the album's title track replaced by a hitherto previously unreleased shorter mix (5.00 as apposed to the original 5.45 mix). No single mixes were included on this re-issue. *Strange Charm* was the final release from Numa Records as Gary dissolved the label following his return to the British top 20 in March of 1996 with a re-issue of 'Cars.'

FAN CLUB AND MAIL ORDER RELEASES
Gary Numan's fan club came into existence shortly after his initial burst of success. Unlike most however, it was a family run affair that guaranteed a genuine personal service. Gary's fan club operated much the same as any other by distributing newsletters, yearbooks, magazines and posters as well as a varied selection of Numan related merchandise. The fan club was also used to make available to fans music and interviews that were never destined to be sold commercially (for instance, in 1991 every date of the 'Emotion Tour' was made available to fans for purchase). This section of 'The Numa Years' will take a look at some of the material Numan issued through the club.

THE IMAGES SERIES
With Numan's understandable mistrust of the media it was deemed to be a far better idea to release a series of albums featuring Gary answering a range of questions presented by long time fan Peter Gilbert. These albums were entitled *Images* and came housed in the same covers with the only exception being each one was numbered and each featured a four page booklet of black and white photos. These albums ran from 1986 until 1992 with the final one released (*Images 11*) being the first and final one to emerge on CD.

The following includes details for each of the six releases: *Images 1&2*, 1986 (Cat No: 2LP GNFCDA1), this release concentrated on Gary's early life, his journey through an assortment of semi-professional bands, his huge breakthrough success in 1979 and his first big tour. Both albums featured snippets of many songs from this time period. *Images 3&4*, 1986 (Cat No: 2LP GNFCDA2), this release concentrated on the 1980/1981 period (from the release of *Telekon* up to the round the world solo flight) and featured snippets of many of the songs associated with that period (interestingly 'I Die; You Die' was represented by the ultra rare alternative mix and not the regular single version). In addition to the studio material, live tracks from Gary's farewell show at Wembley were also included as well as several instrumental B-sides. *Images 5&6*, May 1987 (Cat No: GNFCDA3), this release included – amongst snippets of songs taken from both *I, Assassin* and *Warriors* – early demos of 'This Is My House', 'She Cries', 'White Boys And Heroes' and 'Noise Noise.' Also included were the US remix of 'White Boys And Heroes', an unreleased 7-inch mix of 'Warriors' as well as all three pieces of music Gary recorded for the soft drinks company *7Up* in 1982. *Images 7&8*, December 1987 (Cat No: GNFCDA4), this release concentrated on the years 1984 to 1986 and featured snippets of tracks from Numa's first three studio albums as well as one or two of the acts Gary signed to the label. In addition, this release also included the previously unreleased 1984 recording of 'On Broadway', a track that featured an unlikely duet with Leo Sayer. All of these albums ran for 1 hour and 30 minutes. *Images 9&10,* November 1988 (Cat No: GNFCDA5), this release concentrated on the time period 1987 through 1989 and had its running time reduced to 1 hour after fans complained that the sound quality on some of the previous releases was poor. Interestingly, aside from including many songs from this time period this release also featured unreleased demos of 'This Is Emotion' and 'Devious.'

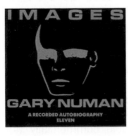

IMAGES 11
(**Cat No:** GNFCCD11)
Formats: CD.
Released: 1992.
Content: 'Voices'/ 'I'm On Automatic'/ 'Cold Metal Rhythm'/ 'Survival' (live '88)/ 'Down In The Park'(live '88)/ 'Creatures' (live '88)/ 'I Die; You Die' (live '88)/ 'Shame'/ 'Interval 1'*/ 'Intro 4'*/ 'Waiting'*/ 'Chaser'*/ 'Funeral'*/ 'Sexomania'*/ 'Asylum 2'*/ 'Harmonos.'

* Previously unreleased out-takes from the September 1990 recording sessions for *The Unborn* soundtrack (*Human*). *Images 11* was the final interview album to be released and the only one issued on CD, the running time on this release was reduced to 70 minutes. All the music included was excerpts only and not the full songs.

GHOST
(**Cat No:** UK Numa1007)
Formats: double vinyl album, Numad1007-Gatefold sleeve.
Released: March 1988.
Foreign formats: none.
Re-issued: October 1992 (see 'Numa Re-issues'), September 1999 and March 2003 (see 'The Eagle Records Years').

Musicians: Gary Numan – Vocals/ Chris Payne – Keyboards and viola/ John Webb – Keyboards, saxophone and backing vocals/ RRussell Bell – Guitar/ Nick Davis – Bass/ Greg Brimstone – Drums/ Val Chalmers – Vocals/ Emma Chalmers – Vocals.
Engineered by Tim Summerhayes and Smudger.
Mixed at The Factory by Tim Summerhayes and Gary Numan.
Produced by Gary Numan.
Recorded at The Hammersmith Odeon, London on the 25th and 26th of September 1987.
Recorded on the RAK mobile.
Record One, tracks: 'Ghost' 1.40/ 'Call Out The Dogs' 4.00/ 'I Die; You Die' 3.35/ 'Creatures' 5.05/ 'I Can't Stop' 3.40/ 'Me! I Disconnect From You' 3.10/ 'Tricks' 5.35/ 'The Sleeproom' 5.10/ 'My Breathing' 6.05/ 'Cars' 4.40.
Record Two, tracks: 'Metal' 3.10/ 'Sister Surprise' 6.05/ 'This Disease' 4.10/ 'We Take Mystery (To Bed)' 6.15/ 'We Are Glass' 4.35/ 'Down In The Park' 4.55/ 'Are "Friends" Electric?' 6.30/ 'My Shadow In Vain' 2.30/ 'Berserker' 5.35.

Taped exclusively from Numan's 1987 'Exhibition Tour', this fan club only double album perfectly captured for prosperity both Numan and fans clearly still reeling from the sudden and unexpected top 20 hit re-issue of 'Cars.' Although already an understandably high-spirited concert tour, this recording (taken from concluding two nights at the Hammersmith Odeon) featured a raft of exemplary performances and captured both Gary and the band in fine form. The set-list for the tour was cleverly balanced to show Gary's Numa years material – although sadly less well received than his Beggars Banquet recordings – which was still every bit as good as his more well known stellar earlier works. Pitched against a backdrop of classics like 'We Are Glass', 'Metal', 'Down In The Park', 'My Shadow In Vain' and a thoroughly majestic rendition of 'Are "Friends" Electric?', Numan performed choice cuts from all three of his Numa funded studio albums, the best of which was the funky as hell 'Tricks' (*The Fury*), the menacing and rumbling *Berserker* title track as well as three tracks (all debut performances) taken from Gary's final Numa studio album *Strange Charm* (the storming 'My Breathing', the slow-burning anthem 'The Sleeproom' as well as former single 'I Can't Stop'). With a heady mix of both old and new, *Ghost* was one of Gary's finest and certainly liveliest live recordings thus far. Following this tour Gary signed on with IRS Records.

★★★☆☆

THE RADIAL PAIR

(**Cat No:** UK Salvation Records SACD1)
Formats: CD.
Released: August 1994.
Foreign formats: none.
Tracks: 'Kiss Me And Die' 5.49/ 'Mission' 3.02/ 'Dark Rain' 2.47/ 'Cloud Dancing' 3.48/ 'Virus' 3.04/ 'Cold House' 3.33/ 'Red Sky' 3.18/ 'Machine Heart' 2.26.
All songs by Gary Numan.

Released as the audio soundtrack to the aviation video of the same name, these eight instrumentals were credited as being the very roots that Numan's 'return to form' album *Sacrifice* emerged from. This CD is now extremely rare.

THE BABYLON SERIES

The *Babylon* series afforded Numan the opportunity to transfer much of the long lost 12-inch mixes and B-sides from his days recording for his own imprint Numa Records. Seven mini-CDs were eventually released and each one moved chronologically from the label's debut in 1984 up to the final releases in 1995 when it was discontinued (a proposed *Babylon 8* never materialised). All these releases were issued on the fan club only label Salvation Records and all shared the same cover photo, each CD cover had the same typeset presented in a different colour for each of the 7 discs. Bizarrely, most of the 7-inch mixes for each single remained un-transferred until 1999 when Eagle compiled and issued the Numa singles collection *New Dreams For Old* (see 'The Eagle Records Years').

BABYLON 1
(**Cat No:** UK SACD1/2)
Formats: CD.
Released: August 1995.
Colour of typeset on cover: Red.
Tracks: 12-inch versions of 'Berserker' and 'My Dying Machine' were included as well as the three B-sides from that period ('Empty Bed, Empty Heart', 'Here Am I' and 'She Cries'). The final track on the disc 'Rumour' did not originate from this period instead coming from 1987 (itself a Radio Heart B-side).

Fans, although pleased to finally see these recordings appear on an official Numan endorsed CD, were disappointed that the two previously unreleased tracks performed on the *Leo Sayer Show* ('This Is New Love' and 'On Broadway') did not appear here. Sadly it's since come to light that both these recordings may have been erased following the show's transmission, however, Gary has confirmed the existence of a later recording of 'This Is New Love.' Whether this was the version that was performed

on *The Lulu Show* just prior to the release of *Berserker* or a hitherto as yet unheard recording is unknown. In addition, the Italian remix of 'My Dying Machine' that found its way onto the *Numa Records Year 1* compilation album was eventually located and due for release on *Babylon 8*. However, this disc has yet to surface.

Early versions of Babylon 1 & 2.

BABYLON 2
(**Cat No:** UK SACD2/2)
Formats: CD.
Released: August 1995.
Colour of typeset: red.
Tracks: both 12-inch mixes of 'Your Fascination' and 'Call Out The Dogs' were included along with the 12-inch mix of 'We Need It.'* Two B-sides from this project ('Anthem' and 'This Ship Comes Apart') were included, however, two further flip sides ('No Shelter' and the original version of 'The Fear'**) remained untransfered. One oddity was the inclusion of the Radio Heart US B-side 'Mistasax (1)' originally released in 1987. The version included here was slightly different to the 1987 version and was actually 'Mistasax (2).' More material from *The Fury* sessions could be found on the next mini-CD released, *Babylon 3*.
* 7-inch mix also untransfered.
** A remixed version of this song appeared on *Babylon 3*.

BABYLON 3
(**Cat No:** UK SACD2/3)
Formats: CD.
Released: August 1995.
Colour of typeset: blue.
Track list: 'Miracles' (12-inch)/ 'I Still Remember' (1986 new version-7-inch mix)/

'The Fear' (1995 remix)/ 'Puppets' (1995 remix)/ 'Tribal' (previously unreleased)/ 'Shame' (B-side to the 1991 single 'Heart').

Rather a scrappy, messy assemblage of tracks with two remixes taking precedence over the original recordings ('The Fear' and 'Puppets' were both redone due to the loss of the original master tape) as well as the final track originating instead from Gary's days under the IRS umbrella as apposed to Numa. The one find on the disc was an early take of 'Call Out The Dogs' entitled 'Tribal'; this version of the song sounded closer in style to material from the *Berserker* album and was probably a late demo from those sessions.

Missing from this concluding round-up of *The Fury* B-sides and 12-inch material was the 12-inch mix of 'I Still Remember' from 1986.

BABYLON 4
(**Cat No:** UK SACD2/4)
Formats: CD.
Released: August 1995.
Colour of Typeset: purple.
Track list: 'This Is Love' (12-inch/ album mix)/ 'I Can't Stop' (10-inch club mix)/ 'Survival' (B-side to 'This Is Love')/ 'Faces' (B-side to 'I Can't Stop')/ 'Time To Die' (12-inch mix)/ 'Mistasax (2).'

The material on this disc, bar one, originated from the sessions for Gary's 1986 album *Strange Charm*. Missing though were both the 7-inch and 12-inch mixes of 'New Thing From London Town', the 12-inch mix of 'I Can't Stop' (only slightly longer that the 10-inch club mix) and the original 7-inch mix of 'Time To Die.' Final track, 'Mistasax (2)' was actually the originally released version that found its way onto the B-side of the US version of 'Radio Heart'; this version was mistakenly dubbed 'Mistasax (2).' Both versions were just two different takes that were submitted to Gary with the differences only slight so it's perhaps understandable how confusion had arisen over the two takes.

BABYLON 5
(**Cat No:** UK SACD2/5)
Formats: CD.
Released: November 1995.
Colour of Typeset: purple.
Tracks: all three singles released by IRS Records ('New Anger', 'America' and 'Heart') as well as four relevant B-sides ('I Don't Believe', 'Children', 'Icehouse' and 'Tread Careful').

Rather bizarrely included on this mini-CD were 7 tracks originating from Gary's time spent under the wing of IRS Records. Missing from this disc though were the two US only remixes of 'My World Storm' as well as the 'Rockers Uptown' – Renegade Sound Wave remix of 'Are "Friends" Electric?'

BABYLON 6
(**Cat No:** UK SACD2/6)
Formats: CD.
Released: November 1995.
Colour of typeset: green.
Track list: 'The Skin Game (Digi mix)'/ 'Emotion' (album version)/ 'Dark Mountain'

(B-side to 'The Skin Game')/ 'In A Glasshouse' (B-side to 'Emotion')/ 'Hanoi' (B-side to 'Emotion')/ 'River' (B-side to the Radio Heart single 'All Across The Nation').

All the material featured originated from the sessions for the album *Machine + Soul* with the exception of the final track 'River' that emerged in 1987.

Missing from this disc were the Lycra mix of 'The Skin Game', the extended mix of 'Emotion', 'Machine + Soul' B-sides '1999', 'Wonder Eye' and 'Cry Baby.' In addition, all the various mixes of the track 'Machine + Soul' bar one* as well as the six live tracks recorded in September and October 1991 that were included on two of the formats of that single were also omitted.

* One 'Machine + Soul' mix available on final *Babylon 7* disc.

BABYLON 7
(**Cat No:** UK SACD2/7)
Formats: CD.
Released: February 1996.
Colour of typeset: Green.
Track list: 'Machine + Soul (Mix 4)'/ 'A Question Of Faith (Devout edit)'/ 'The Hauntings' ('Machine + Soul' B-side)/ 'Metal Beat' (previously unreleased demo from the *Sacrifice* sessions)/ 'Whisper Of Truth' (B-side to 'Absolution')/ 'Play Like God' (B-side to 'Absolution')/ 'Absolution' (unreleased extended mix).

Final *Babylon* CD featured two tracks from the sessions for *Machine + Soul* and five tracks from the *Sacrifice* time period.

Missing from this disc were both remixes of the *Sacrifice* track 'Magic' (Trick mix and the extended mix that featured as a B-side to the single 'Absolution').

AUDIO CD
The following fan club releases emerged during the latter part of Gary's days signed to the Eagle imprint.

PURIFIED
(**Cat No:** UK TPACD01)
Formats: CD.
Released: February 2001.

Special CD sold initially during the UK / US and Canadian Leg of the 'Pure Tour.' The disc featured five music clips including three 'work-in-progress' tracks that didn't make it onto the *Pure* record, the demos for 'Walking With Shadows' and 'Rip' as well as Gary answering fifty questions.

PHOTO CD 1
(No Catalogue number)
Formats: CD.
Released: October 2001.

Includes fifty photographs taken from Gary's 2001 UK tour in support of the album *Pure* as well as a further twelve photos taken from the 2001 Euro rock Festival in Belgium.

PHOTO CD 2
(No Catalogue number)
Formats: CD.
Released: May 2002.

Features Gary's tour diary from the 2001 North American tour. Also included were audio clips of Numan answering fan questions, off stage and on stage video clips, photos as well as demos for the *Pure* album used as background music.

ALIEN MAGAZINE

In 1999 Gary decided to convert the long running Gary Numan fan club into an all-encompassing magazine. Going by the name *Alien*, the magazine ran until 2002 when it was discontinued due to Gary's rapidly ascending career. The main reason, however, was down to the fact that Nuworld, Numan's own official website would always be far more up to date than a magazine ever could be so it was decided to plough all Numan related information into that instead.

MEMORABILIA

The following pages gather together some of the memorabilia that emerged during the years that Numa Records was in operation.

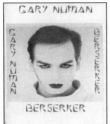

Foreign issue of *UK extended cassette issue of both* Berserker *and* The Fury, *also included is*
Berserker. *the standard cassette issue. Note that the extended issue of* The Fury *was*
mis-spelt as "extented mixes."

Original CD issues of both The Fury *and* Strange Charm.

Both sides of the 7-inch picture disc released via Zig Zag
Records (Zigpro 001), includes UK mix and the specially
commissioned remix.

12-inch Italian remix of "My Dying
Machine."

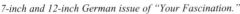

7-inch and 12-inch German issue of "Your Fascination."

Debut release from Numa
Records – "Venus In Furs" by the
late Paul Gardiner.

German issue of The Fury *album, note the pink shaded inner sleeve.*

Spiral Scratch *magazine with Numan featured on the cover pictured live from "The Fury Tour."*

Inside the Fury Tour photo book.

Berserker *pin.*

Fan club poster. Painting by Nick Theato.

Sound On Sound, *August 1986.*

Fan produced Numan clock.

Record Collector, *Dec '85, included a detailed Gary Numan discography.*

10-inch club mix + free flexi-disc.

German sleeve for this single slightly different. 12-inch "Maxi 45" also issued.

Selection of yearbooks.

Slightly different cassette covers for the original Dream Corrosion *album.*

Mid '80's box set featuring an interview CD, a set of photos and an interview 7-inch single.

Double pack 12-inch issue of "This Is Love" and "Call Out The Dogs."

The "Seed Of A Lie" single given away free with the vinyl issue of Sacrifice.

Left (above and below): Two Sacrifice era mugs. Above: March 1992 Issue of Aircraft Illustrated.

SECTION ONE

PART THREE

THE IRS RECORDS YEARS

When Numan signed a new recording contract with Miles Copeland's IRS / Illegal Records, fans breathed an understandable, collective sigh of relief. Back on something of a major label, it was hoped that the disappointing memories of Numa Records could be laid to rest and IRS would put an end to Numan's dwindling fortunes by putting him not only back in the spotlight but back into the upper reaches of the charts. In truth, by 1988, Numan was viewed as a fading star of the early 80s and in desperate need of a chart storming hit, one that would instantly re-tune the public's perception of Gary to the present tense rather than the lingering memories of his early 80s synth-heavy pop music and ever changing images.

Gary's three years spent as a recording artist on his own independent label had passed by virtually un-noticed by the public at large and fans as well as Numan's organisation were hoping that IRS could buck the downward spiral. Unfortunately the label fundamentally failed to grasp the importance of Numan's comeback, worse, they fatally under-estimated his decline. Add to that the label also seemed to possess a remarkable inability to even understand either Numan's fans or his music. With that knowledge, any hope of Gary being re-established in his homeland and around the world, evaporated right there. In the end Numan's three and-a-half years spent under the IRS imprint would prove to be a frustrating experience for all concerned, with the label's suggestions of inappropriate cover versions and unwanted dance mixes being rightfully dismissed by Gary who just wanted them to do the one thing he needed the most, and that was to promote him. Had they done that, the music buying public of the mid-80s would have heard a radically different sounding Gary Numan to the one before with both *Metal Rhythm* (1988) and *Outland* (1991) being heavily influenced by American dance/ rock giants like Prince and Janet Jackson. Numan's new US flavoured sound was a world away from the outwardly bombastic, synth god stance of the early 80s, yet the reluctance of IRS to promote Gary to anyone but his dwindling fan base saw him finally begin to slip from the mainstream and further into the background. It was something of a relief when following inner label turmoil in the middle of 1991, IRS and Gary Numan (amongst many others on the label) parted company for good.

ORIGINAL ALBUMS
1988 – 1991

METAL RHYTHM
(**Cat No:** UK ILP035)
Formats: vinyl*, cassette (ILPMC035) and CD. (ILPCD035).
Released: September 1988.
Foreign formats: US, European and Far East version re-titled *New Anger* featuring revised cover artwork. European version also included a short (typed) Gary Numan biography.
Re-issued September 1999 on CD.
Special note: released as a limited edition picture disc. (ILPX035 – 5000 print run).
* Limited edition gatefold sleeve, cover artwork for this issue altered slightly.
Musicians: Gary Numan – Vocals, keyboards and drum programming/ Keith

Beauvais – Guitar/ Ian Herron – Percussion/ Mike Smith – Keyboards/ Andy Coughlan – Bass/ Dick Morrissey – Saxophone/ Peter Haycock – Guitar and slide guitar/ RRussell Bell – Guitar/ Martin Elliott – Bass/ Chris Payne – Violin/ Tessa Niles – Vocals.

Engineered by Ted Miller, Ray Hedges and Tim Summerhayes, assisted by Julie Gibson.

Mixed at Popps farm by Nick Smith and Ben Fanner, assisted by Robin Black.

Recorded at Black Barn Studios, Studio house, The Factory and Rock City Sound Studios.

Produced by Gary Numan.

Side One, Tracks: 'This Is Emotion' 3.59/ 'Hunger' 4.28/ 'New Anger' 3.19/ 'Devious' 4.15/ 'America' 3.30.

Side Two, Tracks: 'Voix' 4.56/ 'Respect' 4.07/ 'Young Heart' 3.00/ 'Cold Metal Rhythm' 4.25/ 'Don't Call My Name' 3.42.

All songs by Gary Numan.

Singles: 'New Anger' and 'America'. In addition, 'Respect' issued as a double-sided 12-inch promo In North America.

Videos: none.

Metal Rhythm was Gary's first studio record in two years and his strongest and most cohesive set since *Warriors* back in 1983. During his time spent away, (aside from a few minor side projects) Gary had been busy evolving his trademark sound to incorporate a more contemporary, hard hitting, dance rock sound, a style popularised by the likes of Janet Jackson, Michael Jackson, Prince and Cameo in the mid to late 80s. On *Metal Rhythm*, Numan shared common ground with these artists giving his new material an aggressive and edgy vibe that ran in tandem with his own metallic proto-industrial backdrops. Although the album was hard hitting, it was still commercial enough for mass appeal with tracks like 'Respect', 'Cold Metal Rhythm', 'Young Heart' and 'Hunger' being obvious singles; the latter two tracks showed Gary had also learnt new ways to use his voice with his vocals coming across softer and far less stylised that normal. However, Gary hadn't totally forsaken his hardcore fan base with tracks like the nerve shredding 'Voix,' the pumping synth pop of 'America' and the caustic 'Cold Metal Rhythm' (the album's original 'in-full' title) providing older fans with music that operated on much more familiar territory.

Gary's best shot at the charts and standout track on the record was the infuriatingly catchy anthem 'Devious.' Unfortunately, IRS ignored it and chose 'New Anger' as the album's first single, itself a good enough song but nowhere near what was needed to spark Gary's much-anticipated big comeback. When 'New Anger' faltered outside the top 40 singles chart it effectively torpedoed the album delivering it a fatal blow that it would never recover from. A second single, 'America', was met with indifference charting even lower than 'New Anger' had the month previous, virtually sealing the record's fate.

The failure of *Metal Rhythm* was a cruel blow, especially with the record being one of the best of his career, its lush backdrops, superb musicianship and fabulous usage of backing vocals and saxophones thoroughly deserved to be heard by a much wider audience than it was ultimately privy to. It's fanciful to speculate what would have been the possible outcome had IRS marketed the record more aggressively with glossy promo's for the album's two singles and a bigger promotional push through TV and magazines. As it was, *Metal Rhythm* merely continued Numan's slide from the mainstream.

Metal Rhythm entered the charts at a peak position of No 48 spending just 3 weeks on the top 75.

Far East CD and the original US 'long box' issue, back cover to Far East CD differs slightly to US by featuring altered artwork and a removable Japanese language sticker.

US version of *Metal Rhythm* (re-titled in the States as *New Anger*, Cat No: IRS WD82005 – vinyl and IRS D82005 – CD), released with a slightly altered cover in June 1989. Track list altered to feature a superbly remixed 'Devious' as the album's opening track followed by: 'America' (original album version), 'Cold Metal Rhythm,' 'This Is Emotion,' 'Don't Call My Name,' 'Voix,' 'Respect', 'New Anger,' 'My Dying Machine'(William Orbit mix) and finally 'A Child With A Ghost.' This change, as well as the inclusion of the additional material, came at the loss of both 'Young Heart' and 'Hunger.'

THE SKIN MECHANIC – LIVE
(**Cat No:** UK EIRSA1019)
Formats: vinyl*, cassette** (EIRSAC1019) and CD (EIRSACD1019).
Released: October 1989.
Foreign formats: US CD released in a long cardboard box – Cat No: IRD82023. (All American late 80s and early 90s CDs came housed like this).
* Vinyl version omits the tracks 'I Can't Stop' and 'I Die; You Die.'
** Cassette version omits the track 'I Can't Stop.'

★★★☆☆

Musicians: Gary Numan – Vocals/ RRussell Bell – Guitar/ Andy Coughlan – Bass/ Chris Payne – Keyboards and violin/ Ade Orange – Keyboards and saxophone/ Cedric Sharpley – Drums/ John Webb – Saxophone/ Val Chalmers – Vocals/ Emma Chalmers – Vocals. Produced by Gary Numan.
Recorded at The Dominion Theatre, London on the 28th of September 1988.
Tracks: 'Survival' 2.12/ 'Respect' 4.09/ 'Call Out The Dogs' 4.05/ 'Cars' 5.21/ 'Hunger' 4.31/ 'Down In The Park' 5.18/ 'New Anger' 3.17/ 'Creatures' 5.07/ 'Are "Friends" Electric?' 7.40/ 'Young Heart' 5.03/ 'We Are Glass' 5.23/ 'I Can't Stop' 3.32./ 'I Die; You Die' 3.50.
Singles: none.
Videos: none. However, *The Skin Mechanic – Live* was released on video in 1990.
Special note: unlike Numan's last two live albums (*White Noise* and the fan club released *Ghost*); *The Skin Mechanic – Live* (a record drawn exclusively from the previous year's 'Metal Rhythm Tour') was only issued as a single disc featuring

twelve concert highlights from the taped show at the Dominion Theatre.

The Skin Mechanic – Live was taped from a concert tour that had been, in many ways, largely overshadowed by the frustrating and disappointing failure of one of Gary's best albums in years. As grim news as this obviously was, bizarrely, Numan's commercial downturn was having little impact on the live front with Gary actually moving from strength to strength both musically and visually. Of the twelve tracks included, four were taken from Gary's latest album with the rest being a balanced and measured collection of past classics. Highlights included spirited performances of 'We Are Glass', 'Call Out The Dogs', 'Cars', 'I Die: You Die' and newie 'Respect' as well as a simply stunning rendition of 'Down In The Park.' This album was also backed up with a short UK-only tour (see Gary Numan 'Live' section).

The Skin Mechanic – Live entered and peaked at No 55 spending two weeks on the charts.

★★★☆☆

OUTLAND

(**Cat No:** UK EIRSA1039)

Formats: vinyl, cassette (EIRSAC1039) and CD (EIRSACD1039).

Released: March 1991.

Foreign formats: matched the UK.

Musicians: Gary Numan – Vocals, keyboards, drum/ percussion programming, samples, acoustic guitar, fretless bass and bass sampler/ Mike Smith – Keyboards, toms, guitar samples*, percussion programming, slide guitar, brass, bongos, saxophone samples and stick samples/ Keith Beauvais – Guitar/ Cathi Ogden – Vocals/ Nick Beggs – Stick and bass/ Dick Morrissey – Saxophone/ Tim Whitehead – Saxophone/ RRussell Bell – Guitar ('Outland')/ Paul Harvey – Rhythm and slide guitar.

* *Outland* was awash with samples from many of the big Hollywood movies of the 80s with snippets from films such as *Predator, Bladerunner, Red Heat, Aliens* and *Terminator* being woven into various songs spread across the album as well as a number of B-sides.

Engineered and mixed by Gary Numan.

Recorded by Gary Numan at Outland studios.

Produced by Gary Numan.

Tracks: 'Interval' 1 1.13/ 'Soul Protection' 3.36/ 'Confession' 4.17/ 'My World Storm' 3.44/ 'Dream Killer' 4.21/ 'Dark Sunday' 4.04/ 'Outland' 4.07/ 'Heart' 4.06/ 'Interval 2'. 0.19/ 'From Russia Infected' 4.30/ 'Interval 3'. 0.39/ 'Devotion' 4.13/ 'Whisper' 4.20. All songs by Gary Numan.

Singles: 'Heart', 'My World Storm' – the latter released in the US as a limited edition 12-inch promo containing newly commissioned remixes.

Videos: 'Heart.'

Outland picked up pretty much where *Metal Rhythm* left off walking the same hard hitting US style dance/rock path laid down by its predecessor. However, the musical climate of 1991 was a markedly different place to the one *Metal Rhythm* emerged in. By 1991 the cultures of dance and indie music had exploded, both these genres were busy laying waste to the dying flame that was the 80s. Radio too was now noticeably hostile to anything and anyone even associated with the 1980s, preferring instead to champion the stars of this new decade. All this did not bode well for Numan who was already struggling to get back into the top 40. In *Outland* though, Gary had justifiable cause to be optimistic. A musically strong record with an abundance of quality material on board to keep fans happy, the record opened impressively enough with a chilling instrumental (one of three on the disc), but by track two, ('Soul Protection') the album was suddenly knocked off course, it being just about the weakest track on the record. Seemingly this track had been added at the 11th hour, apparently in place of the suddenly withdrawn Prince cover '1999' (this track later found it's way on to the B-side of the 1992 single 'Machine + Soul').Thankfully this proved to be only a minor blip on an otherwise fine album.

Potential singles were not in short supply on *Outland* with hard hitting anthems like 'Confession' and 'My World Storm' being beautifully offset by two stellar melodic ballads ('Dream Killer' and 'Heart'). By far the standout track on the album though was the closing 'Whisper', a stripped back, semi-acoustic slowie that wasn't that far removed from the format of *MTV*'s celebrated show *Unplugged*. When it came to promotion for the record however, Numan and his label did not see eye to eye. In fact, prior to the eventual and much delayed release of *Outland* (the record was due to drop in the late Autumn of 1990 preceded by a single 'Shame') the record had undergone a number of record company requested remixes, tweaks and re-recordings (earlier versions of this album that hit the bootleg market clearly showed a record that, over time, had in fact been gradually watered down). In the end, a heavily re-recorded and vastly altered mix of the album appeared in the early spring of 1991, preceded by the album's only single 'Heart' ('Shame' having been relegated to feature as a mere B-side). Not surprisingly, this single quickly settled into a predictable pattern by stalling just outside the UK top 40 singles chart before vanishing.

Over in the states, however, a special 12-inch only single was issued, this release included remixes of both 'Are "Friends" Electric?' and *Outland* album track 'My World Storm.' These remixes were said to have formed part of an early attempt by IRS to issue a Gary Numan remix album, a project that did not materialise and appeared to have been abandoned as the year wore on.

Outland entered and peaked at No 39 spending two weeks on the top 75.

Following the conclusion of the 'Outland UK Tour', worrying news began to filter out from the label. With music giant EMI expressing an interest in the company, the label's future as well as Gary's record contract suddenly looked far from certain. Despite assurances to the contrary, within months of this unexpected upheaval, Gary found himself for the second time in his career minus a record deal.

ORIGINAL SINGLES
1988 – 1991

★★★★☆

NEW ANGER
1. 'New Anger' 3.20. 2. 'I Don't Believe' 3.22. (non-album track).
(**Cat No:** UK ILS1003)
Formats: 7-inch*, 12-inch** and CD single.
Released: August 1988.
Foreign formats: matched the UK.
* 7-inch poster bag also released (ILSP1003).
**Two 12-inch versions released featuring the extra track

'Children' 3.08 (non-album track) – gatefold sleeve (ILSG1003) and the regular version (ILST1003).
1. 'New Anger' 3.20. 2. 'I Don't Believe' 3.22 (non-album track). 3. 'Creatures' 4.33 (live 1987). 4. 'I Can't Stop' 3.38 (live 1987) – both live tracks taken from the fan club released live album *Ghost*.
(**Cat No:** UK ILSCD1003)
No promo video.

Following three frustrating years struggling as an independent artist, as well as a flurry of side projects from the likes of Radio Heart and Sharpe and Numan, it was no surprise to learn that fans were more than anxious to see Numan resume his solo career as soon as possible. Now he was back on a major label, nothing short of a block-busting comeback would do and with advance word on the new album being encouragingly good, fans were understandably beside themselves with anticipation.

Unfortunately, IRS dropped a clanger with their first single from *Metal Rhythm* by selecting the completely wrong song for the UK market. 'New Anger,' although a good enough track, was far too rocking for the UK singles chart, which was by the late 80s far more used to the delicate pop ditties peddled by the likes of Stock, Aiken and Waterman prodigies Kylie Minogue and Jason Donavan. 'New Anger''s guitar-heavy, aggressive chops were much better suited to the American market; had IRS chose either 'Hunger' or 'Devious' as Gary's first UK single, the outcome would, in all probability, have been very different. As it was, 'New Anger''s brash, metallic riffs were shunned and with no video or TV exposure, the track hovered briefly just outside the top 40 before departing for good.

Fold-out sleeve for the 'New Anger' single.

To further fans' disappointment and annoyance, flipping the single over revealed a gem of a track entitled 'I Don't Believe,' a soaring, synth pop anthem that was far too good to be languishing as a mere B-side. Fans were stunned; within the space of a few short weeks, what was hoped to be Gary's big, major label comeback now looked more like a complete disaster.

'New Anger' entered and peaked at No 46 spending two weeks on the top 75.

AMERICA
1. 'America' (remix) 3.00. 2. 'Respect' (live '88) 4.22.
(**Cat No:** UK ILS1004)
Formats: 7-inch*, 12-inch (ILST1004) ** and CD(ILSCD1004).***
Released: November 1988.
Foreign formats: matched the UK.
* Also released as a 7-inch picture disc (ILSPD1004).

** Includes an extra track, 'New Anger' (live '88) 3.24.

*** Four-track CD single, included 'Call Out The Dogs' (live '87) 3.58 – this track was taken from the fan club released live album *Ghost*.

Special note: CD single sleeve slightly different to the 7-inch and 12-inch releases. No promo video.

Perhaps in a bid to rescue the project, 'America' was quickly remixed and became the second single to be drawn from the *Metal Rhythm* album. Gary, with the help of Andy Piercy and Chris Sheldon, managed to transform the pulsating, metallic nature of the track into a driving, glittering, synth pop anthem complete with chirpy female backing vocals, rendering it probably the most commercial single release from Gary since 'I Can't Stop' back in 1986. Yet IRS funded no video and hardly promoted the single. Fans could barely hide their dismay when 'America,' like 'New Anger' before it, stalled predictably just outside the top 40.

'America' entered and peaked at No 49 spending one week on the charts.

HEART

1. 'Heart' 4.06. 2. 'Ice House' 3.17 (non-album track).

(Cat No: UK NUMAN1)

Formats: 7-inch*, cassette (NUMANC1) **, 12-inch (NUMANTX1) and CD single (NUMANCD1).

Released: March 1991.

Foreign formats: matched the UK.

Special note 1: 12-inch featured; 'Heart' 4.06 2. 'Are "Friends" Electric?' (The Renegade Soundwave remix) 5.14 (non-album track) 3. 'Tread Careful' 4.08 (non-album track).

Special note 2: CD single featured 1. 'Heart' 4.06. 2. 'Ice House' 3.17 (non-album track). 3. 'Tread Careful' 4.08 (non-album track).

*Second 7-inch single released on red vinyl (NUMANCV1) featuring 1. 'Heart' 4.06. 2. 'Shame' 4.39 (non-album track).

** Cassette tracks matched NUMAN1.

Promo video shot.

With five different formats for fans to choose from, on the surface 'Heart' looked like a concerted effort from IRS to get Numan back into the British top 40. The track itself was a pretty, piano-led ballad reminiscent of 'This Is Love.' Over on the B-side was yet another gem of a track entitled 'Icehouse,' itself exclusive to this single and not included on *Outland*. The release of this single was something of a compromise following Gary's refusal to allow *Outland* album track 'My World Storm' to be turned into a 'smiley-faced' dance track. Sadly, 'Heart', when released, quickly settled into a by now familiar pattern by stalling just outside the top 40.

'Heart' entered and peaked at No 43 spending two weeks on the top 75.

RE-ISSUE CAMPAIGN
ALBUMS

All three albums released via IRS were finally re-issued in late 1999; all were digitally re-mastered featuring expanded artwork, detailed sleeve notes and additional bonus material.

METAL RHYTHM
(**Cat No:** EMI 7243-5-2213320)
Formats: CD.
Released: September 1999.
Foreign formats: matched the UK.
Re-issued cover artwork shaded darker to the originally issued UK album artwork.

This re-issue featured the full ten-track album along with five bonus cuts. 'I Don't Believe' (B-side to 'New Anger') and 'Children' (B-side to the 12-inch version of 'New Anger'). This release also enabled US and Far East fans to finally own the original UK version of this album and in particular both 'Young Heart' and Hunger,' two tracks that were excised from the original US/Far East edition and were both previously unreleased until now. In addition, EMI included two of the three US / Far East only remixes that originally appeared on the 'New Anger' album. Both William Orbit's remix of 'My Dying Machine' and Andy Piercy's remix of 'Devious' were superb, easily eclipsing the original versions (in fact, in the case of 'My Dying Machine', the song was transformed into a US flavoured, jaunty club track enhanced by additional guitar and synthesizer embellishments). Not included though were the live B-sides added to the flipside of 'America.' These were included 'uncut' on *The Skin Mechanic – Live* CD. Also not included were the live versions of 'Creatures,' 'Call Out The Dogs' and 'I Can't Stop', these were originally B-sides to both 'New Anger' and 'America' and lifted from the fan club live album *Ghost*. Another rather curious omission (and supposedly third remix on *New* Anger) was the long rumoured Andy Piercy remix of 'New Anger.' This track, although listed as a remix on both the US and Japanese versions of *New Anger* failed to appear on the *New Anger* album itself leaving fans to conclude that it was listed this way as no more than just a simple typing error. However, fans remain convinced that the remix does in fact exist and has simply been 'misplaced.' One final omission was 'A Child With A Ghost', included on the US version of 'Metal Rhythm' and originally taken from Gary's 1984 album *Berserker*.

All in all though, this was a superb effort from EMI enabling fans the opportunity to own virtually both versions of the *Metal Rhythm/ New Anger* album.

THE SKIN MECHANIC – LIVE
(**Cat No:** EMI 7243-5-21406-26)
Formats: CD.
Released: September 1999.
Foreign formats: matched the UK.
Cover artwork was altered slightly on this re-issue.
Special note: track list on both the back cover and the CD booklet was incorrect. Out of the thirteen tracks listed two ('Young Heart' and 'Are "Friends" Electric?') were printed the wrong way round. 'Are "Friends" Electric?' in fact preceded 'Young Heart' and not the other way round.

This re-issue featured the original thirteen-track album; no bonus material was added which was something of a disappointment for fans who had hoped that this album would receive the 'full concert' treatment as had the Beggars Banquet CD re-issue of *Living Ornaments '79* the previous year. Like *Metal Rhythm*, an expanded CD booklet was also included featuring detailed sleeve notes and archive photographs.

OUTLAND
(**Cat No:** EMI 7243-5-21405-27)
Formats: CD.
Released: September 1999.
Foreign formats: matched the UK.
Cover remained unchanged from the original.
Special note: an early acetate of this re-issue featured both remixes of 'My World Storm' linked together as one track (Running time 9.25).

This re-issue featured the original thirteen-track album and five bonus tracks, those were; 'Shame,' 'Ice-House,' 'Tread Careful' (all three, B-sides to the single 'Heart'). Also included were two US only remixes of 'My World Storm.' The first was a dance mix entitled 'US Promo Mix' (5.44), the second was a rock mix entitled 'Alternative Mix' (3.41). Not included on this re-issue was the 'Rockers Uptown' remix of 'Are "Friends" Electric?' that also appeared on the 12-inch US promo that had included both the remixes of 'My World Storm.'

Top left: Japanese issue of Outland.
Left to right: original US 'long box' issue of Outland *along with a rare hand painted* Metal Rhythm *era T-shirt.*
Below: fold-out poster of the 'New Anger' single and an official 'Skin Mechanic Tour' scarf.

Original magazine ads for both "New Anger" and "America."

Left to right: Vinyl, picture disc and 12-inch issue of "America."

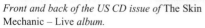

Front and back of the US CD issue of The Skin Mechanic – Live *album.*

Pair of fridge magnets.

US 12-inch promo (Cat No: IRS v-13824), released June 1991. Tracks: "My World Storm" 5.44 (mix by Rockers Uptown), "My World Storm" 3.41 (instrumental), "Are "Friends" Electric?" 5.14 (Renegade sound wave 1991 remix), "Are "Friends" Electric?" 5.14 (instrumental).

This 12-inch actually made an appearance on the US Billboard dance charts.

Canadian 12-inch promo from 1989 (Cat No: IRS8925) – played the Metal Rhythm track " Respect" on both sides.

Music Technology Dec 89.

N/Y single "Adrenalin" (B-side – "Love Is The Doctor" – Cat No: IRS ADREN1). A-side was produced by Yen and Numan. B-side co-written with Numan, issued in Feb 1990.

Selection of IRS era yearbooks.

Vinyl sleeve for the Metal Rhythm album, note the altered artwork.

SECTION ONE

PART FOUR

THE SHARPE AND NUMAN YEARS

Numan had in the past aligned himself with some fairly unexpected and unusual recording artists (Dollar, Robert Palmer, and Leo Sayer). Teaming up with Bill Sharpe, founder member of the coffee table soul/ pop act Shakatak to release a single was, on the surface, a bizarre pairing. This liaison though resulted in a huge amount of media attention and a much needed career boost for Gary at a time when he had just suffered the worst selling record of his career (1984's *Berserker*). What was initially a one-off outing culminated in a flurry of singles as the pair recorded sporadically over the course of five years, ending with an album mid-way through 1989.

Recording as Sharpe and Numan gave Gary the unique opportunity to record chart oriented pop music entirely separate from his own career. Bizarrely, under this guise, Numan experienced positive press attention, radio airplay as well as TV invites to plug the latest Sharpe and Numan release (something unthinkable with his own solo efforts in the mid to late 80s).

Although the duo's first single, 'Change Your Mind', was a big hit, the pair failed to replicate that success with subsequent releases and by the time they got round to issuing a full album, interest in Sharpe and Numan had dwindled. Following promotional duties for that record, Sharpe and Numan parted company for good.

ORIGINAL SINGLES
1985 – 1989

CHANGE YOUR MIND
1. 'Change Your Mind' 4.12. 2. 'Remix, Remake, Remodel'* 3.58.
(**Cat No:** UK Polydor POSP722)
1. 'Change Your Mind' (extended version) 8.24. 2. 'Remix, Remake, Remodel'* 3.58. 3. 'Fools In A World Of Fire'* 3.42.
(**Cat No:** UK Polydor POSPX722 – Picture disc)
Formats: 7-inch and 12-inch.
Released: February 1985.
Foreign formats: Spanish sleeve slightly different. Canadian 12-inch had a slightly different cover. In addition, promo DJ 12-inch issued (DJP149) featuring the extended UK mix and the single mix; this release was re-credited to 'Gary Numan And Bill Sharpe (of Shakatak).'
* Bill Sharpe only.

All three tracks released were included on the Bill Sharpe solo album *Famous People*. German CD version of this album (Cat No: 825 497-2) included – along with the record's standard ten tracks, one which ('Famous People') had been remixed for the US market – two additional remixes namely the extended 12-inch mix of 'Change Your Mind' and the Razormaid extended mix of 'Famous People.'

Special note: Additional 7-inch picture disc released (POSPP722) – same tracks as the regular 7-inch version. In addition, a rare 12-inch PolyGram promo was issued (Cat No: 883 061) featuring a remix of 'Change Your Mind.' This was undertaken by Joseph Watt and the track list for this release was: 1. 'Change Your Mind' 7.30 (the Razormaid mix). 2. 'Change Your Mind' (UK single mix). 3. 'Change Your Mind' (UK 12-inch mix.). In addition, two magazines, *Electronic Music Maker* and *Soundwave* carried a free cassette featuring an unreleased mix of 'Change Your Mind.'

Promo video shot.

Special note: a sheet music magazine for this single was available to buy shortly after its release.

'Change Your Mind' arrived unexpectedly at a time when Gary's career had taken a turn for the worse following the crushing failure of his *Berserker* project. The song immediately caught the attention of the media who never expected Numan to join forces with such an unlikely partner and deliver a pop song of such style, flair and conviction. 'Change Your Mind' quickly rewarded the duo with a smash top 20 hit, the tracks menacing, futuristic dance grooves wormed their way onto everything from daytime radio and television as well as the nation's dance floors. While Numan certainly benefited from this unusual pairing and bathed in the warm glow of its success, returning to his solo career was, if anything, a jolt back to reality.

'Change Your Mind' entered the charts at No 43 climbing all the way to No 17 spending 8 weeks on the chart.

NEW THING FROM LONDON TOWN
2nd single from Sharpe and Numan.
(see **'SECTION ONE, PART ONE – THE NUMA YEARS'**)

★★★☆☆

NO MORE LIES
1. 'No More Lies' 3.24. 2. 'Voices' 3.48.
(**Cat No:** Polydor POSP894)
1. 'No More Lies' (extended mix) 7.46. 2. 'Voices' 3.48.
(**Cat No:** Polydor POSPX894)
Formats: 7-inch*, 12-inch* and CD single (features the same tracks as the 12-inch adding both 7-inch versions of 'Change Your Mind' and 'No More Lies'** – POSPCD894).
Released: January 1988.

Foreign formats: German version of this single issued 'Voices' as the chosen A-side relegating 'No More Lies' to the flipside (**Cat No:** 887613-2), however, this single (available as a regular 7-inch, a 4 track CD and as an extended, 4 track 12-inch) wasn't available for long and was quickly withdrawn.

* Both the 7-inch and 12-inch were also released as picture discs (POSPP894). In addition, the 7-inch version was also released on coloured vinyl (white vinyl – POSPW894, blue vinyl – POSPB894 and finally clear vinyl – POSPT894).

**CD single artwork stated that 'No More Lies' was the single mix, this was incorrect, the correct version included was the extended 7.46 mix.

No promo video.

A third Sharpe and Numan single emerged in the early weeks of 1988. Fans though were less taken by this release citing it as by far the weakest of the three singles released thus far. 'No More Lies' was very lightweight 'coffee table pop' and hardly sounded like Gary Numan at all. The single's weak and throwaway nature saw it passed up by radio and with no video it hardly troubled the charts either. On the B-side was a track that sent a bolt of electricity through Gary's fan base. 'Voices' was a classic Numan anthem, metallic, hard-hitting and just about the best new song from Numan in two years. Fans argued that this track should have been the single's A-side, a sentiment shared in Germany where 'Voices' was indeed promoted (for a short time anyway) as the third single from the duo.

'No More Lies' entered the charts at No 35 climbing one place higher the following week before departing after three weeks on the top 75.

This was the final single featuring Gary Numan (other than the 1996 re-issue of 'Cars') to enter the UK top 40 singles chart until 'Rip' in May of 2002.

'No More Lies' picture discs.

I'M ON AUTOMATIC

1. 'I'm On Automatic' 4.06. 2. 'No More Lies' (1989 mix) 3.59.
(**Cat No:** Polydor POPB43 This format available as a poster sleeve)

1. 'I'm On Automatic' (extended mix) 7.37. 2. 'Love Like A Ghost' 3.28 (non-album track). 3. 'Voices' (1989 mix) 5.35.*
(**Cat No:** Polydor PZ43, PZCD – picture disc)

Formats: 7-inch (two versions released, the second featured 'Love Like A Ghost' on the flip side, Cat No: PO43 – This version was also issued as a picture disc 7-inch with 'Love Like A Ghost' on the flip side Cat No: POPD43), 12-inch (two versions) and CD single (PZCD43 – same tracks as 12-inch, CD cover printed above).

* Previously issued in 1988 in Germany only, artwork for this CD single incorrectly states that this version of 'Voices' features on the *Automatic* album.

Released: June 1989.

Foreign formats: matched the UK.

No promo video.

Special note: both the extended version of 'Voices' and 'Love Like A Ghost' were included on a bootleg CD version of the 'Automatic' album in the US.

'I'm On Automatic' was a substantial improvement over 'No More Lies' being much closer in spirit to the duo's debut hit 'Change Your Mind.' This single also featured another strong track on the flipside entitled 'Love Like A Ghost', a lullabying slowie that featured one of the best vocal performances from Gary yet, proving that underneath his trademark snarl, he actually possessed a great singing voice.

'I'm On Automatic''s melodic, radio-friendly rhythm track was beautifully complimented by Numan's assured, dusky, melancholic vocals and all looked set for another sizable hit for the pair. Fans too were also hoping that a return to the Sharpe and Numan franchise would at least feature somewhere in the UK top 40 and keep Numan in the public eye. Yet despite securing daytime radio airplay (a bizarre Sharpe and Numan phenomenon) the single climbed no higher than its point of entry (predictably just outside the top 40) before falling away.

'I'm On Automatic' entered and peaked at No 44 spending two weeks on the top 75.

It was now clear that by 1989, Gary had lost a significant number of his fan base and no longer had the power to punch new releases straight into the British top 40. This was obviously not just very bad news for Gary but bad news for both Numan and Bill

'I'm On Automatic' 7-inch poster sleeve and cover.

who were mere weeks away from releasing their first album together.

ORIGINAL ALBUM

★★★☆☆

AUTOMATIC
(**Cat No:** Polydor 839-5202)
Formats: CD, vinyl (839-5201) and cassette (839-5204).
Released: June 1989.
Foreign formats: matched the UK.
Special note 1: CD version of *Automatic* featured two extra tracks added to the album's track list (see below).
Special note 2: album actually recorded in the early spring of 1988.
Musicians; Gary Numan – Vocals/ Bill Sharpe – Keyboards/ Roger Odell – Drums/Tessa Niles – Backing vocals/ Linda Taylor – Backing vocals ('Change Your Mind' only)/ Synth programming – John Davis/ Mitch Dalton – Guitar.
Tracks: 'Change Your Mind' 4.14/ 'Turn Off The World' 3.58/ 'No More Lies' (1989 mix) 4.02/ 'Breath In Emotion' 3.25/ 'Some New Game' 4.01/ 'I'm On Automatic' 4.08/ 'Rip It Up' 4.13/ 'Welcome To Love' 3.30/ 'Voices' 3.50 (original 1988 mix)/ 'Nightlife' 3.41.

CD bonus tracks: 'No More Lies' (original 12-inch mix) and 'I'm On Automatic' (original 12-inch mix).

All songs by Bill Sharpe and Gary Numan.

Engineered by Nick Smith, except 'Breathe In Emotion' (engineered by John Davis).

Mixed by Nick Smith, except 'Change Your Mind' (mixed by Wally Brill).

Recorded at Scratch Studios, Rock City, Maison Rouge and Marcus Studios.

Produced by Bill Sharpe.

Singles: 'Change Your Mind', 'New Thing From London Town'*, 'No More Lies' and 'I'm On Automatic.' In addition, 'Turn Off The World' emerged as a 7-inch promo in South Africa featuring 'Voices' as its B-side (T. Music Promo 38).

Videos: 'Change Your Mind'. In addition, 'Change Your Mind' was performed on *Top Of The Pops*. 'No More Lies' was performed on the *ITV* chart show, *The Roxy*. 'I'm On Automatic' was performed on the TV show, *Club X*.

* Originally released via Numa Records, this single also had a promo video shot.

Special note: all releases (bar 'Change Your Mind' and 'New Thing From London Town') were credited to Sharpe + Numan.

Automatic, the debut album from Bill Sharpe and Gary Numan finally appeared in June of 1989 some five years after the duo began their recording partnership. For fans, it was an opportunity to enter the realms of pure pop with the music on board cutting a clear path somewhere between coffee table, white boy soul and radio friendly danceable pop. Of the ten tracks on the record, only 'Voices' harked back to the biting, metallic anthems Numan was better associated with, the rest followed the template laid down by previous Sharpe and Numan singles. Quality material though was at a premium, with the likes of the gorgeous pop of 'Breathe In Emotion' and 'Turn Off The World' indicating that the record had an abundance of potential future singles on board. However, the standout track on this record and an obvious single (aside from 'Change Your Mind') was the winsome slowie 'Welcome To Love', a beautiful piece of music featuring a superb duet between Gary and Tessa Niles. Sadly, the poor reception offered to the album when it was released curtailed any hopes from long time fans that further singles would be lifted from the album.

Automatic entered and peaked at No 59 spending 1 week on the top 75.

With Gary now seemingly losing even the vital support of his fan base – everything being released was hovering just outside the top 40 before vanishing – this was unknown to the public at large who just assumed Numan had retired, preferring to plough his energies into his other well publicized passion for aeroplanes. To long time fans, however, it was all becoming extremely frustrating as increasingly Numan's late 80s career appeared confused and aimless as he alternated wildly between solo endeavours and side projects with alarming regularity. The failure of this album seemingly brought an abrupt end to the Sharpe And Numan partnership. However, rumours still persist that further recording was undertaken in 1990 with talk of a second album being recorded and shelved.

On the next page are one or two pieces of memorabilia from the era of Sharpe and Numan.

7-inch and 12-inch German release of "Voices", extended version of "Voices" was exclusive to the German market. Other tracks on the 12-inch issue were: "No More Lies"(7-inch mix), "Change Your Mind" (7-inch mix) and "Voices" (regular UK mix).

Slightly different cover for the Spanish release of this single.

"Change Your Mind" picture disc single.

Back cover of the US issue of "Change Your Mind" featuring an exclusive. addition remix.

Picture disc for "I'm On Automatic."

Alternative sleeves for "I'm On Automatic."

US bootleg CD of "Automatic", includes two extra tracks.

SECTION ONE

PART FIVE

THE NICHOLSON AND NUMAN YEARS

At the time of the demise of Numa records in early 1987, Gary's former label manager there (Matt Nicholson) put Gary in touch with one of his relatives, Hugh, who along with his brother David, had formed a new record label entitled GFM Records. The pair were keen to get Gary to sing guest vocals on a track that they felt lent itself well to Numan's musical style. Although not entirely struck with the song, Numan eventually accepted the offer and with his vocals added, the track was quickly issued as a single in the early part of the year. Entitled 'Radio Heart', the song was quick to pick up radio airplay and became a minor top 40 hit prompting Gary to agree to appear as guest vocalist on a further two singles. However, these additional songs were substandard in comparison and failed to emulate the heights scaled by the first single. At the end of 1987 the group issued an album that rather misleadingly gave the impression that Gary had sang on every track (he in fact only appeared on the project's three singles), this was quickly withdrawn and re-promoted later stating exactly who sang what.

Fans' reaction to the Radio Heart liaison was lukewarm at best with Gary's fan base being not overly struck with the chart-oriented material recorded (a feeling shared by Numan as well it later appeared). Oddly, seven years later, Numan recorded another song with the Nicholson writing team entitled 'Like A Refugee (I Won't Cry)', a track inspired by the then Bosnian refugee crisis. When this single vanished without trace it effectively put paid to any further collaborations.

ORIGINAL SINGLES

RADIO HEART
1. 'Radio Heart' 3.40. 2. 'Radio Heart' (instrumental) 4.20.
(**Cat No:** UK GFM109)
Formats: 7-inch* and 12-inch.**
Released: March 1987.
Foreign formats: French sleeve different. American 12-inch released via Critique Records (**Cat No:** 0-96758) featuring the extended and single mix along with another new track entitled 'Mistasax (2).' This was released in a blue cover (Alternative **Cat No:** GFMR109).
* Second 7-inch version available in a blue sleeve (sleeve same as the US 12-inch released through Critique Records) advertising the track 'Mistasax (2)' as its B-side, it in fact played (like the first 7-inch) the instrumental version of 'Radio Heart.'
** Extended mix increased to 6.00, B-side same as the 7-inch (Cat No: GFMT109).
Special note: Both formats were released in a flurry of different picture discs with the 7-inch having two (GFMP109 and GFMG109. The latter was a radio shaped disc) and the12-inch also having two (GFMX109 and GFMTP109).
This single was credited to 'Radio Heart featuring Gary Numan.'
Three promo videos shot. The 7-inch and 12-inch versions of this video featured Gary clad in a black suit performing in front of the Radio Heart band, the third was a 'night' version complete with extra footage that could only be screened after 9 pm.

1987 saw Numan quickly re-emerge following the dissolving of his Numa imprint under the guise of a new collaboration. Like Sharpe and Numan before it, 'Radio

Heart' featured Numan as the guest vocalist, the track in question, when released, was instantly added to radio play lists and resulted in a minor top 40 hit. Fans though were not entirely struck with the song. Although a fairly moody pop song, it featured an unusually brittle, ghostly and rather strained vocal performance from Gary leaving fans speculating that perhaps even Numan himself wasn't entirely thrilled with it either.

'Radio Heart' did, however, briefly re-ignite Gary's American profile with the single climbing into the Billboard charts providing Numan with his first real stateside hit since 'Cars' back in 1980.

'Radio Heart' entered the UK charts at No 50 peaking at No 35 with a six week run on the top 75.

LONDON TIMES

1. 'London Times' 3.45. 2. 'Rumour' 2.45 (non-album track).
(**Cat No:** UK GFM112)
Formats; 7-inch* and 12-inch** (GFMT112 – 'London Times' extended to 5.30. B-side same as the 7-inch).
Released: June 1987.
Foreign formats: matched the UK.
* Flexi disc issued with this format.
**Two picture discs also released (GFMP112 and GFMX112 – the latter was a square shaped disc).

No promo video.

Special note: 'Rumour' was credited to Gary Numan only.

Long time fans were stunned when 'London Times' emerged in the summer months of 1987, its over the top, bouncy, pop hooks and bright and perky chorus had them shaking their heads in utter disbelief. 'London Times' was clearly an ill-advised dalliance into the realms of pop music and succeeded only in thrusting a wedge ever deeper between Numan and his fan base.

'London Times' entered and peaked at No 48 spending two weeks on the top 75.

ALL ACROSS THE NATION

1. 'All Across The Nation' (Radio mix) 4.00. 2. 'River' 3.33 (non-album track).
(**Cat No:** UK NBR NBR1)
Formats: 7-inch, 12-inch*and CD single.**
Released: November 1987.
Foreign formats: matched the UK.
* Includes an extended 5.31 mix of the A-side as well as the instrumental version and the track 'River' (Cat No: NBE1. In addition, a second 12-inch emerged featuring a second remix of the A-side, other tracks conformed to the first 12-inch. This release appeared in a blue sleeve (Cat No: NBRX1).
** This was the first ever Gary Numan CD single and featured the extended version of the A-side, the 7-inch version and the instrumental version as well as the track 'River' (CDNBR1).

No promo video.

Following Gary's return to the top 20 with the 'E REG Model' version of 'Cars', the last of the three songs Gary recorded with the group Radio Heart emerged as a single. Entitled 'All Across The Nation', it was by far the weakest lacking anything near the hooks of the previous two. Despite it being the first CD single from Numan, 'All Across The Nation' failed to enter the top 75, the first single to do so since 'Down In The Park' way back in 1979.

LIKE A REFUGEE (I WON'T CRY)
1. 'Like A Refugee (I Won't Cry)' 3.54. 2. 'Like A Refugee (I Won't Cry)' 5.35 (extended mix). 3. 'Like A Refugee (I Won't Cry)' 4.33 (acoustic mix).
(**Cat No:** UK The Record Label SPIN D1)
1. 'Like A Refugee (I Won't Cry)' 3.54. 2. 'Like A Refugee (I Won't Cry)' 4.37 (Pandemonium mix). 3. 'Like A Refugee (I Won't Cry)' 3.54 (instrumental mix). 4. 'Machine + Soul' (live)* 6.20.

(**Cat No:** UK The Record Label SPIN R1)
Formats: 12-inch vinyl (SPIN T1), two-track cassette and 2 CD singles.
Released: April 1994.
Foreign formats: issued in Germany on the Global Satellite label.
This single was credited to 'Numan and Dadadang.'
* 'Machine + Soul' was taken from the then forthcoming live record *Dream Corrosion*, in addition, both CD sleeves were slightly different from one another.
Promo video shot.

In a surprise move, Numan unexpectedly re-united with the writing team responsible for the mid 80s Radio Heart project. For fans though, the resurrection of this particular side project was enough to cause them genuine concern, especially as the recently performed 'Dream Corrosion Tour' had seen Gary virtually reborn as a credible artist bringing previously disillusioned fans flocking back in their thousands. Although long time fans were not relishing yet another ill-advised move into the realms of pop music, any of those fears were quickly brushed aside by the sheer brilliance of the new song recorded; entitled 'Like A Refugee (I Won't Cry)', it was by far the best song to emerge from the pen of principle writer Hugh Nicholson. 'Like A Refugee (I Won't Cry)' was a masterpiece, an emotionally charged anthem to the displaced peoples of Yugoslavia who were, by the mid-90s, in the midst of social and political turmoil. Unfortunately the single was completely ignored when released and failed to chart.

'Like A Refugee (I Won't Cry)' is regarded by fans as a genuinely lost classic, however, the song would have been a sizable hit for Gary had it emerged at any other time. As it was, by 1994, Numan was then firmly out of the public eye and struggling to raise his profile after releasing the worst selling album of his career (*Machine + Soul*). The failure of this single halted any further Nicholson and Numan collaborations.

The following items of memorabilia are from the era of Radio Heart.

US 3 track 12-inch.

"Radio Heart" picture disc.

Original CD release of the
Radio Heart *album.*

"Radio Heart" picture disc.

*Alternative sleeve for "Radio"
promo single.*

Cassette single.

Both versions of the "London Times" picture discs.

*Alternative sleeve for this 12-
inch single.*

ORIGINAL ALBUM

RADIO HEART
(**Cat No:** UK NBRLP1)
Formats: vinyl*, cassette (NBRC1) and CD. (CDNBR1).
Released November 1987.
Foreign formats: Swedish version featured extra tracks.
* Picture disc released. (NBRLPX1).
   Full title for the album was 'Radio Heart featuring Gary Numan- special guest Elton John.'
Tracks Side One: 'Radio Heart' 3.44/ 'Blue Nights' 4.39/ 'Starlight Jingles' 4.10/ 'Strange Thing' 4.29.
Tracks Side Two: 'All Across The Nation' 4.01/ 'I'm Alive' 4.09/ 'Mad About The Girl' 3.49/ 'London Times' 3.44/ 'The Victim' 4.00.
Produced by Hugh and David Nicholson.
All songs written by Hugh Nicholson.
Single: 'Radio Heart', 'London Times' and 'All Across The Nation.'
Videos: 'Radio Heart' (three versions). In addition, 'Radio Heart' was performed on German TV and *The Des O'Connor Show* in the UK.

The *Radio Heart* album was withdrawn almost as quickly as it appeared with only the vinyl version ever making it to the shops. This was due to concerns from Gary that as he was depicted on the record's cover, fans would assume that he sang on every track when in fact he only appeared on the three singles that had been lifted from the project. The album was typical of the mid-80s, poppy and very lightweight.

This album's three formats are now quite rare and hard to find.

Radio Heart failed to chart.

Ultra rare French release of the 'Radio Heart' single, this version issued in an alternative cover.

RE-ISSUE CAMPAIGN
ALBUMS

RADIO HEART Featuring GARY NUMAN
(**Cat No:** The Record Label SPINCD2003)
Formats: CD.
Released: August 1999.
Foreign formats: matched the UK.
Re-issued in a new cover.

This re-issue featured the original *Radio Heart* album from 1987. Aside from a newly commissioned (and once again, rather misleading) front cover, no other differences could be detected. New cover photo was a reversed still from the 'Radio Heart' video reprinted here in black and white.

NICHOLSON/ NUMAN 1987 – 1994
(**Cat No:** The Record Label SPINCD2005)
Formats: CD.
Released: August 1999.
Foreign formats: matched the UK.
Special note: fans obtaining this CD direct from the label's online address received a free remix mini-album (see below) featuring remixes of the 'Radio Heart' song. These mixes had previously been issued on a limited edition CD in 1997 (see 'Remix projects'). In addition, fans could also buy a plain-sleeved three-track video featuring two versions of the 'Like A Refugee (I Won't Cry)' video as well as the 'Radio Heart' single promo itself.

Tracks: 'Thrill Me' ('Radio Heart' demo) 4.03/ 'Radio Heart' (radio mix) 3.40/ 'Radio Heart' (extended mix) 6.00/ 'Hearts And Minds' ('London Times' original demo) 3.31/ 'London Times' (radio mix) 3.43/ 'London Times' (extended mix) 5.23/ 'Nuits Francaise' ('All Across The Nation' original demo) 3.11/ 'All Across The Nation' (radio mix) 4.02/ 'All Across The Nation' (extended mix) 5.39/ 'Over On The Other Side' ('Like A Refugee (I Won't Cry)' original demo) 4.00/ 'Like A Refugee (I Won't Cry)' 4.32 (acoustic mix)/ 'Like A Refugee (I Won't Cry)' 3.53 (radio mix)/ 'Like A Refugee (I Won't Cry)' 4.37 (Pandemonium mix)/ 'Tragedy In Blue' (demo) 3.55.

This release included all the various mixes of the four singles that emerged with Gary on vocals. In addition, the original demos for each single featuring the vocals of Hugh Nicholson were also included. Missing though were the instrumental versions of each single. The final track, 'Tragedy In Blue,' again featured Hugh on vocals and was ear-marked to be offered to Gary (along with previously unreleased track entitled 'Run'). Unfortunately events conspired against these plans and Numan never got to hear either track.

'Radio' CD.

SECTION ONE

PART SIX

THE BBC SESSIONS

Tubeway Army had, by the end of 1978, released two singles and one album, all of which had met with a wall of relative public indifference. John Peel, late night DJ at Radio One, however, was sympathetic to the group's strangely garage rock/ electronic sound and invited them to the station to record a session for his show in January 1979. This the band duly did and the finished recordings threw up three work-in-progress versions of 'Me! I Disconnect From You', 'Down In The Park' and 'I Nearly Married A Human.' All these songs eventually found their way onto the group's second album *Replicas*. This session, alongside their appearance on *The Old Grey Whistle Test* shortly after, was also the final time the group would perform live. A second session took place in May of 1979, by this time Jess Lidyard had departed with Gary augmenting the line-up with a new rhythm section. The music too had changed with the former gritty garage rock sound now totally overrun with an all-encompassing synthesizer sound.

The four new songs recorded in May, as well as the three previous tracks from January, lay in the *BBC* vaults (or more accurately boxed up in a hallway with other sessions) until The Strange Fruit label (part launched by John Peel) began releasing a wide spectrum of these forgotten sessions including Tubeway Army.

Interestingly, in 2001, Gary returned to the *BBC* to record a new session for the station. Fresh from recording his stunning new record *Pure*, Gary delivered an electrifying set in front of a live audience that was heavy with selections from his latest album as well as older more familiar numbers (a further reading of 'Are "Friends" Electric?' was aired on John Peel's *Festive Fifty* bash). These latest recording have, so far, not been released officially although superb bootlegs are easily obtained (see 'Bootlegs').

ORIGINAL RELEASES
1987 and 1989

THE PEEL SESSIONS – TUBEWAY ARMY
(**Cat No:** Strange Fruit SFPS032)
Formats: 12-inch vinyl and cassette. (SFPSC032).
Released: August 1987.
Foreign formats: Canadian 12-inch issued via PolyGram.
Special note: prior to this release, two bootleg 7-inch singles found their way onto the market place featuring both of the sessions from the band in 1979 (see 'Bootlegs').
Tracks: 'Me! I Disconnect From You' 3.07/ 'Down In The Park' 4.19/ 'I Nearly Married A Human' 6.36.
Musicians: Gary Numan – Vocals, guitar and keyboards/ Paul Gardiner – Bass/ Jess Lidyard – Drums.
Produced by Bob Sargeant.
Engineered by Neil Burn.

Tubeway Army's experimental take on synthesised rock had caught the attention of noted Radio One DJ John Peel and this release featured all three songs that the band recorded for the station in the early part of January 1979. The session saw the band moving away from the garage rock template and into a more electronic environment; first track, 'Me! I Disconnect From You', was a perfect example of a group in transition, welding the dynamics of rock to the otherworldly drone of electronics. The final two tracks took this idea to its logical conclusion with 'Down In The Park' enveloped in a haunting and chilly synthesised backdrop. Final track, 'I Nearly Married A Human', was a stark, bleak instrumental that was more akin to the work of Germany's premier electronic act Kraftwerk than anything the band had previously attempted.

Numan's singular vision was steering the band into fairly uncharted waters and although no one realised it at the time, Tubeway Army were about to open the floodgates to a veritable revolution in popular music.

GARY NUMAN – TUBEWAY ARMY

(**Cat No:** Strange Fruit SFPMA202)
Formats: vinyl, cassette (SFPMAC202) and CD (SFPMACD202).
Released: July 1989.
Special note: this release included the previously released session issued in 1987.
Tracks: 'Cars' 3.15/ 'Airlane' 3.20/ 'Films' 2.55/ 'Conversation' 6.45/ 'Me! I Disconnect From You' 3.07/ 'Down In The Park' 4.19/ 'I Nearly Married A Human' 6.36.
Musicians: Gary Numan – Vocals/ Chris Payne – keyboards/ Cedric Sharpley – Drums/ Billy Currie – Keyboards/ Paul Gardiner – Bass.
Produced by Tony Wilson.
Engineered by Mike Robinson.

Numan's second John Peel session was recorded on the 25th of May 1979 and aired shortly after both 'Are "Friends" Electric?' and *Replicas* had stormed the UK charts. This session revealed that the transition to an all synthesiser sound was now complete. Four new songs were recorded, all of which found their way onto Numan's debut solo album *The Pleasure Principle* a few months later. Of the four songs recorded, both 'Airlane' and 'Conversation' were not radically different from their eventual album counterparts. 'Cars' and 'Films', however, were very much work in progress, being less bombastic than the finally recorded versions that appeared on the album.

This release, complete with the earlier John Peel session, were both fascinating snapshots of a group on the cusp of international stardom and were a worthy addition to the Numan canon.

12-inch vinyl issue.

RE-ISSUE CAMPAIGN

THE RADIO ONE RECORDINGS
(**Cat No:** Strange Fruit SFRSCD081)
Formats: CD.
Released: April 1999.
Foreign formats: released in the US as *The BBC Sessions*.
Musicians and studio details for tracks 1 to 7, see previous releases.
Musicians, tracks 8 to 10: Gary Numan – Vocals/ Paul Gardiner – Bass/ Chris Payne – Keyboards/ Second keyboardist: unknown though likely to be Dennis Haines/ RRussell Bell – Guitar, keyboards and viola/ Jess Lidyard – Drummer
Tracks 8 to 10 Produced by Jeff Griffin.
Tracks 8 to 10 Engineered by Chris Lycett.
Sleeve notes by Steve Malins.

This re-issue came complete with sleeve notes and included both the sessions that had appeared in 1989 (SFPMA202) as well as three live tracks that were recorded on the 30th of November 1979 at the Wembley Arena *Year Of The Child* concert. Fans listening to the trio of newly discovered live tracks ('Me! I Disconnect From You' 3.06, 'Metal' 3.28 and 'Down In The Park' 5.04) soon realised that they were identical to the recordings found on *Living Ornaments '79*. This meant that although the band appeared live at the charity concert, they were in fact miming to a previously recorded live tape. A closer inspection of the photos from this concert also revealed that Cedric Sharpley was not on stage at this event either, the vacant drum stool being occupied by original Tubeway Army drummer Jess Lidyard.

Below are two items of Strange Fruit memorabilia.

Right: US version of SFRSCD081. This CD was re-titled The BBC Sessions *due to the unfamiliarity of Radio One in America. Released via Varese/ Fuel Records (Cat No: 61064-6/00. This CD was also known as* BBC In Concert, The Best Of The Gary Numan Band Live.

Cassette version of SFPMA202 Full title for this release was Double Peel Session, Gary Numan-Tubeway Army. Two Complete Sessions.

SECTION ONE

PART SEVEN

THE EAGLE RECORDS YEARS

With Numan back in the British top 20 in the early part of 1996 with a Beggars Banquet era 'greatest hits' collection and another hit re-issue of 'Cars', Gary opted to pull the plug on his Numa imprint for the second (and final time) in favour of securing a new recording contract. Keen to drum up interest in his new music, several labels were approached. The response, however, was lukewarm at best but Gary eventually signed up with a new company called Eagle and settled down to completing his first record of new material in three years. A second boost to Numan's profile appeared in the middle of 1997 when a two CD tribute album hit the shops. Entitled *Random*, the project featured artists as diverse as Republica, Gravity Kills and The Magnetic Fields delivering fresh interpretations of Gary's past work. Critics may have scratched their heads but all this fresh attention helped Gary's first album for Eagle, *Exile*, breach the top 50 when released in the autumn of 1997. If this wasn't great news in itself, the accompanying tour was even better as for the first time in years Gary felt confident enough to extend his reach beyond the confines of the UK taking in European territories as well as, for the first time since 1980, the United States.

Amidst all this live activity, Eagle and its US counterpart Cleopatra Records got down to the task of re-issuing (and in some cases re-packaging) Gary's extensive Numa catalogue making 1998/1999 a bonanza period for fans as long deleted albums from Numa, Beggars Banquet and EMI as well as others flooded onto the marketplace.

In 2000, Gary issued his second studio record for Eagle entitled *Pure* and the response from fans, as well as the press, was overwhelmingly positive. In fact, *Pure* not only united press and fans behind him, it marked the start of Gary's return to the mainstream in a big way. However, as good news as that was, it did present Numan with a new problem, his label. In truth, Eagle Records is primarily home to artists whose glory days are firmly behind them, it's certainly not the kind of company a mainstream artist would or should be signed to and when the *Pure* campaign was over, Numan and Eagle, not surprisingly, parted company with Gary quickly signing to the hip imprint Artful Records (itself an offshoot of the mighty Universal group).

Eagle was arguably a major milestone in Gary's career with the label issuing not only two of his best latter-day albums but also re-issuing much of his independently released works from the 80s and 90s. Its likely more records are in the pipeline with fans speculating that more studio material will be re-issued as well as previously unreleased live recordings from Gary's time on the label emerging too.

ORIGINAL ALBUMS
1997 – 2000

EXILE
(Cat No: UK EAGCD008)
Formats: CD and cassette.
Released: October 1997.
Foreign formats: US version included extra track, 'Down In The Park' (live version taken from *Ghost*), released via Cleopatra. Japanese version featured the extended versions of 'Dominion Day' and 'The Angel Wars' as extra tracks.
Re-issued November 1998 as an extended release.

Extended running times were: 'Dominion Day' 7.45/ 'Prophecy' 8.57/ 'Dead Heaven' 7.48/ 'Dark' 7.29/ 'Innocence Bleeding' 6.50/ 'The Angel Wars' 9.35/ 'Absolution' 6.23/ 'An Alien Cure' 9.45/ 'Exile' 8.54 (Cat No: EAGCD067).

Special note: promo CD + insert released. (EAGCD008P). In addition, bootleg copies of an earlier 'Numa version' of *Exile* (featuring slightly different mixes of the album's nine tracks) have also emerged.

Musicians: Gary Numan – Vocals and all other instruments/Mike Smith – Additional keyboards on 'Prophecy', 'Dark', 'An Alien Cure' and 'Exile'/Steve Harris – Guitar on 'Innocence Bleeding', 'An Alien Cure' and 'Exile'. Additional guitar on 'Dead Heaven.'

Tracks: 'Dominion Day' 4.50/ 'Prophecy' 5.05/ 'Dead Heaven' 5.22/ 'Dark' 4.30/ 'Innocence Bleeding' 4.25/ 'The Angel Wars' 5.05/ 'Absolution'* 4.59/ 'An Alien Cure' 6.09/ 'Exile' 6.47.

All songs written, performed, engineered and mixed by Gary Numan.

* Re-recorded version of the 1995 single.

Assistant engineer Gemma Webb.

Recorded at Outland studios, England.

Singles: 'Dominion Day.'

Videos: 'Dominion Day'. In addition, 'Absolution' performed on both *SKY TV's* UK *Living* and *ITV's Richard And Judy Show*. Satellite music station *VH1* also screened Numan performing the track 'Dark' alongside two older songs. ('Friends' and 'Noise Noise'). 'Dominion Day' performed on *N.B.C.*

Utilizing the gothic, industrial template laid down by the previous album *Sacrifice*, Numan entered the sessions for what would be the follow-up with a renewed enthusiasm and vigour. The resulting opus entitled *Exile* saw Numan honouring his pledge to continue his bone chilling, cyber rock sound, though this recording was a far darker affair than *Sacrifice*; its nine tracks loosely revolving around a quasi-religious theme, were both sombre and brooding. However, on first listen, the record seemed one long melodic, sludgy wall of looped industrial beats and rhythms. The songs themselves though were cunningly designed to crawl under the skin of the listener, planting memorable melodies that were not easy to dislodge. Layered over the top of this was Numan's exquisite, seductive voice making *Exile* a deceptively beautiful body of work. From the oppressive and deeply rhythmic opener 'Dominion Day' to the un-nerving and disturbing 'The Angel Wars' and 'Prophecy', *Exile* sounded uncannily like the soundtrack to the most sinister movie never made, it's no surprise that one track, the vampire-like mournful gloom of 'Dark' was quickly added to both the soundtrack to the movie *Dark City* as well as the Lara Croft computer game *Tomb Raider 2*. Other notable highlights were the ominous windswept balladry of 'Innocence Bleeding', the startling new version of former single 'Absolution', here, a vast improvement over the original and the album's masterful title track.

Original Cleopatra Records poster.

With the acquisition of a new recording contract and a steady flow of artists from across the musical spectrum name checking and publicly voicing their admiration for Gary through interviews and cover versions. It was gratifying to see *Exile* return Numan to the British top 50 when released and it was clear that the chinks of light that had begun with *Sacrifice* were, three years later, quickly re-igniting Numan's once struggling career.

Exile entered and peaked at No 48 spending one week on the top 75.

PURE
(**Cat No:** UK EAGCD078)
Formats: CD.
Released: October 2000.
Foreign formats: US version released via Spitfire Records in November 2000
(**Cat No:** 5088-2).
Re-issued: February 2001 in the UK with an additional disc featuring remixes and live tracks (see 'Memorabilia' section). In addition, there exists an extended version of this album but sadly Eagle saw no commercial value with

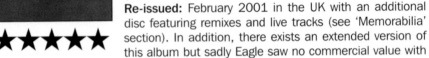

its release and shelved the idea. However, copies (if authentic) have slipped out on to the bootleg market. New running times were: 'Pure' 8.00/ 'Walking With Shadows' 7.06/ 'Rip' 8.34/ 'My Jesus' 7.38/ 'Listen To My Voice' 6.54/ 'Torn' 7.48 and 'I Can't Breathe' 7.13. Both 'Little Invitro' and 'One Perfect Lie' were unchanged. 'Fallen', however, was here represented by a new alternative take of the song. Not included though was 'A Prayer For The Unborn' (see 'Bootleg' section).

Musicians: Gary Numan – Vocals, keyboards, guitar and programming/ Monti – Drums, programming and keyboards/ Rob Holiday – Guitar and keyboards/ Steve Harris – Guitar/ Richard Beasley – Drums.

Tracks: 'Pure' 5.08/ 'Walking With Shadows' 5.52/ 'Rip' 5.06/ 'One Perfect Lie' 4.35/ 'My Jesus' 5.45/ 'Fallen'* 2.31/ 'Listen To My Voice' 5.12/ 'A Prayer For The Unborn' 5.43/ 'Torn' 5.10/ 'Little Invitro' 4.28/ 'I Can't Breathe' 5.45.

All songs by Gary Numan except 'I Can't Breathe' – Music, Gary Numan and Sulpher.* Lyrics by Gary Numan.

Engineered and mixed by Gary Numan.

Recorded and mixed at Alien Studios, England.

All songs produced by Gary Numan and Sulpher** except 'Fallen' and 'Torn', produced by Gary Numan.

* Used in the cinematic trailers for the movie *Thirteen Ghosts*.

** Sulpher comprised of Rob Holliday and Monti.

Singles: none from this album although 'Rip' emerged as a single in 2002 via Artful/ Jagged Halo Records. In addition, Spitfire Records issued a two track CD single promo (CDPRO-5088-D) featuring: 'Listen To My Voice' 3.55 (edit)/ 'Listen To My Voice' (album mix).

Videos: 'Rip'. In addition, live versions of 'Pure', 'Rip' and 'Cars' recorded in 2000 at the Brixton Academy were also made available. (All three added to the US release of *Scarred*). 'Cars' and 'Rip' performed on Japan's Fuji TV in Dec 2000.

Although a cloud of personal tragedy hung heavy over the recording of this album, far from de-railing the project, the sessions for *Pure* saw Numan pour his pain back into the recording resulting in not only some of the best music of his career but quite possibly his best record thus far. *Pure* truly was a mesmerising record, its eleven tracks bubbled and seethed with a relentless and oppressive edge that quickly saw it elevated into the same category as past Numan masterpieces like *Replicas*, *Telekon* and *The Pleasure Principle*. Keen to show off his new musical muscles, album opener, 'Pure', laid down the template that would set the tone for the rest of the record. Following a deceptive, melodic intro, the album's title track exploded into life with big rock riffs and an anthemic chorus. It didn't stop there either, techno rock stormers like the creepy and malevolent 'Rip', the frighteningly riveting 'My Jesus' as well as the truly shattering, concluding track 'I Can't Breathe' all helped push Numan into the kind of bracket occupied by the likes of Nine Inch Nails, Marilyn Manson and Filter.

Highlights of the record were firstly a trio of superb moody ballads ('A Prayer For The Unborn', 'Little Invitro' and 'One Perfect Lie'). Although all three were fairly downbeat each was a lyrical triumph for Numan and musically amongst the best of his career. Secondly, and perhaps the single most stunning piece of music on the record was the icy yet melodic, gothic anthem 'Walking With Shadows', a track that featured a towering vocal performance from Gary and was without doubt one of the best songs of Numan's career thus far. Surprisingly, amidst this album's pulsating, aggressive grooves, metallic beats and claustrophobic moods sat one track that showed Numan could still pen classic, modern pop when the mood took him. This album's most commercial moment was undoubtedly 'Listen To My Voice', an assured dance-floor-bound, gothic slice of anthemic, cyber pop.

Pure resulted in some of the best press coverage for Gary in years with the written media in total agreement that the album's throbbing bass, serrated guitars and bouts of metallic noise as well as the quality song count contributed to *Pure* being a stunning return to form and easily one of the best records of Gary's career.

A year after the record emerged though it was clear to all concerned that Eagle did not possess the required clout to carry Gary's career any further and following the conclusion of promotional duties for it, Numan and Eagle parted company.

Pure entered and peaked at No 58 spending one week on the top 75.

2001-tour edition of Pure *included a poster and bonus disc including two remixes and five live tracks (see 'Memorabilia').*

ORIGINAL SINGLE

DOMINION DAY
1. 'Dominion Day' (video version) 3.40. 2. 'Voix' 4.45 (20th anniversary version*). 3. 'Dead Heaven' 7.49 (extended mix). 4. 'Cars' 3.26 (live '97).
(**Cat No:** UK EAGXS008)
1. 'Dominion Day' 7.45 (extended mix). 2. 'Metal' 4.07 (20th anniversary*). 3. 'Down In The Park' 5.15 (20th anniversary*). 4. 'Dominion Day' 5.15 (live '97).
(**Cat No:** UK EAGXA008)
Formats: 2 CD singles, cassette also released.
Released: April 1998.
Foreign formats: released in the US as an eight track mini-album. In addition, released in Australia featuring 'Dark' as a bonus track.
Special note: both live tracks recorded at the Shepherds Bush Empire on the 9th of November 1997.
* Newly recorded versions.
Promo video shot.

'Dominion Day' was Numan's first single of new material in two years and fans were more than surprised that Eagle chose to even consider releasing a single from a record as fiercely uncommercial as *Exile*. 'Dominion Day's' riffy, alternative rock complete with Gary's gothic and seductive vocals was, in truth, unlikely to breach the UK top 40 but at least stood a good chance of returning Numan to the lower reaches of the top 75; unfortunately with CD1 and CD2 failing to be released simultaneously, the single failed to chart. However, in Germany following a month long European tour, the single breached the alternative rock chart going top 5 in the process. This event gave Gary his biggest hit in mainland Europe in over a decade.

US issue of Live At Shepherds Bush Empire.

COMPILATION ALBUM
Licensed: UK

NEW DREAMS FOR OLD 84 – 98

(**Cat No:** UK EAMCD096)
Formats: CD.
Released: October 1999.
Foreign formats: US version released in January 2000 via Spitfire Records (Cat No: 5052-2).
Tracks: 'Dominion Day' (single version) 3.40/ 'Metal' (20th anniversary version) 4.07/ 'The Skin Game' (single edit) 4.09/ 'America' (single mix) 3.00/ 'Berserker' (single edit) 4.05/ 'Down In The Park' (20th anniversary version) 5.15/ 'Call Out The Dogs'** (single edit) 3.13/ 'New Anger' 3.20/ 'Absolution' (single version) 4.35/ 'My Dying Machine' (single edit) 3.22/ 'New Thing From London Town'* (single edit) 3.30/ 'Cars' (live '84 – single edit) 3.25/ 'A Question Of Faith' (single edit) 3.45/ 'Your Fascination' (single edit) 3.31/ 'Magic' (Trick mix) 4.08/ 'Voix' (20th anniversary version) 4.45/ 'I Can't Stop'** (single edit) 3.25/ 'I Still Remember'** (1986 re-recording) 4.00/ 'Tribal' 4.44.

All songs by Gary Numan except* – music by Bill Sharpe, lyrics by Roger Odell.
Produced by Gary Numan except** (Gary Numan and The Wave Team). In addition, 'New Thing From London Town' produced by Bill Sharpe and Nick Smith, 'Your Fascination' produced by Gary Numan and Colin Thurston.
Executive producer for this compilation – Steve Malins.
Special note: 'New Thing From London Town' re-mastered from an un-played vinyl copy of the single due to the master tapes for this track being unavailable.

To round off Eagle's campaign to re-issue the five Numa studio albums, a compilation emerged. Entitled *New Dreams For Old*, it consisted of virtually all Gary's Numa released singles as well as a number of other rarities and obscurities. For fans, it was a dream come true as for years most of these single edits and mixes had either been long out of print or in the case of 'New Thing From London Town', completely lost.

Although a veritable goldmine, the compilation wasn't perfect, with fans feeling space should have been allocated for the single mixes of 'Emotion', 'Machine + Soul' and 'This Is Love', all of which were at the time of this compilations arrival out of print. In addition, for some reason, the 1985 released 'Live EP' was here represented by the live version of 'Cars' instead of the lead track 'Are "Friends" Electric?', however, these were only minor gripes. With superb liner notes from Steve Malins and excellent packaging that consisted of many rare photographs, *New Dreams For Old* was an excellent post

Magazine advert 2000.

Beggars Banquet singles compilation easily eclipsing the dozens of shoddy Numa based collections that were appearing with alarming regularity at this time.

New Dreams For Old failed to chart.

COMPILATION ALBUM
Licensed: US

REMODULATE – THE NUMAN CHRONICLES 1984-1995
(**Cat No:** Cleopatra CLP0335-2)
Formats: CD and limited edition vinyl.
Released: August 1998.
Foreign formats: None.

★★★★☆

Disc 1 – THE NUMA YEARS.
Tracks: 'My Breathing' 6.39/ 'Your Fascination' 5.11 (extended version)/ 'A Question Of Faith' 4.52 (album version)/ 'The Secret' 6.40 (extended version)/ 'Call Out The Dogs' 4.42 (album version)/ 'Love And Napalm' 5.07 (album version)/ 'Cold Warning' 6.55 (extended version)/ 'Bleed' 6.12 (album version)/ 'Berserker' 4.00 (single edit)/ 'I Wonder' 4.28 (album version)/ 'New Thing From London Town' 7.57 (extended version)/ 'My Dying Machine' 7.38 (Italian 12-inch remix).

DISC 2 – THE LIVE CHRONICLES.
Tracks: 'Stormtrooper In Drag' 4.54/ 'The Dream Police' 4.37/ 'Every Day I Die' 4.28/ 'Listen To The Sirens' 3.01 – All tracks taken from the live album *Dark Light*. 'Metal' 3.17/ 'Down In The Park' 4.50/ 'Are "Friends" Electric?' 6.42/ 'I Die: You Die' 3.45/ 'We Are Glass' 4.39 – All tracks from the live album *Ghost*. 'The Iceman

Two US trade adverts from 1997.

Comes' 4.37/ 'Cars' 3.36/ 'Me! I Disconnect From You' 3.22 – All tracks from the live album *White Noise*. 'We Are So Fragile' 3.02/ 'Jo The Waiter' 6.33/ 'The Machmen' 3.43 – All tracks taken from the live album *Dream Corrosion*.

Released in the middle of the Cleopatra, Numa re-issue campaign, this compilation was set out in two parts. The first disc was a fairly run of the mill collection of studio tracks, however, both the 12-inch mix of 'New Thing From London Town' and the Italian remix of 'My Dying Machine' were completely new to CD. The second disc, took an intelligent and quirky look at the four live albums released through Numa by selecting a handful of tracks from each one.

RE-ISSUE CAMPAIGN
Licensed: UK

When Numan signed to Eagle Records, the label also picked up the option to re-issue Gary's Numa catalogue. In the US, Eagle licensed this catalogue to the dark wave/ gothic specialist label Cleopatra who, like Eagle, eventually re-issued the bulk of the albums released originally under Numa in new sleeves featuring a plethora of value for money bonus tracks.

GARY NUMAN – THE NUMA YEARS
(**Cat No:** UK EAGBX025)
Formats: five CD box set. (Limited edition).
Released: June 1998.

Book shaped box set comprising of five studio albums: *Berserker* (1984), *The Fury* (1985), *Strange Charm* (1986), *Machine + Soul* (1992) and *Sacrifice* (1994).

Each disc featured the original album in full with relevant B-sides added as bonus tracks.

Berserker featured five bonus tracks: 'Empty Bed, Empty Heart', 'Here Am I', 'She Cries', 'Rumour' (originally the B-side to the 1987 Radio Heart single 'London Times') and 'This Ship Comes Apart' (originally the B-side to the 1985 Gary Numan single 'Call Out The Dogs').

The Fury featured five bonus tracks: 'We Need It' (extended mix), 'Anthem,' 'No Shelter,' 'Puppets' (originally the B-side to the 1986 version of 'I Still Remember') and 'The Fear.'

Strange Charm featured five bonus tracks: 'Survival', 'Faces', 'Time To Die' (extended mix), 'River' and 'Mistasax (2).' The latter two tracks were originally B-sides to two Radio Heart singles ('Radio Heart' – US version and 'All Across The Nation').

Machine + Soul featured six bonus tracks: 'Hanoi', 'Dark Mountain', 'The Hauntings', this track actually comprises of two instrumentals ('Embryo' and 'We Fold Space') taken from the soundtrack to the movie *The Unborn.* '1999', 'Cry Baby' and 'Wonder Eye' (this disc omitted 1991 B-side 'In A Glasshouse').

Sacrifice featured four bonus tracks: 'Play Like God', 'Whisper Of Truth', 'Metal Beat' and 'Absolution' (single mix).

Each of the five discs came printed with the *Exile* logo.

Within the box set were several pages of sleeve notes that gave an insight into each album, with a wealth of historical photographs (including the original album sleeves).

The Numa Years box set was an excellent start to the Eagle re-issues campaign.

Eagle's UK re-issue campaign swung into action proper in February 1999 with the five albums that had featured on *The Numa Years* box set being issued separately. Although the CDs were identical to the box set versions, the packaging for each album was significantly different with additional sleeve notes and all but one having a new cover.

Extended versions of four of the five albums* were not included in this campaign. In addition, bar the album *Sacrifice*, no single mixes were included.

* *Strange Charm* was not issued as an extended album when it originally appeared in 1986.

BERSERKER
(**Cat No:** UK EAMCD072)
Formats: CD.
Released: February 1999.
Foreign formats: issued in the US via Cleopatra in a new cover May 1999.
UK cover artwork unchanged from the original.

Track list the same as the box set disc. One glaring omission, however, was the 12-inch Italian remix of 'My Dying Machine' (of which a further two separate edits exist) that had found its way onto the 1986 *Numa Records Year One* compilation and the US compilation *Remodulate: The Numan Chronicles 1984-1995*. Fans were also disappointed that the two original versions of 'This Is New Love' that were performed on TV prior to *Berserker* emerging (not to mention the Leo Sayer/ Gary Numan duet of 'On Broadway' that was also performed on TV) were not included. Another track fans would have liked to have seen was the appearance of the original Numan demos for 'My Dying Machine' (issued as a promo in 1986) and 'The Picture' (included as the B-side to the Caroline Munroe single 'Pump Me Up.'

THE FURY
(**Cat No:** UK EAMCD073)
Formats: CD.
Released: February 1999.
Foreign formats: issued in the US via Cleopatra in a new cover November 1998.
New UK cover commissioned.
Special note: all artwork included altered Numan's red

dickie-bow tie to white.

Track list the same as the box set version. Of the nine tracks on this version of *The Fury*, the original album version of 'Call Out The Dogs' was removed and bizarrely replaced with the 12-inch extended mix. Two tracks not included were the edited mix of 'We Need It' and the extended mix of 'The Fear.' New cover artwork was the fifth so far for this album. No other differences were detected.

STRANGE CHARM
(**Cat No:** UK EAMCD074)
Formats: CD.
Released: February 1999.
Foreign formats: issued in the US via Cleopatra in a new cover April 1999.
New UK cover artwork commissioned.

Track list same as the box set version. Tracks from the recording sessions for this album not included were: 'I Can't Stop' (extended and 10-inch mix), 'New Thing From London Town' (extended mix), 'Time To Die' (edit) and the extended mix of 'Puppets.' New cover artwork was the fifth so far for this album. No other differences were detected.

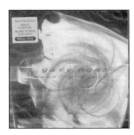

MACHINE + SOUL
(**Cat No:** UK EAMCD0750)
Formats: CD.
Released: February 1999.
Foreign formats: issued in the US via Cleopatra in a new cover May 1999, album also re-titled as *Machine And Soul*.

New UK cover artwork commissioned. Album remained titled in the UK as *Machine + Soul,* however, inner sleeve printed the album's title track as both 'Machine And Soul' and 'Machine & Soul.'

Track list same as the box set version. Tracks not included from the recording sessions for this album were: 'Emotion' (extended mix), 'The Skin Game' (the lycra mix), 'Machine + Soul' (mixes 1, 3 and 4 as well as promo mix 1 and 2). In addition, the six live tracks recorded in both the UK and Brussels on the 1991 'Emotion Tour' were also omitted. This album featured new artwork that originated from the 1988 *Metal Rhythm* sessions. This was the third cover artwork so far for this album (excluding the extended cover). No other differences were detected.

SACRIFICE
(**Cat No:** UK EAMCD076)
Formats: CD.
Released: February 1999.
Foreign formats: issued in the US via Transmit Discs in February 1997 as *Dawn* in a new cover (see 'Memorabilia'), re-issued August 1998 via Cleopatra in another new cover.

Cover artwork was altered from its black and white print to a grey tint. This was the fifth cover artwork for this album. (Excluding the extended cover).

Track list same as the box set version. Tracks not included from the recording sessions for this album were: 'A Question of Faith' (extended mix) and 'Magic (both the extended mix and trick mix). Aside from the cover artwork, no other differences were detected.

The next batch of re-issues from Eagle centred on the four live albums that had emerged via Numa namely: *White Noise*, *Ghost*, *Dream Corrosion* and *Dark Light*. All four live albums eventually emerged in the first half of 2003. All came housed in unifying cover artwork complete with sleeve notes by Dominic Jones. CD booklets included: tour dates, ticket stubs, programmes, relevant photos and most of the originally released artwork.

This campaign also added two new live recordings that had been taped during Gary's time spent under Eagle though these have been included in the 'From The Vaults' section. Originally a box set was to emerge in November 2002 entitled *Decadence Gary Numan Live 1984-2000* (Cat No: EAGBX241) containing all four live albums as well as a single live disc recorded in 2000, this idea though was scrapped. (Box set later emerged in 2004 re-designed to include all six live albums).

WHITE NOISE
(**Cat No:** UK EDMCD158)
Formats: 2CD.
Released: March 2003.
Foreign formats: issued in the US via Cleopatra in a new cover January 1998.
New UK cover artwork commissioned.

An excellent package, however, the sleeve notes did carry one or two factual errors from Dominic Jones. The claim that only four songs were performed from the *Berserker* album on the 'Berserker Tour' failed to take into account that a fifth, 'The Secret', was also performed. This track did not last long in the set and was dropped after the first date of the tour. In addition, 'Sister Surprise' was not the first single from the 1983 album *Warriors* and 'The Live EP' from 1985 in fact entered the charts at the No 40 position, not No 27 as stated in the booklet.

The original album artwork was reprinted within giving fans the option to choose which cover they wanted to front the CD. (The cover reprinted here was a scan of a signed copy).

GHOST
(**Cat No:** UK EDM159)
Formats: 2CD.
Released: March 2003.
Foreign formats: issued in the US via Cleopatra in a new cover September 1999.
New UK cover artwork commissioned.

Released simultaneously with *White Noise*, sleeve notes carried one factual error by stating that 'Cars, The E REG Model' released in 1987 entered the charts at No 26; the single had in fact entered the charts at No 35.

DREAM CORROSION
(**Cat No:** UK EDM160)
Formats: 2CD.
Released: April 2003.
Foreign formats: issued in 1995 through the US label Alex Records. Bizarrely overlooked by Cleopatra Records however during their US Numa reissue campaign of 1998/99.
New UK cover artwork commissioned.

Released simultaneously with the live album *Dark Light*, again like the re-issue of *White Noise*, the cover artwork printed within the CD booklet had been originally signed by Gary Numan.

DARK LIGHT
(**Cat No:** UK EDM161)
Formats: 2CD.
Released: April 2003.
Foreign formats: Issued in the US via Cleopatra in a new cover August 1998. Re-issued again in the US in February 2001 via Big Eye Records.
New UK cover artwork commissioned.
Back cover repeated the tour date error that had featured on the original 1995 issue.

Dark Light was recorded at the Hammersmith Apollo on the 5th of November 1994 as apposed to the stated date of the 12th (this date was in fact the final night of the 'Sacrifice Tour' with the venue being the London Astoria 2). In addition, the sleeve note incorrectly listed one of the songs performed ('Listen To The Sirens') as 'Please Listen To The Sirens' as well as highlighting tour incidents that in fact occurred on the previous year's 'Dream Corrosion Tour.' Some of the songs (most notably 'Stormtrooper In Drag') had been partially reworked in the studio due to the tour being beset with problems and glitches throughout.

Within each CD booklet was the offer of a free collectors case that was designed to hold the four re-issued albums as well as both the *Scarred* and *Live At Shepherds Bush* CDs.

RE-ISSUE CAMPAIGN
Licensed: US

CLEOPATRA RECORDS
Since leaving Beggars Banquet in the early 80s, little of Numan's independent works had surfaced in the states. Cleopatra Records were finally granted the task of issuing Gary's vast Numa Records catalogue in the United States (a move ironic in itself as Numan had earlier backed out of a deal with Cleopatra as he felt the label were a back catalogue specialists only). The label re-packaged and released all Gary's Numa albums (bar the extended UK versions) and added bonus material that differed greatly from the UK Eagle Records re-issues. As with Eagle, no single mixes were included.

WHITE NOISE
(**Cat No:** US CLP0303-2)
Formats: 2CD.
Released: January 1998.
Foreign formats: none.
Cover artwork altered to include a new typeset.
Liner notes by Dave Thompson.
Track list identical to the UK.

EXILE
(**Cat No:** US CLP0200-2)
Released: February 1998.
Foreign formats: none.
Cover artwork identical to the UK.

    Exile emerged in the US featuring an extra track ('Down In The Park' – live 1987, taken from the album *Ghost*) added to the album's running order. This addition though did not sit well with Gary who expressed his annoyance at the time of its release.

    One year later (March 1999) the extended version of *Exile* emerged in the US (Cat No: CLP0522-2): this though was identical to the UK version.

DARK LIGHT
(**Cat No:** US CLP0334-2)
Formats: 2CD.
Released: August 1998.
Foreign formats: none.
Re-issued in February 2001 via Big Eye Records.

    Aside from the newly commissioned cover artwork, this release was identical to the UK release of 1995. This live set had been previously issued in the US in July of 1995 (along with *Dream Corrosion)* via Alex Records.

SACRIFICE
(**Cat No:** US CLP0336-2)
Formats: CD.
Released: August 1998.
Foreign formats: none.
Re-issued in May 2001 via Big Eye Records, bizarrely, the cover artwork was altered yet again (see 'Memorabilia').

    This re-issue featured the *Sacrifice* album in full with four bonus tracks: 'A Question Of Faith' 8.43 (extended mix), 'Love And Napalm' 8.26 (extended mix), 'Metal Beat' 3.05 and 'Play Like God' 6.55. Unfortunately, 'Magic' (both Trick mix and the extended mix), 'Whisper Of Truth' and the single mix of 'Absolution' were omitted from this US release.

DOMINION DAY
(**Cat No:** US CLP0347-2)
Formats: CD.
Released: September 1998.
Foreign formats: none.

This release coupled together both CD singles that had been released in the UK making a convenient eight track mini-album for the US market. Later pressings (see right) dropped the 'Dominion Day' edit and also altered the artwork to state that the EP 'contains 7 exclusive tracks.'

THE FURY

(**Cat No:** US CLP0389-2)
Formats: CD.
Released: November 1998.
Foreign formats: none.
Cover artwork altered to include a new typeset.

This re-issue featured *The Fury* album in full with five bonus tracks: 'Call Out The Dogs' 6.42 (extended mix), 'I Still Remember' 5.20 (extended mix), 'Anthem' 3.23, 'Tribal' 5.57 (demo)* and 'The Fear' 6.14 (1995 remix).* This disc also re-instated the regular album version of 'Call Out The Dogs' (omitted from the UK Eagle re-issue). However, three B-sides from this era were not included ('We Need It' (7-inch and 12-inch), 'No Shelter' and 'This Ship Comes Apart') along with both extended mixes of 'Your Fascination' and 'Miracles.'

'Tribal' was a different, extended mix to the version that first appeared in the UK.
* 'The Fear' although marked as a 1995 remix was actually the regular 1985 mix, the extended mix of this track was not included.

STRANGE CHARM

(**Cat No:** US CLP0534-2)
Formats: CD.
Released: April 1999.
Foreign formats: none.
Cover artwork altered to include new typeset.

This re-issue featured the *Strange Charm* album in full with five bonus tracks: 'New Thing From London Town' 7.57 (extended mix), 'Time To Die' 4.19, 'I Can't Stop' 6.30 (original 10-inch DJ club mix), 'Faces' 4.54 and 'Survival' 5.12. Omitted from this issue were: 'Time To Die' (edit), 'Puppets' (edited and extended mixes) and 'I Can't Stop' (extended mix).

BERSERKER

(**Cat No:** US CLP0536-2)
Formats: CD.
Released: May 1999.
Foreign formats: none.
Cover artwork altered to include new typeset.

This re-issue featured the *Berserker* album in full with four bonus tracks: 'Berserker' 6.40 (extended mix),

'Empty Bed, Empty Heart', 'My Dying Machine' 9.04 (extended mix) and 'Here Am I.' Omitted, however, were: 'My Dying Machine' (Italian remix and demo), 'Here Am I' (German edit), B-side 'She Cries', 'This Is New Love' (original version), 'On Broadway' (Leo Sayer duet) and Gary's original demo of 'The Picture.'

MACHINE AND SOUL
(**Cat No:** US CLP0541-2)
Formats: CD.
Released: May 1999.
Foreign formats: none.
Cover artwork was a cropped and altered version of the UK Eagle Records version.

This re-issue featured the *Machine + Soul* album (re-titled here as *Machine And Soul*) with seven bonus tracks: 'Hanoi' 2.06, 'In A Glasshouse' 4.12, 'Wonder Eye' 4.02, 'Cry Baby' 4.17, 'The Hauntings' 4.10, '1999' 4.53 and 'Dark Mountain' 3.13. Omitted, however, were: 'Emotion' (extended mix), 'The Skin Game' (Lycra mix) and 'Machine + Soul (mixes 1, 3 and 4 as well as promo mix 1 and 2). In addition, like the UK Eagle re-issue, the six live tracks recorded in both the UK and Brussels on the 1991 'Emotion Tour' were also not included.

GHOST
(**Cat No:** US CLP0680-2)
Formats: 2CD.
Released: September 1999.
Foreign formats: none.
Cover artwork altered to include new typeset.

Aside from the new cover, this album was identical to the original 1988 UK issue. *Ghost* was the final Numan licensed product to be handled by Cleopatra Records with Spitfire Records stepping into the role for the US release of *New Dreams For Old* and *Pure*.

FROM THE VAULTS

Following Numan's departure from the label, aside from continuing to re-issue Gary's Numa catalogue, Eagle also dug into their archives and issued two live albums (one in 2003 and one a year later). Both these albums were part of a six album live box set that included *White Noise*, *Ghost*, *Dream Corrosion* and *Dark Light*. All four of these albums were also re-issued in early 2003.

SCARRED
(**Cat No:** UK EDGCD242)
Formats: 2CD.
Released: January 2003.*
Foreign formats: issued in the US via Eagle featuring a bonus section that included live videos for 'Rip', 'Cars' and 'Pure' (the latter track was an official live promo video). All live clips were taken from the Brixton Academy

October 2000.

Special note: CD booklet unfolded to reveal a nine-picture poster, all photographs taken from the Brixton show. In addition, a peel off sticker was added to the front of the album that stated the recording was from the 'Pure Tour.'

* *Scarred* was due to be released at the end of 2002, however, this did not occur due to Gary's former label Beggars Banquet re-issuing both *I, Assassin* and *Warriors* on CD thus completing their Numan studio albums campaign. The original cover for *Scarred* was scrapped in the run up to its eventual release; this can now be found in the memorabilia section for 'The Eagle Records Years.'

Musicians: Gary Numan – Vocals and guitar/ Ade Orange – keyboards and bass/ David Brooks – Keyboards/ Steve Harris – Guitar/ Richard Beasley – Drums. Engineered, mixed and produced by Gary Numan.

CD 1, – Tracks: 'Intro' 2.27/ 'Pure' 4.13/ 'Me! I Disconnect From You' 3.00/ 'The Angel Wars' 5.04/ 'My Jesus' 5.43/ 'Films' 3.36/ 'Magic' 4.57/ 'Rip' 5.05/ 'Cars' 3.17/ 'Metal' 4.05/ 'Little Invitro' 4.25/ 'Down In The Park' 5.13.

CD 2, – Tracks: 'This Wreckage' 5.37/ 'Dead Heaven' 5.22/ 'I Can't Breathe' 5.42/ 'Are "Friends" Electric?' 5.56/ 'A Prayer For The Unborn' 5.42/ 'Listen To My Voice' 5.22/ 'Replicas' 5.02/ 'Observer' 2.34/ 'Dance' 2.04/ 'Tracks' 3.10.

Singles: none.

Videos: two clips from the Brixton Academy surfaced (see US version of this album). Although the concert was professionally filmed, it has yet to be released officially.

This album also featured superb sleeve notes from Fear Factory front man Burton C Bell.

Although this record was issued long after Gary's defection from the Eagle stable, *Scarred* – a recording taped mere weeks after the launch of the masterful *Pure* opus – was Numan's first official live outing since 1995's double release *Dark Light*. However, where that record documented Numan at the very beginning of his long climb back from the musical wilderness, *Scarred* saw Numan on the very brink of a heroic mainstream return.

Like *Pure*, *Scarred* was a thunderous, aggressive and shuddering musical statement with each song replete with pounding drums, menacing bass and filthy distorted guitars. Of the 21 tracks aired, a good portion (seven in all) had been lifted from Gary's latest (and for once) critically lauded new studio album with the juggernaut pace of tracks like 'Listen To My Voice', 'My Jesus' and the album's title track slipping effortlessly into a live set already packed with an arsenal of re-grooved and re-worked Numan classics, the best of which came in the shape of the edgy update of 'Replicas', the exciting and breathless take of 'Me! I Disconnect From You' and the spirited renditions of both 'Are "Friends" Electric?' and 'Cars.' However, the set was not an all out attack with two of the tracks included (both from *Pure)* being a brace of heartfelt and touching ballads. The first, the fraught and delicate 'Little Invitro' did a fine job of bringing a lump to the throats of the assembled crowd, the second – 'A Prayer For The Unborn' – was simply stunning, a song good enough to rank amongst the very best of Numan's outstanding recorded legacy.

Although this album failed to chart when released, *Scarred* captured Numan at a pivotal and important turning point in his career.

★★★★★

LIVE AT SHEPHERDS BUSH EMPIRE
(**Cat No:** UK EDGCD162)
Formats: CD.
Released: April 2004.
Foreign formats: issued in the US in a new cover and re-titled 'Live In London.'
Recorded live on the 9th of November 1997 at Shepherds Bush Empire in London.
Musicians: Gary Numan – Vocals and guitar/ Steve Harris – Guitar/ Richard Beasley – Drums/ David Brooks – Keyboards/ Ade Orange – Keyboards and bass.

CD 1, Tracks: 'Intro'/ 'Down In The Park'/ 'Dominion Day'*/ 'Friends'/ 'Films'/ 'A Question Of Faith'/ 'Voix'/ 'Every Day I Die'/ 'Dark'/ 'You Walk In My Soul.'
CD2, Tracks: 'Noise Noise'/ 'An Alien Cure'/ 'Cars'*/ 'Absolution'/ 'Dead Heaven'/ 'Metal'/ 'Bleed'/ 'Are "Friends" Electric?'/ Band introductions – 'We Are So Fragile'/ 'Jo The Waiter.'
Special note: including *Scarred,* the CD spines of this album as well as the four live albums re-issued by Eagle in the UK in 2003 all featured the Exile logo.
* Edited versions previously released on the 1998 'Dominion Day' single.
Engineered, mixed and produced by Gary Numan.

After missing a number of release dates, *Live At Shepherds Bush Empire* finally appeared (over a year later than originally scheduled) in the early spring of 2004 as an expansive 2CD set (previous information surrounding the album stated that it was to be issued as a highlights only single disc). Like the earlier Eagle re-issued live albums sleeve notes came courtesy of Dominic Jones who once again provided some excellent and informative liner notes. However, Dominic did make a number of minor errors. The claim that *Exile* spent two weeks on the top 75 was incorrect, the album in fact only charted for one. In addition, Dominic stated that the single 'Absolution' was issued to promote the extended version of the album *Sacrifice,* this was also incorrect. Although both the album and single were released in early 1995, neither was issued together with *Sacrifice* emerging in January and 'Absolution' emerging two months later in March.

This release, the final instalment of Eagle's Gary Numan live albums extravaganza was a superb atmospheric souvenir from 'The Exile Tour' featuring stunning renditions of songs from Gary's halcyon early days as well as including the best material from both his return to form 90s albums *Exile* and *Sacrifice.*

Live At Shepherds Bush Empire failed to chart.

MEMORABILIA

The following pages are dedicated to some of the merchandise that emerged during Numan's days signed to Eagle Records.

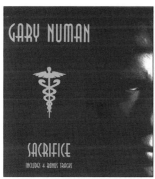

Slightly different cover for
Sacrifice. *This version released by*
Big Eye Records in February 2001
(Cat No: 4135).

US only promo issue of Pure.

Sacrifice *emerged in the US as*
Numan Dawn *in February 1997.*
New artwork came from Joseph
Michael Linsner, illustrator for the
US comic book Crypt Of Dawn
CD booklet comprised of 12 pages
of artwork and lyrics.

Drive *magazine 1998.*   Magic Feet *magazine 1998.*

Extended version of Exile *(Cat No:*
EAGCD067), issued in the UK,
Nov 98.

Magazine advert for the Pure *album.*

Pure the tour edition issued in the UK (Cat No: EDGTE-078) February 2001, this re-issue included the full *Pure* album alongside a bonus disc of live material and exclusive remixes. This release also included a screen saver and a poster. All the tour editions were individually numbered.

CD2, Tracks: 'Pure' 6.42/ 'My Jesus' 5.53/ 'Rip' 5.08/ 'Cars' 3.23/ 'Replicas' 5.13. All five tracks recorded live at the Brixton Academy October 20th 2000. 'A Prayer For The Unborn' 8.35 (Grayed up mix)*/ 'Listen To My Voice' 7.59 (Grayed up mix), both remixes by Andy Gray.

* An edited version of this track was scheduled for release as a single in 2001, however, Eagle bizarrely backed out of the idea as the year progressed (much to Numan's annoyance) with the finished edited mix finally appearing as a B-side to the Artful/ Jagged Halo single 'Rip.'

Original cover for the live record Scarred.

Back page poster of the Crypt Of Dawn comic

Crypt of Dawn *issue 4. Published by Sirius comics in 1998. This issue featured a colour centrefold story written by "The Dark One" based on the* Exile *track "Dark."*

Another US variation of the Pure *album.*

In store poster for the Crypt Of Dawn *and* Numan Dawn *Projects.*

Two track Eagle promo.

US only three track single drawn from the Numan Dawn *album featuring: 1. "Magic" 4.42. 2. "You Walk In My Soul" 4.39. 3. "Play Like God" 6.55. Released January 1997 Transmit Discs (Transmit 01). An additional promo single of "A Question Of Faith" also emerged.*

SECTION ONE

PART EIGHT

THE ARTFUL RECORDS YEARS

Within weeks of Numan's departure from Eagle Records, he was quickly courted by the Universal spin off label Artful Records and eventually signed with them at the tail end of 2001. In addition to signing this new deal, Gary also started a brand new label entitled Jagged Halo Records. This label would be the vehicle used to issue all Numan's new music, though unlike Numa, Jagged Halo would have the backing and support of a major record company behind it. Surprisingly, the first task of Jagged Halo/ Artful Records was to release a retrospective compilation album that although only picked up modest sales, neatly laid the foundations for Gary's much anticipated return to the mainstream. In the early summer, Artful managed to do with ease what many long time Numan fans thought they would never see again, Gary Numan back in the British top 40 with a new song. By harnessing Numan's loyal fan base and using the latest marketing strategies (limited edition singles, hip associations through guest appearances and celebrity remixes) Numan suddenly found himself not only rubbing shoulders with the likes of Kylie Minogue and Linkin Park but more importantly, back on *Top Of The Pops*.

To arrive at this point had been a long, hard road both for Gary and his dedicated fan base but with, at last, the media in full support, and a newly appreciative, younger audience on board it seemed the world's most unconventional pop star had finally come full circle. Sadly, in scenes that echoed Gary's time spent with both IRS and Eagle, relations between Artful and Numan soured in 2004 with Gary opting to vacate the label in favour of going it, once again, alone.

ORIGINAL SINGLES
2002-2003

RIP
1. 'Rip' 5.02 (album version). 2. 'A Prayer For The Unborn' 3.47 (Andy Gray edit). 3. 'M.E.' (new version) 4.36. 4. 'Rip' (video).*
(**Cat No:** UK JHCDS1)
Formats: CD only.
1. 'Rip' 5.02 (album version). 2. 'This Wreckage' 4.48 (Metalmorphosis mix). 3. 'Are "Friends" Electric?' 5.16 (Metalmorphosis mix).
(**Cat No:** UK JHCDSX1)
Formats: CD only.
Released: July 2002.
Foreign formats: matched the UK.
* Many fans complained that they had trouble opening the video included with CD 1 (most notably owners of older computers like Windows 95 and 98).
Promo video shot.

'Rip' was Numan's first single in four years. Although the track itself originally appeared two years back on the *Pure* album, here it had been lifted from the Artful compilation *Exposure, The Best Of Gary Numan 1977-2002*. However, this single would perhaps never have appeared had an unexpected chain of events not occurred at the time *Exposure* emerged. Numan's fortunes were given a sudden boost when 'Rip,' having been previously rejected and ignored by all the other music video channels, found itself championed by the new satellite rock channel *Kerrang TV.* Within days the clip had become the most requested video on the station (as well as the channel's most popular ringtone) ultimately spending two weeks at the No 1 spot and over a month inside the top 10 (the song later enjoyed a second run a year later when *Kerrang TV* added the video to their 'Legends' week). A second boost arrived in the shape of UK all girl pop act, the Sugababes, who shot to No 1 in the national UK singles chart with a heavily sampled 'Are "Friends" Electric?' interwoven into the track 'Freak Like Me'. In a bizarre month, Numan found himself at No1 with two completely different songs from two completely different eras of his career. Artful though, quickly scheduled 'Rip' for release as a single, limiting each of the two formats to 5000 copies only. In addition, the exclusive B-sides attached (with the exception of 'A Prayer For The Unborn') all pertained directly to the recent Numan sampled singles that had hit the charts (both 'M.E' and 'This Wreckage' had been sampled on to the UK dance act Basement Jaxx single 'Where's Your Head At?' and 'Are "Friends" Electric?' being sampled for the Sugababes recent hit). Finally, in the week the single emerged, Gary undertook a gruelling spate of in-store signing sessions. All this good luck and effort finally paid off when 'Rip' crashed into the UK singles chart returning Numan to the British top 40 for the first time (1996 re-issue of 'Cars' excepted) since 'No More Lies,' the third Sharpe and Numan single that hit the No 34 position in January 1988.

'Rip' entered the charts at a peak position of No 29 spending two weeks on the top 75 singles chart.

CRAZIER
1. 'Crazier' 3.19 (Steve Osborne mix). 2. 'Listen To My Voice' 5.16 (Rico's Hybrid mix). 3. 'Ancients' 7.08 (Grayed out seriously alternative mix). 4. 'Crazier' (video). (**Cat No:** UK JHCDV6)
Formats: CD.
This CD single was released as CD1 ('The Ride').

1. 'Crazier' 4.46 (Rico alternative slide mix). 2. 'Big Black Sea' 5.28. 3. 'Garden Man' 3.59. 4. 'Crazier' (*Arte TV*, live footage May 6th restricted to 2 minutes only by UK chart rules).
(**Cat No:** UK JHCDX6)
Formats: CD.
This single was released as CD2. ('The Slide').

1. 'Crazier' 3.24 (acoustic glide mix). 2. 'Ancients' 6.22 (demo version). 3. 'A Prayer For The Unborn' 5.26 (*Arte TV*, live mix). 4. 'A Prayer For The Unborn' (*Arte TV*, live footage May 6th).
(**Cat No:** UK JHCDS6)
Formats: CD.
Released: June 2003.
Foreign formats: matched the UK.
This single was released as CD3. ('The Glide').*
All three formats were limited to 3000 copies only.

Credited to 'Gary Numan Vs Rico.'
* This CD was to originally feature the previously unreleased Loni Gordon remix of
'Dominion Day.' This though was pulled shortly after for unspecified reasons and
replaced with the two spectacular live versions of 'A Prayer For The Unborn.'
Promo video shot.

After something of a lengthy and frustrating delay (this single was originally
scheduled for release much earlier in the year), June finally saw the release of
'Crazier' as the first single to be lifted from the remix album *Hybrid*. The song
had been superbly remixed for single release by Steve Osborne who turned the
Hybrid recorded grungey, 'Nu-metal' stomper into a pop-encrusted dance floor
anthem. *Kerrang TV* immediately play-listed the video for the track and within a
week it was the second most requested video (behind the mighty Metallica) on
the station. The following week it was No1, staying there for a full three weeks.
In addition, 'Crazier' was also voted the second most popular ring tone. Once
again this vital exposure and careful marketing (the single was issued over three
formats, all featuring exclusive B-sides) enabled the song to crash into the
British top 15 within a week of its release giving Numan his biggest hit single in
21 years.

'Crazier' entered and peaked at No 13 spending three weeks on the top 75.

COMPILATION ALBUMS
Licensed

EXPOSURE – THE BEST OF GARY NUMAN 1977 – 2002
(**Cat No:** UK JHCD002)
Formats: CD.
Released: May 2002.
Foreign formats: matched the UK.
Special note: five track promo issued featuring: 'Are
"Friends" Electric?', 'Cars', 'Rip', 'My Jesus' and 'I Die:
You Die.'
Singles: 'Rip'. In addition, two-track CD promo issued
featuring 'A Prayer for The Unborn' and 'Rip' (**Cat No:**
JHCDS1).

Videos: 'Rip'. In addition, 'Rip' was performed on *Top Of The Pops 2* alongside a
suitably revamped 'Are "Friends" Electric?'
CD1 Tracks: 'Films' 4.09/ 'I Die: You Die' 3.43/ 'Are "Friends" Electric?' 5.22/
'Pure'* 5.09/ 'Dead Heaven' 5.21/ 'Down In The Park' 4.24/ 'Me! I Disconnect
From You' 3.22/ 'Metal' 3.29/ 'She's Got Claws' 4.56/ 'Magic' 4.44/ 'We Are Glass'
4.46/ 'Music For Chameleons' 6.57 (extended version, previously unreleased on
CD)/ 'My Shadow In Vain' 3.19 (newly recorded version)/ 'Every Day I Die' 4.20
(newly recorded version).
CD2 Tracks: 'My Jesus'* 5.44/ 'Cars' 3.57/ 'Dominion Day' 4.49/ 'Complex' 3.11/
'We Are So Fragile' 2.53/ 'Rip'* 5.04/ 'M.E.' 5.36/ 'We Take Mystery (To Bed)'
3.40/ 'Dark' 4.30/ 'Remember I Was Vapour' 5.10 (Original 1980 version)/ 'Listen
To My Voice'* 5.11/ 'Deadliner' 4.30/ 'Exposure' 2.46 (Instrumental, previously
unreleased)**/ 'Voix' 4.44 (20th anniversary version)/ 'A Prayer For The Unborn'
8.33 (Grayed up remix).

15 tracks licensed from Beggars Banquet, 11 tracks licensed from Eagle and 3 tracks licensed from Jagged Halo/ Artful Records.
All songs by Gary Numan.
All songs produced by Gary Numan except * Additional production by Sulpher.
** This track originally surfaced as the intro instrumental on the 1997 UK 'Exile Tour.'
Executive producer Steve Malins.

Rare five track promo along with a two-track promo single.

Signing to Artful Records finally afforded the opportunity to assemble a broader and much more comprehensive compilation of Gary's 25 year recording career. *Exposure* included a flurry of tracks from Numan's last three studio albums as well as reaching as far back as 1979 (although the album mistakenly gives the impression that tracks were culled from as far back as 1977). Long time fans though were less keen to see yet another compilation hit the shops especially as they already owned most of the material included anyway. Instead, fans concentrated on the four sweeteners that had been included with the package. For this release, Gary had gone back to the original 1978 *Tubeway Army* album and recorded new versions of both 'Every Day I Die' and 'My Shadow In Vain' for inclusion on the compilation. Neither though merited much interest although fans felt that the new version of 'My Shadow In Vain' was clearly the better of the two. Beggars Banquet also weighed in with the long lost 12-inch mix of 'Music For Chameleons,' appearing here on CD for the first time. Lastly, one new track was also included; an eerie instrumental entitled 'Exposure' that ultimately went on to provide the backbone for the new version of 'M.E.' (see 'Rip' single).

With stunning artwork and superb sleeve notes from Steve Malins, the album achieved its aim of presenting a fresh spin on the recorded works of Gary Numan.

Exposure, The Best Of Gary Numan 1977-2002 entered and peaked at No 44 spending 1 week on the top 75.

French in-store poster.

RESONATOR (PIONEER OF SOUND)
(**Cat No:** Pychobaby/ Fulfill PBZ008)
Formats: CD.
Released: March 2004.
Foreign formats: issued in the US and Japan in April 2004.
Limited UK availability.
Special note: initial copies featured a peel-off sticker that drew attention to the fact that this compilation included Numan's 2003 top 20 UK hit 'Crazier.'
Tracks: 'Exposure'*/ 'Crazier' (Rico slide mix)**/ 'Big Black Sea'**/ 'Ancients'***/ 'Me! I Disconnect From You'***/ 'Cars'***/ 'Down In The Park'***/ 'Are "Friends" Electric?' (Grayed out electronic mix-previously unreleased)/ 'Every Day I Die'*/ All I Know' (previously unreleased on CD)****/ Crazier' (Steve Osborne mix)**/ 'Ancients' (Grayed out mix).**

* Taken from the double compilation album *Exposure*.
** Taken from the single 'Crazier.'
*** Taken from the double remix album *Hybrid*.
**** Taken from the DVD *Mutate*.

Although a somewhat disjointed assemblage of Numan's Artful era recordings this compilation CD did however manage to deliver two sweeteners for hard core fans in the guise of the previously unreleased 'electronic mix' of 'Are "Friends" Electric?' and the alternative rock mix of 'Ancients' (re-titled 'All I Know') that was included on the 2003 *Mutate* DVD. This CD was later withdrawn on Numan's request who explained online through the NuWorld website that he considered the track list to be very poor featuring none of the songs he expected to see on it.

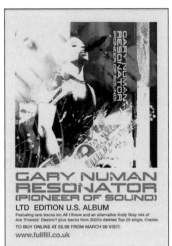

Magazine advert.

SECTION ONE

PART NINE

MISCELLANEOUS RELEASES

MISCELLANEOUS RELEASES
(I) SOUNDTRACK ALBUMS

Fans may be interested to learn that the soundtrack to the early 90s horror movie *The Unborn* (*Human* CD, released in 1995) was not Gary's first appearance on a movie soundtrack, here are a few others that are also worthy of note.

TIMES SQUARE
(**Cat No:** UK RSO2658145)
Formats; vinyl and cassette.
Released: 1980.
Foreign formats: matched the UK.
　　Movie starred Trini Alverado and Robin Johnson as two teenage runaways attempting to break into the music industry.
　　Soundtrack was *New Wave* themed and featured an early demo of 'Down In The Park.' The song was credited to Gary Numan alone and not Tubeway Army.

RIDING HIGH
(**Cat No:** UK JAMBO JAM2)
Formats: vinyl and cassette.
Released: 1981.
Foreign formats: none.
　　Made for TV movie that starred Eddie Kidd.
　　Soundtrack that featured an early 3 minutes and 46 seconds take of 'Remember I Was Vapour,' this album is now extremely rare.

URGH! A MUSIC WAR
(**Cat No:** UK A&M AMLX64692)
Formats: double tape and vinyl, also issued on CD years later missing a few tracks (video also released).
Released: October 1981.
Foreign formats: matched the UK.
　　This movie was just one long multi-artist concert featuring a string of *New Wave* era bands like The Police and the Dead Kennedy's. Also included was the *Living Ornaments '80* rendition of 'Down In The Park.'

SPEED
(**Cat No:** UK FOX11018)
Formats: vinyl, cassette and CD.
Released: June 1994.
Foreign formats: matched the UK.
　　Movie starred Keanu Reeves, Dennis Hopper and Sandra Bullock desperately trying to prevent a rigged bus from exploding should its speed drop below 50 mph. The film was loosely based on the Japanese thriller *Bullet Train*. Soundtrack featured the 1993 Sprint remix of "Cars." Album also available as the original film score.

DARK CITY
(**Cat No:** TVT Records TVT8160-2)
Formats: CD.
Released: 1998.

Ambitious, yet relatively odd, Sci-fi thriller starring Rufus Sewell and Kiefer Sutherland. Plot concerned alien experiments on human memory.

Included the superb *Exile* track 'Dark', a song that had previously been used on the trailers for a few other Hollywood movies during 1998 (*Romeo Must Die, The Astronauts Wife*) but eventually found a home with this film.

(II) REMIX PROJECTS
RAZORMAID

Razormaid comprised of a number of independent DJ's that, aside from providing danceable remixes for artists like New Order and Depeche Mode, also remixed a number of Numan tracks. The first Numan related remix they undertook was a US only 12-inch mix of 'Change Your Mind' (Cat No: PolyGram promo 88306-1, see Sharpe and Numan). More 12-inch remixes followed, those being: 'My Dying Machine' 12-inch US DJ promo mix 6.50 released on red vinyl 1989 (Cat No: RM005), 'This Disease' 12-inch US DJ promo mix 6.36 released 1989 (Cat No: RM0012), 'No More Lies' 12-inch US DJ promo mix 6.30, no picture sleeve, released on yellow vinyl 1989 (Cat No: RMD19), 'Cars' (Class X mix) CD US DJ mix 6.10, no picture sleeve, released in 1989 (Cat No: CX03) and finally 'I'm On Automatic' 12-inch US promo mix 6.50, no picture sleeve, released 1989 (Cat No: RMZ3).

Razormaid also issued two remix compilation CDs, the first was entitled *Prehistoric Razormaid* (see right) and featured another two Numan remixes namely: 'This Disease' 6.46 (90s mix) and 'Change Your Mind' 7.41 (90s mix). This 2CD affair included many of the DJ mixes from over the years and was released in 1990 (**Cat No:** RMCD11).

The second compilation, however, was entirely devoted to the world of Gary Numan.

HEIGHTENED ANXIETY
(**Cat No:** unknown)
Formats: CD.
Released: November 1999.
Foreign formats: none.
Tracks: 'This Disease' 6.50 (1990 remix)/ 'I'm On Automatic' 6 50 (1989 mix)/ 'I Can't Stop' 6.16 (previously unreleased)/ 'No More Lies' 6.30 (1989 mix)/ 'Change Your Mind' 7.30 (Chapter 7 mix, 1985 remix re-titled)/ 'My Dying Machine' 6.12 (edit) – previously unreleased/ 'Cars' 6.10 (Class X mix)/ 'Harlequin Tears' 7.14 (this track by the group, Harlequin)/ 'This Disease' 4.14 (this was a previously unreleased dub mix featuring only Tessa Niles/ 'Change Your Mind' 7.45 (CD mix) – previously unreleased/ 'Harlequin Tears' 6.53 (R1 mix),

final track by the group, Harlequin.

Released to perhaps cash in on the late 90s resurgence of interest in Numan, this compilation is now quite rare.

The following are some of the other remix projects that emerged in the last few years.

TECHNOARMY Featuring Gary Numan
(**Cat No:** UK Castle Communications WENCD006)
Formats: CD.
Released: April 1996.
Foreign formats: none.
Special note: this album was preceded by a 12-inch vinyl single featuring remixes of 'Cars' (**Cat No:** WENT 1010).
Tracks: 'Are "Friends" Electric?' 5.39/ 'Cars' 4.14/ 'We Are So Fragile' 4.20/ 'We Are Glass' 5.33/ 'She's Got Claws' 4.11/ 'I Die: You Die' 4.26/ 'Deadliner' 4.09/ 'Machine And Soul' 4.20/ 'Emotion' 5.12/ 'A Question Of

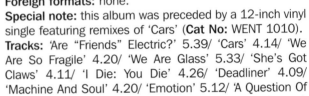

Faith' 4.09/ 'U Got The Look' 4.17/ 'Cars' 4.17 (Rush hour skadiva) This track features the original 1979 vocal./ 'Cars' 5.39 (Talla 2xlc remix). Final two tracks issued as a 12-inch single.

European styled dance versions of a selection of re-sung Numan tracks, best of which were two superb new mixes of 'Cars' as well as a further two dance orientated reinterpretations of 'Emotion' and 'A Question Of Faith.' Most of the material on this album was later remixed again for inclusion on the Cleopatra Records *The Mix* album.

NUMANIA VOL 1
(**Cat No:** UK Flag recordings FLAGCD001)
Formats: 12-inch and CD.
Released: 1997.
Foreign formats: none.
This release was credited to 'The Borg.'
Tracks: 'Are "Friends" Electric?' 6.50/ 'Replicas' 6.01/ 'We Are So Fragile' 3.57.

Not much is known about The Borg or this three-track promo that emerged, but the remixes, however, were rather good although nothing has been heard from this project since.

CARS (THE WITCHMAN REMIXES)
(**Cat No:** UK Beggars Banquet CARS001)
Formats: 2x 12 inch vinyl.*
Released: March 1996.
Foreign formats: none.
* Released in green vinyl (500 copies pressed) and orange vinyl (1000 copies pressed).
Tracks: 'Cars' 6.24 (Astral body mix)/ 'Cars' 8.52 (Witchman's freebase assault mix).

Released at the same time as the 'Premier Hits' mix of

'Cars', this 12-inch DJ only promo went on to be something of an underground club hit eventually sparking the idea for a full album of 'clubby' style dance remixes.

CARS
(**Cat No:** UK Beggars Banquet GNNYC1)
Formats: CD.
Released: 1997.
Foreign formats: none.
Tracks: 'Cars' 3.55 (original 1979 single version)/ 'Cars' 5.12 (Dave Clarke 1997 remix)/ 'Cars' 3.50 (Native soul 1993 remix)/ Cars 6.27 (Astral body 1996 extension mix*).
* Same as the previous 'Astral body' mix).

This promo CD single was released prior to the *Random 2* project and featured a number of the various remixes of 'Cars' floating around at the end of the 90s.

RADIO
(**Cat No:** UK The Record Company SPIN006)
Formats: CD (two different covers).
Released: 1997.
Foreign formats: none.
Promo video shot (sadly this video was never released).
Tracks: 'Radio' 3.40 (radio mix)/ 'Radio' 4.53 (extended mix)/ 'Radio' 3.53 (Heart mix).

This ultra rare promo CD was remixed by 'NRG Inc.' The three tracks were basically superb dance mixes of the 1987 song 'Radio Heart.' These mixes are still available to buy direct from The Record Label website.

RANDOM (02)
(**Cat No:** UK Beggars Banquet BBQLP197)
Formats: 4x 12-inch albums.
Released: October 1997.
Foreign formats: none.

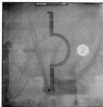

These four, 12-inch releases featured various Numan tracks drastically remixed for the underground club scene and they were all issued separately as follows: *Random 2.1* (red vinyl featuring 'Metal' and 'Dans Le Park'), released October

1997, *Random 2.2* (green vinyl featuring 'I Die: You Die' and two versions of 'Cars'), released November 1997, *Random 2.3* (blue vinyl featuring 'Warriors', 'Are "Friends" Electric?' and 'Remember I Was Vapour'), released January 1998 and finally *Random 2.4* (clear vinyl featuring 'We Are Glass', 'Films' and 'The Iceman Comes'), released February 1998.

One month later the entire project was issued as a single compilation CD (see below).

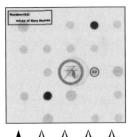

RANDOM (02)
(**Cat No:** UK Beggars Banquet BBQCD197)
Formats: CD.
Released: March 1998.
Foreign formats: matched the UK.
Tracks: 'Metal' 5.59 – Robert Armani/ 'Dans Le Park' 7.36 – DJ Hell/ 'I Die: You Die' 7.35 – Greenhaus/ 'Cars' 6.16 – Mike Dearborn/ 'Cars' 5.12 – Dave Clarke/ 'Warriors' 5.18 – Dave Angel/ 'Are "Friends" Electric?' 6.48 – Liberator D.J.'s/ 'Remember I Was Vapour' 6.06 – Steve Stroll/ 'We Are Glass' (Broken glass mix) 6.19 – Claude Young/ 'Films' 5.26 – Alex Hazzard/ 'The Iceman Comes' – Peter Lazonby.

★☆☆☆☆

Fans listening to all the remixes commissioned as a whole quickly saw the folly of this project. Hardcore dance remixes from hardcore dance DJ's these may have been, but the simple fact was that a full album of 'Bangin choons' would drive any relatively normal person pretty much close to insanity. In short, *Random 2*, aside from the just about bearable remixes of 'I Die: You Die' and 'The Iceman Comes,' had very little to recommend about itself.

THE MIX
(**Cat No:** US Cleopatra CLP 0192-2)
Formats: CD.
Released: April 1998.
Foreign formats: US Import only.
Sleeve notes by Dave Thompson.
Tracks: 'Are "Friends" Electric?' 4.58 (Leather strap mix)/ 'Cars' 4.51 (Spahn Ranch mix)/ 'We Are So Fragile' 4.35 (Death ride 69 mix)/ 'We Are Glass' 4.50 (Transmutator mix)/ 'A Question Of Faith' 5.00 (Anubian lights mix)/ 'I Die: You Die' 3.52 (Information society mix)/ 'Cars' 4.53

★★☆☆☆

(Talla 2xlc mix)/ 'We Are Glass' 5.01 (Astralasia mix)/ 'Deadliner' 4.09 (Spaceship eyes mix)/ 'Cars' 4.00 (JLAB mix)/ 'Emotion' 4.58 (Kill...klick mix)/ 'She's Got Claws' 4.42 (Biokraft mix)/ 'Are "Friends" Electric?' 4.43 (Ikon mix)/ 'We Are So Fragile' 4.58 (LCD mix).

Appearing at roughly the same time as the UK *Random 2* project, this US only release was one of the first albums that Cleopatra issued in the states as they began their re-issue campaign of Numan's Numa catalogue. This album was basically a remixed version of the *Techno Army* project and although it was better than *Random 2* featuring dance mixes that people could at least dance to, it was still a very flawed project of very little merit.

★★★★☆

HYBRID

(**Cat No:** UK Artful/ Jagged Halo JHCD005)
Formats: 2CD and 16-track double vinyl album.
Released: February 2003.
Foreign formats: US version issued in a slightly different cover.
Re-issued in the UK August 2003 featuring an additional DVD entitled *Mutate*, this release was limited to 3000 copies only. Re-issued in Sept 2004 on Ltd edition vinyl.
CD1, Tracks: 'Hybrid' (Sulpher)/ 'Dark' (Andy Gray)/ 'Crazier'* (new song, previously unreleased)/ 'Bleed' (Sulpher)/ 'Torn' (Sulpher)/ 'Down In The Park' (Curve)/ 'Every Day I Die' (Andy Gray)/ 'Absolution' (Andy Gray)/ 'Cars' (Flood).
CD2, Tracks: 'Ancients'** (new song, previously unreleased)/ 'Dominion Day' (Sulpher)/ 'A Prayer For The Unborn' (Andy Gray edit)/ 'Me! I Disconnect From You' (Andy Moulder)/ 'Listen To My Voice' (Rico)/ 'Rip' (Andy Gray)/ 'This Wreckage' (New Disease)/ 'Are "Friends" Electric?' (Andy Gray)/ 'M.E.' (Gary Numan)/ 'Down In The Park' (Sulpher).

Special note: bonus DVD *Mutate* issued with the re-promoted edition of *Hybrid* featured nine audio-only tracks along with six promotional videos. Tracks included were: 'Crazier' (Steve Osborne single mix)/ 'All I Know' ('Ancients' alternative version – previously unreleased)/ 'Rip' (single version)/ 'Cars' (Fear Factory version featuring Gary Numan – not included on the US *Mutate*. / 'Are "Friends" Electric?' (Metalmorphosis mix)/ 'Dominion Day' (single mix)/ 'Crazier' (*Arte TV* live version)/ 'A Prayer For The Unborn' (*Arte TV* live version)/ 'Ancients' (Grayed out mix***). All these tracks were listed as part of the 'Sound' portion of the DVD.

Tracks listed as part of the 'Vision' portion of the DVD were: 'Crazier'/ 'Rip'/ 'Cars' (Fear Factory featuring Gary Numan) – not included on the US *Mutate*. / 'Dominion Day' – all promotional videos. 'Crazier'/ 'A Prayer For The Unborn' – all live footage sourced exclusively from Numan's appearance on the *Arte TV* channel.
Brackets denote the name of the producer/ remixer on CD1 and CD2.
* Written by Rico and Gary Numan.
** Written by Gary Numan and Andy Gray.
*** Actually the original demo version.
All other songs written by Gary Numan. (Except 'Hybrid' written by Gary Numan and Sulpher).
Executive producer Steve Malins with inspiration from Zakaroo.
Singles: 'Crazier'. 'Ancients' issued in the US and Germany as a radio only single. In addition, edited version also included with UK *Future Music* magazine.
Videos: 'Crazier'. In addition, 'Crazier' performed on *The Dom Joly Show* (alongside 'Are "Friends" Electric?') as well as an appearance on *Top Of The Pops*.

To celebrate Numan's 25 years as a professional musician, *Hybrid*, a 2CD part remixed, part re-recorded compilation album emerged. With 19 tracks spread over two discs it was clearly an ambitious project, but the end result far exceeded not only fans expectations but also Numan himself who expressed his delight with the project in the album's sleeve notes. The bulk of the mixes came from both Andy Gray and Sulpher with additional material coming from Rico, Alan Moulder, Curve, New Disease and the legendary Flood. Classics old and new went under the knife with tracks like 'Hybrid' (a re-titled 'Pure'), 'Bleed', 'Torn', 'Dominion Day', 'Absolution' and 'Rip' re-emerging in vastly different guises. Also receiving stunning updates were the new Curve version of 'Down In The Park' and New Disease's take on 'This Wreckage' but by far the standout track on the entire project was the Flood remake of 'Cars.' The version that appeared here sounded nothing like the original, coming across more like a malevolent religious chant complete with flutes than its former synth pop counterpart. Yet with a project of this size it was perhaps inevitable that some of the mixes provided would fall somewhat short of the desired target area, and certainly Alan Moulder's icy and detached take of 'Me! I Disconnect From You' was rather underwhelming, as were both Andy Gray's new version of 'Are "Friends" Electric?' and Sulpher's somewhat shambolic take of 'Down In The Park' (the only track here to appear twice). *Hybrid* also featured two new songs, 'Crazier' and 'Ancients'; both were excellent and gave fans an early indication of the direction that Gary's new album would be heading in. Sadly though, when originally released *Hybrid* did not enter the top 75, perhaps indicating fans were not that sold on the idea of yet another Gary Numan remix album especially after the atrocious results delivered by both *Random 2* and *The Mix*. The subsequent re-issue featuring the bonus DVD also failed to chart.

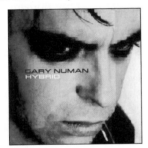

US cover for Hybrid.

Re-issued UK cover. (Cat No: JHCD007).

UK Mutate *cover. This DVD was later issued separately in the UK.*

US Mutate *cover.*

Hybrid *re-issued in the US re-titled as* Mutate.

(III) HOMAGES
Cover versions, samples and tribute albums.

For other musicians to record other artist's material is, in itself, not unusual, however, with the explosion in easy to use new technologies in the last 10 years or so as well as the proliferation of the Internet, the cover version has developed into a fascinating side industry. Gary Numan, however unlikely it seemed, was not immune to this phenomenon. In Numan's case though quite a diverse subculture has unfolded over the years with everyone from the terminally obscure to the incredibly famous tackling Gary's work. Obviously it would be impractical to list every Numan cover (not to mention impossible) as there are so many out there, instead this section will highlight the ones that would be of interest to fans.

Some of the very first Gary Numan/Tubeway army covers appeared on a series of late 70s/early 80s compilation albums. These albums were full of the hits of the day, yet instead of using the original songs, sound-alikes were drafted in to attempt to replicate the singer on any given track, often with hilarious results. These albums always featured scantily clad models on the cover and are fairly easy to get a hold of in second hand vinyl stores these days. Three of Numan's singles were used in this practice and fans interested in these albums will find 'Are "Friends" Electric?' on *Top Of The Poppers* from 1979, 'Complex' from *Parade Of Pops* from 1980 and lastly, 'We Are Glass' from *Top Of The Poppers* from 1980. Mercifully this practice was soon abandoned in favour of officially licensed music compilations.

CLUES by Robert Palmer
(**Cat No:** UK Island ILPS90493-2)
Format: Vinyl and cassette album.
Released: September 1980.
Track: 'I Dream Of Wires.'
Special note: Numan also co-wrote two tracks with Robert that appeared as B-sides namely: 'Style Kills' and 'Found You Now.' With critical hatred for Numan's synth drenched pop music gathering pace, it was something of a surprise to see soft rock crooner Robert Palmer cover one of Gary's songs for inclusion on his own album *Clues*. 'I Dream Of Wires' eventually found its way onto Numan's own 1980 album *Telekon*.

'PUMP ME UP' by Caroline Munroe.
(**Cat No:** UK Numa NU5)
Formats: 7-inch and 12-inch single.
Released: April 1985.
Tracks: 'Pump Me Up'/ 'The Picture.'
Special note: an Italian 7-inch and 12-inch remix was also released.

Caroline was an ex *TV* presenter and former 'Bond' girl who approached Numan with aspirations to be a pop star. 'Pump Me Up' had originally appeared on Gary's 1984 album, *Berserker* (there titled 'Pump It Up') and actually lent itself well to Caroline's voice. The B-side was a brand new Numan penned track entitled 'The Picture.' So far the original Numan led vocal for this song has not materialised.

'INTOLERANCE' By Tik & Tok.
(**Cat No:** UK Survival SURLP008)
Formats: vinyl* and cassette album (XCSUR8).
Released: August 1984.
Track: 'A Child With A Ghost.'
* Picture disc also released. (SURPX8).

Tik and Tok had originally been a part of the dance group Shock but by the mid-80s the duo had gone solo appearing on TV with Numan in 1984 as two cone-headed characters during an early performance of the song 'This Is New Love.' Later in the year they released their debut album featuring the Numan penned track 'A Child With A Ghost'; this song would eventually surface again three months later on Numan's own *Berserker* album.

'GHOST OF A WHITE FACE CLOWN, A TRIBUTE TO GARY NUMAN' – Various Artists.
(Cat No: US Northwest Elektro-Industrial Coalition)
Formats: CD and cassette.
Released: 1995.
Special note: Released in the US only.
Tracks: 'Down In The Park' 5.01 – Offworld/ 'Bleed' 4.48 – Silence/ 'Are "Friends" Electric?' 5.03 – Kill Switch...Klick/ 'Praying To The Aliens' 5.11 – Einer Ask And The Same/ 'Warriors' 4.26 – 'Jon The Beloved'/ 'Listen To The Sirens' 4.28 – Nocturnal/ 'Change Your Mind' 4.35 – Henry's Life In Hell/ 'This Is New Love' 6.24 – Schweigen Project/ 'Cars' 4.38 – Bytet/ 'Down In The Park' 4.18 – Faith And Disease.

★★★☆☆

Intriguing ten-song tribute album that was recorded mostly in Seattle area of Washington. Certainly the first all Gary Numan tribute album to appear. The covers themselves were mostly excellent with Silence and Jon The Beloved delivering the most faithful re-interpretations. This album is now virtually impossible to find.

'GIRL POWER' by Shampoo.
(Cat No: UK CDFOOD76)
Formats: CD and cassette.
Released: July 1996.
Track: 'Cars' (B-side). Other tracks on this single were 'Girl Power' (A-side) and 'Don't Call Me Babe' (B-side).

Released in the middle of the *Britpop* era reaching No 25 in the singles chart, Shampoo were a short lived 'Fem-punk' outfit who added a spunky, bratty version of 'Cars' to the B-side of this single.

'LUNCHBOX (EP)' by Marilyn Manson.
(Cat No: UK Interscope B00000IY88)
Formats: CD.
Released: January 1995.
Track: 'Down In The Park' (B-side), other tracks: 'Lunchbox', 'Next Mother F**ker', 'Brownbag', 'Metal' (not the Numan song) and 'Lunchbox (High School Dropouts).'

At this point Manson was an underground artist and was yet to embrace his antichrist persona. The Marilyn Manson version of 'Down In The Park' was a typically creepy affair adding a new dimension to the track.

'MONKEY WRENCH' by Foo Fighters.
(**Cat No:** UK Roswell CDCLS7880)
Formats: Part two of a two CD set.
Released: May 1997.
Track: 'Down In The Park' (B-side). Other tracks on the single were 'Monkey Wrench' (A-side) and 'See You' (B-side).
Special note: 'Down In The Park' originally featured on the *X Files* soundtrack album *Songs In The Key Of X*.

Here, 'Down In The Park' was given the alternative rock treatment, which suited the song rather well, easily one of the better versions of this seminal track.

'RANDOM' – Various Artists.
(**Cat No:** UK Beggars Banquet BBQCD195 1&2)
Formats: 2CD.
Released: June 1997.
Special note: Australian version featured a slightly altered cover. In addition, early press pack* came with a poster (see. below). Japanese issue included a lyric sheet and Obi.
* Included black folder (with album logo), press cuttings and an A5 cardboard ad.

CD1, Tracks: 'Stormtrooper In Drag' 7.43 – St Etienne*/ 'We Have A Technical' 3.20 – Matt Sharp and Damon Albarn/ 'Poetry And Power' 3.18 – Gravity kills/ 'I Can't Stop' 4.02 – Peck Slip/ 'Are "Friends" Electric?' 4.06 – An Pierle/ 'We Are Glass' 4.05 – EMF/ 'I Die: You Die' 3.10 – The Magnetic Fields/ 'We Are So Fragile' 3.44 – Jesus Jones/ 'She's Got Claws' 3.16 – Posh/ 'M.E.' 3.55 – Earl Brutus/ 'Films' 7.05 – Underdog/ 'Me! I Disconnect From You' 3.00 – Sukia/ 'Jo The Waiter' (Bon appetite remix) 9.44 – The Orb.
CD2, Tracks: 'I'm An Agent' 4.15 – Kenickie/ 'Down In The Park' 6.31 – Jimi Tenor/ 'Are 'Friends' Electric?' 6.28 – Moloko/ 'Remember I Was Vapour' 3.16 – Chris Holmes/ 'Metal' 5.05 – Towering Inferno/ 'Every Day I Die' 3.40 – Dubstar/ 'Absolution' 3.52 – Amanda Ghost/ 'Replicas' 5.11 – Deadsy/ 'Friends' 3.55 – Pop Will Eat Itself/ 'Are "Friends" Electric?' 5.39 – Republica (With Gary Numan)/ 'War Songs' 3.39 – Windscale/ 'We Are So Fragile' 2.59 – Bis/ 'Cars' 5.12 – Dave Clarke.
* Edited version (5.26) of this song included on the Saint Etienne album *Continental*.

Tribute albums are mostly dire affairs usually warranting no more than a cursory listen, not so with *Random*. This lavish 2CD set not only featured an amazingly good selection of quality re-interpretations but a stellar cast of high profile luminaries from just about the full spectrum of the music business. *Random* had originally come about as a direct response to the sudden upsurge in name bands (particularly big American alternative rock acts) not only publicly voicing their long felt admiration for Numan but actually covering some of his songs. Both Marilyn Manson and the Foo Fighters had covered Gary's 1979 classic 'Down In The Park' with acts like Weezer, The Smashing Pumpkins and Hole all airing Numan songs at their concerts.

When released, *Random* immediately garnered rave reviews and provided Numan with another vital stepping stone on his way back to the mainstream. The album's 26 tracks featured a wealth of diversity with the project swinging wildly from the avant-garde to pop, rock, dance and the just plain weird. So, impressed with the project, Numan appeared on TV (most notably *MTV*) to promote the album. Fans too were similarly impressed, feeling a sense of pride that after years of flying the Numan flag alone, here was an album that proved Numan's influence and style had in fact permeated way beyond his doggedly loyal and fiercely protective fanbase.

'CARS' by Fear Factory.
(**Cat No:** UK Roadrunner RR2189-3)
Formats: CD.*
Released: September 1999.

Original poster.

Foreign formats: Australian artwork different (see below).
Special note: Numan also appeared with the band in the promotional video.
Promo CD (Cat No: RR396) featured the slightly shorter

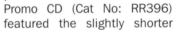
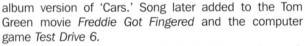

album version of 'Cars.' Song later added to the Tom Green movie *Freddie Got Fingered* and the computer game *Test Drive 6*.

Right: Australian single artwork.

Tracks: 'Cars' 3.39 (remix)/ 'Descent' 4.38 (Falling deeper mix)/ 'Edge Crusher' 4.3 (Urban assault mix). Last two tracks do not feature Gary Numan.

Superb 'Nu-metal' version of Numan's long standing classic single did much to sell Numan to a new, younger, more contemporary audience. Voted the No 1 song of the year in the UK's *RockSound* magazine and No 3 in *Kerrang* magazine.

'REPLICAS RUBATO' by Terre Thaemlitz
(**Cat No:** UK Demille Plateaux MPCD71)
Formats: CD.
Released: October 1999.
Special note: this album features a variety of Numan compositions re-interpreted on the piano.
Tracks: 'Stormtrooper In Drag' 5.44/ 'Down In The Park' 6.24/ 'A Dream Of Siam' 6.13/ 'Friends' 2.39/ 'Sister Surprise' 4.24/ 'Cars' 6.18/ 'Cry The Clock Said' 9.44/ 'Praying To The Aliens' 6.13/ 'Slowcar To China' 3.29/ 'Jo The Waiter' 4.23/ 'Please Push No More' – 'Down In The Park'* (Synth version) 8.03.
* Included on the CD but not listed on the album packaging itself.

A bizarre, yet fascinating, piano instrumental tribute album. One single ('Stormtrooper In Drag') was lifted from this album.

'THE CHURCH OF GARY NUMAN' by Jim Collins
(**Cat No:** UK Orchard 2419)
Formats: CD.
Released: November 2000.
Released: in an alternative cover (see below).
Special note: issued more covers in 2004 as 'I Am Gary Numan.'
Tracks: 'Jo The Waiter' 3.18/ 'I Dream Of Wires' 4.08/ 'Cars' 4.24/ 'Stories' 3.17/ 'Down In The Park' 5.45/ 'A Question Of Faith' 3.54/ 'Dominion Day' 4.39/ 'Love Is Like Clock Law' 4.12/ 'Metal' 3.46/ 'You Are In My Vision' 2.39/ 'I Still Remember' 3.30/ 'Cars' 5.38 (Jazz mix).

American one-man tribute album, one or two interesting covers though hardly essential.

Second cover artwork for this album.

'KOOCHY' by Armand Van Heldon.
(**Cat No:** UK FCDP379)
Formats: CD, cassette and vinyl single.
Released: May 2000.
Special note: promo 12-inch also issued (see right) featuring additional mixes.

Fantastic torn apart dance mix made up of the synth riff from 'Cars'.' Better still, apart from being a top 10 hit, the track was performed on *Top Of The Pops* featuring *Touring Principle* era Numan clones dancing along to the song.

'TUBEWAY NAVY' by Reload (Brian Applegate).
(**Cat No:** Unknown)
Formats: CD.
Released: June 2000.
Tracks: 'Me! I Disconnect From You' 3.01/ 'Bombers' 3.56/ 'Check It' 3.01/ 'Are "Friends" Electric?' 4.35/ 'We Are So Fragile' 2.56/ 'Down In The Park' 4.57/ 'Listen To The Sirens' 3.01/ 'My Shadow In Vain' 3.22/ 'Critics' 1.48/ 'Metal' 3.08.

Similar to the tribute album *The Church Of Gary Numan* featuring a couple of interesting covers.

'THINGS FALLING APART' by Nine Inch Nails.
(**Cat No:** UK Nothing/ Interscope AA694907441)
Formats: CD.
Released: November 2000.
Track: 'Metal.' Other tracks were a series of remixes taken from the group's last studio record *The Fragile*.

Nine Inch Nails main-man Trent Reznor had long voiced his admiration for Gary Numan and its reported that the album *Telekon* has been a major influence. The group's version of 'Metal'(recorded during the early sessions for *The Fragile)* had originally been heard earlier in the year as a sample on one of Numan's Nu-music telephone lines. The track eventually found its way onto this Nine Inch Nails remix album. Interestingly, yet another version of this track has found its way into fandom with fans actually preferring this mix over the *Things Falling Apart* version.

'WHERE'S YOUR HEAD AT' by Basement Jaxx.
(**Cat No:** UK XLT140)
Formats: CD and cassette.
Released: November 2001.
Track: 'Where's Your Head At.'

This track took samples from Numan's 1979 classic 'M.E.' as well as the 1980 single 'This Wreckage.' The end result was a hard driving Prodigy-like dance track centred on a rumbling synth riff. The single climbed into the top 10 and featured a completely bizarre video involving human/ape experiments.

'FREAK LIKE ME' by Sugababes
(**Cat No:** UK Universal/ Island CID798/ 582898-2)
Formats: CD and cassette.
Released: April 2002.
Special Note: rare bootleg mix of this track featuring Numan's original vocal as well as the Sugababes vocal also issued.

Although Sugababes ultimately took this wonderful 'Are "Friends" Electric?' hybrid to the No 1 spot, the song itself dated back to the year 2000.

'Girls On Top' single.

Originally released as a bootleg (courtesy of Richard X) by Girls On Top, the song then was called 'Are Freaks Electric?' and took its vocal from a 1995 track by Adina Howard entitled 'Freak Like Me.' Although this track passed by largely unnoticed, a resurrected version of the all girl pop act Sugababes re-recorded it as their comeback single and wound up with an enormous Europe-wide hit.

(IV) GUEST APPEARANCES
Numan has also accepted quite a number of invitations to appear on other artists recordings (Sharpe and Numan, Radio Heart), but this section will highlight some of the lesser well known moments.

'FIRST NIGHT IN NEW YORK' by Claire Hamill.
(**Cat No:** UK WEA K18440)
Formats: 7-inch vinyl.
Released: February 1981.
Track: 'Ultraviolet Light' (B-side).
　　This single featured Numan playing the synths on the B-side.

'STARS' by Nicky Robson
(**Cat No:** UK Scratch SCR006)
Formats: 7-inch and 12-inch (SCRT0060 – A side of this format extended.
Released: October 1981.
Tracks: 'Stars' 4.44 (12-inch mix 8 27)/ 'Eye To Eye' 3.28.
　　This single was recorded and mixed at Numan's Rock City Studios; in addition, Numan also produced this single.

'FOR FUTURE REFERENCE' by Dramatis
(**Cat No:** UK Rocket Records TRAIN 18)
Formats: vinyl and cassette.
Released: January 1982.
Track: 'Love Needs No Disguise.'
　　Made up of former members of Numan's band, Dramatis (RRussell Bell, Dennis Haines, Chris Payne and Cedric Sharpley) received a big boost when Numan recorded the lead vocal for the track 'Love Needs No Disguise.' Sadly, the band failed in their bid for stardom and eventually split with most of the members re-joining Gary for the *Warriors* project in 1983.

Right: Original magazine advert taken out by Dramatis following the April 1981 farewell concerts.

Below: The Dramatis album has been issued twice on CD. First re-issue, August 2000 via Metro (Metro 457) and second re-issue, June 2003 via Teenie (Teenie 060).

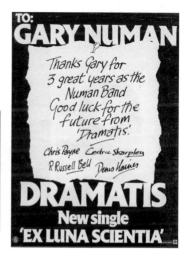

First re-issue.　　*Second re-issue.*

'BREAKING SILENCE' by James Frued.
(Cat No: UK Carrere CAL134)
Formats: vinyl and cassette album.
Released: March 1982.
Track: 'Automatic Crazy.'
   'Automatic Crazy' was produced by Numan and released as a single in Australia through Mushroom Records. The single was credited to 'James Frued and Berlin.'

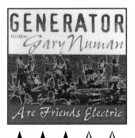

'ARE "FRIENDS" ELECTRIC?' by Generator.
(Cat No: JVO Records JVO001)
Formats: 7-inch, 12-inch and cassette single.
Released: 1994.
Tracks: 'Are "Friends" Electric?' (radio mix)/ 'Are "Friends" Electric?' (Eccentric mix)/ Bring Back The Love'*/ 'Going Home.'*
*Numan does not feature on these tracks.
Special note: mixes of this song featuring Numan only vocals were due to have been included on the fan club issued *Babylon* 8, sadly, this disc has yet to appear.
   This single features a guest appearance on vocals from Numan although when the single, not surprisingly, did nothing in the charts, the group quickly faded from view.

'I CANT BELIEVE IT'S NOT PLANKTON' by The High Kings of Tara.
(Cat No: Minority One MIN09CD)
Formats: CD album.
Released: September 1998.
Track: 'Mars (Is Heaven).'
   Numan provided some strange 'Sci-fi' vocals for one of the tracks on this British oddball, electro outfit. The man at the centre of the group was one Shane O'Neill who is presumed to be the brother of Gary's wife Gemma.

'THE SELF SAME THING' by Dubstar
(Cat No: UK CDFOODS133)
Formats: CD single.
Released: August 2000.
Track: 'Redirected Mail.'* Other tracks were: 'Self Same Thing' (A-side), 'And When You Laugh' (B-side) and 'Victoria' (B-side).
* B-side 'Redirected Mail' featured a guest appearance from Numan.

'HYACINTHS AND THISTLES' by The 6THS
(**Cat No:** MERGE MRG485)
Formats: CD album.
Released: September 2000.
Track: 'Sailor In Love With The Sea.'*
*Numan provided the vocal for this album track.

'RADIO JXL, A BROADCAST FROM THE COMPUTER HELL CABIN' by Junkie XL.
(**Cat No:** UK Roadrunner RR8380-8)
Formats: 2CD.
Released: June 2003.
Track: 'Angels.'*
Special note: second disc featured a 12-inch mix of 'Angels' amongst other tracks from the album, a third disc was available direct from Junkie's website featuring further remixes from the project.

* Junkie's album featured a stellar cast of guest vocalists including The Cure's Robert Smith, Grant Nicholas from Feeder and Depeche Mode's Dave Gahan. Numan sang the lead vocal for the track entitled 'Angels', a fantastic, anthemic dance track that was not too dissimilar in style to the Bryan Adams/ Chicane single from a few years back. Numan's voice actually lent itself extremely well to this kind of music and the track itself received an extremely positive reaction from Gary's hardcore fanbase.

'EARGASM' by Plump DJ'S
(**Cat No:** UK FLRCD007)
Formats: CD.
Released: July 2003.
Track: 'Pray For You.'

Much like the Junkie XL album, *Eargasm* featured a number of guest vocalists. 'Pray For You' harked back in sound to the early 80s *New Romantic* era with Numan once again turning in another superb, dusky vocal performance. Later issued as a single (see below).

Left: Promo CD and 12-inch issue of 'Pray For You', tracks included were: 'How Much Is Enough (non-Numan track) and three fresh mixes of the A-side (Plump DJs dub, Lee Coombs vocal and Lee Coombs dub).

(V) BOOTLEGS

Bootlegs are counterfeit product and as such are highly illegal; nevertheless for hardcore fans of any artist they are much sought after. Bootlegs are mostly made up of live material and can be split into three distinct groups. The first is sourced from audience recordings and as a result are usually fairly poor quality while the second is sourced direct from the sound board or the mixing desk and these tend to be just about as good as an official release. The last type is radio broadcasts and these are almost always of superior quality. Some bootlegs can contain studio material and these are mostly made up of studio out-takes that are usually unfinished/work in progress studio tracks that have been spirited away by unscrupulous studio engineers, but the quality of these, however, can vary dramatically. Bootlegs also usually suffer from poor packaging like incorrect track lists, dates, venues and studio information. Obviously it would be impractical to feature here every single bootleg that has emerged, as there are so many. Instead this section will highlight the most well known Numan bootlegs that have surfaced over the years.

LIVE RECORDINGS
(I) TUBEWAY ARMY

LIVE AT THE ROXY – 1977
GARY NUMAN/ TUBEWAY ARMY
(**Cat No:** TUBE101).
Released: 1981.
Re-issued 1982.
Bootleg type: audience recording.
Special note: issued on vinyl and limited edition cassette.
Musicians: Gary Numan – Vocals and guitar/ Paul Gardiner – Bass/ Bob Simmonds – Drums.
Tracks: 'Motherless Faces'*/ 'Boys'/ 'Blue Eyes'/ 'You Don't Know Me'/ 'My Shadow In Vain'/ 'Me, My Head'/ 'That's Too Bad'/ 'Basic Joe'*/ 'Do Your Best'/ 'Didn't I Say'*/ 'I'm A Poseur'/ 'White Light/ White Heat'**/ 'Pure St Joy."*
* Incorrect song titles (see 1998 *Tubeway Army* CD re-issue for corrections).
** This track was missing from the back cover packaging.

This was, and still is, the only known live Tubeway Army recording to have ever appeared (although rumours of a further two live recordings have surfaced in recent years). The first version emerged sometime in 1981, wrapped in a plain white cardboard sleeve featuring handwritten recording details but no track list. It's understood that the pressing originated in France and was limited to as little as 50 copies, and perhaps understandably, this version of *Live At The Roxy-1977* is virtually impossible to find now. The second version appeared a year later featuring a printed sleeve (see above) as well as a track list; the print run for this version is unknown.

The cover states that the recording comes from 1977, however, this cannot be as Gary can be clearly heard informing the attendant audience that the next track, 'That's Too Bad,' is the band's new single putting the time frame for the recording to February 1978. Also it's doubtful the recording was taken from the Roxy with most fans feeling that the venue in question was in fact the Rock Garden in London on the 21st of February.

This bootleg has since been added to the 1998 CD re-issue of *Tubeway Army* and has been subsequently cleaned up featuring all the correct song titles.

(II) GARY NUMAN

THE TOURING PRINCIPLE 1979/ 1980
UK LEG 1979
Except for the 1981 officially released *Living Ornaments '79* album (and as of 1998, the full concert 2CD set), only audience recordings are in circulation from this leg of the 'Touring Principle.'

US LEG 1980

TOURING PRINCIPLE IN CANADA '80
(**Cat No:** Unknown)
Included were a trio of new songs namely the classical instrumental 'Trois Gymnopedies' as well as 'Remind Me To Smile' and 'I Die: You Die.'

GARY NUMAN LIVE 1980
(**Cat No:** LIVEDISCS 005)
Released: 1980.
Date of recording: Twenty-first of February 1980 at the Providence Ocean State Theatre.
   Original tape had no sleeve, now available on CD.
Bootleg type: mixing desk recording.
Tracks: identical to the *Touring Principle In Canada '80* bootleg (see above).
Special note: like the *Touring Principle In Canada '80*, the sound quality was superb.

TRANSCRIPT
(**Cat No:** NEU Records NEU1)
Released: 1980.
Date of recording: Ninth of March 180 from the Santa Monica Civic Hall, Los Angeles.
Bootleg type: radio broadcast.
Tracks: 'Airlane'/ 'Me! I Disconnect From You'/ 'Praying To The Aliens'/ 'M.E.'/ 'Films'/ 'Fragile'*/ 'Are "Friends" Electric?'/ 'Conversation'/ 'Metal'/ 'Cars'/ 'I Die: You Die'/ 'Down In The Park.'
* Abbreviated, full title of song 'We Are So Fragile.'
   US radio broadcast that was pressed onto vinyl and used as a radio transcription disc, this concert was aired in the UK on the *BBC Radio One Rock Hour*. The sound quality was superb. Recording now available on bootleg CD.

SOUTHERN HEMISPHERE '80
AUSTRALIA

THE TOURING PRINCIPLE '80
(**Cat No:** unknown)
Release date unknown.
Date of recording: 31st May 1980 from the Capital Theatre.
Bootleg type: radio broadcast.
Tracks: 'Intro'/ 'Airlane'/ 'Me! I Disconnect From You'/ 'Praying To The Aliens'/ 'M.E.'/ 'Films'/ 'We Are So Fragile'/

'Are "Friends" Electric?'/ 'Conversation'/ 'Remind Me To Smile'/ 'Replicas'/ 'Remember I Was Vapour'/ 'Trois Gymnopedies'/ 'Cars'/ 'I Die: You Die'/ 'Bombers'/ 'Tracks'/ 'We Are Glass.'

Final date of the 'Touring Principle World Tour', tape was of superb sound quality.

THE TELETOUR '80
UK LEG

Except for the 1981 released (and currently in limbo) *Living Ornaments '80* album, only one mixing desk recording (featuring equally superb sound quality) has ever surfaced in fandom. Other recordings floating around from the 19/ 20* date UK trek were all audience recordings of varying sound quality.

* Second date of the tour on the 5th of September featured a matinee and evening performance at the Birmingham Odeon.

TELETOUR '80
(**Cat No:** unknown)
Release date unknown.
Date of recording: The 7th of September 1980 at the Manchester Apollo.
Bootleg type: soundboard recording (2CD).
Tracks: 'This Wreckage'/ 'Remind Me To Smile'/ 'Complex'/ 'Telekon'/ 'Me! I Disconnect From You'/ 'Conversation'/ 'Airlane'/ 'M.E.'/ 'Every Day I Die'/ 'Stories'/ 'Are "Friends" Electric?'/ 'The Joy Circuit'/ 'I Die: You Die'/ 'I Dream Of Wires'/ 'Down In The Park'/ 'Tracks'/ 'We Are Glass.'

Superb sound quality soundboard mix, interestingly, the early portion of this tour featured an early take of a new song entitled 'Stories' (a track that would ultimately be included on the 1981 album *Dance*).

US LEG

To date no mixing desk/soundboard recordings have found their way into fan circles from the US, the best audience recordings have been Boston's Orpheum Theatre, The New York Palladium, Pittsburgh's Stanley Theatre and The LA Forum (see below).

LA WELCOMES GARY NUMAN!
(**Cat No:** unknown)
Release date unknown
Date of recording: 1st of November 1980 at the Forum, Los Angeles.
Bootleg type: audience recording.
Tracks: identical to the UK set list with the only alteration being the removal of 'Stories' in favour of a returning 'Remember I Was Vapour' positioned between 'Every Day I Die' and 'Are "Friends" Electric?' The sound quality on this recording was surprisingly good for an audience recording.

THE FAREWELL SHOWS, UK

WEMBLEY 1981
(**Cat No:** unknown)
Release date unknown.
Date of recording: the 26th of April 1981 at Wembley Arena London.
Bootleg type: mixing desk recording (2CD).
This recording was similar to the 1998 2CD official release *Living Ornaments '81*, but was from the second night and unlike the official release featured the track 'Conversation' instead of 'Complex.' Of the three nights only one mixing desk recording has surfaced in fan circles. In addition, all three nights were also available as audience recordings and of course the final night of the farewell concerts has since been immortalised on video as well as CD.

THE AMERICAN I, ASSASSIN TOUR
Of the 18 dates performed on US soil in late 1982, only audience recordings have ever filtered down into fan circles. However, footage from the UK music show *The Tube* featured professionally shot video footage of Numan live at Perkins Palace at the start of the tour which meant it was highly likely that some of the shows were also being audio taped as well. The best audience tape in circulation was the show performed at The Ritz in New York (see below).

LIVING ORNAMENTS '82
(**Cat No:** unknown)
Release date unknown.
Date of recording: The 26th of October 1982 at The New York Ritz, New York.
Bootleg type: audience recording.
Tracks: 'This Is My House'/ 'I, Assassin'/ 'Remind Me To Smile'/ 'Films'/ 'Crash'/ 'Music For Chameleons'/ 'She's Got Claws'/ 'Every Day I Die'/ 'Down In The Park'/ 'White Boys And Heroes'/ 'Cars'/ 'Warsongs'/ 'We Take Mystery (To Bed)'/ 'This Wreckage'/ 'We Are Glass'/ 'Tracks.'
The sound quality for this show was pretty good for an audience recording.

THE WARRIORS TOUR 83

WARRIORS TOUR
(**Cat No:** unknown)
Released: 1983.
Date of recording: 20th of September 1983 at the Glasgow Apollo, Scotland.
Bootleg type: radio broadcast.
Tracks: 'Sister Surprise'/ 'Warriors'/ 'Remind Me To Smile'/ 'She's Got Claws'/ 'Love Needs No Disguise'/ 'I Die: You Die'/ 'We Take Mystery (To Bed)'/ 'Cars'/ 'Are "Friends" Electric?'/ 'Tracks'/ 'We Are Glass.'
This bootleg was made up of a one-hour radio broadcast originally transmitted

by *Clyde Radio* in the UK. The show was from the opening night of the tour and the sound quality for this bootleg was superb.

NUMAN LIVE! '83
(Cat No: unknown)
Released: 1983.
Date of recording: same as above.
Bootleg type: audience recording (2CD).
Tracks: 'Sister Surprise'/ 'Warriors'/ 'Remind Me To Smile'/ 'Metal'/ 'This Prison Moon'/ 'Down In The Park'/ 'Films'/ 'She's Got Claws'/ 'Love Needs No Disguise'/ 'I Die: You Die'/ 'Me! I Disconnect From You'/ 'Love Is Like Clock Law'/ 'The Iceman Comes'/ 'Rhythm Of The Evening'/ 'This Is My House'/ 'I Am Render'/ 'Warsongs'/ 'My Centurion'/ 'The Tick Tock Man'/ 'We Take Mystery (To Bed)'/ 'Cars'/ 'Are "Friends" Electric?'/ 'Tracks'/ 'We Are Glass.'

    This bootleg contained the full show of the opening night of the tour. Sound quality was average.

LIVING ORNAMENTS '83
(Cat No: unknown)
Release date unknown.
Date of recording: The 6th of October 1983 at The DeMontfort Hall, Leicester.
Bootleg type: mixing desk recording (2CD).
Tracks: 'Sister Surprise'/ 'Remind Me To Smile'/ 'Metal'/ 'This Prison Moon'/ 'Down In The Park'/ 'This Is My House'/ 'My Centurion'/ 'Warriors'/ 'She's Got Claws'/ 'Love Is Like Clock Law'/ 'The Iceman Comes'/ 'Films'/ 'I Am Render'/ 'Warsongs'/ 'Cars'/ 'We Take Mystery (To Bed)'/ 'I Die: You Die'/ 'Me! I Disconnect From You'/ 'Love Needs No Disguise'/ 'Are "Friends" Electric?'/ 'Tracks'/ 'We Are Glass'/ SFX interview.

    Excellent mixing desk recording from the 15th date of the 'Warriors Tour'; note that only five tracks from the *Warriors* album had survived in the set at this point.

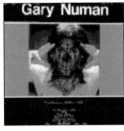

GARY NUMAN
(Cat No: unknown)
Released: 1984.
Date of recording: 14th of October 1983 at the Hammersmith Odeon, London.
Bootleg type: radio show.
Tracks: 'Remind Me To Smile'/ 'Metal'/ 'This Prison Moon'/ 'Down In The Park'/ 'This Is My House'/ 'The Iceman Comes'/ 'Films.'

    For some unfathomable reason the cover for this release sported Fish, the lead singer with progressive rockers Marillion. The recording was also incorrectly listed as being from 1982 and some of the track listing was wrong, however, the sound quality was superb.

IN CONCERT SERIES
(**Cat No:** unknown)
Release date unknown.
Date of recording: same as above.
Bootleg type: this was a 'Transmission disc' pressed up for UK radio programmers.
Tracks: same as above except featuring an additional five tracks, those being: 'Cars'/ 'We Take Mystery (To Bed)', 'I Die: You Die', 'Me! I Disconnect From You', 'Love Needs No Disguise' and 'Are "Friends" Electric?' This recording was transmitted again on *Digital Radio* in the fall of 2002 and sparked a flurry of new bootlegs onto the market.

NUMAN
(**Cat No:** unknown)
Release date unknown.
Date of recording: the 15th of October 1983 at the Hammersmith Odeon, London.
Bootleg type: audience recording.
Tracks: 'Sister Surprise'/ 'Remind Me To Smile'/ 'Metal'/ 'This Prison Moon'/ 'Down In The Park'/ 'This Is My House'/ 'My Centurion'/ 'Warriors'/ 'She's Got Claws'/ 'Love Is Like Clock Law'/ 'The Iceman Comes'/ 'Films'/ 'Warsongs'/ 'Cars'/ 'We Take Mystery (To Bed)'/ 'I Die: You Die'/ 'Me! I Disconnect From You'/ 'Love Needs No Disguise'/ 'Are "Friends" Electric?'/ 'Tracks'/ 'We Are Glass.'

Despite this bootleg being an audience recording, the sound quality was very good. Recording taken from the 3rd night at the Hammersmith Odeon.

THE BERSERKER TOUR '84
The 1984 'Berserker Tour' produced nothing but audience recordings with the best tape in circulation being from the 3rd night of the tour on the 24th of November at the Birmingham Odeon. However, with the officially released *White Noise* double live album released shortly after the tour, demand for 'Berserker Tour' bootlegs has never been a priority for even die-hard fans.

THE FURY TOUR '85

THE FURY TOUR
(**Cat No:** unknown)
Release date unknown.
Date of recording: 1st of October 1985 at the Hammersmith Odeon, London.
Bootleg type: mixing desk recording.
CD 1, Tracks: 'Intro'/ 'Tricks'/ 'Me! I Disconnect From You'/

'Creatures'/ 'Metal'/ 'Berserker'/ 'Are "Friends" Electric?'/ 'Miracles'/ 'Down In The Park'/ 'Cold Warning.'
CD 2, Tracks: 'I Die: You Die'/ 'Sister Surprise'/ 'This Disease'/ 'We Take Mystery (To Bed)'/ 'Call Out The Dogs'/

'Cars'/ 'My Shadow In Vain'/ 'We Are Glass.'

The only mixing desk recording to emerge from 'The Fury Tour.' Also issued as 'Electric Friends' through Cemetary Greats. **Cat No:** CG003 (see previous page, bottom right).

GARY NUMAN – IPSWICH
(**Cat No:** TRL002)
Release date unknown.
Date of recording: The 5th of October 1985 at the Gaumont, Ipswich.
Bootleg type: audience recording.
Tracks: 'No Shelter'/ 'Tricks'/ 'Me! I Disconnect From You'/ 'Creatures'/ 'Metal'/ 'Berserker'/'Are "Friends" Electric?'/ 'Miracles'/ 'Down In The Park'/ 'Cold Warning.'

Special note: This bootleg's first 400 copies came with a free album featuring a further four songs from this show. The tracks on this album were: 'I Die: You Die', 'Sister Surprise', 'This Disease' and 'We Take Mystery (To Bed).'

THE EXHIBITION TOUR '87

RADIO SHOW '87
(**Cat No:** ATTM009)
Release date unknown.
Date of recording: 21st of September 1987 at the Barrowlands, Glasgow.
Bootleg type: one hour broadcast from *Radio Clyde*.
Tracks: 'Call Out The Dogs'/ 'I Die: You Die'/ 'Creatures'/ 'I Can't Stop'/ 'Me! I Disconnect From You'/ 'My Breathing'/ 'Cars'/ 'Metal'/ 'Sister Surprise'/ 'We Take Mystery (To Bed)'/ 'We Are Glass.'

Wrongly listed as being recorded in 1985 and credited to Gary Neuman, however, the sound quality was excellent.

THE METAL RHYTHM TOUR '88

NEW ANGER LIVE
(**Cat No:** HUT004)
Release date unknown.
Date of recording: The 11th of October 1988 at the Astoria, London.
Bootleg type: audience recording.
Tracks: 'Intro'-('Survival')/ 'Respect'/ 'Call Out The Dogs'/ 'Me! I Disconnect From You'/ 'I Die: You Die'/ 'I Can't Stop'/ 'Tricks'/ 'Metal'/ 'Creatures'/ 'Down In The Park'/ 'Hunger'/ 'Sister Surprise'/ 'Are "Friends" Electric?'/ 'We Take Mystery (To Bed)'/ 'We Are Glass'/ 'New Anger'/ 'Cars'/ 'Young Heart'/ 'My Shadow In Vain'/ 'My Breathing'/ 'Devious'/ 'Young Heart'/ 'This Is Emotion' (latter three tracks were all demos from *Metal Rhythm*).

Excellent audience recording that featured the entire show as well as three previously unreleased demos from 1988.

THE SKIN MECHANIC TOUR '89

LIVE IN LONDON
(**Cat No:** LOAD1)
Release date unknown.
Date of recording: 12th of October 1989 at the Dominion Theatre, London.
Bootleg type: audience recording.
Tracks: 'Intro'-('God Only Knows')/ 'America'/ 'Me! I Disconnect From You'/ 'Respect'/ 'I Die: You Die'/ 'Creatures'/ 'This Is Emotion'/ 'Cars'/ 'This Is Love'/ 'Down In The Park'/ 'Hunger'/ 'Devious'/ 'Tricks'/ 'I Can't Stop'/ 'We Take Mystery (To Bed)'/ 'Are "Friends" Electric?'/ 'Call Out The Dogs'/ 'New Anger'/ 'My Shadow In Vain'/ 'We Are Glass.'

A good audience recording of the full show with highlights video also taken from this tour (see 'Official video cassettes').

THE OUTLAND TOUR '91
Numan's next tour, the 14 date 'Outland Tour' of 1991 (in support of the similarly titled album) has so far only turned up as audience recordings, none of which feature anything other than average sound quality and therefore were hardly essential purchases for fans.

THE EMOTION TOUR '91

EUROPEAN TOUR 91
(**Cat No:** SFX-ET100)
Release date unknown.
Date of recording: 14th of September 1991 at the Ancienne Belgique, Brussels.
Bootleg type: mixing desk recording.
Tracks: 'Hanoi' – ('Intro')/ 'Me! I Disconnect From You'/ 'Call Out The Dogs'/ 'Your Fascination'/ 'Outland'/ 'Respect'/ 'Cars'/ 'Devious'/ 'The Sleeproom'/ 'Are "Friends" Electric?'/ 'Soul Protection'/ 'Confession'/ 'From Russia Infected'/ 'My World Storm'/ 'Emotion'/ 'Metal Rhythm'/ 'America'/ 'Young Heart.'

All 19 dates of the 'Emotion Tour' were mixing desk recordings and were available to buy direct from Numan's fan club. This bootleg recording was derived from one of those tapes but was wrongly labelled as being taped from a European tour when in fact only one date was performed in mainland Europe on this trek. All the recordings from this tour were of superb sound quality.

ISOLATE TOUR '92

NUMAN LIVE! – ISOLATE TOUR 1992
(**Cat No:** Media Industries MI01)
Release date unknown.
Date of recording: 1st of April 1992 at the Corn Exchange, Cambridge.
Bootleg type: Audience recording.
Tracks: 'Intro'/ 'Respect'/ 'Devious'/ 'Confession'/ 'Me! I Disconnect From You'/ 'America'/ 'Call Out The Dogs'/ 'Soul Protection'/ 'Outland'/ 'Your Fascination'/ 'Time To Die'/ 'Cars'/ 'From Russia Infected'/ 'My World Storm'/ 'The Skin Game'/ 'Emotion'/ 'Are "Friends" Electric?'/ 'We Are Glass'/ 'U Got The Look'/ 'Metal

Rhythm'/ 'Young Heart.'
One of the better audience recordings from this brief 13-date UK tour.

THE DREAM CORROSION TOUR '93

Numan's next outing was the 'Dream Corrosion Tour', again, only audience recordings
have surfaced and with a superb double live album eventually taken from the tour
(*Dream Corrosion*), fan demand for any of the other 13 dates has always been fairly
low. Similarly, the 7 dates performed as support to O.M.D. at the end of 1993 have
also thrown up a number of audience recordings, though these were average at best.

THE SACRIFICE TOUR '94

THE SACRIFICE TOUR '94
(Cat No: NU003)
Released: 1995.
Date of recording: 6th of November 1994 at the Town
Hall, Birmingham.
Bootleg type: audience recording.
Tracks: 'Pray'/ 'A Question Of Faith'/ 'I Dream Of Wires'/
'Noise Noise'/ 'Listen To The Sirens'/ 'Every Day I Die'/
'Desire'/ 'Friends'/ 'Scar'/ 'Magic'/ 'M.E.'/ 'Replicas'/
'Stormtrooper In Drag'/ 'Deadliner'/ 'Bleed'/ 'Love And Napalm'/ 'I'm An Agent.'

Fairly good audience recording and one of the first Numan bootlegs to emerge
on CD, a sound check CD from this date has also emerged in recent years.

PREMIER HITS TOUR '96

LIVE IN CONCERT '96
(Cat No: LIVEDISCS LDCD5)
Release date unknown
Date of recording: the 30th of March 1996 at the
Glasgow Pavilion.
Bootleg type: audience recording.
CD1, Tracks: 'Prophecy' (false start)/ 'Prophecy'/ 'Noise
Noise'/ 'A Question Of Faith'/ 'Me! I Disconnect From You'/
'Replicas'/ 'The Seed Of A Lie'/ 'An Alien Cure'/ 'Are
"Friends" Electric?'/ 'Films.'

CD2, Tracks: 'Bleed'/ 'Every Day I Die'/ 'Are You Real?'/ 'Dark'/ 'Absolution'/ 'Cars'/
'Love And Napalm'/ 'We Are Glass'/ 'Remind Me To Smile.'
One of the better audience recordings from this tour.

FESTIVALS '96

DOWN IN THE PARK –LIVE FROM VICTORIA PARK

(Cat No: STONEBOLTT 001)
Release date unknown.
Date of recording: the 16th of August 1996 at Victoria Park, Warrington.
Bootleg type: audience recording.
Tracks: 'Dark'/ 'Noise Noise'/ 'A Question Of Faith'/ 'Scar'/ 'Are "Friends"

Electric?'/ 'An Alien Cure'/ 'Dead Heaven'/ 'Every Day I Die'/ 'Dominion Day'/ 'Cars.'
Fairly average audience recording.

THE EXILE TOUR '97/ '98

LIVE IN THE UK THE EXILE TOUR
(**Cat No:** ZEE T2)
Release date unknown.
Date of recording: 31st of October 1997 at the Pavilion, Glasgow.
Bootleg type: audience recording.
Tracks: 'Dominion Day'/ 'Films'/ 'A Question Of Faith'/
'Voix'/ 'Dark'/ 'You Walk In My Soul'/ 'Noise Noise'/ 'Cars'/
'Bleed'/ 'This Wreckage'*/ 'The Joy Circuit'*/ 'On
Broadway'**/ 'This Is New Love' (*The Leo Sayer Show*
version)/ 'Your Fascination' (7-inch single mix).
* Taken from *Living Ornaments '80*, both tracks jump.
** Taken from the free live single issued with *Telekon* in 1980.
The first half of this bootleg comprises of a selection of live tracks from the
Pavilion with the other half taking in tracks from a variety of sources.

EXILE USA
(**Cat No:** NUMAN TXOOO3)
Release date unknown.
Date of recording: 11th of March 1998 at the Metro, Chicago.
Bootleg type: audience recording.
Tracks: 'Intro'/ 'Friends'/ 'Dominion Day'/ 'Cars'/ 'Films'/ 'A Question Of Faith'/ 'Voix'/
'Every Day I Die'/ 'Dark'/ 'Noise Noise'/ 'An Alien Cure'/ 'Down In The Park'/
'Absolution'/ 'Dead Heaven'/ 'Metal'/ 'Are "Friends" Electric?'/ 'Replicas'/ 'We Are So
Fragile'/ 'Me! I Disconnect From You.'
One of the many good audience recorded CDs that emanated from Gary's first
US live shows in 17 years. Other good quality shows floating around were: The
Philadelphia Theatre (1.5.98), The New York Plaza (2.5.98), The Pittsburgh Club
Larga (6.5.98), Toronto's Lees Place (7.5.98), Cleveland Odeon (8.5.98), Portland,
Oregon Berbatis Pan (16.5.98) and finally Orlando Sapphire Club (26.5.98).
Numan's next outings were a series of one-off shows at various points throughout
1999/2000. Again, only fairly average audience recordings emerged on to the
bootleg market, similarly the brief European and UK 'Pure Tours' were also
represented by less than spectacular audience recordings.

THE SECRET SHOW
(**Cat No:** Radio Archives RAX007)
Released: March 2001.
Date of recording: the 7th of February 2001 at the BBC
Studios.
Bootleg type: FM digital recording.
Tracks: 'Rip'/ 'Metal'/ 'Pure'/ 'My Jesus'/ 'Cars'/ 'Listen To
My Voice'/ 'I Can't Breathe'/ 'Down In The Park'/ 'A Prayer
For The Unborn.'
This bootleg was taken from Gary's appearance on John Peel's radio show; the

live session was from the Maida Vale studios in London. Other variations of this recording also include Numan's run through of 'Are "Friends" Electric?' from the John Peel *Festive Fifty Show*. Bootleg video footage also exists from this appearance although it was very, very poor quality.

THE PURE TOUR – US LEG 2001

NUMAN LIVE AT THE HOUSE OF BLUES
(**Cat No:** TRAX: TXCD6785-45)
Released: 2001.
Date of recording: the 28th of April 2001 at the House of blues, Chicago.
Bootleg type: audience recording.
Tracks: 'Intro'/ 'Pure'/ 'Films'/ 'Rip'/ 'Listen To My Voice'/ 'Cars'/ 'Dark'/ 'Down In The Park'/ 'Walking With Shadows'/ 'Metal'/ 'My Jesus'/ 'A Question Of Faith'/ 'I Can't Breathe'/ 'Are "Friends" Electric?'/ 'Remind Me To Smile'/ 'A Prayer For The Unborn.'
    Pretty good recording from this 16-date US trek.

LIVE READING FESTIVAL 2001
(**Cat No:** Underground CD2001)
Released: September 2001.
Date of recording: the 24th of August 2001 at the Reading Festival.
Bootleg Type: audience recording.
Tracks: 'Intro' – 'My Jesus'/ 'Pure'/ 'Cars'/ 'A Question Of Faith'/ 'Listen To My Voice'/ 'Rip'/ 'Are "Friends" Electric?'/ 'Dead Heaven'/ 'I Can't Breathe'/ 'A Prayer For The Unborn'/ 'Dark.'
    Pretty good audience recording.

live manchester 2002

LIVE MANCHESTER 2002
(**Cat No:** LIVE! N2)
Released: April 2002.
Date of recording: the 5th of April 2002 at the Academy, Manchester.
Bootleg type: audience recording.
Tracks: 'M.E.'/ 'My Jesus'/ 'Metal'/ 'Absolution'/ 'Dark'/ 'Down In The Park'/ 'Remember I Was Vapour'/ 'Pure'/ 'A Prayer For The Unborn'/ 'Every Day I Die'/ 'Exile'/ 'My Shadow In Vain'/ 'Rip'/ 'I Can't Breathe'/ 'This Wreckage'/ 'Voix'/ 'Cars'/ 'Are "Friends" Electric?'
    An excellent live recording.

THE 25th ANNIVERSARY SHOWS 2003

25th ANNIVERSARY TOUR
(**Cat No:** NUSHOWS NU5)
Released: February 2003.
Date of recording: the 9th of February 2003 at the Academy, Manchester.
Bootleg type: audience recording.
Tracks: 'Hybrid'/ 'My Shadow In Vain'/ 'M.E.'/ 'My Jesus'/

'That's Too Bad'/ 'Ancients'/ 'Every Day I Die'/ 'Torn'/ 'Down In The Park'/ 'Please Push No More'/ 'It Must Have Been Years'/ 'Crazier'/ 'Pure'/ 'I Can't Breathe'/ 'Rip'/ 'A Prayer For The Unborn'/ 'Cars'/ 'Are "Friends" Electric?'/ 'Bleed'/ 'I Die: You Die'/ 'We Are Glass.'

KOLA/ COLOGNE 2003
(**Cat No:** ARTE1)
Released: March 2003.
Date of recording: the 17th of February 2003 for German TV channel *Arte TV.*
Bootleg type: TV / audio transfer.
Tracks: 'Rip'/ 'Dark'/ 'Crazier'/ 'A Prayer For The Unborn'/ 'I Can't Breathe'/ Interview segments.

Superb sound quality transfer, bootleg video of Gary's appearance was also made available.

LONDON ASTORIA-2XCD-20.09.03
(**Cat No:** Astoria 01)
Released: October 2003.
Date of recording: the 21st of September 2003.
Bootleg type: audience recording.

Spread over the two CDs included was the full concert from the 21st of September, one of the two dates performed in this month (the other show being performed in Manchester), and although only an audience recording the sound quality was still very good.

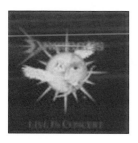

DRAMATIS LIVE IN CONCERT
(**Cat No:** Unknown)
Released: November 2003.
Date of recording: 1983.
Bootleg type: radio broadcast.
Tracks: 'Sand And Stone'/ 'I Only Find Rewind'/ 'Face On A Wall'/ 'I Can See Her Now'/ 'Turn'/ 'Love Needs No Disguise'/ 'Pomp And Stomp And Stamp'/ 'The Shame.'

This Radio One recording took place prior to the band re-joining Numan for the *Warriors* album.

STUDIO

Many Numan bootlegs have featured an assortment of rare, remixed and previously unreleased studio tracks. In addition, radio and TV interviews have emerged on vinyl and CD in recent years. Bootleg remixes and cover versions of Numan's material can also be obtained (usually via the Internet). However, this final part of the bootleg section will highlight the more well-known and fan-recognisable bootlegs that have emerged in recent years.

THE PLEASURE PRINCIPLE SESSIONS
(**Cat No:** PPS234-45)
Release date unknown.
Bootleg type: work-in-progress studio tapes.

These recordings have been floating around for a number of years and feature 45 minutes of early *Pleasure Principle* recordings. These consist of various takes of 'Cars'*, 'Observer', 'Tracks' and 'Conversation'. Some copies came complete with an interview from Australia recorded in 1980, however, the sound quality was average. Some variations of this recording have also included demos for 'Cry The Clock Said,' 'She's Got Claws' and 'Moral' (all three from 1981).

* Separate bootleg CD issued (see right) featuring five different takes of 'Cars.' Tracks included were: 1. The lead vocal mix. 2.Vocal dub mix. 3/4. Instrumental mixes 1 & 2. 5. The lead vocal plus bass and keyboards mix).

WHITE LIGHT, WHITE HEAT (LIVE '78)
(**Cat No:** NEU Records 002)
Released: September 1982.

This bootleg 7-inch single was limited to just 1000 copies and was lifted from the bootleg live album *Vortex Live*. Interestingly, the B-side to this single came from Numan's old band Mean Street performing the track 'Bunch Of Stiffs.'

Vortex album (NES115) – Issued on dark red vinyl.

VOLUME ONE JOHN PEEL SESSION – JANUARY 1979
(**Cat No:** Stigma Records)
Released: 1987.
Credited to 'Gary Numan and the Tubeway Army.'
Tracks: 'I Nearly Married A Human'/ 'Down In The Park'/ 'Me! I Disconnect From You.'
Cover photo was taken from the 'Teletour' in 1980.

This bootleg 7-inch single came housed in a fold out poster bag and featured the first three session tracks Tubeway Army recorded for John Peel in early 1979.

VOLUME TWO JOHN PEEL SESSION – AUGUST* 1979
(**Cat No:** Stigma Records)
Released: 1987.
Credited to 'Gary Numan and the Tubeway Army.'
Tracks: 'Films'/ 'Airlane'/ 'Conversation.'
* Correct date for session was the 25th of May 1979.

This bootleg 7-inch featured the second session recorded by Gary (although minus 'Cars'). Again it came housed in a fold out poster bag.

ZERO BARS (MR SMITH)
(**Cat No:** Budkon Records)
Release date unknown.
Six inch square flexi disc.
　　One of literally dozens of different coloured Russian flexi-discs that emerged; all came housed in a black and white paper sleeve.

RAZORMAID PRESENTS GARY NUMAN
(**Cat No** and release date unknown)
Tracks: 'This Disease' (mixes 1 and 2)/ 'I'm On Automatic'/ 'I Can't Stop'/ 'No More Lies'/ 'Change Your Mind' (mixes 1 and 2)/ 'My Dying Machine'/ 'Cars' (class X)/ 'Harlequin Tears' (mixes 1 and 2).
　　Collection of remixes from the Razormaid stable.

PURE (THE EXTENDED MIXES)
(**Cat No:** SRT007)
Release date unknown.
　　Never officially issued due to Numan's then record company Eagle Records showing zero interest it, where this extended recording actually came from was the subject of much heated fan debate with many feeling that it was in fact nothing more than a fan generated remix.

CARS
(**Cat No:** Unknown)
Release date unknown.
Tracks: Cars (original 1979 version)/ Cars (E Reg Model mix)/ Cars (live).
　　This CD single emerged in the US at the end of the 80s. This was primarily a 'radio only' promo and was unlikely to have been an official release.

Back cover and CD itself.

SECTION TWO

VIDEO

(I) OFFICIAL VIDEO CASSETTES

Towards the end of the 1970s, home video players and recorders became affordable for the public to buy and with that grew a major entertainment market to cater to the whims of the movie and music connoisseur. Numan's inroads into this new market gave him the unique distinction of releasing the world's first 'all music video cassette' (*The Touring Principle '79*) that the public could actually buy. More video cassettes followed throughout the 80s and into the early 90s although now the majority of these cassettes are long deleted. However, Numan has expressed a desire to re-issue the bulk of his video catalogue, this time onto the far superior DVD format though legal wrangling over just who owns the copyright to these recordings and even tape deterioration may ultimately prevent these videos from ever seeing the light of day again. Perhaps understandably, tired of waiting, fans have in recent years begun converting their own copies of Numan's videos to the DVD format (see 'bootleg DVDs').

The one positive piece of news concerning these videos came courtesy of UK retro pop show *Top Of The Pops 2*, in the middle of 2002 – with Numan back in the top 30 with 'Rip' – the show screened the original promo video for 'I Die: You Die' featuring, for the first time, the original single mix of the song (previously seen versions had all featured the rare, alternative promo mix). On the show's pop up information box, Gary claimed that he had 'just recently found the clip having lost it for many years.' This news did much to fuel fans hopes concerning the likelihood of any eventual re-appearance of these promo videos.

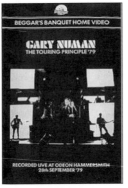

★★★★☆

THE TOURING PRINCIPLE — '79

(**Cat No:** PEVN0001/ Beggars Banquet/ Warners)
Released: April 14th 1980.
Formats: Betamax, VHS, U-Matic, Phillipes and VCD.
Foreign formats: US Betamax version (**Cat No:** IN4021). Recorded at the Hammersmith Odeon on the 28th of September 1979.
Running time: 60 minutes.
Re-issued in 1981 and 1988* via Palace video.
* **Cat No:** PVC 3002B.
Special note: this cassette was available via mail-order from Beggars Banquet in the months prior to its release.
Musicians: Gary Numan – Vocals/ Paul Gardiner – Bass/ Chris Payne – Keyboards/ Cedric Sharpley – Drums/ Billie Currie – Keyboards/ RRussell Bell – Guitar.
Tracks: 'Cars' (promotional video)/ 'Me! I Disconnect From You'/ 'M.E.'/ 'We Are So Fragile'/ 'Every Day I Die'/ 'Conversation'/ 'Remember I Was Vapour'/ 'On Broadway'/ 'Down In The Park'/ 'My Shadow In Vain'/ 'Are "Friends" Electric?'/ 'Tracks.'

Boasting the proud claim 'A video journey into rock's electronic future,' *The Touring Principle '79* immediately pushed Numan to the forefront of the embryonic video market through being the first artist anywhere to issue an all music, long form video to buy. The cassette culled 11 superb live tracks (as well as including the promo video for 'Cars') from Gary's triumphant sold out UK tour of 1979. The tour itself was a glittering, neon encrusted return to the glory days of show business featuring a futuristic and startling stage set complete with pulsing lights and flashing panels of neon tubing that blinked in time to the beat of the music. The film footage too was, like Numan, fairly ground breaking stuff having been treated with what the video cassette explained as 'a variety of generated images which supplement the themes of his (Numan's) music.' This process was relatively new and at the time regarded as innovative. These days, however, technology has obviously moved on and *The Touring Principle's* treated film footage now looks somewhat dated.

Special mention should also be given to the fact that this video cassette featured the two new tracks that were aired on the UK tour namely: 'Remember I Was Vapour' and 'On Broadway.' The former was a brand new track that ultimately found its way onto Numan's next studio album *Telekon*. The latter track, however, was a cover of a song originally made popular by the American group The Drifters. On this track keyboard player Billie Currie brought the song to a close with an inspired and beautiful synthesiser solo. It's this solo that fans have since wittily quipped was probably Billie's way of re-auditioning for the re-united, Midge Ure-fronted version of Ultravox!

The Touring Principle'79 has been deleted since the late 80s and can now only be found either via fans or internet auction sites like *EBay*. A release on DVD looks extremely unlikely; in its present state *The Touring Principle'79* is nothing more than a curio now. A move to DVD should, at the very least, include (like the 1998 re-issue of *Living Ornaments '79*) the full concert with perhaps the addition of relevant TV interviews and all three promo videos shot for *The Pleasure Principle* album.

The Touring Principle '79 reached the No1 spot on the UK video charts.

Re-issued new cover for The Touring Principle '79 (UK).

Video CD version of The Touring Principle '79 (UK).

1988 re-issue.

MICROMUSIC
(Beggars Banquet/ Palace video)
Released: April 1982.
Formats: VHS, Betamax, Laserdisc and VCD.
Foreign formats: Japanese version released in a new cover, Dutch and German version also released in a new cover (see below).
Recorded at the Wembley Arena on 28th April 1981.
Running time: 1 hour and 54 minutes.
Re-issued 1988 via Palace video (Cat No: PVC3001).
Special note: this recording was initially available to buy by sending Palace video a blank, two hour video cassette.
Musicians: Gary Numan – Vocals, keyboards and guitar/ Chris Payne – Keyboards and viola/ Cedric Sharpley –

Drums/ Dennis Haines – Keyboards/ Paul Gardiner – Bass/ RRussell Bell – Guitar.
Special guests: Nash The Slash and dance troupe Shock.
Tracks: 'Intro'/ 'This Wreckage'/ 'Remind Me To Smile'/ 'Metal'*/ 'Me! I Disconnect From You'/ 'Complex'/ 'The Aircrash Bureau'/ 'Airlane'/ 'M.E.'/ 'Every Day I Die'/ 'Films'/ 'Remember I Was Vapour'/ 'Trois Gymnopedies (First movement)'/ 'She's Got Claws'/ 'Cars'/ 'I Dream Of Wires'/ 'I'm An Agent'/ 'The Joy Circuit'/ 'I Die: You Die'/ 'Cry The Clock Said'/ 'Tracks'/ 'Down In The Park'/ 'My Shadow In Vain'/ 'Please Push No More'/ 'Are "Friends" Electric?'/ 'We Are Glass'/ 'Outro.'
* Featured new lyrics.

Micromusic was taped from the concluding night of Gary's three farewell shows in April 1981 and over 20 years later this footage is still pretty spectacular eye candy. For anyone wanting to see for themselves just how big a phenomenon Numan had become in the early part of the 80s then *Micromusic* was the ideal place to view it. These shows witnessed Numan at the very height of his powers with each one a jaw-dropping, OTT fantasy made flesh. The set-list itself read like a who's who of Gary Numan classics and for nearly two gruelling hours Numan dazzled and rocked the assembled crowds at Wembley for what was to be the last time. In amongst the tried and tested classics were three new songs namely: 'She's Got Claws', 'Cry The Clock Said' and 'Moral' (the latter song, a lyrical swipe at the UK based *New Romantic* scene was rather bizarrely welded to the original backing track for Numan's '79 classic 'Metal'). These new songs not only gave fans an early indication of the direction his new material would be taking but reassured The Numan army (some of which thought Numan was retiring for good) that although Gary was bowing out of the concert circuit, his recording career would definitely continue.

Two versions of *Micromusic* exist; the first was an edited highlights version that was screened on British television one Sunday afternoon shortly after the completed concerts were performed in 1981. The other was the standard full concert.

The edited version was mainly sold in foreign markets and featured the following track list: 'Intro'/ 'This Wreckage'/ 'Airlane'*/ 'M.E.'/ 'She's Got Claws'/ 'Cars'/ 'I'm An Agent'/ 'The Joy Circuit'/ 'I Die: You Die'/ 'Tracks'/ 'Down In The Park'/ 'Are "Friends" Electric?'/ 'We Are Glass'/ 'Outro.'

* This was wrongly spelt on the packaging.

Since the late 80s both versions of *Micromusic* have been out of print and are now, like the preceding video cassette *The Touring Principle '79*, quite rare.

Of all Gary's early videos *Micromusic* is the one fans would most dearly like to see back on sale but for now this cassette looks like remaining out of print for some time to come.

Below are the various versions of *Micromusic* that have emerged over the years.

Picture left:
The video CD version.

Picture right:
Dutch and German version,
Released: November 1983
(Cat No: Atlas 8129).

Japanese version issued in 1984.

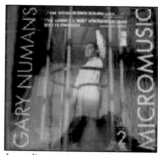

Laserdisc version.

1988 UK re-issued version.

NEWMAN NUMAN – THE BEST OF GARY NUMAN

(Beggars Banquet/ Palace video)
Released: November 1982.
Formats: VHS.
Foreign formats: matched the UK.
Running time: 45 minutes.
Re-issued 1988 via Palace video (Cat No: PVC3003M).*
* *Newman Numan*, along with *The Touring Principle '79* and *Micromusic*, were all simultaneously re-issued in 1988 following Gary's entire Beggars Banquet back catalogue emerging on CD for the first time in the UK, the re-issued cover for *Newman Numan* was virtually identical to the original. (see below).

Direction and production credits: 'I Die: You Die'*, 'Cars', 'Complex', 'Down In The Park', Are "Friends" Electric?', 'We Are Glass' and 'This Wreckage' directed and produced by Kate and Derek Burbridge for Zoetrope Ltd. 'Music For Chameleons', 'Love Needs No Disguise' and 'We Take Mystery (To Bed)' directed by Jeff Baynes, produced by Tattooist. 'She's Got Claws' directed by Julian Temple, produced by Chrissie Smith. Video compilation directed by John Vernon, edited by Neil Patience.
* Video version different to the single issued version.
Tracks: 'The 1930's Rust'/ 'I Die: You Die'/ 'Music For Chameleons'/ 'Cars'/ 'She's Got Claws'/ Brief interview – 'We Take Mystery (To Bed)'/ 'Complex'/ 'Love Needs No Disguise'/ 'Down In The Park' (Live 1979)/ Are "Friends" Electric?' (Live 1979)/ 'This Wreckage' (Live 1980)/ 'We Are Glass.'

Originally released to coincide with the release of the licensed 'greatest hits' compilation of the same name, this video cassette gathered together, for the first time, all but one of Gary's promo videos up to this point (the one promo not included being the one-off video that was shot for 'Metal'). Also included on the cassette was a small selection of brief interview segments. It should be pointed out that hardly any of the promos are complete (something that angered Numan at the time) with some even inter-cut with footage of Gary's early 80s airborne escapades. Also worthy of note with the inclusion of an edited mix of the *I, Assassin* album track 'The 1930's Rust', this version was previously unreleased and rumoured to have been put forward by Beggars Banquet as a potential single as early as February 1982. This idea, however, was nixed by Gary who chose 'Music For Chameleons' instead as his first single of the year. This track, like many of the rest on this compilation was also incomplete and in addition, did not feature a promo video, playing instead along to privately shot footage of the attractions of Las Vegas.

This cassette has been deleted since the late 80s and is unlikely to ever resurface officially. The promos themselves however are likely to re-emerge in the future as part of a possible archive DVD from the Numan camp though Gary's well documented (and in some cases justified) disdain for the majority of his early 80s videos means any kind of release is not likely to be soon.

1988 re-issued cover.

★★★☆☆

THE BERSERKER TOUR
(Peppermint video – **Cat No:** 6121-5)
Released: January 1986.
Formats: VHS and video CD.
Foreign formats: Japanese issue featured an alternative track list to the originally released UK version (see below). Recorded at the Hammersmith Odeon, London on 11th December 1984.
Running time: 60 minutes.
Re-issued May 1987 via The Video Collection (VC4010), August 1990 via Castle/ Hendring (HEN2266), December 1993 via 4Front video and finally onto DVD in July 2002 via Sanctuary (see 'Official DVD's').
Special note: promo version of the video featured an extra track.

Musicians: Gary Numan – Vocals/ Chris Payne – Keyboards and viola/ RRussell Bell – Guitar and violin/ Andy Coughlan – Bass/ John Webb – Keyboards and sax/ Cedric Sharpley – Drums/ Karen Taylor – Backing vocals.
Tracklist: 'We Are Glass' – Interview segment/ 'Berserker'/ 'Remind Me To Smile'/ 'Sister Surprise'/ 'Music For Chameleons'/ 'The Iceman Comes'/ 'Cold Warning'/ 'This Prison Moon'/ 'My Dying Machine'/ 'We Take Mystery (To Bed)'/ 'This Is New Love.'

Of all Numan's 80s video cassettes, *The Berserker Tour* is by far the easiest to track down having been re-issued a number of times since its original 1986 issue. The cassette featured 10 live tracks culled from Numan's 'Berserker Tour' of 1984 along with a short opening interview sequence. Viewing the footage, however, only emphasised to fans just how far Numan had slid in the years since the Wembley shows of 1981. The 'Berserker Tour' shows were definitely lacking in Numan's previous innate sense of spectacle and pizzazz. With a stage set resembling an all white Roman coliseum as well as a rather bored looking band all decked out in uniform white and a far from inspired set list, *The Berserker Tour* video has sadly gone on to become something of a visual snapshot of a rather awkward misstep in Numan's career.

Bizarrely, the UK 1990 re-issue of this cassette featured an alternative track list from the taped show although the back cover to the cassette still stated the original cassette's tracklist. Revised track list included: 'Berserker'/ 'Metal'/ 'Remind Me To Smile'/ 'The Iceman Comes'/ 'Cold Warning'/ 'Down In The Park'/ 'I Die: You Die'/ 'My

Dying Machine'/ 'Cars'/ 'We Are Glass'/ 'This Is New Love'/ 'Are "Friends" Electric?'
Special note: this video cassette has, as of 2002, been re-issued again rather controversially this time onto DVD by Sanctuary entertainment much to the Numan camp's obvious annoyance and displeasure, making a full concert official re-issue seem ever more remote.

Below are the various re-issues of The Berserker Tour *video.*

May 1987 re-issue via Video Collection

August 1990 re-issue via Castle/Hendring, note the back cover features the original tracklist when the tape inside actually played the revised concert tracklist.

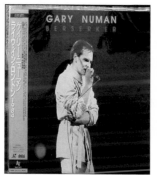

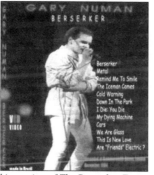

Japanese VCD release, tracklist for this version of The Berserker Tour was identical to the UK Castle/Hendring re-issue. This VCD was re-issued again in December 1993 and December 1996.

December 1993 via 4Front video

THE SKIN MECHANIC – LIVE
(PMI Video **Cat No:** MVP99-1217-3)
Released: June 1990.
Formats: VHS.
Foreign formats: matched the UK.
Recorded at the Hammersmith Odeon, London on the 26th of October 1989.
Running time: 60 minutes.
Deleted February 1992.
Re-issued on DVD via Classic Rock Productions in September 2003 (see 'Official DVDs').

This concert was shown on *Central Television* shortly after its release.

★★★★☆

Musicians: Gary Numan – Vocals/ RRussell Bell – Guitar/ Andy Coughlan – Bass/ Chris Payne – Keyboards/ Ade Orange – Keyboards/ Cedric Sharpley – Drums/ Cathi Ogden – Backing vocals/ Diana Wood – Backing vocals.
Tracklist: 'Intro' – ('God Only Knows')/ 'America'/ 'Me! I Disconnect From You'/ 'Creatures'/ 'Cars'/ 'Down In The Park'/ 'Devious'/ 'I Can't Stop'/ 'Are "Friends" Electric?'/ 'Call Out The Dogs'/ 'We Are Glass.'

Taped from the 1989 tour of the same name, *The Skin Mechanic-Live* video was one of Numan's most visually stunning outings to date, indeed on the live front, a tanned and relaxed Numan was certainly not letting his worsening record sales affect his concert performances or even allowing his limited finances to put the brakes on his lofty ideas for more elaborate and visually stunning shows. The tour saw Gary totally revamp his image in a bid to perhaps appeal to a much broader audience than before. Indeed Numan's move into the mainstream saw him taking a leaf out of the books of glossy pop acts like Duran Duran and Spandau Ballet by utilizing not only attractive female backing singers/ dancers but also presenting himself and the band within the framework of a modern stylish pop group.

The Skin Mechanic-Live video was, like *The Touring Principle '79* and *The Berserker Tour* before it, a highlights only release. With only 10 tracks on offer, the video was hardly an accurate representation of the tour set list which actually lent heavily on Gary's last studio album *Metal Rhythm* with a full six tracks lifted from that record. Fans hopes for a future re-issue of this video on DVD including, for the first time, the full uncut concert were dashed in September of 2003 when Classic Rock Productions licensed the edited live footage for a rather dubious DVD entitled *Gary Numan* (see 'Official DVDs).

SHADOWMAN
(NUMA/ Machine Music **Cat No:** NumaVID01)
Released: November 1992.
Formats: VHS.
Foreign formats: none.
Running time 50 minutes.
Special note: only available to buy via the Gary Numan website and the Gary Numan fan club.
Back cover featured all the single sleeves except 'Machine And Soul'*, this was represented by the *Machine + Soul* album cover.
* Re-titled 'Machine And Soul' on this video cassette.

Direction and production credits: 'Warriors' directed by Gary Numan, 'Your Fascination' directed by Terry Braun, 'Berserker' and 'My Dying Machine' made by Trilion Pictures, 'Call Out The Dogs' directed by Adrienne Sharp, 'Heart' directed by David Rose, 'I Can't Stop', 'This Is Love' and 'New Thing From London Town' made by Kadek Vision and finally both 'Emotion' and 'Machine And Soul' directed by Tracy Adams.

Track list: 'Warriors'/ 'Your Fascination'/ 'Berserker' (live promo)/ 'Call Out The Dogs'/ 'Heart'/ 'This Is Love'/ 'New Thing From London Town'/ 'Emotion'/ 'I Can't Stop (7-inch version)/ 'My Dying Machine' (live promo)/ 'Machine And Soul.'

Shadowman neatly picked up where the previous video compilation *Newman*

Numan left off in 1982. For this cassette, 11 promos were assembled ranging from the original video shot for the 1983 single 'Warriors' all the way up to Gary's latest offering, 'Machine And Soul.' *Shadowman*, however, did not include the videos shot for 'Miracles', 'I Still Remember' and the extended promo for 'I Can't Stop.' Also omitted were the promos shot for the Sharpe and Numan single 'Change Your Mind' as well as the 1987 self-titled 'Radio Heart' single. All the videos presented were in full and uncut.

DREAM CORROSION

(NUMA/ Machine Music – **Cat No:** NumaVID03)
Released: August 1994.
Formats: VHS.
Foreign formats: none.
Running time: 2 hours and 15 minutes.
Recorded at the Hammersmith Apollo on the 6th of November 1993.
Special note: cover photo was actually taken from Gary's appearance at the OMD shows in December 1993.
Musicians: Gary Numan – Vocals and guitar/ John Webb – Keyboards and saxophone/ Ade Orange – Keyboards and bass/ Kipper – Guitars/ Richard Beasley – Drums/ T.J. Davies – Backing vocals.

Tracklist: 'Intro' – 'Mission'/ 'Machine And Soul'/ 'Outland'/ 'Me! I Disconnect From You'/ 'We Are So Fragile'/ 'Respect'/ 'Shame'/ 'Films'/ 'Dream Killer'/ 'Down In The Park'/ 'My World Storm'/ 'The Machmen'/ 'Generator'/ 'Noise Noise'/ 'Cars'/ 'Voix'/ 'You Are In My Vision'/ 'It Must Have Been Years'/ 'That's Too Bad'/ 'Remind Me To Smile'/ 'I'm An Agent'/ 'Are "Friends" Electric?'/ 'My Breathing'/ 'I Don't Believe'/ 'Bombers'/ 'Jo The Waiter'/ 'We Are Glass'/ Interview segment.

Complimentary video released to accompany the 2CD live album of the same name, 'The Dream Corrosion Tour' saw Numan temporarily halt his career to give fans a concert tour they would never forget. For over two hours Numan entertained his loyal fan base with a live set made up of rarely performed album tracks and long lost B-sides. Almost every era of Gary's recording career got a look in on the 'Dream Corrosion' trek with the likes of 'Jo The Waiter', 'The Machmen', It Must Have Been Years', 'Noise Noise', 'I Don't Believe', 'Shame', 'Machine And Soul', 'Voix', 'Dream Killer' and 'Generator' all being aired for the very first time. What was also remarkable was the fact that Numan seemed to be really enjoying himself on this tour, even indulging in a few spots of impromptu headbanging. The *Dream Corrosion* video was an excellent release, one that captured a real turning point in Gary's troubled and beleaguered career.

(II) MISCELLANEOUS VIDEOS AND DVDS

Portions of Numan's songs have been included in a number of movies over the years (*Times Square, Dark City, In The Heat Of Passion, Point Of Interest, Buying The Cow* and *Speed*), however, the following videos and DVDs feature more than brief excerpts and therefore should be of interest to fans.

URGH! A MUSIC WAR
(Trimark Pictures)
Released: January 1981.
Formats: VHS, laserdisc and Betamax.
Foreign formats: matched the UK.
Directed by Derek Burbridge.
Running time: 104 minutes.

Video concert featuring Gary Numan performing 'Down In The Park' live on the 1980 'Teletour' (see 'Soundtrack albums'). In addition, the 1979 *Touring Principle* live clip of this track was also included on the 1980 punk documentary *Punk And its Aftershocks*. This was eventually re-issued on video in 1992.

Two other variations of the Urgh! A Music War *cassette as well as a promo poster.*

GARY NUMAN'S GREAT WARBIRDS AIR DISPLAY
(**Cat No:** unknown)
Released: June 1984.
Formats: VHS.
Foreign formats: none.

Filmed at the West Malling air show in 1983, this video features lots of aerobatics as well as complimentary gun camera footage from The Second World War. In amongst this, Gary can be seen interviewing various pilots from the air display itself. Following this event, Numan invested in his own Harvard aeroplane in a bid to move himself up from a simple club pilot to a fully-fledged air display pilot.

Original advert.

CARS/ WE ARE GLASS

(Chart Attack – videocassette single, **Cat No:** VCS008)
Released: December 1987.
Formats: VHS.
Foreign formats: none.
Special note: 'We Are Glass' was a previously unreleased, alternative video version taken from the 1981 *Micromusic* live VHS cassette.

Released following the return of 'Cars' to the British top 20, other recording artists had promo videos released on this short-lived video single format.

THE RARE GROOVE MIX

(**Cat No:** SVO 863)
Released: 1988.
Formats: VHS.
Foreign formats: none.
Running time: 60 minutes.
Special note: also issued on vinyl, cassette and CD.

This 20+ track video compilation featured 'We Are Glass' as part of its track list and the entire recording was edited into one long continuous mix.

SKI SCHOOL

(Movie store entertainment)
Released: 1991.
Formats: VHS.
Foreign formats: matched the UK.
Running time: 89 minutes.

Saucy comedy starring Ava Fabian and Dean Cameron. Movie was of interest to Numan fans due to the inclusion of the remixed version of the *Metal Rhythm* track 'Devious.'

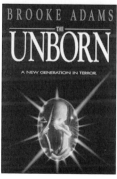

THE UNBORN

(RCA/ Columbia pictures)
Released: 1991.
Formats: VHS.
Foreign formats: matched the UK.
Running time: 82 minutes.

Horror movie directed by Rodman Flender (Executive producer: Mike Elliott) starring Brook Adams. This movie featured music composed by Gary Numan

Rare movie poster.

and Michael R Smith (see 'Numa Albums Part Two 1992-1995').

THE RADIAL PAIR
(Numa/ Machine music NUMAVID02)
Released: 1992.
Formats: VHS.
Foreign formats: none.
Special note: only available via Numan's website and the Gary Numan fan club.
Track list: 'Kiss Me And Die'/ 'Mission'/ 'Dark Rain'/ 'Cloud Dancing'/ 'Virus'/ 'Cold House'/ 'Red Sky'/ 'Machine Heart.' All songs are instrumentals.

This video took the viewer into the Numan cockpit for a seat-of-the pants trip into the frightening world of the air display pilot. The video featured formation aerobatics, low-level flying and much more besides. The music from this video was eventually released in its own right as a CD mini-album. Both items can still be obtained from Numan's website as well as the Gary Numan fan club.

MIDNIGHT TEASE
(New Horizon)
Released: 1994.
Formats: VHS.
Foreign formats: matched the UK.
Running time: 76 minutes.

Suspense/ Mystery thriller starring Cassandra Leigh, Rachel Reed and Edmund Halley. Movie was of interest to Numan fans due to the inclusion of the *Machine + Soul* album track 'Love Isolation.'

THE BEST OF THE OLD GREY WHISTLE TEST
(Road show/ BBC)
Released: April 2002.
Formats: double DVD and twin VHS cassettes.
Running time: 190 minutes.
No of discs: two.

Exhaustive trawl through the show's extensive archives. This video/ DVD delivered a vast array of artists and performances, primarily of interest to fans of Gary Numan and Tubeway Army due to the inclusion of the live performance of 'Are "Friends" Electric?'

VHS issue.

Special note: *The Old Grey Whistle Test* version of 'Down

In The Park' was included on one of the spin-off albums from the show in the early 80s.

(I) OFFICIAL DVDS

DVD added itself to the market place in the late 90s and this new format was a vast improvement over the traditional video cassette by delivering crystal clear visuals on basically a standard compact disc. With optional extras like alternative camera angles, out-takes and commentary to name but a few its no surprise that this format has proved to be a big hit with the general public at large. Indeed it's expected that DVD will completely replace videotape in the not-too-distant future.

BERSERKER
(Sanctuary Visual Entertainment **Cat No:** SDE3012)
Released: July 2002.
DVD optional extras: DVD VJ – track-by-track audio review*, aspect ratio: 4:3.
Running time of main feature: 60 minutes.
Main feature filmed and recorded at the Hammersmith Odeon, London on the 11th of December 1984.
Main feature previously released on VHS video cassette/ Video CD (see 'Official video cassettes').
* VJ Simon Greenall incorrectly states that in early 1980 both Gary and bassist Paul Gardiner flew to the Bahamas to record 'Remind Me To Smile' with Robert Palmer. Although this trip did take place the actual Numan penned track recorded was 'I Dream Of Wires', a song that was mooted (though eventually rejected) at the time as the likely first single from Gary's then impending second solo album *Telekon*.

Tracks: 'We Are Glass' ('Intro')/ 'Berserker'/ 'Remind Me To Smile'/ 'Sister Surprise'/ 'Music For Chameleons'/ 'The Iceman Comes'/ 'Cold Warning'/ 'This Prison Moon'/ 'My Dying Machine'/ 'We Take Mystery (To Bed)'/ 'This Is New Love.'

The first official Gary Numan DVD arrived in the summer months of 2002 and it was essentially a re-issue of Numan's mid-80s live video *The Berserker Tour* complete with the added VJ section (see above). Unfortunately, its very appearance caused frustration and dismay in the Numan camp, who up to that point were understood to be readying their own DVD release of *The Berserker Tour* video. Numan felt that the footage from this concert had long since reverted back into his ownership. However, Sanctuary disagreed and released it without Numan's permission.

The version used for the DVD was the original 10-song video with the addition of commentary on each individual track. The narration was provided by Simon Greenall who could be viewed reading, quite frankly, laughably incorrect text from a piece of paper in front of him.

Although eagerly snapped up by fans, Numan's debut official DVD was rather disappointing, hopefully a future release of this concert will feature, for the first time, the show in full as well as extras in the way of archive interviews, behind the scenes footage and promos.

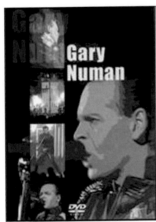

GARY NUMAN
(Classic Rock Legends CRL 1150)
Released: September 2003.
DVD optional extras: none.
Running time: 50 minutes.
Main feature: see *The Skin Mechanic-Live* video for details.
Main feature previously issued on VHS cassette (see 'Official video cassettes').
Tracks: see *The Skin Mechanic-Live* video.

Originally issued in the US in the early part of 2003, the back cover artwork listed all 21 tracks that had originally been performed in concert on 'The Skin Mechanic Tour.' Bizarrely, the front cover was not a shot taken from the 1989 tour but rather a live photo of Gary during the 1980 'Teletour' (see right).

Sadly, fans purchasing this DVD soon discovered that it was in fact not the full concert footage but a direct copy of the same 10-track show transmitted via *Central Television* in the early 90s. Although the taped footage was in excellent condition, fans were extremely disappointed when it was discovered that this second 'official' Numan DVD was just another straight re-issue of a previously released item.

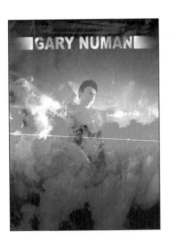

HOPE BLEEDS
(Mortal)
Release due November 2004.

(II) BOOTLEG DVDS
In recent years unofficial DVDs have begun to appear in the marketplace alongside the more commonly seen bootleg videos. These DVDs have ranged from typically poorly shot live camcorder footage to rather excellent digital conversions of previously available video compilations. Some though have been exceptional, put together so professionally that the end product has been as good as an official release and this section will highlight the very best fan generated DVDs that have appeared in recent years.

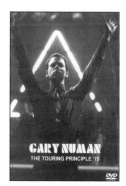

THE TOURING PRINCIPLE – '79
(Cat No and release date unknown)

Standard digital conversion that included a menu that allowed the viewer to access the original 1980 video, a track selection or nine in-concert photographs from the 1979 tour. The video footage was sourced from VHS cassette and was in excellent condition.

MICROMUSIC
(Cat No and release date unknown)

Standard digital conversion that included a menu that allowed the viewer to access the original two-hour concert, information about the band members and a brief biography detailing the history of the event. In addition, the 'monitor mix' version of 'Conversation' was also included. This had originally been added to the 1998 2CD release of

Yet another bootleg DVD of Micromusic, this one appears to be of US origin,

Living Ornaments '81. The concert footage had been sourced from laserdisc.

Special note: the only format that this UK DVD would not play properly on was the *Sony Playstation 2*; concert footage would only playback in black and white.

GARY NUMAN LIVE
(Cat No and release date unknown)

This DVD includes *The Skin Mechanic-Live* video, the menu gave access to the full concert, a track selection as well as the 1989 'Skin Mechanic' tour dates. This recording was taken from the *Central Television*, late night concert programme *Bed Rock* and was a far superior cut of the eventual show issued on DVD by Classic Rock Promotions in September 2003. Unlike that release, this fan-produced recording included the intro tape 'God Only Knows.'

SHEPHERDS BUSH EMPIRE

(Cat No and release date unknown)

Recorded live on the 9th of February 2003 as part of Gary's 25th anniversary shows.

Tracks: 'Hybrid'/ 'My Shadow In Vain'/ 'M.E.'/ 'My Jesus'/ 'That's Too Bad'/ 'Ancients'/ 'Every Day I Die'/ 'Torn'/ 'Down In The Park'/ 'Please Push No More'/ 'It Must Have Been Years'/ 'Crazier'/ 'Pure'/ 'I Can't Breathe'/ 'Rip'/ 'A Prayer For The Unborn'/ 'Cars'/ 'Are "Friends" Electric?'/ 'Bleed'/ 'I Die: You Die'/ 'We Are Glass.'

Running Time: 2 hours and 30 minutes.

    This DVD included the full show as well as including the full set from support band Sulpher. Of all the bootleg camcorder footage in the marketplace, this was easily the best. Recorded on a digital camera mounted on a steady tripod. Highly recommended.

TOP OF THE POPS 1979-2002

(Cat No and release date unknown)

Tracks: 'Are "Friends" Electric?' (five performances)/ 'Cars' (four performances)/ 'Music For Chameleons' (two performances)/ 'This Wreckage'/ 'Warriors'/ 'Sister Surprise'/ 'Berserker'/ 'Change Your Mind'/ 'Rip'/ 'White Boys And Heroes'/ 'We Take Mystery (To Bed).'

Running time: 70 minutes.

    This superb DVD contained every Gary Numan performance from the UK pop show *Top Of The Pops*. The disc featured a menu where the

viewer could access either the whole programme or track selections. In addition, the show's theme music was included as well as chart positions for each of the singles. However, most of these were incorrect. A second version of this DVD appeared at the end of 2003 featuring Gary's 2003 *Top Of The Pops* appearance performing 'Crazier' as well as a brief interview from the show, this re-issue sported a brand new cover (see right).

TV APPEARANCES 1981-1982

(Cat No and release date unknown)

Tracks: *Swap Shop* interview/ *BBC* news report on crash landing/ *Razzmatazz* interview/ 'Music For Chameleons' – *Top Of The Pops*, version one/ 'Music For Chameleons' – *Top Of The Pops*, version two/ 'We Take Mystery (To Bed)' – *Top Of The Pops* performance/ Interview on the *Numanair* plane/ Russell Harty interview on Concorde/ *Late Night On 2* – interview/ *Tiswas* – interview/ *Jim'll Fix it* – 'Music For Chameleons', live performance/ *The Tube* – interview/ 'White Boys And Heroes' – *Top Of The Pops* performance/ 'Music For Chameleons' – *Razzmatazz* performance/

American *MTV* interviews – two features*/ Canadian TV – *New Music* report.*
Running time: 90 minutes.
* Included as bonus features, this footage was not of the high standard of the rest of the clips included on this DVD. Menu also plays four Numan audio tracks: 'This House Is Cold', 'You Are, You Are', 'Warsongs' and the rare US 12-inch remix of 'White Boys And Heroes.'

Utterly fantastic fan produced DVD, an essential purchase for any hardcore fan.

GARY NUMAN'S CARS

(Cat No and release date unknown)

This DVD included all six episodes of the *Men And Motors* show – *Gary Numan's Cars*. Each programme saw Numan test-driving a different vehicle as well as exclusive interviews from his *Alien Studios*. DVD menu also allows the viewer to access a series of photographs as well as one music video.

THE MUSIC VIDEO ANTHOLOGY

(Blitz productions, Cat No and release date unknown)
Formats: DVD and VHS cassette.
Running time: one hour.
Special note: this release appeared to be of US origin.
Tracks: 'Cars'/ 'Down In The Park' (live)/ 'I Die: You Die'/ 'She's Got Claws'/ 'We Take Mystery (To Bed)'/ 'Change Your Mind'/ 'Cars' (Fear Factory version)/ 'Dominion Day'/ 'Cars' (Information window version)/ 'Cars' (Pop-up video version)/ 'Cars' (live in New York '80)/ 1998 documentary/ 2003 profile.

This dubious collection of videos emerged in the middle of 2003; despite the appalling cover, the production team behind it did manage to include all the promos totally uncut, something that would obviously be of high interest to long time fans that have only ever seen the *Newman Numan* versions of these video clips.

GARY NUMAN – THE VIDEOS 1979 – 2003

(Cat No and release date unknown)
Formats: DVD.
Running time: 1 hour 30 minutes.
* Cover actually incorrectly states time frame as 1970 – 2003.

This superb DVD had obviously been a true labour of love, on this disc were all of Numan's 29** promo videos. The recording runs chronologically from 'Cars' (Numan's debut video) right up to 'Crazier.' Four bonus videos were also included, those were: 'Metal'/ 'Cars' (Fear Factory version)/ 'We Take Mystery (To Bed)' – *Top Of The Pops* version/

'White Boys And Heroes' – *Top Of The Pops* version.

** Video for 'This Wreckage' was not the original live promo, rather it was the live version taken from the 1982 video cassette *Micromusic*.

The disc came complete with an interactive menu that played Numan background music as well as options to either select tracks for viewing, or to simply play the full recording. All the video's were in excellent condition and were sourced from Gary's previously available video collections (*Newman Numan*, *Shadowman*) as well as television and CD singles.

SACRIFICE – THE 1994 UK TOUR

(Cat No and release date unknown)
Formats: DVD and VHS cassette.
Running time: I hour 50 minutes.
 Fan-shot camcorder footage.

This DVD emerged in the middle of 2003 and was an upgraded version of the originally issued bootleg video. Like the original, the DVD features the whole show from the Hammersmith Labbats Apollo on the 5th of November.

MUSIC PLANET 2 NITE

(Cat No unknown)
Released: June 2003.
Formats: DVD.
Running time: one hour.

This DVD featured Gary's 'live in the studio' performance on the German TV channel *Arte*, songs performed were: 'Rip', 'Dark', 'Crazier', 'A Prayer For The Unborn' and 'I Can't Breathe.' Also included were three interview segments (one undertaken with Nick Rhodes of Duran Duran and former vocalist with the band Steven 'Tin Tin' Duffy). Menu gave the viewer the opportunity to play the full programme (complete with second band The Devils) or just Numan's performance. In addition, both the promos for 'Rip' and 'Crazier' were included.

GARY NUMAN TV APPEARANCES 1986

(Cat No and release date unknown)
Formats: DVD.
Tracks: Interview (*Lunchtime Live*)/ The Day Of Protest (*UK News*)/ 'This is love'& Interview (*Nightline*)/ Interview at Rock City (*My Weekend Feature*)/ R.S.P.C.A. interview (*BBC Breakfast News*)/ 'I Can't Stop' (*Wogan*)/ Numan feature (*Get Fresh*)/ R.S.P.C.A. interview (*Granada Reports*)/ Interview (*Cable TV*)/ One hour feature (*Cable TV 'Flights Of Fancy'*)*/ 'I Can't Stop' (Club Mix Video).

* Separate DVD (see right) issued featuring this programme. Show featured Gary interviewed by Amanda

Reddington with the conversational topics ranging from Gary's flying antics to his music career. The programme also featured a whole host of promo videos (although none are complete) including 'Change Your Mind', 'She's Got Claws' and the rarely seen video for his 1985 single 'Miracles.' DVD also included the rarely seen extended video for the club mix version of 'I Can't Stop.'

ANTHOLOGY

(Cat No and release date unknown)
Formats: DVD.
Running time: 3 hours.

Included on this disc were: 'Your Fascination'/ 'I Can't Stop'/ Interview 1986/ 'This Is New Love'/ 'Call Out The Dogs' (live 1985 – clip only)/ 'Are "Friends" Electric?' (Old Grey Whistle Test performance)/ Segments of both Dream Corrosion and The Touring Principle '79 videos as well as the complete alternative tracklist of The Berserker Tour video.

Worth seeking out for the first appearance of the second version of *The Berserker Tour* video footage on DVD.

GARY NUMAN 1980

(Cat No and release date unknown)
Tracks: 'Replicas', 'I Die: You Die' and 'Down In The Park.' Live pro-shot footage from the La Palace show in March 1980/ Toronto Music Hall interview/ 'Praying To The Aliens' and 'Cars' from *Saturday Night Live*/ *Swap Shop* interview/ 'I Die: You Die' from *The Kenny Everett Show*/ *Check It Out* interview/ 'This Wreckage', 'Remind Me To Smile' and 'Down In The Park.' Live pro-shot footage from the UK leg of 'Teletour'/ Newcastle City Hall interview/ *Top Of The Pops* performance of 'This Wreckage'/ 'Down In The Park' Hybrid version of both the 1979/ 1980 recordings. This version was taken from the European television channel *Rage*/ Canadian interview (Bonus footage).

Another superb DVD filled with long lost archive interviews and performances. Surprisingly the clips included were in excellent condition and an essential purchase for any fan.

GARY NUMAN LIVE

(Cat No and release date unknown)
This DVD features both *The Touring Principle '79* and the alternative track list version of *The Berserker Tour.*

GARY NUMAN DVD COMPILATION
(Cat No and release date unknown)
Tracks: 'Cars' (*TOTPS* '87 and '96)/ The Warriors Tour sound check/ 'Berserker' (*TOTPS* and *Razzamatazz*)/ 'My Dying Machine' (*Razzamatazz*)/ *Heaven And Earth* interview/ The Berserker Tour – backstage/ 'Your Fascination' – promo/ The Warriors Tour – concert clip/ FM interview '97 and 2000/ *ITN* newsreel (vintage aircraft)/ *The LuLu Show* and *The Leo Sayor Show*/ 'Warriors' promo/ 'Rip' promo/ 'This Is Love' promo/ 'Films' – live 1981/ 'New Thing From London Town' promo/ 'Tracks' – live 1981/ 'I Can't Stop' promo/ 'Emotion' promo/ 'Heart' promo/ Are "Friends" Electric?' – live 1981/ 'Call Out The Dogs' promo/ 'Berserker' promo/ Are "Friends" Electric? – live 1984/ 'Call Out The Dogs' and 'We Are Glass' – live 1989/ Interactive section featuring a discography.

Fairly disjointed DVD compilation, does feature, however, a number of rarities. In addition, the quality of the clips are all excellent.

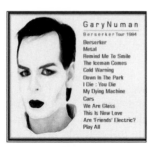

BERSERKER TOUR 1984
(Cat No and release date unknown)
This DVD features the alternative *The Berserker Tour* video

NUMAN – THE DISCO TAPES 2003
(**Cat No:** Unknown)
Released: April 2004
Tracks: 'No More Lies' (*The Roxy*)/ 'Absolution' (*This Morning*)/ 'I Can't Stop' (*Wogan*)/ 'My Dying Machine'-German T.V. / Interview clip (*Late Night On 2*)/ 'Cars' (*Saturday Night Live*)/ 'Sister Surprise' (*Top Of The Pops*)/ 'Change Your Mind' (*Top Of The Pops*)/ 'Music For Chameleons' (*Late Night On 2*)/ Interview clip (*Jack Docherty Show*)/ 'Scar' (*In Bed With Me Dinner*)/ HMV signing session in 2002/ 'Metal' (promo video)/ 'Warriors' (*The Saturday Show*)/ 'Berserker' (*Razamatazz*)/ Interview clip (*Stars And Their Cars*)/ Are "Friends" Electric? (*The White Room*)/ 'On Broadway' (*The Leo Sayer Show*)/ 'We Take Mystery (To Bed)' (*Top Of The Pops*)/ 'Noise Noise' (*Take It To The Bridge*)/ 'This Is New Love' (*The Leo Sayer Show*)/ 'Friends' (*Tom Binns Munchies*)/ 'I Die: You Die' (*The Kenny Everett Show*)/ 'Cars (The Premier Mix)' (*Top Of The Pops*)/ 'Crazier' (new 'fan produced' promo).

Another superb collection of archive Gary Numan TV appearances from across the years. Best of all, this expertly assembled DVD also included a brand new fan sourced promo video for 'Crazier'*, for this clip literally hundreds of TV appearances, live performances and promo videos had been chopped up and used to assemble a unique and utterly fantastic 'Numan through the years' promo video. All the clips included on this DVD were in excellent condition.

* One of three that emerged in the spring of 2004, the others being: 'My World Storm' and 'We Are So Fragile.'

GARY NUMAN TV APPEARANCES – Volume 2

(Cat No and release date unknown)

Running time: 1hour & 5 minutes

Tracks: 'Friends' & interview (*Tom Binn's Munchies*)/ 'Are "Friends" Electric?', 'Rip' and 'Crazier' (*T.O.T.P.S. 2*)/ 'Are "Friends" Electric?' and 'Crazier' (*This Is Dom Joly*)/ 'Are "Friends" Electric?' and interview (*Graham Norton*)/ Interview (*Rise*)/ Music clip (*Never Mind The Buzzcocks*).

An excellent compilation.

GARY NUMAN ON TV

(Cat No and released date unknown)

Running time: 1 hour.

Tracks: 'Are "Friends" Electric?' 1979 and 2002. 'Rip' and 'Crazier' (all clips from *TOTP 1 and 2*)/ 'Dominion Day' (promo)/ 'Rip' (promo)/ 'Cars' (Fear Factory promo)/ 'Crazier' (promo)/ Interviews (*Heaven And Earth, Jo Whiley, Graham Norton and Liquid News*)/ 'Are "Friends" Electric?' (*Old Grey Whistle Test*)/ 'Cars' (*Saturday Night Live*)/ 'Friends' (*Tom Binns Munchies*)/ 'Are "Friends" Electric?' (*Graham Norton*)/ 'Crazier' and 'Are "Friends" Electric?' (*This Is Dom Joly*)

Plenty of good quality Numan footage and all expertly assembled.

GARY NUMAN TV APPEARANCES Volume 1

(Cat No and release date unknown)

Running time: 1 hour and 5 minutes.

Tracks: Numan clip from a Human League programme/ Gary Numan feature (*I love 1979*)/ 'Cars premier mix' (*TOTP*)/ 'Cars premier mix' (*TOTP2*)/ 'Cars' (*Noels House Party*)/ Carling Premier TV Ad1 and Carling Premier TV Ad2/ Premier Hits TV Ad/ 'Are "Friends" Electric?' TV Ad/ 'Cars' and 'Are "Friends" Electric?'(*The White Room*)/ 'Absolution' and interview (*This Morning*)/ Interview (*Rock Mania*)/ Interview (*Adam And Joe Show*)/ Interview (*Liquid News*)/ Interview (*He's Got To Have It*)/ Interview (*Kerrang Awards*)/ An incomplete clip from the Reading festival/ 'Koochy' video clip/ 'I Die: You Die' (*TOTP2*).

Another bumper package of rare and hard to find Numan clips.

GARY NUMAN TV APPEARANCES Volume 6

(Cat No and release date unknown)

Running time: 1 hour and 7 minutes.

Tracks: 'I'm On Automatic' and interview (*Club X*)/ Interview 1992 (*Breakfast TV*)/ 'Are "Friends" Electric?' promo video (Nancy Boy) and interview/ Interview (*Light Lunch*)/ 'Koochy' (*TOTP*)/ Interview (*Channel 4 Top Ten Electro Acts*)

Another fine compilation.

GARY NUMAN TV APPEARANCES 1983

(Cat No and release date unknown)

Running time: 1 hour.

Tracks: 'Warriors' (*TOTP*)/ TV appearance (*Summer Run*)/ Interview (*Kid Jenson – Mad About*)/ Interview (*Razzamatazz*)/ 'Warriors' (*Crackerjack*)/ News item (*Granada TV*)/Interview (*CBTV*)/ Interview (*Calender*)/ 'Warriors' and interviews (*The Saturday Show – four separate programmes*)/ News item (*ITN News*)/ Brief interview (*Rock Around The Clock*)/ 'Sister Surprise (*TOTP*)/ Interview (*Switch*)/ Interview (*Southeast At Six*)/ 'Remind Me To Smile'

Cine camera footage with additional 'radio sourced' soundtrack.

Absolutely superb, an essential purchase for any fan.

GARY NUMAN TV APPEARANCES 1984

(Cat No and release date unknown)

Running time: 50 minutes.

Tracks: 'Berserker' (*TOTP and Razzamatazz*)/ A roadies life (*The Oxford Roadshow*)/ 'My Dying Machine' (*Razzamatazz*)/ 'This Is New Love' (*The Main Attraction and The Leo Sayer Show*)/ Interview and 'On Broadway' (*Leo Sayer Show*)/ TV appearance (*Names And Games*).*

Another fan produced professional DVD.

* Separate DVD issued featuring this TV appearance (see right).

GARY NUMAN TV APPEARANCES 1985
(Cat No and release date unknown)
Running time: 90 minutes.
Tracks: Intro page: Razormaid remix of 'This Disease'/ 'My Dying Machine' (*German TV*)/ 'Berserker' (*Swiss TV*)/ 'Change Your Mind' promo video plus Sharpe & Numan interview (*Saturday Superstore*)/ 'Change Your Mind' (*TOTP*)/ 'Are "Friends" Electric?' plus Interview (*The Old Grey Whistle Test*)/ 'Your Fascination' (*Italian TV.*)/ Interview (*TV Eye*)/ Interview (*TV AM*)/ Interview (*Northern Life*)/ The Fury Rehearsals (*The Wide Awake Club*)/ Interview (*Southampton today*)/ Interview (*Lees place*)/ Cine camera footage from 'The Fury Tour' featuring B-side 'Puppets' as its soundtrack/ 'Harlequin Tears' – Hohokam promo video.

Another superb collection of hard to find vintage Numan clips.

IMPORTANT TELEVISION APPEARANCES

Although radio was reluctant to give Numan's music much airplay, television on the other hand was one medium that was always much more receptive to the Gary Numan cause, allotting time and space for him whenever he had new product to promote. This section will take a chronological look back over some of Gary's more notable TV interviews and performances that fans would be interested in.

OLD GREY WHISTLE TEST (UK)
BBC 2, 23rd of May 1979.
Subject: live in the studio performance of 'Down In The Park' and 'Are "Friends" Electric?'

This was Tubeway Army's debut TV appearance and the nation's first glimpse of the enigmatic Gary Numan. *The Old Grey Whistle Test* was a long established 'serious' music show more inclined to show acts less likely to enter the British top 40. For the show, Gary had augmented the group's line-up to a five piece including one time Ultravox! keyboard player Billie Currie. This appearance was the group's first live performance in front of a real TV audience.

TOP OF THE POPS (UK)
BBC 1, 24th of May 1979.
Subject: mimed performance – 'Are "Friends" Electric?'

With good fortune on their side, Tubeway army were asked to perform their new single on the show's 'Bubbling under' section, and clad in black and immersed in stark white light, 'Are "Friends" Electric's' throbbing drone and relentless motorised beat entranced a nation. Within weeks the single found itself rocketing to the top slot staying there for a full four weeks, making Numan an instant overnight star.

SATURDAY NIGHT LIVE! (US)
NBC, 16th of February 1980
Subject: live performance – 'Cars' and 'Praying To The Aliens.'*
* The screening of this song rather bizarrely featured subtitles.

With an estimated viewer potential of 50 million, this was Numan's golden opportunity to break into the lucrative US market; following this appearance, 'Cars' and its parent album *The Pleasure Principle* both went on to become huge stateside smashes.

TELETOUR FOOTAGE (UK)
Various, 1980.
Subject: three live promo's: 'Down In The Park', 'Remind Me To Smile' and 'This Wreckage.'
   Much to the obvious frustration of fans, only three clips have ever surfaced from Gary's spectacular 1980 'Teletour', regarded by fans as the very zenith of Numan's early 80s powers. Should the full video ever appear it will no doubt be greeted with hysteria from Numan's long time fans.

THE KENNY EVERETT VIDEO SHOW (UK)
Originally filmed in 1980, finally aired 1981.
Subject: Performance – 'I Die: You Die.'
   Kenny Everett was a popular comedian whose show was a chaotic mixture of sketches and live performances. Controversially, Numan's performance, of his then new single 'I Die: You Die', was removed from its Christmas slot and re-scheduled for later the next year (see Gary Numan autobiography *Praying To The Aliens* for details). The version performed was a hitherto previously unreleased 4th version of the track and to date has not re-surfaced.

CHECK IT OUT (UK)
ITV and Tyne Tees television, April 1980.
Subject: interview.
   This interview was conducted by Paul Gambaccini on the set for Gary's then upcoming new single 'We Are Glass.' The interview itself was interesting as it gave an insight into the embryonic world of the video market (then a brand new medium). As Numan was the first artist anywhere in the world to release an all-music, long-form video to buy, Paul was keen to quiz Gary about his thoughts over its potential success or failure, and it's during this interview that Gary confirmed rumours that he was considering bringing an end to his live career to concentrate on making primarily music and videos. A great interview, but fans were not impressed by the extremely unprofessional attitude of one member of the show's closing presenters who commented 'Amazing what you can do with a puppet these days' when the piece ended.

THE FAREWELL SHOWS (UK)
ITV television, June 1981.
Subject: edited highlights from the Wembley Arena shows.
   Following the conclusion of the farewell concerts back in April, *ITV* television screened an edited 45-minute concert one Sunday afternoon; this footage was eventually released as a video and sold exclusively in foreign markets as an alternative to the UK released *Micromusic* video that featured the full uncut concert.

PLANE CRASH (UK)
Subject: various news reports 29th of January 1982 from the BBC and ITV.
   Fans tuning in to the news on this particular evening would have been stunned

to see a rather breathless and dazed Gary Numan being interviewed in the middle of a road with a shattered aircraft just behind him. The reasons behind the actual crash turned out in the end to be mechanical failure but the press, thrilled to finally have the opportunity to totally humiliate the star printed their own invented versions of this unfortunate mishap over the following days and weeks. The legacy of this event has hung over Gary ever since and still dogs him to this day.

TOP OF THE POPS (UK)
BBC 1, June and August 1982.
Subject: specially commissioned *Top Of The Pops* promos for 'White Boys And Heroes' and 'We Take Mystery (To Bed).'
    With Numan residing in the USA in 1982, *Top Of The Pops* travelled to both New York and Los Angeles to film two promo videos for Gary's next two singles. Fans have since pointed out that the clip shot for 'We Take Mystery (To Bed)' was actually much better than the official video that was shot for the song.

THE TUBE (UK)
Channel 4 television, September 1982.
Subject: interview.
    With Numan preparing for his American concerts in support of the album *I, Assassin*, Channel 4 music show *The Tube* despatched presenters Jools Holland and the late Paula Yates to conduct a series of interviews. Gary seemed relaxed and highlighted his admiration for his parents (who were also with Gary in the states and also interviewed during the piece) and revealed plans for a return to performing in the UK the following year. Also shown during the programme was professionally shot live footage of Gary on stage performing 'Music For Chameleons' leading fans to speculate that this tour, like previous outings, was also periodically video taped. Fans hope more video footage from this trek will surface in the future as part of a complimentary video/ DVD compilation.

THE LEO SAYER SHOW (UK)
ITV television, June 1984.
Subject: interview and performance.
    Numan's first TV appearance of 1984 came courtesy of Leo Sayer. Leo had been a hugely successful solo artist with a string of hits and here in the mid-80s had his own prime time TV show. The interview followed film of Gary landing a WW2 Dakota named 'Vera Lynne' and took place on the grass just off the runway. Gary appeared relaxed in Leo's presence and this made for an excellent interview; later the pair climbed into the aircraft for a quick complimentary jaunt round the airfield. This segment gave way to the pair back at the TV studios dressed as tramps who were clearly somewhat intoxicated. The pair performed an unlikely duet of the Numan early 80s live favourite 'On Broadway', and it was during this song that Gary shocked both audience and fans by finally removing his hat to reveal his newly dyed electric blue hair! The final song was performed without Leo and was a fantastic brand new track entitled 'This Is New Love.' Sadly, fans' hopes of a release for this track as a single faded over the course of the next few months, although a little later in the year another version of this track was performed on *The Main Attraction*. Neither mixes of this track or the 'On Broadway' duet have ever been granted an official release.

TOP OF THE POPS/ RAZZAMATTAZ (UK)
BBC 1 and Channel 4, November 1984.
Subject: performance of 'Berserker.'

Numan's return to the pop scene was something of a shock, not only for fans but the public at large, and regular viewers of both shows tuning in were greeted to a heavily made up Numan clad in clown white make-up, blue hair, blue lipstick and blue eye shadow. The shocks didn't end there either as musically Numan had also dramatically changed; gone was the previously anthemic, yet simplistic synth pop attack replaced here with a shuddering slab of proto-industrial noise complete with a cracked and ragged vocal performance from Gary layered over the top. The song's thunderous grooves found little favour amongst the Duran Duran/ Wham! – weaned pop kids of 1984 and quietly entered and slipped from the lower reaches of the UK top 40.

TV EYE (UK)
BBC 1, 1985.
Subject: interview as part of a political documentary.

Perhaps the most career damaging moment for Gary was to agree to be interviewed for a documentary concerning the political climate of the mid-80s. Also contributing interview segments were Paul Weller and Billy Bragg, both of whom were supporters of 'Red Wedge', a left-wing Labour movement. Numan's interview segments were manipulated to make it appear is if he was a hard line Tory supporter (an extremely unpopular position to be in at this point in time) and off-set against Weller and Bragg's comments, the producers succeeded in making Gary appear foolish, ill-informed, rude and very arrogant. When aired, it angered many and did much to cement a negative opinion about Gary that lingered for years after.

THE DAY OF PROTEST (UK)
BBC 1, 9th of August 1986.
Subject: news report.

For much of Numan's career, attempting to secure vital radio airplay on the nation's premier station Radio One had always proved extremely difficult even during Numan's most popular years. However, by 1986 Gary's career had settled down somewhat and being now in charge of an independent record company, radio airplay was now more sought after than at any time before. Radio One though, wouldn't budge, refusing to play-list Gary Numan singles full stop. By the middle of 1986 fans had had enough; having watched in anger two of Gary's finest singles barely graze the top 30 ('This Is Love' and 'I Can't Stop') they took matters into their own hands and demonstrated outside Broadcasting house itself. The event picked up some media attention and even Gary himself was said to be touched, sadly though, despite the good intentions, the day of protest only succeeded in polarising opinions at the station, virtually blacklisting Numan for good from daytime airplay.

THE ROXY (UK)
ITV television, January 1988.
Subject: performance of the new Sharpe and Numan single 'No More Lies.'

Another pivotal moment in Gary's career arrived in early 1988 with the release of a 3rd Sharpe and Numan single entitled 'No More Lies.' Unsure of the track to begin with, when it came time to perform the song on the new *ITV* chart show *The Roxy*, Numan all but walked off the set. Fans watching the show at home were stunned, gone was Gary's trademark style and sound replaced by the kind of weak, lightweight pop pap that was paraded on both *The Roxy* and *Top Of The Pops* week in week out. Not surprisingly fans neglected to buy the single and it made little impression on the charts; in fact 'No More Lies' was Gary's last visit to the UK top 40 singles chart (bar the 1996 re-issue of 'Cars') for many years.

TOP OF THE POPS/ THE WHITE ROOM/ NOEL EDMUNDS HOUSE PARTY (UK)
Various channels, January 1996.
Subject: performances of 'Cars.'

Following the high profile beer commercial that used 'Cars' as part of its advert, the song was a sudden and unexpected smash all over again. Gary found himself back in demand once more and duly appeared on a glut of shows either being interviewed or performing his two biggest hits 'Are "Friends" Electric?' and 'Cars.' This sudden exposure put Gary on the long road to recovery and following promotional duties for the single and its accompanying compilation *Premier Hits* he signed a new record deal with Eagle Records and made a return to the charts in his own right with a new studio album *Exile* at the end of 1997.

THE BIG BREAKFAST (UK)
Channel 4, 1997.
Subject: interview.

Gary appeared on the *Channel 4* flag-ship show *The Big Breakfast* to be interviewed by regular host Johnny Vaughan. Vaughan's warm and witty interview technique quickly put Gary at ease and both were soon sharing jokes (most of which were at Numan's expense). Subjects touched upon ranged from his early career to fans stealing his garden fish and flowers. Also revealed for the first time (and much to the embarrassment of an off camera Gemma Webb) was the fact that she too had later confessed to Gary to being responsible for removing birthday cards from his car as a young fan. This was a great interview and did much to change the public perception of Gary, expelling any lingering, negative opinions.

JACK DOCHERTY (UK)
Channel 4, 1997.
Subject: interview.

Gary appeared as a guest on this late night chat show to talk mainly about his early career. The topic was fairly lightweight with Gary taking the incessant leg-pulling from the host of the show all in his stride, in fact, throughout the interview Numan revealed himself to be something of a comedian, playfully rebuffing Jack's endless jokes and wind-ups. Also worthy of note was Gary's frustrations concerning his archive of video material that was then, apparently, under the ownership of Derek Burbridge despite Numan confessing he had no recollection of ever selling them to him in the first place.

MTV – SELECT (EUROPE)
1997.
Subject: interview.

For the release of the 2CD tribute album *Random* Gary was invited into the *MTV* studios and duly appeared on the video request programme *Select*. Numan admitted he was initially taken aback upon hearing of the project but thrilled with the end product. Other topics raised were his upcoming autobiography, getting married and even a spot of acting. Its worth pointing out that Eve, the *MTV* host, admitted to having been quite nervous prior to meeting Gary and commented after the interview how refreshingly down to earth and nice he was in the flesh.

GRAHAM NORTON (UK)
Channel 4, May 2002.
Subject: interview.

With the Sugababes at No1 with the 'Are "Friends" Electric?' sampled single 'Freak Like Me', Norton invited Gary onto his late night chat show for an interview. Gary was full of praise for the single and admitted he thought it actually eclipsed his own 1979 version. Norton also poked fun at some of the outfits Gary wore in the 80s, which Gary seemed happy to play along with. The show concluded with an edited new live version of 'Are "Friends" Electric?'

TOP OF THE POPS/ KERRANG TV (UK)
BBC 1 and Satellite television, May 2002.
Subject: two singles at No1 at the same time, one, a semi-cover version and the other a brand new song.

The video for the song 'Rip' had been shot over a year ago and had, at the time, been ignored and shelved by Gary's label Eagle Records. Following his move to Artful Records in late 2001 the clip was duly licensed from Eagle and sent in the spring of 2002 to the newly launched interactive music channel *Kerrang TV* who immediately play-listed it. Within weeks it had become the channel's most requested video and rocketed to the No1 spot. At the same time all girl pop act Sugababes released their 'Are "Friends" Electric?' sampled new single 'Freak Like Me' and also scored an instant No1 giving Gary the unique accolade of having two different songs at No1 at the same time. 'Rip' was eventually released as a single in its own right and returned Gary to the British top 30 for the first time in over a decade.

TOP OF THE POPS 2 (UK)
BBC1, August 2002.
Subject: live performance.

Top Of The Pops 2, sister show to the long established *Top Of The Pops* invited Gary to the studio to perform both his new single 'Rip' and his former and recently Sugababes re-activated 1979 classic 'Are "Friends" Electric?' The performance of both songs went extremely well with Numan warmly received by the assembled audience.

HEAVEN AND EARTH (UK)
BBC 2, June 2002.
Subject: interview.

Heaven And Earth was a current affairs show that transmitted on a Sunday morning, its tone was semi-religious though not overbearing. Fans expressed considerable surprise when news filtered through that Gary was booked to appear on the show as a guest, especially as he was well known for his outspoken views of all organised religions. Transmitted in two parts, the interview was conducted by Alice Beer and filmed from Gary's country retreat. Subjects under the spotlight were the recent mega hit with the Sugababes, his turbulent post-success years, flying, religious persuasion and finally his feelings for his wife Gemma. Numan appeared relaxed throughout the interview and Alice seemed genuinely touched not only by Gary's affections for his wife but also his down-to-earth/ non-rock star attitude jokingly chastising him for being the exact opposite of his dark and mysterious public image.

Easily one of the best latter day Gary Numan television interviews with Gary coming across as personable and extremely likable, characteristics that are somewhat rare within the entertainment industry.

MUSIC PLANET TONIGHT (Germany)
ARTE TV, February 2003.
Subject: live performances and interview segments.

Superb in-the-studio TV concert that included some fabulous interview segments conducted by former MTV VJ Ray Cokes who was clearly thrilled to have Gary on the show. Questions put to Gary ranged from his feelings surrounding his current high profile, other acts covering his material, his mild form of Aspergers Syndrome, a condition that can make him feel somewhat uncomfortable in the company of strangers as well as his long documented affections for his wife Gemma. Of the screened performance footage, the five songs selected out of the nine originally performed all concentrated on the Gary Numan of now (in fact the oldest track performed was 'Dark' a track originally found on Gary's 1997 studio album *Exile)* with set highlight going 'A Prayer for the Unborn', performed here in its edited Andy Gray remixed guise.

THIS IS DOM JOLY (UK)
BBC 3, July 2003.
Subject: performance of both 'Crazier' and 'Are "Friends" Electric?' with two brief interviews/ sketches.

Rather a surreal moment in front of the cameras for Numan on this occasion, primarily there to promote his then, upcoming single 'Crazier' as well as deliver yet another run through of 'Are "Friends" Electric?' Although both performances were excellent, anyone tuning in would have been bemused to see the iconic Gary Numan having to try and keep a straight face with a portion of the studio audience dancing at the front of the stage dressed as grizzly bears!

TELEVISION AND RADIO ADVERTS
Aside from the standard TV and radio adverts commissioned to promote Numan's music, live shows and videos over the years, Gary has also had his music added to a number of non-Numan related products too, the following are a few of the better known ones.

LEE COOPER JEANS – Television advertisement (UK)
Aired: early 1979.
Song: 'Don't Be A Dummy.'

With *New Wave* all the rage towards the end of the seventies, Lee Cooper Jeans commissioned a new advert to tie their product into this relatively new take on punk rock fashion. The music too was suitably *New Wave* themed with the addition of a young, pre-success Gary Numan brought in to sing the brief 20 second clip. Following the meteoric success of 'Are "Friends" Electric?' and *Replicas* a few months later, the team behind the track re-approached Gary with a view to signing him up to sing the lead vocal for the entire track as it was now going to be issued as a single in its own right. However, Numan declined the offer and the song was eventually issued with former Atomic Rooster front man John Du Cann providing the lead vocal instead. The Gary Numan portion of the track can now be found added to the running order for the 1999 CD re-issue of the Gary Numan/ Tubeway Army album *The Plan*.

Original magazine advert for the John Du Cann version of 'Don't Be A Dummy.'

7-UP SOFT DRINKS – Radio advertisement (US)
Aired: never transmitted.
Song: 7-UP.
   At some point in 1982 Numan was approached to sing a radio jingle for the soft drink giant 7-UP, with the company offering £10,000 for his services. Gary felt it was too good an opportunity to ignore and duly obliged, however, the three pieces of music he provided were rejected and the whole project fell through. In recent years the three demo tracks recorded have appeared on the internet and are some of the rarest unofficial Numan recordings available, so rare that when Beggars Banquet was probed about the likelihood of the recordings appearing on their proposed Numan rarities CD, the company claimed to have no knowledge of their existence.

CARLING PREMIER LAGER – Television advert (UK)
Aired: late 1995.
Song: 'Cars (The E Reg Model)', eventually re-titled 'The Premier Mix.'
   As Numan does not drink, fans found it more than a little odd that 'Cars' was used to sell Carling's new *Premier Lager*. For Gary though it was a major career boost thrusting him back into the UK top 20 and back onto *Top Of The Pops*. 'Cars' has also been utilised in the US promoting both Nissan car safety and Debbie's Little Snacks in October 2002. The track was also used a couple of years later in the concluding season episode of the American plastic surgery drama *Nip And Tuck* as well as featuring briefly in an episode of *The Simpsons*!

AMERICAN EXPRESS – Television advertisement (UK and US)
Various channels in the UK and US, Aired: 1999 through 2000.
Song: 'Cars', 1987 remix and 1999 Fear Factory version.
   Having had his own credit card taken away in the mid-80s, it was rather ironic that the self same company commissioned 'Cars' for

their latest round of television adverts promoting their newest credit card, an irony not lost on Gary who allowed himself a chuckle or two during interviews at the time of the advert's run. A second run of the advert substituted the re-worked Fear Factory recording of 'Cars' over the original 'Premier Mix/ E Reg Model' version.

RIMMEL COSMETICS – Television advertisement (UK)
Various channels: summer 2002.
Song: 'Freak Like Me' – by Sugababes.

Shortly after Sugababes had scored their number one hit with the Gary Numan sampled single 'Freak Like Me', cosmetics giant Rimmel commissioned the track to feature in their new glossy TV advert, further boosting the profile of the Numan and Sugababes single in the process.

In addition, Numan provided the music for an undisclosed French perfume commercial; sadly it was never used as the company felt that the end result was far too dark and gloomy, the music eventually found its way onto Gary's return to form album *Sacrifice* at the end of 1994.

SECTION THREE

LIVE

THE FULL CONCERT GUIDE

Gary Numan has been an active live performer since the late 70s just about touring every year since his massive breakthrough success in 1979. Gary's shows have become the stuff of legend, more an event than a straight forward rock concert with his over the top lightshows, stage props and set lists that have always remained fresh and forward looking.

This section will take a chronological look back at these tours, from the very early days gigging as Tubeway Army right up to the present.

(I) TUBEWAY ARMY

When Numan answered an advert requiring a lead guitarist in the summer of 1977, he soon found himself not only joining the ranks of a new group called the Lasers but quickly taking total control of that group within days of their first rehearsal. With the group re-christened Tubeway Army, they began gigging soon after. Exact information on the live history of Tubeway Army has unfortunately never been properly documented but it is clear that the group's first concert took place at the Covent Garden in London supporting Mean Street, a group Gary had been forced out of prior to the formation of Tubeway Army. The band gigged sporadically throughout the late summer and early winter with a succession of fairly fluid line-ups centred in and around the nucleus of Gary and original Lasers bassist/ vocalist Paul Gardiner. The group eventually settled as a three piece with Paul and Gary being joined by Jess Lidyard, uncle to the young Gary Webb, and it's this line-up that recorded the debut three-track 'Tubeway Army' demo in mid-October of that year. Fielding the cassette around various record companies was met with a negative response, eventually though the small independent label Beggars Banquet, liking the three tracks recorded and seeing the band perform at a showcase gig at The Vortex (premiering new drummer Bob Simmons), put pen to paper and duly signed the fledgling new group. More gigs followed with the group playing support slots at The Marquee Club, The Pegasus, The Rochester Castle and the Royal Hotel for acts such as Adam And The Ants and the Skids. Following these stints though, the group's line-up fractured once more with Jess Lidyard returning to deputise on drums in March of 1978. Another new Tubeway Army line-up was assembled in mid-April, this time featuring new boys Barry Benn (Drums) and Sean Burke (Guitar). By now though, the group were beginning to headline at certain venues with further dates being performed in July at the Hope and Anchor in Islington and The White Hart pub in Acton. The latter date was, however, the final live appearance of this version of the group as Gary, tired and weary of the constant unruly behaviour and violence at the shows decided to dispense with live work indefinitely. The group did appear live, however, in the run up to the enormous success of 'Are "Friends" Electric?' before Gary's subsequent decision to dispense with the group name for good. On May the 23rd 1979 the band performed live on the late night adult music show *The Old Grey Whistle Test* with a new line-up including both Paul and Gary with new members Cedric Sharpley (replacing the finally departed Jess Lidyard) on drums, Chris Payne, former Ultravox! man Billie Currie on keyboards and Trevor Grant on guitar. This line-up later appeared live on *Top Of The Pops* to mime along to their new single 'Are "Friends" Electric?' although further appearances on the show saw Trevor Grant (a long time friend of Chris Payne's) dropped from the line-up and replaced by Numan's long time friend Garry

Robson. This would prove to be Gary's final public appearance under the Tubeway Army moniker

(II) GARY NUMAN
THE TOURING PRINCIPLE – 1979/ 1980
UK LEG: 1979

SEPTEMBER
20th Glasgow Apollo/ 21st Newcastle City Hall/ 23rd Coventry Theatre/ 24th Bristol Colston Hall/ 25th Liverpool Empire/ 26th Manchester Apollo/ 27th London Hammersmith Odeon/ 28th London Hammersmith Odeon*/ 30th Birmingham Odeon.

OCTOBER
1st Guildford Civic Hall/ 2nd Southampton Gaumont/ 3rd Ipswich Gaumont/ 5th Brighton Dome/ 6th Aylesbury Friars/ 7th Wolverhampton Civic Hall/ 8th Sheffield City Hall.
* One of the Hammersmith dates contributed £3000 to the 'Save The Whales' Fund.
Musicians: Gary Numan – Vocals/ Cedric Sharpley – Drums/ Chris Payne – Keyboards/ Billie Currie – Keyboards/ RRussell Bell – Guitar/ Paul Gardiner – Bass.
U.K. setlist: 'Intro'/ 'Airlane'/ 'Me! I Disconnect From You'/ 'Cars'/ 'M.E.'/ 'You Are In My Vision'/ 'Something's In The House'/ 'Random'/ 'Every Day I Die'/ 'Conversation'/ 'We Are So Fragile'/ 'Bombers'/ 'Remember I Was Vapour'/ 'On Broadway'/ 'The Dream Police'/ 'Films'/ 'Metal'/ 'Down In The Park'/ 'My Shadow In Vain'/ 'Are "Friends" Electric?'/ 'Tracks.'

With 'Cars' and *The Pleasure Principle* repeating the success of their immediate predecessors ('Are "Friends" Electric?' and *Replicas*) by both vaulting to the coveted No 1 spot in the UK singles and albums chart respectively, the autumn of 1979 finally saw Numan hitting the road following his stunning year of success. Dubbed 'The Touring Principle', Numan's first major headlining tour took in territories as far a field as North America and Japan before bowing out after eight months with a series of shows in both New Zealand and Australia.

The first leg of the tour, not surprisingly, kicked off in the UK and ran for two and a half weeks through September and October. With an estimated 40,000 fans in attendance, this was the nation's first chance to see Numan in the flesh and with demand for tickets high, not surprisingly, every date of the tour was completely sold out. Numan's show brought the long banished, glittering world of show business back to the live circuit signalling the end of Punk rock's four year, anti-star trip reign. Numan's imaginative and innovative stage set was both visually impressive and futuristic in its design. Backed by a powerful, state-of-the-art light show as well as a well rehearsed, tight band, Gary effortlessly delivered on his promise of making his first real tour more an event than just another 'run of the mill' concert tour.

Musically, Numan's synth-dominated sound slotted perfectly into the live arena, allowing Gary to not only add significant muscle but vastly improve both the dynamics and the scope of the songs that were selected for the tour. The set list, although primarily *The Pleasure Principle*-heavy, did include a number of tracks from both the 1978 and 1979 eras of Tubeway Army with five tracks selected from each. In addition, Numan also aired three brand new songs, one, an instrumental ('Random'), one, a cover version ('On Broadway') and one, a brand new track entitled 'Remember I Was Vapour.' The latter was performed as a fairly unusual medley comprising of three tracks, the other two being the aforementioned cover track 'On Broadway' (originally performed by The Drifters) and a virtually unrecognisable take of 'Bombers', originally the second Tubeway Army single. All three tracks shared the same rhythm track and their inclusion made for an entertaining change of pace mid-set.

One month following the conclusion of the UK leg of the tour, the Gary Numan band re-grouped to appear live at the charity concert 'The Year Of The Child.' The event was held at London's Wembley Arena on the 11th of November and the band ran through a brief, three song set. However, neither Billie Currie nor Cedric Sharpley participated, their places filled by Dennis Haines and Jess Lidyard (the three tracks aired can now be found on the 1999 released BBC CD *The Radio One Recordings*-see SECTION ONE, PART SIX, THE BBC SESSIONS). This concert neatly coincided with the release of the second and final single to be lifted from The Pleasure Principle, 'Complex', a song that although a stand-out track on the album, did not feature on the tour. Following the release of this single, the tour was shipped overseas in the New Year for Gary's first visit to the United States.

NORTH AMERICAN LEG: 1980
FEBRUARY

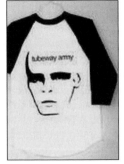

Left: US magazine advert for the 1980 North American tour.
Above: two official T-shirts.

18th Toronto Music Hall/ 19th Montreal St Denny Theatre/ 21st Providence Ocean State Theatre/22nd Philadelphia Tower Theatre/ 23rd Boston Harvard Square Theatre/ 24th New York Palladium/ 26th Pittsburgh Stanley Theatre/ 29th Cleveland Music Hall.
MARCH
1st Detroit Royal Oak Theatre/ 2nd Milwaukee Uptown Theatre/ 3rd Minneapolis Guthrie Theatre/ 8th San Francisco Warfield Theatre/ 9th Los Angeles Santa Monica

Civic Centre.

Overseas setlist: 'Intro'/ 'Airlane'/ 'Me! I Disconnect From You'/ 'Praying To The Aliens'/ 'M.E.'/ 'Films'/ 'We Are So Fragile'/ 'Are "Friends" Electric?'/ 'Remind Me To Smile'/ 'Conversation'/ 'Metal'/ 'Replicas'/ 'Remember I Was Vapour'/ 'Trois Gymnopedies'/ 'Cars'/ 'I Die: You Die'/ 'Down In The Park'/ 'Bombers'/ 'Tracks'/ 'We Are Glass.'

MAINLAND EUROPEAN LEG: 1980
MARCH

21st Brussels Auditorium Q/ 23rd Berlin Hochschule Der Kunste/ 24th Hamburg Musikhalle/ 25th Dusseldorf Philipshalle/ 27th Munich Deutsches Museum/ 29th Paris La Palace.

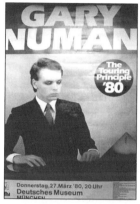
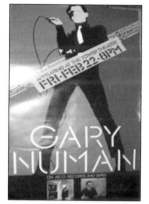

FAR EAST LEG: 1980

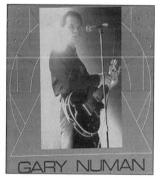

Japanese tour book and April 1980 Far East music magazine.

APRIL

2nd Nagoya Aichi Bunka Kaikan/ 4th Osaka Expo Hall/ 6th Tokyo Sun Plaza/7th Tokyo Shibuya Kokaido/ 8th Tokyo Nihon Seinenkan.

NEW ZEALAND AND AUSTRALIAN LEG: 1980
APRIL

12th Auckland Town Hall/ 14th Christchurch Town Hall/ 15th Wellington Majestic Theatre/ 19th Melbourne Palais Theatre/ 20th Melbourne Palais Theatre/ 22nd Adelaide Opera House/ 23rd Adelaide Opera House/ 25th Newcastle Civic Theatre/ 27th Brisbane Festival Hall/ 29th Sydney Capital Theatre/30th Sydney Capital Theatre/ 31st Sydney Capital Theatre.

The move overseas (now minus Billie Currie, replaced by newcomer Dennis Haines) saw the setlist alter dramatically with virtually all material from 1978 dropped in favour of including one or two different tracks as well as adding a number of recently demoed new songs, in fact, by the tour's finale in Australia, Gary was regularly performing future *Telekon* era tracks like 'I Die: You Die', 'We Are Glass', 'Trois Gymnopedies' and 'Remind Me To Smile' as well as the British debuted 'Remember I Was Vapour.' In addition, a further two tracks from Replicas ('Praying To The Aliens' and the album's title track) were also added to the set.

Although the UK leg of 'The Touring Principle' has long been documented on both album and video cassette, no overseas recordings of this tour have so far been officially released. However, a proposed rarities CD from Gary's former label Beggars Banquet has long been rumoured and fans hope that at least some overseas recordings will materialise on this disc. In addition, video footage from both 'The Toronto Music Hall' concert on the 18th of February in Canada and the 29th of March concert at the 'Le Palace' in Paris were screened on UK and European television. Clips from the concerts were a mixture of rehearsal and 'in concert' footage, whether the full concert footage from either of these shows still exists is unknown.

Left, top to bottom: two T-shirt designs that appeared following the success of Replicas. *Middle to right: official Australian tour poster along with both sides of the official Australian tour T-shirt.*

THE TELETOUR 1980
UK LEG

SEPTEMBER

4th Birmingham Odeon/ 5th Birmingham Odeon (matinee and evening performance)/ 7th Manchester Apollo/ 8th Manchester Apollo/ 10th Southampton Gaumont/11th Southampton Gaumont/ 12th Bristol Hippodrome/ 13th Bristol Hippodrome/ 15th London Hammersmith Odeon/ 16th London Hammersmith Odeon/ 17th London Hammersmith Odeon/ 18th London Hammersmith Odeon/ 21st Brighton Conference Centre/ 22nd Coventry Apollo/ 24th Liverpool Empire/ 25th Preston Guildhall/ 26th Glasgow Apollo/ 27th Edinburgh Playhouse/ 29th Newcastle City Hall.

Musicians: Gary Numan – Vocals/ RRussell Bell – Guitar/ Chris Payne – Keyboards/ Roger Mason* – Keyboards/ Cedric Sharpley – Drums/ Paul Gardiner – Bass.

Setlist: 'This Wreckage'/ 'Remind Me To Smile'/ 'Complex'/ 'Telekon'/ 'Me! I Disconnect From You'/ 'Cars'/ 'Conversation'/ 'Airlane'/ 'M.E.'/ 'Every Day I Die'/ 'Remember I Was Vapour'/ 'Stories'**/ 'Are "Friends" Electric?'/ 'The Joy Circuit'/ 'I Die: You Die'/ 'I Dream Of Wires'/ 'Down In The Park'/ 'Tracks'/ 'We Are Glass.'

* Replaced by a returning Dennis Haines for all overseas dates.

**Only played on a handful of the early dates on the UK leg, subsequently dropped for the remainder of the tour.

Above and left: 'Teletour' scarves and T-shirt.

NORTH AMERICAN LEG: 1980
OCTOBER

14th Toronto Maple Leaf Gardens/ 15th Montreal The Forum/ 17th Boston Orpheum Theatre/ 18th Passaic N.J. Capital Theatre/ 19th New York Palladium/

21st Pittsburgh Stanley Theatre/ 22nd Akron Civic Hall/ 24th Ann Arbor Detroit Hill Auditorium/ 25th Chicago Granada/ 27th Madison Civic Centre/ 28th Milwaukee Auditorium/ 29th St Paul Civic Centre.

NOVEMBER

1st Los Angeles Forum/ 2nd San Diego Fox Theatre/ 6th San Francisco Warfield Theatre/ 8th Vancouver Queen Elizabeth Theatre/ 11th Edmonton Field House/ 12th Calgary Max Bell Arena.

The 1980 'Teletour' saw Numan approaching the very pinnacle of his early 80s career, hugely successful with a growing international profile (a situation resulting in many of the dates performed on this trek being sold out in a matter of days). In the UK, so high was the demand for tickets that double and even quadruple dates had to be booked at some venues. The shows themselves were a visual and musical extravaganza capturing the Numan phenomenon in full flight. Numan wowed audiences with a dazzling and elaborate stage set that included *Telekon* styled, illuminated light panels, neon towers, costume changes and an array of unusual and bizarre stage props, all of this was topped off with a fantastic, state-of-the-art light show. The music too was also out to impress with an armada of synthesisers on hand and a set list jam-packed with the very best of Numan's then recorded material. 'The Teletour' saw Gary updating a number of his songs too with both 'The Joy Circuit' and 'Are "Friends" Electric?' being significantly improved upon. Most memorable of all though were the performances of both 'Every Day I Die' and 'Down In The Park.' The latter had now been twinned with its later recorded piano version and for the song Numan would emerge from beneath the drum riser to sing the main portion of the track seated within a remote controlled futuristic car (interestingly, this car was eventually given away later as part of a competition). The former had also been altered, elevated here into a spine-tingling, synth rock masterpiece.

'The Teletour', aside from featuring brand new material culled from Gary's latest album, also featured a debut airing for 'Complex', a song that had oddly failed to make the set list for 'The Touring Principle' and was here performed as a semi instrumental by Gary knelt at the front of the stage utilizing a lone ARP Odyssey synth. Another live debut came in the shape of a completely brand new track entitled 'Stories', though this song was dropped during the early portion of the tour. Each night the set concluded with a typically pumped up rendition of 'We Are Glass', a song Numan spent much of the tour frequently ad-libbing in places due to his seemingly unfamiliarity with the lyrics.

Following the end of the UK leg, the tour moved overseas in mid-October for a further two-month stint in the US, although this reportedly aggravated Gary's US record company who were still in the middle of their promotional campaign for *The Pleasure Principle*.

Of all Numan's tours, 'The Teletour' is the one cited by fans as his best and most memorable; the *Telekon* image had been an instant hit with his fan base and has become perhaps the most enduring of all Gary's images.

Like 'The Touring Principle', 'The Teletour' was professionally filmed though aside from just three live clips from the tour that were released in the early 80s ('This Wreckage', 'Remind Me To Smile' and 'Down In The Park'), no other live footage has ever materialised. Similarly, other than *Living Ornaments '80*, no other 'Teletour' live

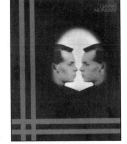

Fan club folder.

recordings, UK or US have ever emerged either. Sadly with Numan's early 80s videos seemingly in limbo and the master tapes for the full show that *Living Ornaments '80* was taken from still lost, the chances of either being released any time soon are remote at best.

THE FAREWELL CONCERTS 1981

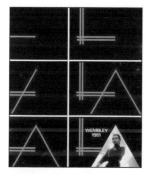

APRIL
26th Wembley Arena, London/ 27th Wembley Arena, London/ 28th Wembley Arena, London.
Musicians and set list: (see 'Official videos' section)
   When Gary Numan officially announced his retirement from live concerts at the beginning of 1981, it instantly made headlines throughout the entertainment industry and beyond. In an attempt to appease his shocked and stunned fan base, two farewell concerts were planned for the end of April (a third being added due to public demand). The show's themselves would all take place at the Wembley Arena in London.
   Although to the public at large Numan's impending retirement from live concerts may have struck some as sudden (Gary had in fact only been famous at this point for a mere two years) the actual seeds for this decision could be traced back as far as early 1980. In fear of overstaying his welcome and worse, suffering a humiliating and ignominious decline, Numan initiated a masterplan (with the album *Telekon* marking the culmination of this pact, the record itself being carefully constructed as the perfect prelude to this long planned 'grand farewell') that involved a gradual phasing out from the music business and a move into both the video and aviation worlds. Gary even publicly reasoned at the time via the press that it was 'Better to commit suicide rather than give someone the chance or opportunity to (commercially) kill me.'
   Of the three concerts, all were completely sold out with 8,000 people in attendance each night to witness Numan treading the boards one final time. The stage set was one of the most spectacular and intricate structures ever assembled on UK soil up to that point. Its motorised multi-level design incorporated both 'The Touring Principle' and 'Teletour' stage sets as well as utilising a number of new additional set pieces and was truly awe inspiring. For two and a half hours Gary performed a 26-song set list drawn mainly from *The Pleasure Principle* and *Telekon* albums with only a handful of tracks culled from Gary's two Tubeway Army albums. In addition, Numan also unveiled tantalising previews of three new songs ('She's Got Claws', 'Cry The Clock Said' and 'Moral' (the latter track bizarrely incorporated

into Gary's 1979 classic 'Metal' with that song's original lyrics substituted for new ones). The final night saw the set list alter slightly with 'Conversation' being dropped in favour of a returning 'Complex', its inclusion on this, the concluding night of the shows, seemed all the more poignant and struck an instant cord with the already emotionally charged audience. Following the final song of the night, Gary came to the lip of the vast stage to thank the fans for the last few years and bid farewell with the rest of the Gary Numan band before departing for good.

A week after the shows though, the ever vicious UK press tore into the star with a predictable vitriolic fury, lambasting the whole event as vapid and meaningless ('Are ends pathetic' being perhaps one of the kinder comments thrust Gary's way), for Numan, however, the shows marked the end of an era. No longer tied to a rigid and exhausting touring schedule, Gary was now free to begin enjoying some of the wealth he had accumulated as well as finally coming to terms with the madness of the last two years.

The final night of the three shows was eventually screened, in edited form, on British television in the early summer of 1981 before being issued complete on video a year later.

 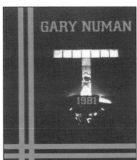 

Australian Juke *magazine from January 1981 announcing Numan's live farewell as well as the official UK tour programme and a commemorative scarf.*

THE I, ASSASSIN AMERICAN TOUR 1982
OCTOBER
8th Pasadena Perkins Palace/ 10th San Francisco Kabuki/ 13th Denver Rainbow Music Hall/ 15th Lubbock Municipal Auditorium/ 17th Houston Cullen Auditorium/ 18th Dallas Agora/ 19th Austin Opera House/ 21st New Orleans The President River Boat/ 23rd Atlanta Agora/ 26th New York The Ritz/ 29th Washington Ontario Theatre/ 30th Providence R.I Main Event/ 31st Boston The Channel.
NOVEMBER
3rd Cleveland Agora/ 4th Detroit Royal Oak Theatre/ 5th Pittsburgh Stanley Theatre/ 7th Cincinnati Bogart's/ 8th Chicago Park West.
Musicians: Gary Numan – Vocals/ Pino Palladino – Bass/ Chris Slade – Drums/ John Webb – Keyboards and saxophone/ Roger Mason – Keyboards/ Rob Dean – Guitar.
Set list: 'This Is My House'/ 'I, Assassin'/ 'Remind Me To Smile'/ 'Films'/ 'Crash'/ 'Music For Chameleons'/ 'She's Got Claws'/ 'Every Day I Die'/ 'Down In The Park'/ 'White Boys And Heroes'/ 'Cars'/ 'Warsongs'/ 'We Take Mystery (To Bed)'/ 'This Wreckage'/ 'We Are Glass'/ 'Tracks.'

In addition, the opening flurry of dates saw Gary performing 'Boys Like Me' and

'I'm An Agent', however, as the tour progressed both of these were dropped.

Following the release of the March 1982 single 'Music For Chameleons' Numan relocated to the United States to become one of the many UK performers driven away by the harsh tax demands imposed upon them. Once there, aside from re-adjusting to the American way of life, Gary gave more thought to the touring aspect of his career and opted to give it all another go. A short club tour (managed by Miles Copeland) was quickly pencilled in for the autumn designed to coincide with the release of Numan's next studio album *I, Assassin*. Once the tour commenced, attendances on a nightly basis fell short of being sold out though this was hardly surprising, as far as the US was concerned, Gary Numan was perceived as a *New Wave* artist and by late 1982, this genre of music was sadly in its death throes. As a result, a proposed visit to Japan, Canada, Australia and Far East countries like Thailand, the Philippines and Singapore did not materialise with Gary preferring to concentrate on recording a new studio record and planning a live comeback on UK soil.

As for the US trek, Gary admitted that he had thoroughly enjoyed the tour and the set list saw him debut nine tracks (two from *Dance* – 'Boys Like Me' and 'Crash' as well as six from *I, Assassin* – 'We Take Mystery (To Bed)', 'Warsongs', 'Music For Chameleons', 'I, Assassin', 'White Boys And Heroes' and 'This Is My House'). The rest of the set was made up of a fair selection of Numan's solo works with only two tracks being included from the days of Tubeway Army ('Every Day I Die' and 'Down In The Park', the latter now featuring altered lyrics with Numan substituting the words 'plane crash' over the normally sung 'car crash' lyric (this alteration obviously related to his recent accident in the UK), something he would continue during the following year's The Warriors Tour). However, curiously absent from this tour was the Tubeway Army mega hit 'Are "Friends" Electric?' although this track as well as both the *Replicas* and the *Tubeway Army* albums were probably overlooked as they were less known outside of the UK. Set highlight went to 'Crash', a song that transformed itself into a guitar heavy, driving rock track live. Its inclusion was an inspired choice and proved to be a strong crowd favourite on the tour. Sadly, 'The I, Assassin Tour' would prove to be Gary's last stateside visit (despite a promised return the following year) for 15 years.

No official document, either audio or video has ever been released to commemorate Gary's low key tour of the US in 1982, the shows themselves, however, are known to have been professionally filmed and its not inconceivable that footage from these shows may yet still appear as part of a future official DVD package.

Above: T-shirt and year book.

THE WARRIORS TOUR 1983

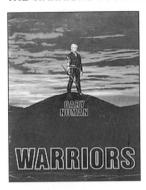

SEPTEMBER
20th Glasgow Apollo/ 22nd Aberdeen Capital Theatre/ 23rd Dundee Caird Hall/ 24th Edinburgh Playhouse/ 25th Sheffield City Hall/ 27th Newcastle City Hall/ 28th Hull City Hall/ 29th Manchester Apollo/ 30th Manchester Apollo.

OCTOBER
1st Derby Assembly Rooms/ 2nd Deeside Leisure Centre/ 3rd Birmingham Odeon/ 4th Birmingham Odeon/ 5th Coventry Apollo/ 6th Leicester De Montfort Hall/ 8th Poole Arts Centre/ 9th Oxford Apollo/ 10th Bristol Colston Hall/ 11th Hemel Hempstead Pavilion*/ 13th London Hammersmith Odeon/ 14th London Hammersmith Odeon/15th London Hammersmith Odeon/ 16th London Hammersmith Odeon/ 18th Middlesbrough Town Hall/ 19th Leeds Victoria Halls/ 20th Blackpool Opera House/ 21st Wolverhampton Civic Centre/ 22nd Nottingham Royal Theatre/ 23rd Hanley Stoke Victoria Hall/ 26th Portsmouth Guildhall/ 27th Margate Winter Gardens/ 28th Southampton Gaumont/ 29th Brighton Conference Centre/ 30th Southend Pavilion/ 31st Ipswich Gaumont.

NOVEMBER
2nd Cornwall Coliseum/ 3rd Gloucester Leisure Centre/ 4th Guildford Civic Hall/ 5th London Dominion Theatre/ 6th London Dominion Theatre.

* This date had been rescheduled due to the stage set being too big to enter the building; this problem was eventually rectified by simply cutting some of the set pieces in half.

Above, Three official T-shirts.

Musicians: Gary Numan – Vocals/ RRussell Bell – Guitar/ Cedric Sharpley – Drums/ Chris Payne – Keyboards/ Joe Hubbard – Bass/ John Webb – Keyboards and saxophone.

Setlist: 'Sister Surprise'/ 'Warriors'/ 'Remind Me To Smile'/ 'Metal'/ 'This Prison Moon'/ 'Down In The Park'/ 'Films'/ 'She's Got Claws'/ 'Love Needs No Disguise'/ 'I Die: You Die'/ 'Me! I Disconnect From You'/ 'Love Is Like Clock Law'/ 'The Iceman Comes'/ 'Rhythm Of The Evening'/ 'This Is My House'/ 'I Am Render'/ 'Warsongs'/ 'My Centurion'/ 'The Tick Tock Man'/ 'We Take Mystery (To Bed)'/ 'Cars'/ 'Are "Friends" Electric?'/ 'Tracks'/ 'We Are Glass.'

With a year of living in relative exile abroad behind him, Numan returned to the UK in the spring of 1983. After receiving a hero's welcome when he landed at Blackbushe airport from his ever-loyal fan base, the star settled down to finalising both his new record and readying himself for his much anticipated comeback tour. For the impending tour, Gary re-united with most of the former members of the original 'heyday' touring line-up (except original Tubeway Army and Gary Numan band bassist Paul Gardiner who declined his invitation to participate and sadly passed away the following year). As a nod of recognition to Dramatis, the defunct group RRussell Bell, Chris Payne and Cedric Sharpley went on to form following the 1981 farewell concerts, Gary opted to include 'Love Needs No Disguise,' the group's only hit into the set list for the tour. Its inclusion went down a storm and was one of many choice moments in an already electrified set. With the tour harking back to 'The Touring Principle' of 1979 by kicking off at the Glasgow Apollo on the same date, many fans felt that the whole *Warriors* project was as much a career re-launch for Gary as it was a genuine comeback. The spectacular stage set (including an innovative computerised lightshow) saw the band performing in and around a nuclear ravaged city with Numan out front looking every inch like pop music's answer to the Mad Max anti-hero 'the road warrior.' The tour ran through much of the autumn and with 40 dates pencilled in, it was certainly Numan's biggest undertaking in the UK yet. Not surprisingly, the bulk of the set lent heavily on the *Warriors* album with the entire record being aired at the start of the tour (although as the tour progressed just six tracks remained in the set). In addition, Gary also included three tracks from his previous album *I, Assassin* ('This Is My House', 'Warsongs' and 'We Take Mystery (To Bed)'), all of which were making their UK debut.

Below: trio of official scarves.

Sadly, even though the tour was a success and the *Warriors* album outselling the 1982 released *I, Assassin*, relations between Gary and his record company took a turn for the worse as the year progressed ultimately resulting in a parting of ways at the tail end of the year (tentative plans to tour the US, Canada, Australia and Japan which had initially been drawn up prior to the UK 'Warriors Tour' were forced to remain on the drawing board). Numan's departure from Beggars Banquet/ WEA sadly began a frustrating cycle of UK-only tours that would last for the next 15 years. Aside from radio broadcasts, no official document either audio or video has ever been released. It is known though that the shows were professionally filmed (Glasgow the 20th is known to have been video taped) and Gary's former record label have, at one time or another, toyed with the idea of issuing a live album from this period at some point in the future, however, no plans for either a concert film or commemorative CD exist at this time.

THE BERSERKER TOUR 1984

NOVEMBER
22nd Cardiff St David's Hall/ 23rd Portsmouth Guildhall/ 24th Birmingham Odeon/ 25th Bristol Colston Hall/ 26th Oxford Apollo/ 27th Leicester De Montfort Hall/ 28th Nottingham Royal Centre/ 30th Blackburn King Georges Hall.
DECEMBER
1st Manchester Apollo/ 2nd Edinburgh Playhouse/ 3rd Glasgow Apollo/ 4th Newcastle City Hall/ 5th Sheffield City Hall/ 6th Guildford Civic Hall/ 8th Ipswich Gaumont/ 9th Southampton Gaumont/ 10th Brighton The Dome/ 11th London Hammersmith Odeon/ 12th London Hammersmith Odeon.

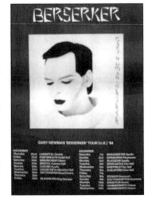

Musicians: Gary Numan – Vocals/ John Webb – Keyboards and saxophone/ Chris Payne – Keyboards and viola/ RRussell Bell – Guitar, keyboards and violin/ Andy Coughlan – Bass/ Karen Taylor – Vocals/ Cedric Sharpley – Drums/ Tik & Tok – Guests.
Set list: 'Intro'/ 'Berserker'/ 'Metal'/ 'Me! I Disconnect From You'/ 'Remind Me To Smile'/ 'Sister Surprise'/ 'The Secret'*/ 'Music For Chameleons'/ 'The Iceman Comes'/ 'Cold Warning'/ 'Down In The Park'/ 'This Prison Moon'/ 'I Die: You Die'/ 'My Dying Machine'/ 'Cars'/ 'We Take Mystery (To Bed)'/ 'We Are Glass'/ 'This Is New Love'/ 'My Shadow In Vain'/ 'Are "Friends" Electric?'

* This track was dropped after the first night of the tour.

Put it down to *Berserker's* shock chart failure or the immense pressure of running a small independent label but somehow the tour that came in support of Gary's first Numa backed album lacked the spark that made previous Numan concerts so riveting. It was, however, clear to all, that by 1984 Gary's days as a superstar were definitely on the wane and it was perhaps fanciful to speculate that the journey back down to earth, so to speak, had knocked some of the wind out of him. With both the *Berserker* album and single failing to return Gary to the British top 20, the subsequent tour pencilled in as support suffered as a result with the shows plagued with fairly poor audience attendances as well as some lacklustre and uninspired band performances – tellingly, only a handful of tracks from the *Berserker* album eventually figured into the set. Unlike 'The Warriors Tour' where that album's nine tracks were all aired live, *Berserker* was represented by just four (a fifth 'The Secret' being dropped after the opening night of the tour) leading fans to conclude that even Gary wasn't that overly struck with this latest recording either. Best of the new tracks aired was the chilling cyber rock of 'Cold Warning.' 'This Is New Love', however, proved every bit as wretched as its studio counterpart with the rest of the set comprising of the by now tried and tested mixed bag of past classics, album tracks and singles.

In addition, the overall look of 'The Berserker Tour' was stark and cold, clearly lacking Gary's previous trademark sense of the spectacular. Aside from the unifying all white stage set and matching costumes, this tour was not destined to be remembered as one of Gary's most lavish or memorable outings.

To commemorate the tour, despite the relatively poor response from fans, Numan issued both a live double album (from which a relatively successful live EP was culled) and a live video the following year, both the album and video are still available with the original VHS cassette recently being re-issued on DVD by Classic Rock Productions.

THE FURY TOUR 1985

SEPTEMBER
20th Oxford Apollo/ 21st Nottingham Royal Concert Hall/ 22nd Cardiff St David's/ 24th Newcastle City Hall/ 25th Sheffield City Hall/ 26th Southampton Gaumont Theatre/ 27th Guildford Civic Hall/ 28th Leicester De Montfort/ 29th Liverpool Empire.

OCTOBER

1st London Hammersmith Odeon/ 2nd London Hammersmith Odeon/ 3rd Cornwall Coliseum/ 5th Ipswich Gaumont/ 6th Bristol Colston Hall/ 7th Birmingham Odeon/ 8th Hanley Theatre Royal/ 9th Manchester Apollo.

Musicians: Gary Numan – Vocals/ RRussell Bell – Guitar/ John Webb – Keyboards and saxophone/ Chris Payne – Keyboards/ Cedric Sharpley – Drums/ Andy Coughlan – Bass/ Kit Rolfe – Backing vocals/ Karen Taylor – Backing vocals.

Setlist: 'Intro – No Shelter'/ 'Tricks'/ 'Me! I Disconnect From You'/ 'Creatures'/ 'Metal'/ 'Berserker'/ 'Are "Friends" Electric?'/ 'Miracles'/ 'Down In The Park'/ 'Cold Warning'/ 'I Die: You Die'/ 'Sister Surprise'/ 'This Disease'/ 'We Take Mystery (To Bed)'/ 'Call Out The Dogs'/ 'Cars'/ 'My Shadow In Vain'/ 'We Are Glass.'

If 'The Berserker Tour' had seen Numan seriously down-sizing his trademark stage sets and cutting back on his over-the-top light shows, then 'The Fury Tour', performed the following year, saw Gary immediately putting matters straight by delivering a tour that was a glorious return to the kind of shows he had always been associated with. The year 1985 had also been a busy one for both fans and Gary with a total of five singles and two albums being released (an additional three mini-albums and one compilation cassette also emerged in the early portion of the year released via Gary's former label Beggars Banquet). Numan had, by this point, dispensed with the white boiler suited, blue haired *Berserker* look, opting instead for a more contemporary and arguably much more comfortable style. With a big powerful stage set behind him and a much improved chart profile thanks to the Sharpe and Numan hit 'Change Your Mind' (curiously not performed on the tour) as well as the unexpected top 30 success of both the 'Live EP' and its parent album *White Noise,* audience figures on this tour were considerably better than those achieved with 'The Berserker Tour.' In all, Gary performed five of the nine tracks found on his latest record alongside a good and varied selection of past classics. With such a positive reaction from fans its surprising that there has been no official document from the shows either on video or audio in recent years, however, a commemorative book of tour photos was released at the end of the year featuring stunning images from the show's (see 'Bibliography').

Official T-shirt and two tour posters.

THE EXHIBITION TOUR 1987

SEPTEMBER

7th Cardiff St David's Hall/ 8th Portsmouth Guildhall/ 9th Southampton Mayflower/ 10th Guildford Civic Hall/ 11th Bristol Colston Hall/ 12th Oxford Apollo/ 14th Leicester De Montfort Hall/ 15th Wolverhampton Civic Hall/ 16th Nottingham Royal Centre/ 17th Cambridge Corn Exchange/ 18th Liverpool Empire Theatre/ 19th Newcastle City Hall/ 21st Glasgow Barrowlands*/ 22nd Sheffield City Hall/ 23rd Preston Guildhall/ 24th Manchester Apollo/ 25th London Hammersmith Apollo/ 26th London Hammersmith Apollo.

* This show was filmed for release as a fan club only video, however, to date this footage has never materialised.

Musicians: Gary Numan – Vocals/ RRussell Bell – Guitar/ Chris Payne – Keyboards and viola/ John Webb – Keyboards/ Nick Davis – Bass/ Greg Brimstone – Drums/ Valerie Chalmers – Backing vocals/ Emma Chalmers – Backing vocals.

Set list: 'Intro – Ghost'/ 'Call Out The Dogs'/ 'I Die: You Die'/ 'Creatures'/ 'I Can't Stop'/ 'Me! I Disconnect From You'/ 'Tricks'/ 'The Sleeproom'/ 'My Breathing'/ 'Cars'/ 'Metal'/ 'Sister Surprise'/ 'This Disease'/ 'We Take Mystery (To Bed)'/ 'Strange Charm'*/ 'We Are Glass'/ 'Are "Friends" Electric?'/ 'Down In The Park'/ 'My Shadow In Vain'/ 'Berserker.'

* Dropped part way through the tour.

'The Exhibition Tour' was Numan's first nation wide trek in two years and came in support of the Beggars Banquet released compilation of the same name. Surprisingly, the set list for the tour was not in any way 'greatest hits' themed with much of the material included emanating mainly from two of Gary's recently released Numa albums (*The Fury* and *Strange Charm*). The three tracks lifted from *Strange Charm* ('I Can't Stop', 'The Sleeproom' and 'My Breathing' – a fourth, the album's title track was dropped early in the tour) were all debut performances and went down exceptionally well alongside evergreen Beggars Banquet material like 'Down In The Park', 'Cars' (performed here in its original 1979 guise) 'Are "Friends" Electric?', 'We Are Glass' and 'I Die: You Die.' Early *Tubeway Army* classic 'My Shadow In Vain' also made a welcome return, however, Gary appeared to have forgotten much of the lyrics to the song, pretty much making them up on the night, much to fans obvious annoyance/ amusement.

Oddly, nothing from Numan's dalliances with either Radio Heart or Sharpe and Numan (Gary's two recent side projects) received an airing on this tour and curiously enough the quota of material from Numan's Beggars Banquet heyday was also kept to a minimum.

For the 'Exhibition Tour', Gary was obviously keen to avoid any accusations from the press and fans alike of performing a (career damaging) 'nostalgia tour' preferring instead to gear the set list to reflect the full scope of his near decade long career by airing a strong cross-selection of music from his very early days recording as Tubeway Army right up to his latest studio album, the 1986 Numa released *Strange Charm*.

Following the conclusion of this tour, Gary performed a one-off concert on the 5th of March at The Flag in London; this was in celebration of his 30th birthday and his 10 years as a professional musician. The setlist for this show was: 'Intro – No Shelter', 'Tricks', 'I Die: You Die', 'Cars', 'Creatures', 'Me! I Disconnect From You', 'Down In The Park', 'The Iceman Comes', 'I Can't Stop', 'Call Out The Dogs', 'We Are Glass', 'Are "Friends" Electric?' and 'My Shadow In Vain.' Released at the same time came a double live album sourced from 'The Exhibition Tour' entitled *Ghost* (see 'The Numa Years'). This was, however, only made available through Gary's fan club and was the final release from Numa for many years with the star eventually inking a new recording contract with IRS Records later in the year.

"Exhibition Tour" T-shirt and Scarf.

THE METAL RHYTHM TOUR 1988

SEPTEMBER
24th Exeter Plaza/ 25th Newport Centre/ 26th Bristol Colston Hall/ 27th Guildford Civic Hall/ 28th London Dominion Theatre/ 29th Oxford Apollo/ 30th Southampton Mayflower Theatre.

OCTOBER
1st Manchester Apollo/ 2nd Birmingham Alexandra Theatre/ 3rd Sheffield City Hall/ 4th Leicester De Montfort/ 6th Glasgow Barrowlands/ 7th Newcastle City Hall/ 8th Hull City Hall/ 9th Liverpool Empire/ 10th London Astoria/ 11th London Astoria/ 12th London Astoria.

Musicians: Gary Numan – Vocals and guitar/ RRussell Bell – Guitar/ Andy Coughlan – Bass/ Chris Payne – Keyboards/ Ade Orange – Keyboards/ Cedric Sharpley –

Drums/ John Webb – Keyboards and saxophone/ Val Chalmers – Backing vocals/ Emma Chalmers – Backing vocals.

Setlist: 'Intro' – ('Survival')/ 'Respect'/ 'Call Out The Dogs'/ 'Me! I Disconnect From You'/ 'I Die: You Die'/ 'I Can't Stop'/ 'Tricks'/ 'Metal'/ 'Creatures'/ 'Down In The Park'/ 'Hunger'/ 'Sister Surprise'/ 'Are "Friends" Electric?'/ 'We Take Mystery (To Bed)'/ 'We Are Glass'/ 'New Anger'/ 'Cars'/ 'Young Heart'/ 'My Shadow In Vain'/ 'My Breathing.'

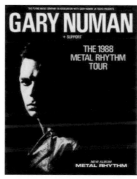

Tenth anniversary T-shirt, Metal Rhythm *Tour poster and T-shirt.*

When *Metal Rhythm*, Numan's first studio album in two years and his first for his new label IRS Records, failed to return him to the spotlight, it stunned not only his fanbase (who had in the meantime quickly hailed the disc as his best album in years) but Numan as well. It was then both ironic and frustrating that the tour – one of Gary's best attended – performed in support of this record was nothing short of stunning with the stage set and lightshow equal to any of his touchstone shows of the early 80s. Four tracks from *Metal Rhythm* made it into the set alongside a strong selection of past classics; sadly the tour lasted only one month and didn't make it overseas despite IRS releasing a new version of the album in the states a few months later.

This tour was eventually documented by a complimentary 'highlights only' live album released the following year, a recent re-issue of this recording emerged through EMI but sadly failed to unearth the full concert tapes.

THE SKIN MECHANIC TOUR 1989

OCTOBER
12th London Dominion Theatre/ 13th Oxford Apollo/ 14th Sheffield City Hall/ 15th

Hull City Hall/ 16th Manchester Apollo/ 18th Bristol Colston Hall/ 19th Newport Leisure Centre/ 20th Glasgow Barrowlands /21st Liverpool Empire/ 22nd Birmingham Alexandra/ 23rd Southampton Mayflower/ 24th Guildford Civic Hall/ 25th London Hammersmith Odeon/ 26th London Hammersmith Odeon.

Musicians: Gary Numan – Vocals/ RRussell Bell – Guitar/ Chris Payne – Keyboards/ Cedric Sharpley – Drums/ Ade Orange – Keyboards/ Andy Coughlan – Bass/ Diana Wood – Backing vocals/ Cathi Ogden – Backing vocals.

Setlist: 'Intro'-('God Only Knows')/ 'America'/ 'Me! I Disconnect From You'/ 'Respect'/ 'I Die: You Die'/ 'Creatures'/ 'This Is Emotion'/ 'Cars'/ 'This Is Love'/ 'Down In The Park'/ 'Hunger'/ 'Devious'/ 'Tricks'/ 'I Can't Stop'/ 'We Take Mystery (To Bed)'/ 'Are "Friends" Electric?'/ 'Call Out The Dogs'/ 'New Anger'/ 'My Shadow In Vain'/ 'We Are Glass.'

In an unconventional, though not entirely surprising move, Numan opted to head out on his final tour dates of the 80s in support of all things, one of his own live albums. The subsequent 'Skin Mechanic Tour' saw Gary airing more material from his well received though under achieving latest album *Metal Rhythm*; of the six tracks performed from that record, three were making their live debut ('This Is Emotion', 'America', and 'Devious'). Another track performed for the first time was 'This Is Love', an excellent Numa era single that strangely had been overlooked in the past until now.

Even though Numan's chart profile was on the slide-1989 being particularly tough (both the recent Sharpe and Numan single and album had suffered a similar fate to *Metal Rhythm* by hovering just outside the top 40 before departing) – on the live front, Gary was going from strength to strength with 'The Skin Mechanic Tour' being hailed by fans as some of his most spectacular shows yet. Gary too was now quite an accomplished live performer slipping into the role with considerably more ease than at any time before.

To commemorate these shows, a highlights only video was issued the following year (the footage was also screened on British television). In 2003 this footage was re-issued on DVD via Classic Rock Productions (see 'Official DVDs').

THE OUTLAND TOUR 1991

MARCH

16th Liverpool Empire/ 17th Glasgow Pavilion/ 18th Manchester Apollo/ 19th Newcastle City Hall/ 20th Sheffield City Hall/ 22nd Birmingham Hummingbird/ 23rd Hull City Hall/ 24th Oxford Apollo/ 25th Southampton Mayflower/ 26th Guildford Civic Hall/ 27th Bristol Colston Hall/ 28th Leicester De Montfort/ 29th London Hammersmith Odeon/ 30th London Hammersmith Odeon.

Musicians: Gary Numan – Vocals and guitar/ Mike Smith – Keyboards/ John Webb – Keyboards and bass/ Cedric Sharpley – Drums/ Keith Beauvais – Guitar/ Jackie Rawe – Backing vocals.

Setlist: 'Intro'/ 'Soul Protection'/ 'Confession'/ 'Respect'/ 'Call Out The Dogs'/ 'Me! I Disconnect From You'/ 'America'/ 'Dark Sunday'/ 'Creatures'/ 'Your Fascination'/ 'Down In The Park'/ 'Cars'/ 'Outland'/ 'Devious'/ 'From Russia Infected'/ 'My World Storm'/ 'Are "Friends" Electric?'/ 'Young Heart'/ 'I Die: You Die'/ 'We Are Glass.'

Special note: this tour had originally been pencilled in to take place in September 1990, unfortunately, with the *Outland* album unfinished the tour was rescheduled for the following year.

If fans were, by and large, disappointed with Numan's latest album *Outland*, the subsequent tour performed in support only confounded matters further with fans witnessing Numan clearly attempting to make a conscious effort to break with his illustrious past once and for all. Visually too, Gary had noticeably toned down on the elaborate stage sets and dazzling light shows preferring a more down to earth and grittier setting for this tour. With the main bulk of the set derived almost exclusively from his last two albums (*Outland* being represented by six tracks and a further four lifted from *Metal Rhythm*) any fans hoping for a good cross section of earlier material would have been sorely disappointed with only five tracks from Gary's heyday selected.

Of the six new tracks aired, all but two remained faithful to a recognisable Numan blueprint ('Confession' and 'My World Storm'), the others

Official T-shirt and tour poster.

only highlighted the fact – as did much of the recently released parent album that although the musicianship could not be faulted, Gary's dance/ rock style change had gone too far threatening the very fabric of his appeal and steadily alienating his already fracturing fanbase. Not surprisingly, fans, which had already given the new album a cautious welcome, were now noticeably beginning to trickle away. Sadly, this depressing and relatively frustrating period in Numan's career was suddenly made significantly worse when Gary's label, IRS Records, imploded in the middle of 1991 leaving Numan once more without a record deal.

To date no official document of 'The Outland Tour' on either audio or video has been released.

THE EMOTION EUROPEAN TOUR 1991

SEPTEMBER
14th Brussels Ancienne Belgique*/ 16th Bristol Bierkeller/ 17th Derby Assembly Rooms/ 18th Folkestone Leas Cliff Hall/ 19th London Camden Electric Ballroom/ 21st Portsmouth South Sea Pier/ 22nd Crewe Victoria Oakley Centre/ 23rd Sheffield Leadmill/ 24th Norwich Waterfront/ 25th Ipswich Corn Exchange/ 26th London Camden Electric Ballroom/ 27th Milton Keynes Woughton Centre/ 28th Wolverhampton Civic Hall/ 29th Leicester Polytechnic/ 30th Leeds Polytechnic.
OCTOBER
1st Manchester International 2/ 2nd Ayr Pavilion (this show suffered a power failure)/ 3rd Newcastle Riverside/ 4th Blackburn King Georges Hall.*
* Three tracks from each of these dates were added to the flip-side of the 12-inch version of the 'Machine + Soul' single. Show at Blackburn also video-taped.
Musicians: Gary Numan – Vocals and guitar/ Mike Smith – Keyboards/ John Webb – Keyboards and bass/ Cedric Sharpley – Drums/ Keith Beauvais – Guitar/ Jackie Rawe – Backing vocals.
Setlist: 'Intro' – ('Hanoi')/ 'Me! I Disconnect From You'/ 'Call Out The Dogs'/ 'Your Fascination'/ 'Outland'/ 'Respect'/ 'Cars'/ 'Devious'/ 'The Sleeproom'/ 'Are "Friends" Electric?'/ 'Soul Protection'/ 'Confession'/ 'From Russia Infected'/ 'My World Storm'/ 'Emotion'/ 'Cold Metal Rhythm'/ 'America'/ 'Young Heart.'

This hastily arranged tour – designed to help promote Gary's new single, the dire 'Emotion' – was performed primarily in clubs with one date in Brussels (hence the European tour heading), sadly, these dates heralded the beginning of the darkest period in Numan's career with the star now operating out of his re-activated Numa imprint, struggling to even get his new releases into the top 75. Although 1991 had been a year of crushing commercial disappointment, Gary's live show remained refreshingly unaffected with 'The Emotion Tour' witnessing Numan not only firing on all cylinders, but delivering superb performances throughout this 19-date tour. The set list was almost exclusively drawn from his *Metal Rhythm* and *Outland* albums with only three tracks ('Cars', 'Are "Friends" Electric?' and 'Me! I Disconnect From You') included from his glory days. In addition, two tracks, (the aforementioned) 'Emotion' and an aggressive take of 'Cold Metal Rhythm' (the latter lifted from the 1988 *Metal Rhythm* album) also made their live debut on this tour as well as a surprise re-appearance of the 1986 *Strange Charm* album track 'The Sleeproom', performed here for the first time since 1987. The addition of Keith Beauvais on lead guitar added a gutsy, riffy, almost heavy metal approach to Numan's classic repertoire with 'Me! I Disconnect from You', 'My World Storm' and 'Young Heart' sounding much more live wire and far fresher than their original studio counterparts. 'Cars' too had also been reworked here featuring an enhanced rhythm track as well as an extended closing dance

segment. Sadly though, much like the previous 'Outland Tour' much of the material included from the *Outland* album struggled in the live arena with the one new track ('Emotion') only compounding matters yet further still.

In all though 'The Emotion Tour' was an intimate and lively club tour that enabled Numan to undertake his first club tour since the very early days of Tubeway Army.

In a pioneering move (not to mention one guaranteed to hinder bootleggers) every date of 'The Emotion European Tour' was recorded and made available to buy on cassette direct from Gary's fan club shortly after the conclusion of the tour.

Official T-shirt.

THE ISOLATE TOUR 1992

MARCH
22nd Liverpool Empire/ 23rd Aston Villa Sports and Leisure Centre/ 24th Leicester DeMontfort Hall/ 25th Sheffield City Hall/ 27th Glasgow Plaza Ballroom/ 28th Manchester Apollo/ 29th Bristol Colston Hall/ 30th Southampton Mayflower Theatre/ 31st Oxford Apollo Theatre.
APRIL
1st Cambridge Corn Exchange/ 2nd Guildford Civic Hall/ 3rd Hammersmith Odeon/ 4th London Hammersmith Odeon.

Musicians: Gary Numan – Vocals and guitar/ Kipper – Guitar/ Mike Smith – Bass and keyboards/ Cedric Sharpley – Drums/ Susie Webb – Backing vocals/ John Webb – Keyboards.

Set list: 'Intro'/ 'Respect'/ 'Devious'/ 'Confession'/ 'Me! I Disconnect From You'/ 'America'/ 'Call Out The Dogs'/ 'Soul Protection'/ 'Outland'/ 'Your Fascination'/ 'Time To Die'/ 'Cars'/ 'From Russia Infected'/ 'My World Storm'/ 'The Skin Game'/ 'Emotion'/ 'Are "Friends" Electric?'/ 'We Are Glass'/ 'U Got The Look'/ 'Cold Metal Rhythm'/ 'Young Heart.'

Two official T-shirts and an official tour poster.

To help promote the just released Numa compilation album *Isolate* as well as the release of a new single entitled 'The Skin Game,' this thirteen date tour was quickly arranged, however, unlike the previous tour, this trek remained strictly UK based.

Aside from the inclusion of 'Emotion', the rest of the tracks that featured on the *Isolate* compilation were culled exclusively from Numan's three Numa studio albums that emerged in the 80s – most of this material had previously either been long out of print or had simply only just been issued on CD in the first place (as was the case with the *Berserker* era tracks) – although bizarrely, the actual tour set list featured very little from this album or even much at all in the way of either Numa or Beggars Banquet era material. Instead, Numan preferred to stick steadfastly to the template laid down by his two previous tours and concentrate almost entirely on material lifted from the two albums he recorded for IRS Records. 'The Isolate Tour' saw Gary cut back again on his classic early 80s material by including just four tracks from that era.

Making their debut on this tour were two brand new tracks, one was a rather underwhelming cover of the Prince single 'U Got The Look', the other was Numan's new single 'The Skin Game.' A third and final track making its live debut was 'Time To Die', a song that originally appeared on the cassette version of the *Strange Charm* album and even though it was a particular Numan favourite, it had failed to make it into the concert set list until now.

To date, no official document of this tour has emerged either on audio or video although tracks culled from this tour and the previous years 'The Emotion Tour' do appear occasionally on the numerous Numa compilation albums that have sprung up in recent years (see 'The Numa Years'). A live album from this tour was scheduled for release in March 1993; however, to date this recording has not surfaced.

THE DREAM CORROSION TOUR 1993

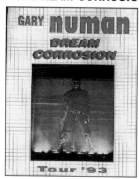

OCTOBER

23rd Brentwood Leisure Centre/ 24th York Barbican Centre/ 25th Leicester De Montfort/ 26th Corby Festival Hall/ 27th Birmingham Town Hall/ 28th London The Marquee/ 29th Mansfield Leisure Centre/ 30th Oxford Apollo/ 31st Manchester Apollo.

NOVEMBER

1st Bristol Colston Hall/ 2nd Guildford Civic Hall/ 4th Portsmouth Guildhall/ 5th Cambridge Corn Exchange/ 6th London Hammersmith Apollo.

Musicians: Gary Numan – Vocals and guitar/ Kipper – Guitar/ John Webb – Keyboards/ Ade Orange – Keyboards and bass/ Richard Beasley – Drums/ T.J. Davis – Backing vocals.

Additional musicians: Charles Pierre and Francis Usmar on 'You Are In My Vision' and 'Bombers.'

Setlist: 'Intro'/ 'Machine And Soul'/ 'Outland'/ 'Me! I Disconnect From You'/ 'We Are So Fragile'/ 'Respect'/ 'Shame'/ 'Films'/ 'Dream Killer'/ 'Down In The Park'/ 'My World Storm'/ 'The Machmen'/ 'Generator'/ 'Noise Noise'/ 'Cars'/ 'Voix'/ 'You Are In My Vision'/ 'It Must Have Been Years'/ 'That's Too Bad'/ 'Remind Me To Smile'/ 'I'm An Agent'/ 'Are "Friends" Electric?'/ 'My Breathing'/ 'I Don't Believe'/ 'Bombers'/ 'Jo The Waiter'/ 'We Are Glass.'

Special note: additional songs aired throughout the tour were: 'Your Fascination', 'Soul Protection' and 'I Die: You Die.'

Official tour poster and T-shirt.

Having been more or less forced to abandon any plans to tour in support of his last record, the poorly received *Machine + Soul*, Numan opted instead to go out on the road promoting the winter 1993 CD re-issue of his Beggars Banquet recorded albums. In the run up to the tour though Gary appeared to have entered into a period of career re-assessment by finally understanding that his fans relentless requests for more early material to be included in his live show was not entirely born out of mere nostalgia but a real desire from them to see the star performing music that was way more 'Numan' in style and content than more recent offerings had been. As a result of this re-appraisal and the re-issue campaign as a whole, an impressive 15 classic era tracks were re-introduced into the live set, many of which had not been played live in years. 'The Dream Corrosion Tour' also saw a total of 10 tracks making their live debut, all of which were mainly overlooked album tracks and obscure B-sides from various points in Numan's recording career. The rest of the set was made up of an assortment of Numa and IRS era tracks that, again, saw lesser-known material being selected in a bid to keep the twenty five-song set list as fresh as possible. It was clear to fans during the course of the two week tour that Gary had seemingly re-discovered himself and genuinely appeared to be enjoying himself every bit as much as his fans.

Official yearbook and T-shirt.

Following the end of the tour, Numan was quickly back out on the road, this time supporting the resurrected OMD on their seven date December 1993 arena tour. Dates played were: Glasgow SECC on the 4th, Sheffield Arena on the 6th, Birmingham NEC on the 7th, Manchester G Mex on the 8th, Cardiff International Ice Rink on the 10th. Bournemouth International Centre on the 11th and finally London Wembley Arena on the 12th. Gary's set for the shows comprised of an abbreviated version of his 'Dream Corrosion' set featuring: 'Intro-Machine And Soul', 'Remind Me To Smile', 'Me! I Disconnect From You', 'Cars', 'Respect', 'Noise Noise', 'My World Storm', 'It Must Have Been Years', 'Films', 'Outland', 'I'm An Agent' and 'Are "Friends" Electric?', the band line-up remained the same as the earlier tour.

A year later a complimentary video and double album taken from the last night on the 'Dream Corrosion Tour' emerged with the record being issued via Gary's re-activated Numa imprint and the video available only through Numan's fan club address.

THE SACRIFICE TOUR 1994

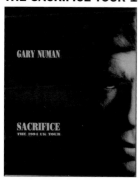

NOVEMBER

2nd Guildford Civic Hall/ 3rd Manchester Apollo/ 4th Southampton Guildhall/ 5th Hammersmith Apollo/ 6th Birmingham Town Hall/ 8th Folkestone Leas Cliff Hall/ 9th Bristol Bierkeller/ 10th Milton Keynes The Sanctuary/ 11th Colchester The CharterHall/ 12th London Astoria 2.*

* After the concert, the band performed a four-song set for the *GAY Club* at the same venue.

Musicians: Gary Numan – Vocals and guitar/ Kipper – Guitar/ Ade Orange – Keyboards and bass/ John Webb – Keyboards/ Richard Beasley – Drums.

Setlist: 'Intro' – ('Pray')/ 'A Question Of Faith'/ 'I Dream Of Wires'/ 'Noise Noise'/ 'Listen To The Sirens'/ 'Every Day I Die'/ 'Desire'/ 'Friends'/ 'Scar'/ 'Magic'/ 'Replicas'/ 'Mean St'/ 'Stormtrooper In Drag'/ 'Deadliner'/ 'Bleed'/ 'Praying To The Aliens'/ 'The Dream Police'/ 'Remind Me To Smile'/ 'Are "Friends" Electric?'/ 'Do You Need The Service?'/ 'Love And Napalm'/ 'Jo The Waiter.'

Additional material performed at various dates was: 'M.E.', 'This Is My House', 'The Hunter', 'I Die: You Die' and 'I'm An Agent.'

Following the release of the album *Sacrifice* (a record which fans felt was a messiah-like return to form), Numan quickly headed out on the road to perform a short two-week tour. Although only brief, 'The Sacrifice Tour' was, like 'The Dream Corrosion Tour' before it, another two hour show packed once more with a virtual treasure trove of long forgotten and long lost Numan classics. The set featured an impressive eight tracks lifted from his new record and a further seventeen coming

Official backstage pass, T-shirt and poster.

from his glorious past. For this trek Gary had finally dispensed with all the IRS era material preferring to concentrate almost entirely (with the exception of the material from his new album) on his late 70s, early 80s recordings. Numan also debuted more rarities at these shows including long forgotten gems like: 'Stormtrooper In Drag', 'Mean St', 'Do You Need The Service?', 'Listen To The Sirens', 'Friends' and 'The Hunter.' Two other tracks making their live return were 'Praying To The Aliens' and 'Replicas', neither of which had been aired since the Australian leg of 'The Touring Principle.'

To commemorate the tour, a double live album emerged although unlike the previous *Dream Corrosion* live release, 'The Sacrifice Tour' was not backed up with a complementary live video.

THE PREMIER HITS TOUR 1996

MARCH
23rd Folkestone Leas Cliff Hall/ 24th London Astoria/ 25th Bristol Colston Hall/ 26th Cambridge Corn Exchange/ 27th Ipswich Regent/ 29th Newcastle City Hall/ 30th Glasgow Pavilion/ 31st Liverpool Empire.
APRIL
1st Nottingham Rock City/ 2nd Southampton Guildhall/ 3rd Guildford Civic Hall/ 4th Birmingham Town Hall/ 5th Manchester Apollo/ 6th Milton Keynes Woughton Centre/ 7th Hammersmith Odeon.
Musicians: Gary Numan – Vocals and guitar/ Ade Orange – Keyboards and bass/ Steve Harris – Guitar/ David Brooks – Keyboards/ Richard Beasley – Drums.
Setlist: 'Prophecy'/ 'Noise Noise'/ 'A Question Of Faith'/ 'Me! I Disconnect From You'/ 'Replicas'/ 'The Seed Of A Lie'/ 'An Alien Cure'/ 'Are "Friends" Electric?'/ 'Films'/ 'Bleed'/ 'Every Day I Die'/ 'Are You Real?'/ 'Dark'/ 'Absolution'/ I'm An Agent'/ 'Cars'/ 'Love And Napalm'/ 'We Are Glass'/ 'Remind Me To Smile.'

Following the sudden and certainly unexpected return of 'Cars' to the British top 20 (this in turn being quickly followed by a Beggars Banquet era singles collection entitled *Premier Hits*), Numan halted progress on his next record and set out on a two week tour to celebrate the success of both of these releases. The subsequent television exposure brought on by these re-issues helped the 'Premier Hits Tour' be one of Gary's best attended in years, convincing him to abandon his Numa imprint once more and search in earnest for a new deal.

The set list, like the previous 'Sacrifice Tour', concentrated purely on a strong selection of early material mixed in with songs from his most recent recordings. In total, ten tracks were culled from his early days – one of which, the 1978 *Tubeway*

1996 yearbook, tour poster and T-shirt.

Army obscurity 'Are You Real?' made its live debut here – with a further eight songs coming from more recent times. Of the newer material, another selection from the *Sacrifice* album ('The Seed Of A Lie') made its live debut here alongside the 1995 Numa single 'Absolution.' Gary also unveiled three brand new tracks-'Prophecy', 'An Alien Cure' and 'Dark' that gave fans a tentative, early preview into the sound and texture of Numan's upcoming new studio album.

Trio of tour flyers from the 1996 festivals.

Following the tour, Numan performed at two outdoor festival shows in the UK during the late summer of 1996, both took place as part of the *V96* festival circuit at Hylands Park in Chelmsford on the 17th of August and Victoria Park in Warrington on the 18th of August, at both, Gary performed in front of a crowd of 35,000 people each day. Preceding these shows, Numan also performed at the Adrenalin Village in London on the 16th of August where he performed a ten song set comprising of: 'Dark,' 'Noise Noise', 'A Question Of Faith', 'Scar', 'An Alien Cure', 'Dead Heaven', 'Every Day I Die', 'Bleed', 'Cars' and 'Dominion Day.' The set list for the following day at Hyland Park remained pretty much the same with the exception of one track ('Bleed') being dropped. The final show at Victoria Park saw the set list increased back up to ten tracks with the inclusion of 'Are "Friends" Electric?' At all three of these dates Gary aired a further two new tracks ('Dominion Day' and 'Dead Heaven') that were due for inclusion on his new studio record.

Although one of the recorded dates on 'The Premier Hits Tour' (Manchester Apollo) was due for release as a souvenir video and CD, to date no official document of either that tour or the three shows above have been officially released.

THE EXILE TOUR 1997/ 1998

UK LEG; 1997
OCTOBER
25th Southampton Guildhall/ 26th London Shepherds Bush Empire/ 27th Bristol Colston Hall/ 28th Guildford Civic Hall/ 29th Cambridge Corn Exchange/ 31st Glasgow Pavilion.

NOVEMBER
1st Southport Theatre/ 2nd Manchester Apollo/ 3rd Newcastle Mayfair/ 4th Birmingham Q Club/ 5th Nottingham Rock City/ 7th Milton Keynes Woughton Centre/ 8th Ipswich Regent/ 9th London Shepherds Bush Empire.*

Musicians; Gary Numan – Vocals and guitar/ Steve Harris – Guitar/ Richard Beasley – Drums/ David Brooks – Keyboards/ Ade Orange – Keyboards and bass.

Setlist: 'Intro'/ 'Down In The Park'/ 'Dominion Day'/ 'Friends'/ 'Films'/ 'A Question Of Faith'/ 'Voix'/ 'Every Day I Die'/ 'Dark'/ 'You Walk In My Soul'/ 'Noise Noise'/ 'Cars'/ 'Absolution'/ 'Metal'/ 'Dead Heaven'/ 'An Alien Cure'/ 'Bleed'/ 'Are "Friends" Electric?'**/ 'Jo The Waiter.'

 * This show was recorded.

** Featured guest vocals from Saffron from Republica.

With *Exile*, Numan's first album for Eagle Records, making a dent in the British top 50 when released and praise for his work pouring in from the likes of The Prodigy, Fear Factory, Nine Inch Nails, The Smashing Pumpkins, Hole and Marilyn Manson (to name but a few), it seemed Numan's years of mainstream exile were finally at an end. With *Exile* being issued throughout the world (Numan's first worldwide release since the IRS era) Gary also felt the time was now right to extend his touring ambitions beyond the confines of the UK with plans quickly drawn up to take 'The Exile Tour' not only to mainland Europe but finally-after a protracted 15-year hiatus – to the United States. However, the first leg of the tour saw Gary perform a fourteen date tour across the UK and with the recent spate of Numan cover versions and tribute albums Gary carefully tailored the set to make a show of some of the tracks that were receiving high profile attention due to this growing phenomenon. To that end, 'Down In The Park' (a track that both Marilyn Manson and The Foo Fighters had recently covered) was re-positioned as the show's set opener though here the song had been radically overhauled to bring forth the track's malevolent, chilling gothic edge. In all, 10 tracks were performed from Numan's touchstone era with both 'Friends' and 'We Are So Fragile' being performed with significantly different rhythm tracks (the former track later morphed completely in to the title track of Numan's 2000 studio album *Pure* and the latter was performed à la Jesus Jones (see *Random* CD), in effect, a cover of a cover!). With only one song plucked from Numan's mid-80s period (a veritable slashing take of 'Voix') the rest of the set was split between tracks lifted from both *Exile* and *Sacrifice*. Numan debuted 5 tracks from his latest album with the riffy 'Dominion Day' and the brooding 'Dark' (a song that later found itself being courted by the Hollywood movie industry) effortlessly eclipsing their somewhat paler studio counterparts. Of the three tracks aired from *Sacrifice,* one, the plaintive and heartfelt slowie 'You Walk In My Soul' – a song written and dedicated exclusively in honour of Gary's partner Gemma-made its concert debut here alongside both 'Bleed' and 'A Question Of Faith', two tracks that sounded better here that when originally performed three years back. One track making a surprise return to the live set after an absence of ten years was Gary's 1979 classic 'Metal' (this song would later be re-recorded along with 'Down In The Park' and added to the flipside of Numan's 1998 single 'Dominion Day'). Add to that a throbbing 'Every Day I Die', a muscular reading of both 'Are "Friends" Electric' and 'Cars' and the superb set closer 'Jo The Waiter' and 'The Exile Tour' soon found itself being performed across the UK to sold out venues filled with fans both old and new.

With the music now twisted into a dense and rhythmic electronic rock sound, on the visual front Gary had also tailored the stage set and look to run in tandem with the overall dark, eerie and gothic imagery conjured up on *Exile*, carefully choreographed lights and bursts of frenzied on stage action all created a tense atmospheric edge that helped make this tour such a memorable and ultimately resounding success. All of this quickly elevated 'The Exile Tour' into the same bracket occupied by a number of Numan's other previously outstanding live outings ('The Teletour', 'The Warriors Tour' and 'The Fury Tour' being just a few) and was quickly proclaimed as Numan's best tour in years with fans citing it as an absolute triumph.

Thrilled with this reaction, Gary agreed to perform a short live set on the 7th of March 1998 at the Forte Posthouse in Milton Keynes as part of a Numan themed convention. Gary's set consisted of; 'Dark', 'Friends', 'Metal', 'Dead Heaven', 'Are "Friends" Electric?' and 'Jo The Waiter' (Gary also performed as part of Ade Orange's own band Dig).

This leg of the tour was later documented when the Shepherds Bush Empire concert from the 9th of November 1997 was issued on CD by Eagle Records in April of 2004.

Special note: both 'Cars' and 'Dominion Day' from the above concert had previously been released and added to the flipside of the 1998 'Dominion Day' single.

EUROPEAN LEG: 1998
MARCH
13th Paris Le Divan Du Monde/ 16th Copenhagen Pumpehuset/ 17th Stockholm Klubben/ 19th Berlin Kesselhaus/ 22nd Frankfurt Batschkapp/ 23rd Munich Incognito/ 24th Cologne Prime Club/ 26th Utrecht Tivoli/ 27th Brussels Ancienne Belgique

Musicians and setlist: same as the UK.

The second leg of 'The Exile Tour' saw Gary perform a nine-date tour across Europe, although none of the shows have so far emerged officially, the concert performed in Stockholm on the 17th was transmitted via the internet.

THE NORTH AMERICAN LEG: 1998
MAY

  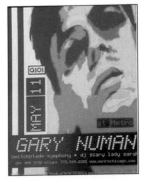

1st Philadelphia Theatre Of Living Arts/ 2nd New York Irving Plaza/ 3rd Cambridge Middle East/ 4th Washington 930 Club/ 6th Pittsburgh Club Laga/ 7th Toronto Lees Place/ 8th Cleveland The Odeon/ 10th Pontiac 7th House/ 11th Chicago The Metro/ 14th Vancouver The Starfish Room/ 15th Seattle The Fenix/ 16th Portland Oregon Berbatis Pan/ 17th San Francisco The Filmore/ 19th Los Angeles The Palace*/ 20th Tempe Bash On Ash/ 22nd The Galaxy/ 23rd Houston Numbers/ 24th Baton Rouge Luna/ 26th Orlando The Club At Firestone/ 27th West Palm Beach Carefree Theatre/ 28th St Petersburg State Theatre/ 29th Jacksonville The Milk Bar/ 30th Atlanta Masquerade/31st Charlotte Baja Club.

Musicians: same as the UK.

* This show was filmed by Cleopatra Records, sadly only a small portion of 'Down In The Park' was ever transmitted with the brief clip being aired on MTV.

Setlist: 'Intro' – ('Closer')/ 'Friends'/ 'Dominion Day'/ 'Cars'/ 'Films'/ 'A Question Of Faith'/ 'Voix'/ 'Every Day I Die'/ 'Dark'/ 'Noise Noise'/ 'An Alien Cure'/ 'Down In The Park'/ 'Absolution'/ 'Dead Heaven'/ 'Metal'/ 'Are "Friends" Electric?'/ 'Replicas'/ 'We Are So Fragile'/ 'Me! I Disconnect From You'/ 'We Are Glass.'*

* Only aired on selected dates.

One month after the mainland European leg, the tour was shipped overseas for Gary's first proper live dates on US soil in 18 years. Numan performed a 24 date tour through the month of May, for these shows, the set was bolstered by the addition of four more tracks ('Replicas', 'Me! I Disconnect From You', 'We Are So Fragile' and 'We Are Glass') many of which had appeared on the tribute album *Random* the previous year.

Of the US dates, Gary admitted to have been extremely worried that he would attract only crowds there purely for nostalgic reasons and the shows themselves would be severely under attended, in fact, almost all the 24 dates were sold out with the crowds in attendance made up of fans both old and new. Crowd favourite on the tour went not to 'Cars' (Numan's only American hit) but 'Down In The Park' with Marilyn Manson himself joining Gary on stage in Los Angeles to duet on the track. Another big star to visit the tour was Nine Inch Nails leader Trent Rezner who greeted Gary after the Baton Rouge date and handed him an early copy of the group's cover of 'Metal', a track that eventually found its way onto the Nine Inch Nails remix album *Things Falling Apart*.

Gary performed his final date of the year on the 12th of September at the Shepherds Bush Empire in London; this was the second of only two shows performed in the UK in 1998.

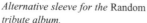

Alternative sleeve for the Random *tribute album.*

Tour poster from the US.

Official T-shirt.

ONE OFF CONCERTS: 1999

April 18th Nottingham Rock City
Setlist: 'Intro'/ 'Friends'/ 'Dead Heaven'/ 'Metal'/ 'Every Day I Die'/ 'Dark'/ 'Desire'/ 'An Alien Cure'/ 'Exile'*/ 'Cars'/ 'The Angel Wars'*/ 'Voix'/ 'Down In The Park'/ 'Dominion Day'/ 'Are "Friends" Electric?'/ 'I Die: You Die'/ 'You Are In My Vision'/ 'Tracks'/ 'Jo The Waiter.'
* Debut performances.

June 12th The London Forum
Setlist: 'Intro'/ 'Films'/ 'Absolution'/ 'Dominion Day'/ 'Friends'/ 'Deadliner'/ 'An Alien Cure'/ 'Are "Friends" Electric?'/ 'The Sleeproom'/ 'Down In The Park'/ 'Every Day I Die'/ 'Dark'/ 'Prophecy'/ 'Metal'/ 'The Angel Wars'/ 'I Die: You Die'/ 'My Shadow In Vain'/ 'Tracks'/ 'Jo The Waiter.'

August 7th Euro Rock Festival Belgium
Setlist: 'Intro'/ 'Films'/ 'Friends'/ 'Dominion Day'/ 'Cars'/ 'Noise Noise'/ 'Metal'/ 'Dark'/ 'Dead Heaven'/ 'Absolution'/ 'Down In The Park'/ 'Voix'/ 'The Angel Wars'/ 'A Question Of Faith.'

November 13th Academy Manchester
'Intro'/ 'Films'/ 'Me! I Disconnect From You'/ 'Dominion Day'/ 'Voix'/ 'Remind Me To Smile'/ 'Metal'/ 'Noise Noise'/ 'I Dream Of Wires'/ 'Down In The Park'/ 'Dark'/ 'Cars'/ 'The Seed Of A Lie'/ 'Remember I Was Vapour'*/ 'Friends/ 'The Angel Wars'/ 'Are "Friends" Electric?'/ 'A Question Of Faith'/ 'We Are Glass'/ 'That's Too Bad'/ 'I Die: You Die.'
* First live airing since Wembley 1981.

These four one-off concert dates were Gary's final performances of the 90s. In addition to these four shows, Gary also appeared live on stage with the US 'cyber metal' band Fear Factory to perform 'Cars' (the group's new single that also featured guest vocals from Gary), this appearance took place at The Brixton Academy on the 31st of October (Halloween).

THE PURE TOUR 2000/ 2001
ONE OFF CONCERTS: UK

Although the campaign to promote Gary's second album for Eagle Records did not get underway proper until the winter of 2000, he did play a one-off show in April on the 15th at the Shepherds Bush Empire in London. The setlist included: 'Intro'/ 'Pure'/ 'This Wreckage'/ 'Films'/ 'The Angel Wars'/ 'M.E.'/ 'A Question Of Faith'/ 'Cars'/ 'Down In The Park'/ 'Hetrodyne'/ 'Remember I Was Vapour'/ 'You Walk In My Soul'/ 'Dark'/ 'Voix'/ 'Sleep By Windows'/ 'Pulse Bass'/ 'Are "Friends" Electric?'/ 'Desire'/ 'Whisper Of Truth'/ 'Deadliner'/ 'Dance'/ 'Jo The Waiter.'

Three brand new tracks figured into the set ('Pure', 'Hetrodyne' and 'Pulse Bass', (the latter two performed under their work in progress arrangements and titles). A fourth, new (ish) song featured at the end of the set, entitled 'Dance', this track turned out to be a newly discovered *Dance* era recording that Gary's former record label were planning to include on the winter re-issue of his 1981 studio album.

In addition, two tracks ('Whisper Of Truth' and 'Sleep By Windows') made their live debut here alongside a resurrected 'This Wreckage' making its return to Numan's live shows after an absence of 18 years.

Following the release of *Pure*, Numan performed another one-off show at the Brixton Academy in London on the 20th of October 2000 (Numan's biggest show since Wembley 1981), the set list for this show featured: 'Intro'/ 'Pure'/ 'Me! I Disconnect From You'/ 'The Angel Wars'/ 'My Jesus'/ 'Films'/ 'Magic'/ 'Rip'/ 'Cars'/ 'Metal'/ 'Little Invitro'/ 'Down In The Park'/ 'This Wreckage'/ 'Dead Heaven'/ 'I Can't Breathe'/ 'Are "Friends" Electric?'/ 'A Prayer For The Unborn'/ 'Listen To My Voice'/ 'Replicas'/ 'Observer'/ 'Dance'/ 'Tracks.'

When finally released, *Pure* detonated a powerful shockwave that resonated not just through Gary's hardcore fan base but also to those in the media quietly observing Numan's miraculous musical rebirth. Within weeks the record was basking in the glow of an impressive amount of critical acclaim (something previously unheard of for a Numan release) turning Gary's previously slow and steady, part nostalgic, part genuine resurrection, into something altogether much more serious. Eagle it seemed were caught on the hop, Numan, however, wasn't and seized this second chance in much the same way that he had the first time around all those years ago. It was then no surprise to see Gary had tailored the *Pure* shows to concentrate almost exclusively on the best from his glory days as well as choice cuts from his last three career reviving albums. An already electrified crowd literally exploded the second the eerie intro music faded as the band powered full tilt into a hard rocking, head banging rendition of the album's title track. In all, seven tracks from *Pure* made it into the set with 'Rip', 'Little Invitro' and 'A Prayer For The Unborn' coming across even more powerful that their studio counterparts. Numan's older live staples had also been toughened up, complete with huge new grooves, loops and beats. Numan also served up more surprises with not only 'Tracks' making a welcome return to the set having not been performed since the early 80s but *The Pleasure Principle* obscurity 'Observer', being dusted down and performed live here for the very first time.

Five tracks from this show were added to the tour edition of the *Pure* album in February 2001 with the full show appearing on CD (entitled *Scarred*) two years later via Eagle Records. In addition, this concert was also filmed with three tracks ('Rip', 'Cars' and 'Pure') added to the US version of this album.

EUROPEAN LEG: 2000

NOVEMBER

20th Germany Cologne Prime Club/ 21st Germany Stuttgart Die Rohre/ 22nd Switzerland Basel Kaserne/ 23rd Austria Vienna Szene Wien/ 24th Germany Munich Metropolis/ 25th Germany Erfurt Centrum/ 26th Germany Berlin Pfefferberg/ 27th Denmark Copenhagen Vega/ 28th Germany Hamburg Schlachthof/ 29th Belgium Brussels Le Botanique.

Musicians: Gary Numan – Vocals and guitar/ Ade Orange – Keyboards and bass/ David Brooks – Keyboards/ Steve Harris – Guitar/ Richard Beasley – Drums.

Setlist: 'Intro'/ 'Pure'/ 'Films'/ 'Rip'/ 'Cars'/ 'Dark'/ 'The Angel Wars'/ 'Down In The Park'/ 'My Jesus'/ 'I Can't Breathe'/ 'Metal'/ 'Walking With Shadows'/ 'Are "Friends" Electric?'/ 'Me! I Disconnect From You'/ 'Listen To My Voice'/ 'Dominion Day'/ 'A Question Of Faith'/ 'A Prayer For The Unborn.'

With *Pure* being acknowledged as Numan's best and most consistent album in 20 years, Gary headed back out on the road in support taking the first leg of the tour to the European mainland. The set chosen for the shows saw Gary playing just six tracks from his early 80s heyday with the rest being made up of more recent recordings including seven songs – one of which, 'Walking With Shadows' (previously performed under the working title 'Hetrodyne' in early 2000) making its proper live debut on this leg of the tour – being

European issue of Pure.

lifted from his new album.

To date no official document of this leg of the tour, either audio or video has been released.

UK / IRELAND LEG: 2001

FEBRUARY

13th Croydon Fairfield Halls/ 14th Southampton Guildhall/ 15th Birmingham Academy/ 17th Dublin Vicar Street/ 18th Belfast Limelight/ 19th Glasgow The Garage/ 20th Nottingham Rock City/ 21st Manchester Academy/ 22nd Sheffield City Hall/ 23rd London The Forum.

Set list: 'Intro'/ 'Pure'/ 'Rip'/ 'Listen To My Voice'/ 'Metal'/ 'Down In The Park'/ 'Walking With Shadows'/ 'My Jesus'/ 'Torn'/ 'Every Day I Die'/ 'Me! I Disconnect From You'/ 'I Can't Breathe'/ 'Are "Friends" Electric?'/ 'Cars'/ 'Voix'/ 'Remind Me To Smile'/ 'A Prayer For The Unborn.'

Special note: two tracks, 'Prophecy' and 'Noise Noise' were aired on the first date of this trek but were dropped for the remainder of the tour.

The second leg of the *Pure* campaign saw Gary not only back on UK soil but also playing his first ever dates in Ireland. The set was also increased with Numan airing more material (ten tracks in all) from the early portion of his career and a further nine from his more recent recordings. One track making its live debut on this leg of the tour was 'Torn' taking the tally of material taken from *Pure* to an impressive eight.

Prior to the UK and Ireland shows, Numan performed a live radio set on the 7th of February for veteran Radio One DJ John Peel, songs performed were: 'Rip'/ 'Metal'/ 'Pure', 'My Jesus', 'Cars', 'Listen To My Voice', 'I Can't Breathe', 'Down In The Park', 'A Prayer For The Unborn.'

Although no official document of this leg of the tour has been released, the show performed in Birmingham at the Academy on the 15th was transmitted via the internet.

In addition, the John Peel recording was eventually aired by Radio One as was a further one-off recording of 'Are "Friends" Electric?' on the John Peel *Festive Fifty* show.

Tour T-shirt.

NORTH AMERICAN LEG: 2001

APRIL

17th Washington D.C. 9.30 Club/ 18th New York Irving Plaza/ 19th Philadelphia Theatre Of Living Arts/ 20th Boston Paradise/ 21st Montreal Café Campus*/ 22nd Toronto Palais Royale/ 24th Royal Oak MI Royal Oak Theatre/ 26th Cleveland The Odeon/ 27th Cincinnati Bogart's/ 28th Chicago House Of Blues/ 29th Minneapolis First Avenue.

MAY

1st Boulder C.O. Fox Theatre/ 4th San Francisco Filmore/ 5th Los Angeles House Of Blues/ 6th San Diego 4th and B Theatre/ 7th Anaheim CA House Of Blues.

* This show was filmed by a local Montreal TV station; footage featured a number of in-concert performances as well as a handful of pre and post show interviews.

Musicians: same as UK / European leg.

Set list: 'Intro'/ 'Pure'/ 'Films'/ 'Rip'/ 'Listen To My Voice'/ 'Cars'/ 'Dark'/ 'Down In The Park'/ 'Walking With Shadows'/ 'Metal'/ 'My Jesus'/ 'A Question Of Faith'/ 'I Can't Breathe'/ 'Are "Friends" Electric?'/ 'Remind Me To Smile'/ 'A Prayer For The Unborn.'

Trio of US only alternative sleeves commissioned for the Pure *album.*

The final leg of the *Pure* campaign paid a visit to the United States in the spring of 2001, there the set list altered little from the UK / European leg with the exception of the *Pure* track 'Torn' being dropped. Most of these shows were also being video taped (both on stage and off) with a view to including some of the footage as part of a new Gary Numan live DVD; however, to date no official document of this leg of the tour has emerged.

ONE-OFF CONCERTS: 2001

On his return from the US, Gary participated in the festival circuit once more performing a total of five shows (sadly minus Ade Orange) during July, August and September. A sixth show (and the final one of 2001) saw Gary performing a full live set at the Shepherds Bush Empire in London.

14th July Arvika Festival Sweden/ 3rd August Eurorock Festival Neerpelt Belgium/ 24th August Reading Festival UK/ 25th August Leeds Festival UK/ 1st September Mera Luna Hildesheim Germany.

Special note: Swedish performance was filmed.

Musicians: Same as 'The Pure Tour.'

Setlist: 'My Jesus'*/ 'Pure'*/ 'Metal'/ 'A Question Of Faith'/ 'Listen To My Voice'*/ 'Are "Friends" Electric?'/ 'Rip'*/ 'Dead Heaven'/ 'Cars'/ 'I Can't Breathe'*/ 'A Prayer For The Unborn'*/ 'Dark.'

*Only these tracks were aired in Germany.

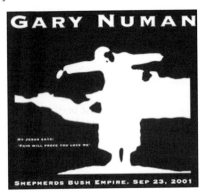 

Concert ad and official tour T-shirt.

September 23rd Shepherds Bush Empire London.

Setlist: 'Intro'/ 'My Jesus'/ 'Pure'/ 'Metal'/ 'Listen To My Voice'/ 'Dominion Day'/ 'Absolution'/ 'Walking With Shadows'/ 'Me! I Disconnect From You'/ 'Love And Napalm'/ 'Rip'/ 'Voix'/ 'A Prayer For The Unborn'/ 'I Can't Breathe'/ 'Films'/ 'Down In The Park'/ 'I'm An Agent'/ 'Are "Friends" Electric?'

To date, none of the one-off concerts performed in 2001 has been released, either on audio or video.

In the months following the show at Shepherds Bush, Numan, feeling his interests would be better served elsewhere, parted company with Eagle Records and quickly signed to Artful/ Universal Records. This event sadly removed any possibility of Numan returning to the US for the promised second leg of the US Pure Tour.

ONE-OFF CONCERTS: 2002

Following the release of the Artful/ Jagged Halo Records compilation album *Exposure*, Numan performed two shows in April. Within a month of the conclusion of these concerts, both 'Are "Friends" Electric?' (via the Sugababes heavily sampled song 'Freak Like Me') and the *Pure/ Exposure* track 'Rip' were hurled to the No1 spots in both the UK national chart and the *Kerrang* video chart.

In September, by way of compensation for there being no new album and no tour booked for the year (and to celebrate the fact that Numan had scored his first top 30 hit single – 'Rip' – in 14 years), a further three UK concerts were performed. April 5th Manchester Academy/ April 6th Shepherds Bush Empire.*

Musicians: same as 'The Pure Tour.'

* This show was also video-taped for a possible live DVD.

Set list: 'M.E.'/ 'My Jesus'/ 'Metal'/ 'Absolution'/ 'Dark'/ 'Down In The Park'/ 'Remember I Was Vapour'/ 'Pure'/ 'A Prayer For The Unborn'/ 'Every Day I Die'/ 'Exile'/ 'My Shadow In Vain'/ 'Rip'/ 'I Can't Breathe'/ 'This Wreckage'/ 'Voix'/ 'Cars'/ 'Are "Friends" Electric?'

September 19th Glasgow University/ 20th Liverpool The Lomax/ 21st London Hackney The Ocean

Setlist: 'Intro'/ 'M.E.'/ 'My Jesus'/ 'My Shadow In Vain'/ 'I Can't Breathe'/ 'This Wreckage'/ 'Dead Heaven'/ 'Pure'/ 'Bleed'/ 'A Prayer For The Unborn'/ 'Walking With Shadows'/ 'We Are So Fragile'/ 'Oh! Didn't I Say'/ 'Listen To The Sirens'/ 'Rip'/ 'Down In The Park'/ 'I Die: You Die'/ 'Moral'/ 'Are "Friends" Electric?'

These three shows were Gary's final concerts of 2002 and followed hot on the heels of his stunning return to the British top 30 a few weeks previously. The set list featured 11 early classics with one, the 1981 track 'Moral', being aired live here for the first time since the farewell shows back in 1981. Also making a surprise return to the live arena were two tracks dating from the very early Tubeway Army days. The first, the 1978 classic 'Listen To The Sirens', had last been aired on 'The Sacrifice Tour' in 1994. The second, 'Oh! Didn't I Say' was originally the B-side to the very first Tubeway Army single 'That's Too Bad' and hadn't been performed since 1978. The remaining eight tracks were all drawn from Numan's last three studio albums, six of which were lifted exclusively from Gary last album *Pure*.

ONE OFF CONCERTS: 2003
THE 25th ANNIVERSARY SHOWS

February 8th Bristol Colston Hall/ February 9th London Shepherds Bush Empire
Musicians: Same as the 'Pure Tour.'
Setlist: 'Hybrid'/ 'My Shadow In Vain'/ 'M.E.'/ 'My Jesus'/ 'That's Too Bad'/ 'Ancients'/ 'Every Day I Die'/ 'Torn'/ 'Down In The Park'/ 'Please Push No More'/ 'It Must Have Been Years'/ 'Crazier'/ 'Pure'/ 'I Can't Breathe'/ 'Rip'/ 'A Prayer For The Unborn'/ 'Cars'/ 'Are "Friends" Electric?'/ 'Bleed'/ 'I Die: You Die'/ 'We Are Glass.'

Two of the official 20th anniversary T-shirts.

To mark his 25 years as a professional musician, Gary performed two anniversary concerts in February of 2003, aside from celebrating this milestone in his career, Numan also took the opportunity to air some of the new remixed versions of his songs that had appeared on the *Hybrid* album. Gary aired a total of 21 tracks at each of the shows with most of the material performed in their newly commissioned/ remixed guises. Numan also performed the two new tracks ('Ancients' and 'Crazier') that had been recorded for the *Hybrid* album, the latter track seeing Glaswegian singer (and co-writer of 'Crazier') Rico join Numan on stage to sing the track live. Three tracks making surprise returns to the live set were Numan's 1980 classic 'Please Push No More', a song last aired an incredible 22 years ago as well as both 'It Must Have Been Years' and 'Bombers', the latter two last aired on 'The Dream Corrosion Tour.'

To date, neither of the two shows has been officially released although a fan generated bootleg video has appeared in fan circles since the conclusion of these shows. Both were also being professionally video-taped with a view to including the footage as part of a new Numan DVD.

In addition, a third live anniversary date was performed one week later, this show though was a little different being instead a live set performed exclusively for German TV on the 17th of February for a show entitled *Music Planet 2Nite*. The group line-up included: Gary Numan – Vocals and guitar/ Steve Harris – Guitar/ Rob Holiday – Bass and guitar/ David Brooks – Keyboards and bass/ Ade Orange – Keyboards/ Richard Beasley – Drums. The set comprised of: 'Hybrid'/ 'Rip'/ 'Dark'/ 'My Jesus'/ 'Crazier'/ 'Down In The Park'/ 'Pure'/ 'I Can't Breathe' and 'A Prayer For The Unborn.' This performance, although recorded within the confines of a TV studio, went extremely well with Gary and the band delivering stunning renditions (none more so than 'A Prayer For The Unborn' here transformed into a stirring, thought provoking Numan anthem) of the nine tracks that had originally been selected. An edited version of the show was eventually screened on May 6th featuring just four of the nine tracks aired ('Rip', 'Dark', 'Crazier', I Can't Breathe' as well as the aforementioned 'A Prayer For The Unborn'). In addition, both 'Crazier' and 'A Prayer For The Unborn' were included on the re-issue of the *Hybrid* album as part of a bonus DVD entitled *Mutate.*

ADDITIONAL ONE-OFF CONCERTS 2003

September 20th Manchester Academy/ 21st London Astoria
Group Line-up: Gary Numan – Vocals and guitar/ Richard Beasley – Drums/ David Brooks – Keyboards/ Steve Harris – Guitar/ Rob Holiday – bass.
Set list: 'Intro' – ('Hybrid')/ 'Pure'/ 'Films'/ 'Moral'/ The Aircrash Bureau'/ 'Dark'/ 'Crazier'/ 'Untitled New Song'/ 'My Jesus'/ 'Down In The Park'/ 'Complex'/ 'Bleed'/ 'I Can't Breathe'/ 'A Prayer For The Unborn'/ 'My Breathing'/ 'Ancients'/ 'Absolution'/ 'My Shadow In Vain'/ 'Are "Friends" Electric?'

Following the success of the Numan Vs Rico single 'Crazier', two one-off shows were quickly scheduled to both celebrate the top 20 success of the recent single and also compensate long time fans over the non-appearance of Gary's long awaited new studio record. Of the two dates, one, the show performed at the Academy, was also being filmed for release as a commemorative (and finally official) live DVD. However, on the eve of the shows Gary suddenly became a father (an event planned for but arriving much sooner than had been expected) and understandably much of the preparation and groundwork for the concerts just about went out of the window (including two of the three hotly anticipated new songs due to be aired). The set list for both shows were, again, another strong selection of past classics and more recent material with the one salvaged 'newie' figuring into the set as an eerie instrumental.

Numan also returned a further three vintage recordings into the set, one of which 'My Breathing' (returning after a 10 year absence) was the only track out of the 19 aired that originated from Numan's much maligned 'mid-period.' The other two songs making welcome returns were 'Complex' and 'The Aircrash Bureau', neither of which had been performed since Gary's farewell show's at Wembley Arena in 1981. Aside from a few minor sound glitches, both shows were excellent.

ONE-OFF CONCERTS 2004

March 3rd Nottingham Rock City/ March 4th Cardiff Barfly*/ March 5th London Shepherds Bush Empire
* For the Cardiff show, Gary performed an intimate set for the 200 strong capacity crowd, the concert was performed in aid of the Shelter and War Child charities with tickets only available to competition winners
Musicians: Gary Numan – Vocals and guitar/ Richard Beasley – Drums/ David Brooks – Keyboards/ Steve Harris – Guitar/ Rob Holiday – bass.
Setlist: 'Exposure'/ 'Films'/ 'Call Out The Dogs'/ 'Crazier'/ 'Rip'/ 'Does God Bleed?'/ 'Metal'/ 'My Jesus'/ 'Walking With Shadows'/ 'Down In The Park'/ 'Haunted'/ 'Prophecy'/ 'I'm An Agent'/ 'Desire'/ 'Jagged Halo'/ 'A Prayer For The Unborn'/ 'M.E.'/ 'Night Talk'/ 'My Breathing'/ 'Are "Friends" Electric?'

Hailed by fans as some of the best Numan concerts in years, this trio of dates captured Gary on the brink of commercial greatness once more, backed by a fantastic lightshow and (this time round at least) an incredible sound. For these shows Numan debuted three brand new tracks ('Does God Bleed?', 'Haunted' and

'Jagged Halo') as well as an additional debut performance of 'Night Talk' a track that was originally the B-side to the 1981 Paul Gardiner single 'Stormtrooper In Drag' (later included on the Numan studio album *Dance*). Of the 20 tracks aired only seven were lifted from Numan's early touchstone era with the lion's share of the set comprising of and concentrating on the best of Numan's recent return to form recordings (although oddly 'Ancients' had been mysteriously excised from the set despite its superb debut live impact in 2003). Two tracks from Numan's mid period also figured into the set, one of which 'Call Out The Dogs' had not been aired since 'The Isolate Tour' and had here been significantly beefed up to dramatic effect.

ADDITIONAL ONE-OFF CONCERTS 2004

September 10th at Birmingham's Carling Academy and London's Shepherds Bush Empire on the 11th
Setlist: 'Intro'/ 'Rip'/ 'Noise Noise'/ 'Voix'/ 'Remind Me To Smile'/ 'My Jesus'/

'Haunted'/ 'Down In The Park'/ 'Ancients'/ 'Replicas'/ 'Jagged Halo'/ 'Listen To My Voice'/ 'Dead Heaven'/ 'Are "Friends" Electric?'/ 'We Are Glass'/ 'A Prayer For The Unborn'/ 'My Shadow In Vain'/ 'Fadeout 1930's'*/ 'I Die: You Die.'*/ 'The Machmen'**/ 'It Must Have Been Years'**/ 'Jo The Waiter.'**

* Only performed at Birmingham's Carling Academy.

** Only performed at The Shepherds Bush Empire.

Following Numan's announcement that his deal with Artful Records was to terminate, Gary performed these two one-off concerts. Both shows were filmed.

SECTION FOUR

APPENDICES

Over the course of the following pages *Electric Pioneer* will take a look at both the many publications and internet websites that have appeared over the years.

APPENDIX I BIBLIOGRAPHY

Since Gary Numan's 1979 breakthrough, a veritable wealth of books, magazines and fanzines have emerged; the bulk of these emerging in the early 80s when Numan was at his early career zenith. The following pages list all the known official publications that have appeared on the market, they are listed in chronological order.

GARY NUMAN BY COMPUTER
Written by Fred and Judy Vermorel.
OMNIBUS PRESS.
Released: 1980.
Typical 'thrown together' book that printed a number of quotes from Gary as a computer type, does include, however, some excellent rare photos over the course of its 64 pages. Although ultimately rather poor it was certainly the first book about Gary Numan to appear on the market following his '79 breakthrough.

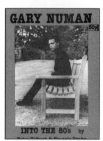

INTO THE 80's
Written by Peter Gilbert and Francis Drake.
Released: 1980.
A 'story so far' booklet that featured fact files on the Gary Numan band members, lyrics to songs (including 'Lucky', a song by Gary's younger brother John aka Johnny Silver) as well as a wealth of excellent photos. Interestingly enough, both writers would ultimately go on to provide the sleevenotes for the 1987 Beggars Banquet compilation *Exhibition*.

GARY NUMAN – AN INTIMATE PROFILE
ROCKSTAR PUBLISHING.
Danacell/ Comag Ltd
Released: 1980.
Fold out magazine that revealed a large poster of Numan during his 'Touring Principle' phase. Magazine also featured a lengthy interview conducted with the star as well as various photos of Gary from 1979.

GARY NUMAN OFFICIAL SONGBOOK – VOLUME ONE
CHAPPEL PUBLICATIONS.
Released: 1982.
Featured the lyrics and music from both *Tubeway Army* and *Replicas*. Additional songs included were three tracks taken from the sessions for *The Plan-1978*: 'Ice', 'The Monday Troop' and 'Critics' as well as both A-sides and B-sides from Tubeway Army's first two 1978 released singles. Separately sold sheet music was later made available for: 'Music For

Chameleons', 'Cars', 'Are "Friends" Electric?', 'This Wreckage' and the Sharpe And Numan hit 'Change Your Mind.'

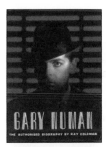

GARY NUMAN – THE AUTHORISED BIOGRAPHY
Written by Ray Coleman.
SIDGWICK AND JACKSON.
Released: 1982.
128 pages.
THIS autobiography chronicles the early part of his career whilst signed to his first label Beggars Banquet. The book included rare family photographs as well as fascinating insights into Gary's pre-success years.

GARY NUMAN WARRIORS TOUR, '83
All photos by Fin Costello.
Released: 1984.
95 pages.
Glossy photographs from Gary's 1983 comeback tour, also featured a tour diary.

GARY NUMAN THE FURY TOUR '85
OFFICIAL PHOTO BOOK OF THE UK TOUR
Released: 1986.
Glossy and stunning photos from Numan's 1985 tour, book was LP sized.

GARY NUMAN – ELECTRIC SHADOWS – A HISTORY IN CUTTINGS: VOLUME ONE
Released: 1986.
60 pages.
This extremely limited edition soft back book featured a whole host of Numan albums and singles running up to 1986 as well as lyrics, interviews and photos. Each copy was individually numbered.

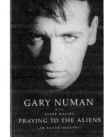 

GARY NUMAN – PRAYING TO THE ALIENS
ANDRE DEUTSCH PUBLISHING
Written by Gary Numan with Steve Malins.
Released: 1997.
Re-issued 1998 complete with an extra chapter (see right).

Gary's autobiography took a look back over his 20-year career to reveal the full story, from his astonishing success, his subsequent slide and his late 90s resurrection. Included excellent sleeve notes and intro chapter from co-writer Steve Malins.

(II) NUMAN ON THE WORLD WIDE WEB

Aside from Numan's own website, there are a plethora of Gary Numan websites online run exclusively by fans. Although great sites like 'Replicants Room', 'Noise Noise' and 'Outland' have faded from view in recent years, an amazing number of excellent new sites have appeared to fill the void left behind. Unfortunately, a lack of space prohibits *Electric Pioneer* from truly doing justice to the many superb sites on the web; this section then will highlight the very best internet sites that would be of interest to fans.

NUWORLD

Address: www.numan.co.uk.

Launched in 1995, Gary's own site is very much hung on the here and now, extremely professional-looking and superbly laid out. Menu includes: up to date news, the online shop *NuStreet*, the latest tour information, interviews, details of Gary's NU phone line service and much, much more besides. Nuworld is also used by Gary (much like the phone lines themselves) to occasionally air demos of work-in-progress new material.

DEAD HEAVEN

Address: myweb.tiscali.co.uk/ deadheaven.

Another extremely professional-looking site that gravitates in the direction of Gary's live work, menu includes: a superb Numan live history, video downloads, live bootlegs (both audio and video), up to date news, screensavers, a vast and highly impressive, past to present photo gallery and so much more besides. Superb.

EXILED TELEKON

Members.tripod.com/ exiledtelekon1.

Another site featuring an excellent in-depth photo gallery*, menu also includes a number of other Numan related topics.

* See also 'ABSOLUTION' (address: www.geocities.com/voix) and 'Gary Numan Scrapbook' (address: www.dubhead.purevision.com/ scrapbook).

NUMANME

Address: homepage.ntlworld.com/Richard Churchward / Numanme.

Another professional and imaginative package, alongside the usual news, Numan links (both fan sites and Yahoo groups), downloadable videos, picture galleries, tour dates and biographies this site features the most detailed text Gary Numan discography on the web. Also included are the sleeves for just about every single and album sleeve either released by Gary or linked to him (although they have all been altered slightly with each picture being digitally curved at the ends). Does, however, feature a small fan forum as well as an excellent Bootleg CD page. With many new and interesting items being added on a weekly basis this is one site definitely worth watching.

* See also 'THE NUMANOID CHANNEL' (www.numanoid007.levillage.org)

THE NORTH AMERICAN GARY NUMAN FAN CLUB
Address: themachman.GaryNuman.info
US site that features, amongst the usual news and reviews, a wealth of rare video and audio downloads. Also has an excellent section devoted to fan produced live photos.*

*See also 'THE MYSTERIOUS ASHLEY X.' (www.ashley.com)

THEGARYCEENUMANPRINCIPLE
Address: http:// groups.msn.com)
This site concentrates on Numan's early career and contains a wealth of hard to find singles and albums as well as an excellent mini photo gallery. In addition, this site includes a number of rare and hard to find magazine covers and posters from across the years all meticulously scanned.*

* See also 'RRWORLD'
(address:http://members:fortunecity.co.uk
/angelnuman/rruworld).

PRAYING TO THE ALIENS
Address: http:// aliens.garynuman.info.
A site packed with excellent Numan related sections and topics. Features the usual tour dates, news and photos as well as a detailed links section to other great sites.

TUBEWAY DAYS
Address: http:// groups yahoo.com/groups/TubewayDays
One of the many superb Yahoo Gary Numan fan sites*, this one differs little from the rest featuring an amazing data base of archive photographs and merchandise as well as additional files and Numan links.

* See also 'Sacrifice' (groups yahoo.com/ Sacrifice).

AFE – THE INTERACTIVE GARY NUMAN SITE
Address: www.afenet.com
Special note: requires a password to access contents.
One of the oldest-running Numan sites on the net. Site includes a small number of Numan links, 'fan sourced' live photo galleries as well as regular polls and live reviews. Jewel in its crown, however, is the site's lively

multi subject fan forum. All in all, superb.

(III) WALKING WITH SHADOWS
To conclude this final section of *Electric Pioneer*, the following pages will highlight the various recordings and videos that, for one reason or another, have not so far returned to the marketplace.

BEGGARS BANQUET
Gary's first label still has some way to go before finally exhausting their Numan archives; the following material is what is thought to be due for release in the near future.

LIVING ORNAMENTS 1980
Having failed to emerge in 1998 alongside both the CD re-mastered versions of *Living Ornaments '79* and *Living Ornaments '81*, an eventual release of the full version of this concert (still misplaced as of 2004) seems a long way off yet, representatives for Beggars Banquet have stated that the search for the original master tapes has now widened to include foreign arms of the label, however, fans hoping for a release any time soon are advised to not hold their breath.

RARITIES CD
A long rumoured project that seems to be edging ever closer to reality, in a recent online interview a representative for the label confirmed that there is enough material in the company's vaults to compile a single CD featuring rare and unreleased tracks.

No tracklist has been put forward but fans speculate it will feature a number of demos, remixes and alternative takes from all Gary's Beggars Banquet albums, tracks likely to feature are: the video mix and the *Kenny Everett Show* version of 'I Die: You Die', an unreleased song from the sessions for the *Warriors* album entitled 'Glasshouse', alternative second takes of both 'Sister Surprise' and 'The Tick Tock Man', the appearance of the long misplaced missing 1983 B-side 'Letters', more Bill Nelson era *Warriors* mixes, an extended, previously unreleased mix (as well as the original demo) of the 1981 track 'Moral', the demo versions of 'She's Got Claws' and 'Cry The Clock Said', the out-of-print 12-inch mix of 'We Take Mystery (To Bed)', a previously unreleased, edited version of 'The 1930's Rust', a previously unreleased, alternative take of the 1981 track 'Boys Like Me', the out-of-print American 12-inch mix of 'White Boys And Heroes', the demos of 'Down In The Park' and 'Remember I Was Vapour' (both of which appeared on two early 80s movie soundtracks), the original vinyl album mixes of 'Remember I Was Vapour', 'Remind Me To Smile'*, 'We Have A Technical' and 'The Joy Circuit' as well as a number of different remixes of 'Cars' from 1987 and 1993. Interestingly an earlier recording of the *Pleasure Principle* album – produced initially by Rikki Sylvian – has recently turned up in fan circles; it remains unclear whether any of these mixes will find a place on the proposed rarities CD.

This CD still has no firm release date at present and fans shouldn't expect a release before at least 2005.

* Replaced in 1998 with a hitherto previously unreleased US mix. This mix was added to the '98 CD issue of *Telekon*.

FURTHER LIVE RECORDINGS

Recordings from both the 'Warriors' and 'I, Assassin' tours are understood to exist (The 'I, Assassin Tour' has one confirmed date recorded on both audio and video and the 'Warriors Tour' itself has a number of live radio broadcasts to its name already) and Beggars Banquet have expressed an interest in issuing both a *Living Ornaments '82* and a *Living Ornaments '83*. In addition, further recordings from the UK leg of the 'Touring Principle' exist thanks to the Scottish radio station *Radio Clyde* recently unearthing a wealth of archive concerts (Numan shows on tape in their vaults are: the 20th of September 1979 ('The Touring Principle'), the 26th of September 1980 ('The Teletour'), the 20th of September 1983 ('The Warriors Tour') and the 21st of September 1987 ('The Exhibition Tour'). Recordings from the overseas leg of the 'Touring Principle' also reside in the Beggars Banquet vaults and it's not unfeasible that material from these shows may yet surface as part of an official future release.

VIDEOS:

Seemingly all footage featured on the three Beggars Banquet era video collections (*The Touring Principle '79*, *Micromusic* and *Newman Numan*) has now reverted back into Gary's ownership following years of legal wrangling; however, fans shouldn't expect any of the three 80s videos to be re-issued in their original states. It's far more likely that Numan will either add selected promotional videos and archive live clips to future DVD packages as bonus material or make the original videos available to buy for a limited period only via the *NuWorld* web site. Similarly, both the 1982 'I, Assassin Tour' and the 1980 'Teletour' were both video-taped, however, although Gary's 5th of November 1982 show at The Stanley Theatre in Pittsburgh still exists, far less is known about either the whereabouts or the actual length of the recording undertaken on the 1980 show that 'This Wreckage', Remind Me To Smile' and 'Down In The Park' were taken from (see *Telekon* album). Similarly, video recordings from 'The Toronto Music Hall' in Canada (snippets aired were: 'Praying To The Aliens', 'Conversation' and 'Me! I Disconnect from You' along with rehearsal footage) as well as a March 1980 show in Paris (tracks aired were: 'Replicas', 'I Die: You Die' and 'Down In The Park' – both of these television shorts were taken from 'The Touring Principle') are known to exist, however, the whereabouts of the actual tapes themselves are currently unknown. Recording details as regards 'The Warriors Tour' are also not known, although at least one full show was known to have been professionally filmed. 'The Warriors Tour' was also professionally filmed by Central Television who broadcast both live and sound check clips on British television around the time of the actual tour. Sadly, neither the Central television nor the professionally filmed footage of 'The Warriors Tour' has ever materialised.

Finally, a long running rumour in fan circles has been a desire on the part of Beggars Banquet to issue all the Tubeway Army/ Gary Numan singles released by the label as CD singles featuring all the original artwork, B-sides and the various mixes housed within box sets. This release would be split into two separate sets and sold via the label's online shop (a similar idea was done for 80s Goth rockers The Cult as well as American Grunge rockers Nirvana). Whether this story has any truth to it is unknown but fan feedback on a Gary Numan singles box set has been overwhelmingly positive.

EAGLE/ NUMA RECORDS

With Eagle now handling both their own Numan archives and overseeing Gary's Numa recordings, more re-issues and releases in general are certain to surface.

EXTENDED RECORDINGS

Currently all Numan's extended albums and singles – both Eagle and Numa releases-are out of print (although some are still available online), its unlikely that the label would see any commercial value in re-issuing these recordings (although fans have pointed out that recently, 80s pop heroes Duran Duran were the subject of a rather successful limited edition, 2CD remix/extended compilation album entitled *Strange Behaviour* that included the group's many extended and remixed releases from across the years).

INSTRUMENTAL ALBUMS

Both *The Radial Pair* (released in 1994) and *Human* (released in 1995) are currently out of print (although copies can still be obtained mail order via the net). There are no plans from Eagle at present to re-issue either of them.

VIDEOS:

The 2002 and 2003 DVD issue of both *The Berserker Tour* and *The Skin Mechanic-Live* videos proved that not all Numan's video footage was safely back under his ownership. The full concert footage for *The Berserker Tour* – along with the *Dream Corrosion* and *Shadowman* videos – are likely to emerge as an in-house, official, Gary Numan DVD at some point in the future, though with Gary's career becoming increasingly busy, fans shouldn't expect either to appear any time soon. Interestingly, both the 'Exhibition' and 'Premier Hits Tour' were video-taped ('The Exhibition Tour' saw three pro-shot clips – 'Call Out The Dogs', 'I Die: You Die' and 'Creatures' – emerge. In the case of the 'Premier Hits Tour', both a live video and CD were to be issued some point in 1998 following the release of *Exile*) however, neither materialised in the end and the footage appears to have been shelved. Whether either of these recordings will ever see the light of day seems highly unlikely at present. In addition, talk of official promotional videos being filmed for the debut US release of the *Sacrifice* album appear to have, in the end, come to nothing with this idea being abandoned in favour of concentrating on the build up to the release of the *Exile* album.

Live video recordings from Gary's time spent under the Eagle imprint are known to exist (both 'Cars' and 'Pure', recorded at the Brixton Academy in October 2000 were added to the US version of *Scarred*) though there are currently no plans to issue any long form live videos or DVDs.

NUMA RARITIES

A number of *Berserker*-era rarities are still outstanding, including: 'My Dying Machine' (demo, originally added to the promo version of the 1986 album *Numa Records Year One*), the Italian remixes of 'My Dying Machine' (originally added to the album *Numa Records Year One*), 'The Picture' (unreleased demo), 'This Is New Love' (*Leo Sayer Show* version as well as the later edited album version) and finally 'On Broadway' (Leo Sayer duet*). Fans doubt that any of these recordings still exist, especially with the 1999 *New Dreams For Old* compilation featuring, amongst its tracks, the 1986 Sharpe and Numan single 'New Thing From London Town' appearing re-mastered from an un-played 7-inch vinyl copy. Rumours of recordings undertaken with Charles Pierre and Francis Usmar of Native Soul have also emerged in recent years with three tracks ('Are "Friends" Electric?', 'Vicious', reputedly the original work-in-progress title for Gary's 1994 studio album and 'Metal Beat') being the only known songs completed. To date none of these recordings has surfaced although 'Metal Beat' was eventually re-recorded during the sessions for the *Sacrifice* album. Finally, rumours of a Gravity kills remix of the album *Exile* appears to have been sadly groundless, the proposed project, according to Gary himself, never materialised. However, hardcore fans have yet to be convinced otherwise. Similarly, Gary's talk of recording a series of purely instrumental albums as well as an 'unplugged' album in late 1996 have so far come to nothing.

* Rumours of further recordings undertaken with Leo Sayer in 1984 have emerged in recent years, however, so far, no recorded material has ever surfaced.

Another Numa era project that never materialised was the long talked about 'Ballads album.' This project only yielded one confirmed track, a remake of the classic *Telekon* era 'Please Push No More.' Sadly, nothing has been heard from this proposed album for a number of years with fans speculating the idea had been ultimately abandoned in favour of recording new music instead.

The much talked about collaboration between Yen and Numan on the *Replicas* classic 'Down In The Park' has also failed to materialise as has a Kipper and Mike Allan take of 'Are "Friends" Electric?

Finally, the single edit of 'This Is Love' is currently the last remaining Numa era single not transferred to Compact Disc; this mix was oddly missed off the 1999 Eagle compilation CD *New Dreams For Old.* It is currently unclear whether there are any plans to include this missing edit on any future Numa era compilations.

POLYDOR RECORDS

There are currently no plans to re-issue any of the Sharpe and Numan recordings with the duo's one album – 1989's *Automatic* – long out of print. A future CD re-issue of this record is likely to include: the 12-inch version of 'Change Your Mind', the Razormaid remix of 'Change Your Mind', B-side 'Love Like A Ghost', the extended 1988/ 89 version of 'Voices', the original 7-inch and 12-inch mixes of 'No More Lies' and the original 12-inch mix of 'I'm On Automatic.' Rumours of a further six Sharpe and Numan recordings made by the duo in 1990 have long circulated in fan circles, however, these songs – recorded it seems for inclusion on a proposed second Sharpe And Numan album – never made it past the demo stage and have long since been shelved by Polydor, as has a 1992, Bill Sharpe remix of 'Change Your Mind.' Time will tell whether these, if any, will ever see the light of day.

BBC

Gary's live radio sessions for John Peel in 2000/ 2001 have been consigned to the station's archives; there are currently no plans to release them.

IRS / EMI

EMI recently completed their three-album re-issue campaign; however, there are still a number of recordings still outstanding.

DEMO MATERIAL

Aside from the originally issued version of Gary's 1991 album *Outland*, two other versions of this recording have long been in circulation in fandom featuring radically different takes of some of the songs that were included on the disc. Oddly, one song that was prepared at the demo stage entitled 'Comsat' failed to materialise. In addition, three demos from *Metal Rhythm* have also surfaced, those being: 'Young Heart', 'Devious' and 'This Is Emotion.' There are currently no plans to issue any alternative takes of songs or any demos from Gary's time under IRS.

LIVE RECORDINGS

The one live album released and re-issued by IRS / EMI (*The Skin Mechanic-Live*) has so far failed to unearth the full 1988 concert recording; there are currently no plans to re-issue this album at present. It's unclear whether any live audio recordings from either the 'Skin Mechanic Tour' or the 1991 'Outland Tour' exist, a release from either on CD (should there be any recordings) would seem extremely unlikely at present.

VIDEO

It's unclear if, like the 'Skin Mechanic Tour', either the 'Metal Rhythm Tour' or the 'Outland Tour' were ever video-taped, a release from either though would seem highly unlikely at present. The 2003 DVD issue of *The Skin Mechanic-Live video*, despite initially advertising the full concert, has to date, failed to materialise. Where the full show is and whether it still exists or not is unknown at present.

In addition, the 1991 'Rockers Uptown' remix of 'Are "Friends" Electric' (originally added to the US 12-inch promo of 'My World Storm') was oddly not included on the 1999 re-issued and re-mastered CD sets. Another curio outstanding was the Andy Piercy remix of 'New Anger', this song was understood to be one of three Piercy remixes that were originally commissioned for the *Metal Rhythm* album, the other two being the thumping, US styled dance mixes that were done for both 'America' and 'Devious.' Although listed on the *New Anger* album in the US and the Far East as remixed the track was in fact nothing more than the regular UK version. Whether this or any of the above will ever surface again is unknown.

OUTRO

THE LAST WORD

'Now it's all over for sure, I'll walk back home.'
(Lyric taken from the 1980 album track 'Please Push No More')

I have really enjoyed writing this manuscript, in doing so it brought me much closer to the music that has had so much bearing on my life. Many times its put me right back to the moment of purchase, remembering that feeling of anticipation as I hurried home with Numan's latest release under my arm. That feeling has never left me, I hope it is still the same for you.

I'm also extremely pleased that this manuscript will see the light of day in the midst of a full Gary Numan resurrection, indeed, since the 1996 smash hit re-issue of 'Cars', Numan has not only successfully rebuilt his once ailing music career but now seems genuinely poised to storm the charts all over again following years of mainstream and critical indifference.

For me though, my self imposed, self-obsessed Gary Numan mission is at an end. I'd like to take this opportunity to thank all the people who helped with this project (one that threatened my sanity on more than one occasion). Gary Numan for kindly taking the time to provide a foreword for this project, Tony Webb for all the advice and encouragement, Sean Body at Helter Skelter Publishing for all his help, my very good friend Nigel Lunn whose kind words, advice and deadly accurate information helped shape the book you now hold in your hands and Harv G, Gary Cee, Frank M (Survival Records), Steve Roper, Wiggy and Madam Stan for sending me stuff that cleared up one of two holes I had in the text. I'd also like to thank my father Geoff for all the things that I am, Chris (Boop) Best for being the nicest bloke in the world, the entire Doyle family (especially Tony and Rosie) for their support and Vicky Robinson for believing in me.

However, more than anything, I'd like to thank my partner Kathy, who trusted my instincts when I first broached her with this idea, supported me when I needed it and probably sighed with relief when I finally completed the last page and switched the computer off.

With *Electric Pioneer* now complete and new book projects fermenting in my mind, I can finally return my vast Numan collection to the confines of my private music vault, freeing (much to my family's relief) all the household televisions and stereos of soaring synth riffs, distorted guitars and black clad gothic rockers.

Now where on earth did I put those "Nine Inch Nails" and "Marilyn Manson" records...?

ABOUT THE AUTHOR.

Paul has been a lifelong fan and an avid collector of Gary Numan music and memorabilia, much of which has been included here in ELECTRIC PIONEER AN ARMCHAIR GUIDE TO GARY NUMAN.

He devotes his spare time to both developing new book ideas and being a family man. His other hobbies include movies, gardening and reading.

Paul lives in North Yorkshire, England with his partner Kathy, their children James and Sarah and two cats Toby and Oliver.

Other Titles available from Helter Skelter

Coming Soon
2005

Rush: The Definitive Biography DUE: AUTUMN 2005
by Jon Collins

Acclaimed Marillion biographer Collins draws on hundreds of hours of new interviews to tell the full in-depth story of the enduring Canadian trio who are one of the most successful cult groups in the world. From early days in Canada to platinum albums, stadium shows and the world's stage, taking in tragedy, triumphs and a wealth of great music, this is the definitive study of one of rock's great enigmas.

Paperback   ISBN 1-900924-85-4   234 X 156mm   16pp b/w photos
UK £14.99   US $19.95

Belle and Sebastian: Just A Modern Rock Story
DUE: SEPTEMBER 2005
by Paul Whitelaw

Formed in 1996, this enigmatic Glasgow band have risen to become one of Britain's most respected bands.

For years, Belle and Sebastian were shrouded in mystery – the 23-piece ensemble led by singer-songwriter Stuart Murdoch refused interviews and the band scarcely ever toured. Their early singles though built them a strong and committed cult following. Their debut mail-order only album *Tigermilk* sold out within a month of its release. The follow-up, *If You're Feeling Sinister*, with its Nick Drake-influenced melodies and dark, quirky lyrics, found favour in alternative circles as far a field as San Francisco, Japan, South America, and especially France where a 1996 poll by influential magazine Les Inrockuptiles placed them above Oasis. The 1998 album, *The Boy With the Arab Strap* entered the UK LP charts at 12. Their latest Trevor Horn-produced album *Dear Catastrophe Waitress* is their highest profile release to date.

This is not only the first biography ever written on the band, but the most official that might ever hit the market. The band have agreed to participate in the project and to give the author extended interviews, paraphernalia and both personal and publicity still photos. Stuart Murdoch himself has agreed to design artwork for the cover.

Paul Whitelaw is an arts writer from Glasgow who has met and interviewed Belle and Sebastian on several occasions and he was the first journalist to champion the band in print.

Paperback ISBN 1-900924-98-6   234 X 156mm   16pp b/w photos
UK £14.99

David Bowie: The Shirts He Wears DUE: SUMMER 2005
by Jonathan Richards

A Bowie book with a difference, this is a study of Bowie as a cultural icon that draws together his music, artworks and fashion to paint a fascinating portrait of one of rock's most important figures.

Paperback   ISBN 1-900924-25-0   234 X 156mm   16pp b/w photos
UK £14.99   US $19.95

John Martyn DUE: SUMMER 2005
by Chris Nickson

First ever biography of the pioneering guitarist best-known for his still-revered 70s album

Solid Air. Draws on interviews with many friends and associates.
Paperback   ISBN 1-900924-86-2   234 X 156mm   16pp b/w photos
UK £14.99   US $19.95

Kicking Against The Pricks: An Armchair Guide to Nick Cave
DUE: SUMMER 2005
by Amy Hanson

Nick Cave is the only artist to emerge from the post–punk era whose music and career can truly be compared with legends such as Bob Dylan or Van Morrison, with a string of acclaimed albums including *Junkyard* (Birthday Party), *Tender Prey* and *The Boatman's Call*.

Cave left Australia to become part of a maelstrom unleashed to awestruck London audiences in the late seventies: the Birthday Party. Miraculously, Cave survived that band's excesses and formed the Bad Seeds, challenging his audience and the Godfather-of-Goth tag: as a bluesman with a gun in one hand, a Bible in the other; a vamp-ish torch singer with echoes of Vegas-era Elvis and a sensitive writer of love songs.

Kicking Against The Pricks chronicles in depth these diverse personalities and the musical landscapes that Cave has inhabited, with a penetrating commentary on all his themes and influences. Cave's memorable collaborations and forays into other media are covered too: duets with Kylie Minogue, PJ Harvey and Shane MacGowan, the acclaimed novel *And The Ass Saw The Angel*, film appearances such as Wim Wenders' *Wings of Desire*, and his stint as Meltdown 2000 curator. Ultimately, it reveals Cave as the compelling and always-relevant musical force he is.
Paperback   ISBN 1-900924-96-X   234 X 156mm   16pp b/w photos
UK £14.99   US $19.95

Save What You Can: The Day of The Triffids and the Long Night of David McComb DUE: SPRING 2005
by Bleddyn Butcher

Finely crafted biography of cult Australian group and their ill-fated front man who was simply the greatest lyricist of his generation.

Charismatic front man McComb's finely crafted tales of misfits and troubled outsiders and lost souls, merged Dylan with Carver and a Perth sensibility to brilliant effect, while his sprawling melodies set against 'Evil' Graham Lee's slide guitar created an achingly beautiful sound best exemplified by critics' favourites, Born Sandy Devotional and Calenture. In spite of rave critical plaudits, the Triffids' sales were mediocre and in 1990 the band split and returned to Australia. McComb put out one excellent solo album in 1994 before the sense of ominous foreboding that lurked throughout his music was proved prescient when he collapsed and was rushed to hospital to undergo a full heart transplant. Months later he was back in hospital with even more agonising intestinal surgery. McComb made a partial recovery, but the medication he was taking kept him in a permanent state of drowsiness. On Saturday, January 30th, 1999, he fell asleep at the wheel of his car. Though McComb survived the crash and discharged himself from hospital, he died suddenly three days later.
Paperback   ISBN 1-900924-21-8   234 X 156mm   16pp b/w photos
UK £14.99   US $19.95

Action Time Vision: The Story of Sniffin' Glue, Alternative TV and Punk Rock DUE: SPRING 2005
by Mark Perry

The legendary founder-editor of *Sniffin' Glue* – the definitive punk fanzine – gives his own account of the punk years. An eyewitness account of the key gigs; an insider's history

of the bands and personalities; the full story of the hugely influential fanzine and the ups and downs of Perry's own recording career with Alternative TV.
Paperback   ISBN 1-900924-89-7   234 X 156mm   16pp b/w photos
UK £14.99   US $21.95

The Who By Numbers DUE: SPRING 2005
by Alan Parker and Steve Grantley
Detailed album-by-album, song-by-song commentary on the songs of one of rock's most important and enduring acts, by Sid Vicious biographer and Lennon expert Parker, teamed with Stiff Little Fingers' drummer, Grantley.
Paperback   ISBN 1-900924-91-9   234 X 156mm   16pp b/w photos
UK £14.99   US $19.95

John Lydon's Metal Box: The Story of Public Image Ltd
DUE: SPRING 2005
by Phil Strongman
In between fronting rock's most iconoclastic group, the Sex Pistols, and re-emerging in the 21st century as a reality TV hero on *I'm A Celebrity*, Lydon led the post-punk pioneers Public Image Ltd who tore up the rulebook and merged disco funk and industrial punk to create coruscating soundscapes with catchy tunes – from *Death Disco* and *Flowers of Romance* to *Rise* and *This Is Not A Love Song* – and caused riots at their gigs. An essential chapter in the growth of post-punk music and one that reveals Lydon as always forward-thinking and always compelling.
Paperback   ISBN 1-900924-66-8   234 X 156mm   16pp b/w photos
UK £14.99   US $19.95

Music in Dreamland: The Story of Be Bop Deluxe and Bill Nelson DUE: SPRING 2005
by Paul Sutton-Reeves
Draws on hours of new interviews with Bill Nelson and other members of the band, as well as admirers such as David Sylvian, Stone Roses' producer John Leckie, Steve Harley and Reeves Gabrel. Cover artwork especially designed by Bill Nelson himself.
Paperback   ISBN 1-900924-08-8   234 X 156mm   16pp b/w photos
UK £14.99   US $19.95

True Faith: An Armchair Guide to New Order DUE: SPRING 2005
by Dave Thompson
Formed from the ashes of Joy Division after their ill fated singer Ian Curtis hung himself, few could have predicted that New Order would become one of the seminal groups of the 80s, making a series of albums that would compare well with anything Joy Division had produced, and embracing club culture a good ten years before most of their contemporaries.

From the bestselling 12 inch single 'Blue Monday' to later hits like 'Bizarre Love Triangle' [featured in the movie *Trainspotting*] and their spectacular world cup song 'World In Motion' the band have continued making innovative, critically revered records that have also enjoyed massive commercial success.

This book is the first to treat New Order's musical career as a separate achievement, rather than a postscript to Joy Division's and the first to analyse in depth what makes their music so great.
Paperback   ISBN 1-900924-94-3 8   234mm X 156mm 256pp 8pp b/w photos
UK £12.99   US $19.95

AUTUMN 2004

Wheels Out of Gear: Two Tone, The Specials and a World on Fire
by Dave Thompson
When the punks embraced reggae it led to a late 1970s Ska revival that began in Coventry
with Jerry Dammers' Two Tone record label and his band, The Specials. Original 60s rude
boy fashions – mohair suits, dark glasses and the ubiquitous pork pie hats – along with
Dammer's black & white themed logo were the emblems for a hugely popular scene that
also comprised hit-making groups such as Madness, The Beat and The Selecter.
Paperback   ISBN 1-900924-84-6   234 X 156mm   256pp, 16pp b/w photos
UK £12.99   US $19.95

Al Stewart: Lights, Camera, Action – A Life in Pictures
by Neville Judd
Best known for his 70s classic 'The Year of The Cat', Al Stewart continues to record and
tour and retains a large and loyal international fan base. This is a unique collection of
rare and unpublished photographs, documenting Al's public and private life from early
days in 1950s Scotland, through to his success in Hollywood and beyond.
Luxury Paperback   ISBN 1-900924-90-0   310 X 227mm   192pp
All pages photos, 16pp of colour
UK £25.00   US $35.00

'77 – The Year of Punk and New Wave
by Henry Bech Poulsen
As 1967 was to the Haight-Ashbury scene, so 1977 was to punk: a year in which classic
singles and albums by all the key bands made it the only musical movement that
counted, and before its energy and potential was diluted and dampened by the forces
of conservatism and commercialism. '77 tells the story of what every punk and new
wave band achieved in that heady year – from The Pistols, Clash and Damned to The
Lurkers, The Adverts and The Rezillos, and everyone in between.
Paperback   ISBN 1-900924-92-7   512pp 245 X 174mm Illustrated throughout
UK £16.99   US $25.00

Linda Ronstadt: A Musical Life
by Peter Lewry
Ronstadt's early backing band became The Eagles and she has had success with songs
by Neil Young, Jackson Browne and Hank Williams. After a US number 1 single and
Grammy winning country rock albums in the 1970s, she has continued to challenge
preconceptions with albums of Nelson Riddle-produced standards, a record of mariachi
songs and a collaboration with Dolly Parton and Emmylou Harris. This is her first ever
biography.
Paperback   ISBN 1-900924-50-1   256pp 234 X 156mm 16pp b/w photos
UK £16.99   US $25.00

Sex Pistols: Only Anarchists are Pretty
by Mick O'Shea
Drawing both on years of research and on creative conjecture, this book, written as a
novel, portrays the early years of the Sex Pistols. Giving a fictionalised fly-on-the-wall
account of the arguments, in-jokes, gigs, pub sessions and creative tension, it documents
the day-to-day life of the ultimate punk band before the Bill Grundy incident and Malcolm
McLaren-orchestrated tabloid outrage turned their lives into a media circus.
Paperback   ISBN 1-900924-93-5   234mm X 156mm 256pp 8pp b/w photos
UK £12.99   US $19.95

Bob Dylan: Like The Night (Revisited)
by CP Lee

Fully revised and updated edition of the hugely acclaimed document of Dylan's pivotal 1966 show at the Manchester Free Trade Hall where fans called him Judas for turning his back on folk music in favour of rock 'n' roll. The album of the concert was released in the same year as the book's first outing and has since become a definitive source.

'A terrific tome that gets up close to its subject and breathes new life into it… For any fan of Dylan this is quite simply essential.' *Time Out*

'Putting it all vividly in the context of the time, he writes expertly about that one electrifying, widely-bootlegged night.' *Mojo*

'CP Lee's book flushed 'Judas' out into the open.' *The Independent*

'An atmospheric and enjoyable account.' *Uncut* (Top 10 of the year)

Paperback   ISBN 1-900924-33-1   198mm X 129mm 224pp 16pp b/w photos
UK £9.99   US $17.95

Everybody Dance
Chic and the Politics of Disco
by Daryl Easlea

Everybody Dance puts the rise and fall of Bernard Edwards and Nile Rodgers, the emblematic disco duo behind era-defining records 'Le Freak', 'Good Times' and 'Lost In Music', at the heart of a changing landscape, taking in socio-political and cultural events such as the Civil Rights struggle, the Black Panthers and the US oil crisis. There are drugs, bankruptcy, up-tight artists, fights, and Muppets but, most importantly an in-depth appraisal of a group whose legacy remains hugely underrated.

Paperback   ISBN 1-900924-56-0   234mm X 156mm 256pp 8pp b/w photos
UK £14.00   US $19.95

Currently Available from Helter Skelter Publishing

This Is a Modern Life
Compiled by Enamel Verguren

Lavishly illustrated guide to the mod revival that was sparked by the 1979 release of *Quadrophenia*. *This Is a Modern Life* concentrates on the 1980s, but takes in 20 years of a mod life in London and throughout the world, from 1979 to 1999, with interviews of people directly involved, loads of flyers and posters and a considerable amount of great photos.

'Good stuff … A nice nostalgic book full of flyers, pics and colourful stories.' *Loaded*

Paperback   ISBN 1-900924-77-3   264mm X 180mm 224pp   photos throughout
UK £14.99   US $19.95

Smashing Pumpkins: Tales of A Scorched Earth
by Amy Hanson

Initially contemporaries of Nirvana, Billy Corgan's Smashing Pumpkins outgrew and outlived the grunge scene with hugely acclaimed commercial triumphs like *Siamese Dream* and *Mellon Collie and The Infinite Sadness*. Though drugs and other problems led to the band's final demise, Corgan's recent return with Zwan is a reminder of how awesome the Pumpkins were in their prime. Seattle-based Hanson has followed the band for years and this is the first in-depth biography of their rise and fall.

'Extremely well-written … A thrilling and captivating read.' *Classic Rock*

'Sex, bust-ups, heavy metal, heroin death and a quadruple-platinum dream-pop double album… The first ever 'serious' Pumpkins biography.' *NME*

'A fascinating story … Hanson has done her research.' *Q*

Paperback   ISBN 1-900924-68-4   234mm X 156mm 256pp 8pp b/w photos
UK £12.99   US $18.95

Be Glad: An Incredible String Band Compendium
Edited by Adrian Whittaker
The ISB pioneered 'world music' on '60s albums like *The Hangman's Beautiful Daughter* – Paul McCartney's favourite album of 1967! – experimented with theatre, film and lifestyle and inspired Led Zeppelin. *Be Glad* features interviews with all the ISB key players, as well as a wealth of background information, reminiscence, critical evaluations and arcane trivia, this is a book that will delight any reader with more than a passing interest in the ISB.
Paperback   ISBN 1-900924-64-1   234mm x 156mm 288pp, b/w photos throughout
UK £14.99   US $22.95

ISIS: A Bob Dylan Anthology
Edited by Derek Barker
ISIS is the best-selling, longest lasting, most highly acclaimed Dylan fanzine. This ultimate Dylan anthology draws on unpublished interviews and research by the *ISIS* team together with the best articles culled from the pages of the definitive Bob magazine. From Bob's earliest days in New York City to the more recent legs of the Never Ending Tour, the *ISIS* archive has exclusive interview material – often rare or previously unpublished – with many of the key players in Dylan's career: friends, musicians and other collaborators, such as playwright Jacques Levy and folk hero Martin Carthy.

Fully revised and expanded edition features additional previously unpublished articles and further rare photos;

'Astounding ... Fascinating... If you're more than mildly interested in Bob Dylan then this is an essential purchase.' *Record Collector*
'This book is worth any Dylan specialist's money.' Ian MacDonald – **** *Uncut*
Paperback   ISBN 1-900924-82-X   198mm X 129mm 352pp, 16pp b/w photos
UK £9.99   US $17.95

Waiting for the Man: The Story of Drugs and Popular Music
By Harry Shapiro
From marijuana and jazz, through acid-rock and speed-fuelled punk, to crack-driven rap and ecstasy and the dance generation, this is the definitive history of drugs and pop. It also features in-depth portraits of music's most famous drug addicts: from Charlie Parker to Sid Vicious and from Jim Morrison to Kurt Cobain.

Chosen by the BBC as one of the Top Twenty Music Books of All Time.
'Wise and witty.' *The Guardian*
Paperback   ISBN 1-900924-58-7   198mm X 129mm 320pp
UK £10.99   US $17.95

Jefferson Airplane: Got a Revolution
by Jeff Tamarkin
With smash hits 'Somebody to Love' and 'White Rabbit' and albums like *Surrealistic Pillow*, Jefferson Airplane, the most successful and influential rock band to emerge from San Francisco during the 60s, created the sound of a generation. To the public they were free-loving, good-time hippies, but to their inner circle, Airplane were a paradoxical bunch – constantly at odds with each other. Jefferson Airplane members were each brilliant, individualistic artists who became the living embodiment of the ups and downs of the sex, drugs and rock 'n' roll lifestyle.

Tamarkin has interviewed the former band members, friends, lovers, crew members and fellow musicians to come up with the definitive full-length history of the group.

"A compelling account of a remarkable band." *Record Collector*
"A superb chunk of writing that documents every twist and turn in the ever-evolving life of a great American band." *Record Collector*

Paperback   ISBN 1-900924-78-1   234mm X 156mm 408pp , 16pp b/w photos
UK £14.99   US No rights

Surf's Up: The Beach Boys on Record 1961-1981
by Brad Elliott
The ultimate reference work on the recording sessions of one of the most influential and collectable groups.

'factually unimpeachable ... an exhausting, exhilarating 500 pages of discographical and session information about everything anybody connected with the group ever put down or attempted to put down on vinyl.' *Goldmine*

Paperback   ISBN 1-900924-79-X   234mm X 156mm 512pp, 16pp b/w photos
UK £25.00   US No rights

Get Back: The Beatles' Let It Be Disaster
by Doug Suply and Ray Shweighardt
Reissued to coincide with the release of *Let It Be ... Naked*, this is a singularly candid look at the greatest band in history at their ultimate moment of crisis. It puts the reader in the studio as John cedes power to Yoko; Paul struggles to keep things afloat, Ringo shrugs and George quits the band.

'One of the most poignant Beatles' books ever.' *Mojo*

Paperback   ISBN 1-900924-83-8   198mm X 129mm 352pp
UK £9.99   No US rights

The Clash: Return of the Last Gang in Town
by Marcus Gray
Exhaustively researched definitive biography of the last great rock band that traces their progress from pubs and punk clubs to US stadiums and the Top Ten. This edition is further updated to cover the band's induction into the Rock 'n' Roll Hall of Fame and the tragic death of iconic front man Joe Strummer.

'A must-have for Clash fans [and] a valuable document for anyone interested in the punk era.' *Billboard*

'It's important you read this book.' *Record Collector*

Paperback   ISBN 1-900924-62-5   234mm X 156mm 512pp, 8pp b/w photos
UK £14.99   US No rights

Steve Marriott: All Too Beautiful
by Paolo Hewitt and John Hellier
Marriott was the prime mover behind 60s chart-toppers The Small Faces. Longing to be treated as a serious musician he formed Humble Pie with Peter Frampton, where his blistering rock 'n' blues guitar playing soon saw him take centre stage in the US live favourites. After years in seclusion, Marriott's plans for a comeback in 1991 were tragically cut short when he died in a house fire. He continues to be a key influence for generations of musicians from Paul Weller to Oasis and Blur.

'One of the best books I've read about the backwaters of rock music.' *Daily Mail*

'A riveting account of the singer's life, crammed with entertaining stories of rebellion and debauchery and insightful historical background... Compulsive reading.' *The Express*

'Revealing... sympathetic, long overdue.' ****Uncut*

'We won't see the like of him again and *All Too Beautiful* captures him perfectly. A right riveting read as they say.' Gary Crowley, BBC London.

'Hewitt's portrayal makes compelling reading.'**** *Mojo*

Hardback   ISBN 1-900924-44-7   234mm X 156mm 352pp 32pp b/w photos
UK £20   US $29.95

Love: Behind The Scenes
By Michael Stuart-Ware

LOVE were one of the legendary bands of the late 60s US West Coast scene. Their masterpiece *Forever Changes* still regularly appears in critics' polls of top albums, while a new-line up of the band has recently toured to mass acclaim. Michael Stuart-Ware was LOVE's drummer during their heyday and shares his inside perspective on the band's recording and performing career and tells how drugs and egos thwarted the potential of one of the great groups of the burgeoning psychedelic era.

Paperback   ISBN 1-900924-59-5   234mm X 156mm 256pp
UK £14.00   US $19.95

A Secret Liverpool: In Search of the La's
By MW Macefield

With timeless single 'There She Goes', Lee Mavers' La's overtook The Stone Roses and paved the way for Britpop. However, since 1991, The La's have been silent, while rumours of studio-perfectionism, madness and drug addiction have abounded. The author sets out to discover the truth behind Mavers' lost decade and eventually gains a revelatory audience with Mavers himself.

Paperback   ISBN 1-900924-63-3   234mm X 156mm 192pp
UK £11.00   US $17.95

The Fall: A User's Guide
by Dave Thompson

A melodic, cacophonic and magnificent, The Fall remain the most enduring and prolific of the late-70s punk and post-punk iconoclasts. *A User's Guide* chronicles the historical and musical background to more than 70 different LPs (plus reissues) and as many singles. The band's history is also documented year-by-year, filling in the gaps between the record releases.

Paperback   ISBN 1-900924-57-9   234mm X 156mm 256pp, 8pp b/w photos
UK £12.99   US $19.95

Pink Floyd: A Saucerful of Secrets
by Nicholas Schaffner

Long overdue reissue of the authoritative and detailed account of one of the most important and popular bands in rock history. From the psychedelic explorations of the Syd Barrett-era to 70s superstardom with *Dark Side of the Moon*, and on to triumph of *The Wall*, before internecine strife tore the group apart. Schaffner's definitive history also covers the improbable return of Pink Floyd without Roger Waters, and the hugely successful *Momentary Lapse of Reason* album and tour.

Paperback   ISBN 1-900924-52-8   234mm X 156mm 256pp, 8pp b/w photos
UK £14.99   No rights

The Big Wheel
by Bruce Thomas

Thomas was bassist with Elvis Costello at the height of his success. Though names are never named, *The Big Wheel* paints a vivid and hilarious picture of life touring with Costello and co, sharing your life 24-7 with a moody egotistical singer, a crazed drummer and a host of hangers-on. Costello sacked Thomas on its initial publication.

'A top notch anecdotalist who can time a twist to make you laugh out loud.' *Q*

Paperback   ISBN 1-900924-53-6   234mm X 156mm 192pp
UK £10.99 $17.95

Hit Men: Powerbrokers and Fast Money Inside The Music Business
by Fredric Dannen £14.99

Hit Men exposes the seamy and sleazy dealings of America's glitziest record companies: payola, corruption, drugs, Mafia involvement, and excess.

'This is quite possibly the best book ever written about the business side of the music industry.' *Music Week*

'This is simply the greatest book about the business end of the music industry.' *Q******

'So heavily awash with cocaine, corruption and unethical behaviour that it makes the occasional examples of chart-rigging and play list tampering in Britain during the same period seem charmingly inept.' *The Guardian.*

Paperback   ISBN 1-900924-54-4   234mm X 156mm 512pp, 8pp b/w photos
UK £14.99   No rights

I'm With The Band: Confessions of A Groupie
by Pamela Des Barres

Frank and engaging memoir of affairs with Keith Moon, Noel Redding and Jim Morrison, travels with Led Zeppelin as Jimmy Page's girlfriend, and friendships with Robert Plant, Gram Parsons, and Frank Zappa.

'Long overdue reprint of a classic 60s memoir – one of the few music books to talk openly about sex.' *Mojo*

'One of the most likeable and sparky first hand accounts.' *Q*****

'Miss Pamela, the most beautiful and famous of the groupies. Her memoir of her life with rock stars is funny, bittersweet, and tender-hearted.' Stephen Davis, author of *Hammer of the Gods*

Paperback   ISBN 1-900924-55-2   234mm X 156mm 256pp, 16pp b/w photos
UK £14.99 $19.95

Psychedelic Furs: Beautiful Chaos
by Dave Thompson

Psychedelic Furs were the ultimate post-punk band – combining the chaos and vocal rasp of the Sex Pistols with a Bowie-esque glamour. The Furs hit the big time when John Hughes wrote a movie based on their early single 'Pretty in Pink'. Poised to join U2 and Simple Minds in the premier league, they withdrew behind their shades, remaining a cult act, but one with a hugely devoted following.

Paperback   ISBN 1-900924-47-1   234mm X 156mm 256pp, 16pp b/w photos
UK £14.99 $19.95

Marillion: Separated Out
by Jon Collins

From the chart hit days of Fish and 'Kayleigh' to the Steve Hogarth incarnation, Marillion have continued to make groundbreaking rock music. Collins tells the full story, drawing on interviews with band members, associates, and the experiences of some of the band's most dedicated fans.

Paperback   ISBN 1-900924-49-8   234mm x 156mm 288pp, illustrated throughout
UK £14.99 $19.95

Rainbow Rising
by Roy Davies

The full story of guitar legend Ritchie Blackmore's post-Purple progress with one of the great 70s rock bands. After quitting Deep Purple at the height of their success, Blackmore combined with Ronnie James Dio to make epic rock albums like *Rising* and *Long Live Rock 'n' Roll* before streamlining the sound and enjoying hit singles like 'Since

You've Been Gone' and 'All Night Long'. Rainbow were less celebrated than Deep Purple, but they feature much of Blackmore's finest writing and playing, and were one of the best live acts of the era. They are much missed.

Paperback   ISBN 1-900924-31-5   234mm X 156mm 256pp, illustrated throughout
UK £14.99 $19.95

Back to the Beach: A Brian Wilson and the Beach Boys Reader
REVISED EDITION
Edited by Kingsley Abbott

Revised and expanded edition of the Beach Boys compendium *Mojo* magazine deemed an "essential purchase." This collection includes all of the best articles, interviews and reviews from the Beach Boys' four decades of music, including definitive pieces by Timothy White, Nick Kent and David Leaf. New material reflects on the tragic death of Carl Wilson and documents the rejuvenated Brian's return to the boards. 'Rivetting!' **** *Q*

   'An essential purchase.' *Mojo*

Paperback   ISBN 1-900924-46-3   234mm X 156mm 288pp
UK £14.99 $19.95

Harmony in My Head
The Original Buzzcock Steve Diggle's Rock 'n' Roll Odyssey
by Steve Diggle and Terry Rawlings

First-hand account of the punk wars from guitarist and one half of the songwriting duo that gave the world three chord punk-pop classics like 'Ever Fallen In Love' and 'Promises'. Diggle dishes the dirt on punk contemporaries like The Sex Pistols, The Clash and The Jam, as well as sharing poignant memories of his friendship with Kurt Cobain, on whose last ever tour, The Buzzcocks were support act.

   'Written with spark and verve, this rattling account of Diggle's time in the Buzzcocks will appeal to those with an interest in punk or just late-1970s Manchester.' *Music Week*

   'This warts 'n' all monologue is a hoot...Diggle's account of the rise, fall and birth of the greatest Manchester band of the past 50 years is relayed with passion and candour...but it works best as a straightforward sex, drugs and rock 'n' roll memoir.' – *Uncut* ****

Paperback   ISBN 1-900924-37-4   234mm X 156mm 224pp, 8pp b/w photos
UK £14.99 $19.95

Serge Gainsbourg: A Fistful of Gitanes
by Sylvie Simmons

Rock press legend Simmons' hugely acclaimed biography of the French genius.

   'I would recommend *A Fistful of Gitanes* [as summer reading] which is a highly entertaining biography of the French singer-songwriter and all-round scallywag' – JG Ballard

   'A wonderful introduction to one of the most overlooked songwriters of the 20th century' (Number 3, Top music books of 2001) *The Times*

   'The most intriguing music-biz biography of the year' *The Independent*

   'Wonderful. Serge would have been so happy' – Jane Birkin

Paperback   ISBN 1-900924-   198mm X 129mm 288pp, 16pp b/w photos
UK £14.99 $19.95

Blues: The British Connection
by Bob Brunning

Former Fleetwood Mac member Bob Brunning's classic account of the impact of Blues in Britain, from its beginnings as the underground music of 50s teenagers like Mick

Jagger, Keith Richards and Eric Clapton, to the explosion in the 60s, right through to the vibrant scene of the present day.

'An invaluable reference book and an engaging personal memoir' – Charles Shaar Murray

Paperback   ISBN 1-900924-41-2   234mm X 156mm   352pp, 24pp b/w photos
UK £14.99 $19.95

On The Road With Bob Dylan
by Larry Sloman

In 1975, as Bob Dylan emerged from 8 years of seclusion, he dreamed of putting together a travelling music show that would trek across the country like a psychedelic carnival. The dream became a reality, and *On The Road With Bob Dylan* is the ultimate behind-the-scenes look at what happened. When Dylan and the Rolling Thunder Revue took to the streets of America, Larry 'Ratso' Sloman was with them every step of the way.

'The *War and Peace* of Rock and Roll.' – Bob Dylan

Paperback   ISBN 1-900924-51-X   234mm X 156mm   448pp
UK £14.99 $19.95

Gram Parsons: God's Own Singer
by Jason Walker £12.99

Brand new biography of the man who pushed The Byrds into country-rock territory on *Sweethearts of The Rodeo*, and quit to form the Flying Burrito Brothers. Gram lived hard, drank hard, took every drug going and somehow invented country rock, paving the way for Crosby, Stills & Nash, The Eagles and Neil Young. Parsons' second solo LP, *Grievous Angel*, is a haunting masterpiece of country soul. By the time it was released, he had been dead for 4 months. He was 26 years old.

'Walker has done an admirable job in taking us as close to the heart and soul of Gram Parsons as any author could.' **** *Uncut* book of the month

Paperback   ISBN 1-900924-27-7   234mm X 156mm   256pp, 8pp b/w photos
UK £12.99 $18.95

Ashley Hutchings: The Guvnor and the Rise of Folk Rock – Fairport Convention, Steeleye Span and the Albion Band
by Geoff Wall and Brian Hinton £14.99

As founder of Fairport Convention and Steeleye Span, Ashley Hutchings is the pivotal figure in the history of folk rock. This book draws on hundreds of hours of interviews with Hutchings and other folk-rock artists and paints a vivid picture of the scene that also produced Sandy Denny, Richard Thompson, Nick Drake, John Martyn and Al Stewart.

Paperback   ISBN 1-900924-32-3   234mm X 156mm   288pp, photos throughout
UK £14.99 $19.95

The Beach Boys' *Pet Sounds*: The Greatest Album of the Twentieth Century
by Kingsley Abbott £11.95

Pet Sounds is the 1966 album that saw The Beach Boys graduate from lightweight pop like 'Surfin' USA', *et al*, into a vehicle for the mature compositional genius of Brian Wilson. The album was hugely influential, not least on The Beatles. This is the full story of the album's background, its composition and recording, its contemporary reception and its enduring legacy.

Paperback   ISBN 1-900924-30-7   234mm X 156mm   192pp
UK £11.95 $18.95

King Crimson: In The Court of King Crimson
by Sid Smith £14.99

King Crimson's 1969 masterpiece *In The Court Of The Crimson King*, was a huge US chart hit. The band followed it with 40 further albums of consistently challenging, distinctive and innovative music. Drawing on hours of new interviews, and encouraged by Crimson supremo Robert Fripp, the author traces the band's turbulent history year by year, track by track.

Paperback   ISBN 1-900924-26-9   234mm X 156mm 288pp, photos throughout
UK £14.99 $19.95

A Journey Through America with the Rolling Stones
by Robert Greenfield
Featuring a new foreword by Ian Rankin

This is the definitive account of The Stones' legendary '72 tour.

'Filled with finely-rendered detail ... a fascinating tale of times we shall never see again' *Mojo*

'The Stones on tour in '72 twist and burn through their own myth: from debauched outsiders to the first hints of the corporate business – the lip-smacking chaos between the Stones' fan being stabbed by a Hell's Angel at Altamont and the fan owning a Stones' credit card.' – Paul Morley #2 essential holiday rock reading list, *The Observer*, July 04.

Paperback   ISBN 1-900924-24-2   198mm X 129mm 256pp
UK £9.99 $19.95

The Sharper Word: A Mod Reader
Edited by Paolo Hewitt

Hewitt's hugely readable collection documents the clothes, the music, the clubs, the drugs and the faces behind one of the most misunderstood and enduring cultural movements and includes hard to find pieces by Tom Wolfe, bestselling novelist Tony Parsons, poet laureate Andrew Motion, disgraced Tory grandee Jonathan Aitken, Nik Cohn, Colin MacInnes, Mary Quant, and Irish Jack.

'An unparalleled view of the world-conquering British youth cult.' *The Guardian*

'An excellent account of the sharpest-dressed subculture.' *Loaded*, Book of the Month

Paperback   ISBN 1-900924-34-X   198mm X 129mm 192pp
UK £14.99 $19.95

BACKLIST

The Nice: Hang On To A Dream by Martyn Hanson
1900924439 256pp   £13.99
Al Stewart: Adventures of a Folk Troubadour by Neville Judd
1900924366 320pp   £25.00
Marc Bolan and T Rex: A Chronology by Cliff McLenahan
1900924420 256pp   £13.99
Razor Edge: Bob Dylan and The Never-ending Tour by Andrew Muir
1900924137 256pp   £12.99
Calling Out Around the World: A Motown Reader Edited by Kingsley Abbott
1900924145§256pp   £13.99
I've Been Everywhere: A Johnny Cash Chronicle by Peter Lewry
1900924226 256pp   £14.99
Sandy Denny: No More Sad Refrains by Clinton Heylin
1900924358 288pp   £13.99
Animal Tracks: The Story of The Animals by Sean Egan
1900924188 256pp   £12.99
Like a Bullet of Light: The Films of Bob Dylan by CP Lee
1900924064 224pp   £12.99
Rock's Wild Things: The Troggs Files by Alan Clayson and J Ryan
1900924196 224pp   £12.99
Dylan's Daemon Lover by Clinton Heylin
1900924153 192pp   £12.00
XTC: Song Stories by XTC and Neville Farmer
190092403X 352pp   £12.99
Born in the USA: Bruce Springsteen by Jim Cullen
1900924056 320pp   £9.99
Bob Dylan by Anthony Scaduto
1900924234 320pp   £10.99

Firefly Publishing: An Association between Helter Skelter and SAF

The Nirvana Recording Sessions
by Rob Jovanovic £20.00
Drawing on years of research, and interviews with many who worked with the band, the author has documented details of every Nirvana recording, from early rehearsals, to the *In Utero* sessions. A fascinating account of the creative process of one of the great bands.

The Music of George Harrison: While My Guitar Gently Weeps
by Simon Leng £20.00
Often in Lennon and McCartney's shadow, Harrison's music can stand on its own merits. Santana biographer Leng takes a studied, track by track, look at both Harrison's contribution to The Beatles, and the solo work that started with the release in 1970 of his epic masterpiece *All Things Must Pass*. 'Here Comes The Sun', 'Something' – which Sinatra covered and saw as the perfect love song – 'All Things Must Pass' and 'While My Guitar Gently Weeps' are just a few of Harrison's classic songs.

Originally planned as a celebration of Harrison's music, this is now sadly a commemoration.

The Pretty Things: Growing Old Disgracefully
by Alan Lakey £20
First biography of one of rock's most influential and enduring combos. Trashed hotel rooms, infighting, rip-offs, sex, drugs and some of the most remarkable rock 'n' roll, including landmark albums like the first rock opera, *SF Sorrow*, and *Rolling Stone*'s album of the year, 1970's *Parachute*.

'They invented everything, and were credited with nothing.' Arthur Brown, 'God of Hellfire'

The Sensational Alex Harvey
by John Neil Murno £20
Part rock band, part vaudeville, 100% commitment, the SAHB were one of the greatest live bands of the era. But behind his showman exterior, Harvey was increasingly beset by alcoholism and tragedy. He succumbed to a heart attack on the way home from a gig in 1982, but he is fondly remembered as a unique entertainer by friends, musicians and legions of fans.

U2: The Complete Encyclopedia by Mark Chatterton £14.99

Poison Heart: Surviving The Ramones by Dee Dee Ramone and Veronica Kofman £9.99

Minstrels In The Gallery: A History Of Jethro Tull by David Rees £12.99

DANCEMUSICSEXROMANCE: Prince – The First Decade by Per Nilsen £12.99

To Hell and Back with Catatonia by Brian Wright £12.99

Soul Sacrifice: The Santana Story by Simon Leng £12.99

Opening The Musical Box: A Genesis Chronicle by Alan Hewitt £12.99

Blowin' Free: Thirty Years Of Wishbone Ash by Gary Carter and Mark Chatterton £12.99

www.helterskelterbooks.com

All Helter Skelter, Firefly and SAF titles are available by mail order from
www.helterskelterbooks.com
Or from our office:
Helter Skelter Publishing Limited
Southbank House
Black Prince Road
London SE1 7SJ

Telephone: +44 (0) 20 7463 2204 or Fax: +44 (0)20 7463 2295
Mail order office hours: Mon-Fri 10:00am – 1:30pm,
By post, enclose a cheque [must be drawn on a British bank],
International Money Order, or credit card number and expiry date.
Postage prices per book worldwide are as follows:

UK & Channel Islands	£1.50
Europe & Eire (air)	£2.95
USA, Canada (air)	£7.50
Australasia, Far East (air)	£9.00

Email: info@helterskelterbooks.com